Sweated Work, Weak Bodies

Sweated Work, Weak Bodies

Anti-Sweatshop Campaigns and Languages of Labor

Daniel E. Bender

Rutgers University Press
New Brunswick, New Jersey, and London

BP45

Library of Congress Cataloging-in-Publication Data

Bender, Daniel E.
    Sweated work, weak bodies : anti-sweatshop campaigns and languages of
labor / Daniel E. Bender.
        p. cm.
    Includes bibliographical references and index.
    ISBN 0–8135-3337–6 (alk. paper)—ISBN 0–8135–3338–4 (pbk. : alk. paper)
    1. Sweatshops—United States—History. 2. Sweatshops—United States—
Prevention—History. 3. Alien labor—United States—History. 4. Garment
workers—United States—History. I. Title.
    HD2339.U6B46 2004
    331.25—dc21

                                                                2003005737

British Cataloging-in-Publication information for this book is available from the
British Library.

Manufactured in the United States of America

1\5\05

To Mimi, in love and in solidarity

Contents

Acknowledgments

Survival in academia, as in any industry, depends on the solidarity and community of one's co-workers. The strengths of this book, indeed, its very publication, are a testimony to the friendship and guidance that I have received in navigating the trials of academic labor and the challenges of research. In graduate school at NYU, Robin D. G. Kelley, Andrew Ross, Lisa Duggan, Liz Cohen, Hasia Diner, Martha Hodes, Chia Yin Hsu, Janet Green, Gerard Fergerson, Walter Johnson, Yonni Kotsonis, Dave Kinkela, Amy Richter, and Jane Rothstein all helped me with critical reads, comments, and questions. My greatest debts are to Daniel J. Walkowitz and Molly Nolan. Molly read numerous drafts of this manuscript and returned them with questions I'm still trying to answer. Danny was a model thesis advisor. Patient and wise, he is at once a role model, guide, and friend.

Many people, outside of the relatively protective environment of graduate school, have also shared with me invaluable comments and help. I would like to thank, in particular, Gene Burns, Tony Coulter, Rosanne Currarino, Liz Faue, Kirsten Fermaglich, Lisa Fine, Anne Igra, Alice Kessler-Harris, Mary Lewis, Howard Markel, Leslie Page Moch, Scott Nelson, Ruth Percy, Peter Rachleff, David Rosner, Fran Shor, Daniel Soyer, Louise Tilly, and Ken Waltzer. Eileen Boris, Miriam Cohen, Patricia Cooper, Richard Greenwald, Howard Markel, and David Offenhall all read the complete manuscript. Their comments, given with grace and intelligence, not only improved the project immeasurably, but also gave me the courage to let it go at last. These scholars demonstrate that academic work done well is so much more than individual accomplishment; it is mentoring, compassion, and friendship.

I am grateful as well for the support and help I received from the Tamiment-Wagner Labor Archives, the Kheel Center archives at Cornell University, and the YIVO Institute for Jewish Research. I would especially like to thank Leo Greenbaum, Andrew Lee, Gail Malmgreen, Fruma Mohrer, and Patrizia Sione. The staff at the Eldridge Street Project and the Tenement Museum of New York helped me think about the public meanings of this research. At Rutgers University Press, I would like to thank Melanie Halkias, Suzanne Kellam, and Brendan O'Malley.

Parts of chapter 6 appeared as "Inspecting Workers: Medical Examination, Labor Organizing, and the Evidence of Sexual Difference," *Radical History Review* 80 (special issue on Health and the Health Professions) (Spring 2001): 51–75.

As any scholar of labor would argue, solidarity in the workplace is intimately linked to community beyond it. I have often, in researching and writing this book, wanted sweatshops to disappear—if only for my own selfish reasons. Eileen Boris, Ardis Cameron, Patricia Cooper, Kirsten Fermaglich, Richard Greenwald, Jon Gold, Tom Jankowski, Stephanie Meyer, Jon Mirsky, David Offenhall—among many other friends and fellow historians—have helped me survive as a scholar.

This book is rooted in my own background. I was raised in one of those Jewish households grounded in a radical tradition of scholarship and politics that helped draw me to the history of anti-sweatshop campaigns. I am extraordinarily lucky to have parents, Carl and Jessica Bender, who understood what this subject meant to me and believed in its importance. My grandparents Rose and Al Bender and Ben Waldbaum never saw this project to its completion. Ben and Al were no longer around when it began. Yet each in person and in their memory conveyed an optimism about the possibility of social change. Mildred Waldbaum remains the kind of sympathetic confidante only a grandmother can be. My family in and around New York, especially Marjorie and Bob Boyer, Alice Schumacher, my brother Michael, and sister-in-law Tamara Koss, knew exactly when to take me away from the desk and archives and exactly what to feed me.

I met my wife, Mimi Halpern, while writing this book. She is my biggest supporter, my best friend, my favorite baker, my best sous-chef, my fellow traveler in life and politics, and my true love. And it is to her that I dedicate this book. Together, we will hope that someone, someday, will be able to write a history of the sweatshop that has a real ending.

Sweated Work, Weak Bodies

Introduction

The Language and the Limits
of Anti-Sweatshop Organizing

George Price left his home in the Ukraine in May 1882 for New York. He was part of a first wave of Eastern European Jewish immigrants who were filling the tenements and workplaces of New York's Lower East Side, the immigrant residential and industrial district in southeast Manhattan. As a new arrival, he felt out of place even in the immigrant Lower East Side. He remembered that "street urchins" ran after him, taunting him for his beard and old country clothing that marked him as an Orthodox Jew. He subsequently cut his hair, shaved his beard, and exchanged his European garb for "American working cloths [sic]."[1] (There is no evidence that he changed his name, though he surely did.)

Price went on to earn a medical degree from New York University and, in 1901, he started his own "School of Sanitation," which trained hundreds of students to pass the civil service exams and become factory inspectors. The author of a number of books and articles on factory sanitation and hygiene, he was the head of investigation for the powerful New York State Factory Investigating Commission, formed in the wake of the disastrous 1911 Triangle Shirtwaist Factory fire that killed 147 garment workers. Even as Price examined factory conditions as far afield as England, France, Belgium, and Soviet Russia, he remained focused especially on the working conditions of Jewish immigrants in New York City.[2] From its inception, Price was the director of the Joint Board of Sanitary Control (JBSC), an innovative experiment in factory inspection and regulation that united Progressive reformers and workers, organized in the International Ladies' Garment Workers Union (ILGWU). Indeed, the JBSC, under Price's eighteen-year guidance, was at the center of

Progressive Era efforts to reform, regulate, and, it was hoped, eradicate sweat-shops. He was praised for his "monumental contribution to the elevation of this trade from the sweatshop category to a plane of comparative dignity and public esteem."[3]

By any account, George Price was a successful immigrant. Gone were his early financial worries. His voluminous writings were now in English, whereas when he first arrived he wrote in Russian and Yiddish. Most significant, he was fully integrated into the highest echelons of the Progressive reform move-ment in New York. In the Factory Commission, for example, Price worked alongside Robert F. Wagner, the future New York senator, and Mary Dreier, an influential leader of the Women's Trade Union League (WTUL), an organi-zation that had long struggled for women's inclusion in unionization.

A career in sanitary science might have seemed a strange road to assimi-lation and Americanization. It diverged widely from the rags-to-riches stories of writers like Abraham Cahan, whose novel *The Rise of David Levinsky* traced the growing prosperity (and deepening loneliness) of an immigrant gar-ment entrepreneur whose background was not unlike that of Price. Why had Price dedicated his career to sanitary reform and not manufacturing, for ex-ample? Perhaps it was his experience in steerage on the boat to New York, where he encountered, as he remembered, "inadequate" ventilation, food, and sanitation.[4] Perhaps he was influenced by his first paying jobs in garment shops in America, where he and his co-workers labored ten hours a day in poor conditions. "The work is tiring, very often unbearable," he recalled, "and brings about an atrophy of the mind." Perhaps Price learned his first lessons in sanitation working under "parasites, who fatten off the work of their em-ployees."[5] Perhaps he felt the pull of "the Federal government, the legisla-tures of individual states and many private social organizations throughout the country [that] vie with each other in numerous inquiries, conferences, in-vestigations, commissions, exhibits, etc., all bearing on the subject of indus-trial and factory conditions."[6] Whatever his motivation, George Price found himself a standard bearer for sanitation among different and sometimes di-vergent groups: immigrant workers, social reformers, and policymakers.

Price was, at once, an immigrant and a leading American authority on sani-tation, a former worker and a doctor. He crossed and obscured lines of class and ethnicity as one of the chief architects of a solution to New York's sweat-shop problem. As perhaps the most influential factory investigator in New York and as a close ally of immigrant unionists, he helped articulate a defini-tion of the sweatshop and its dangers that was acceptable to both workers and outside observers. He himself had experienced the shops of the Lower East Side as a worker and as an inspector. As he recalled, speaking of himself: "The author of these accounts . . . had managed to endure many privations, to suffer. . . . But what he saw during the early days of his duties as Inspector, the sciences which he beheld on every step . . . made him sick. . . . The rooms were damp, filthy, foul and dark; the air was unbearable; the filth impossible, the crowded conditions terrible, particularly in those places where the rooms were used as workshops." He took on the role of a worker, supposedly "accustomed to the poverty and the ghastly conditions of the Russian immigrants," and the task of inspector, distant from and repulsed by the conditions of immigrants' lives and labors.[7] He believed that he could view the workplace through different class lenses. He described and named the alternative to the sweatshop: "the modern factory." For Price, where the sweatshop nauseated outside observers and debilitated workers, the *"model . . . modern factory"* met "high standards in (1) industrial efficiency, (2) economic relations of employer and employes [*sic*], (3) general sanitation, and (4) welfare work."[8]

Industrialization, Anxiety, and the Sweatshop

With all its immediate political concessions about the acceptability of the wage system and more hidden cultural assumptions about class, racial, ethnic, and gender difference, this vision of a "model" shop guided the United States's first anti-sweatshop campaign. For Price, this was a campaign about extremes, about eradicating the "cesspool" of industrial production and replacing it with mechanized, modern factories designed to protect the "health, comfort, and lives of the workers."[9] This was a model, not simply for remaking one industry and protecting a Jewish immigrant community to which Price still belonged, but also for how to eliminate "the evils found in most industrial establishments."[10] The economic conditions surrounding the sweatshop were the side effects of the rapid influx of immigrants who were desperate for wages, the rise of new technologies (like the sewing machine and cutting knife), and unfettered competition. The word "sweatshop" itself, with all its enduring negative connotations, emerged from the way a host of actors understood these social processes and connected them to larger anxieties about the effects of industrialization and immigration.

An examination of the process of defining the sweatshop reveals much about the articulation of social danger at the turn of the twentieth century. This book also explores campaigns against the sweatshop in which workers and reformers forged cross-class coalitions, even as both groups understood social problems in contrasting ways. Finally, this book explores what the defining of the sweatshop and its dangers meant for immigrant garment workers.

George Price's career choice and his activities are crucial because he embodied a remarkable convergence of ideas, politics, and people around the issues of industrial conditions, sanitary science, and, specifically, the sweat-shop. Price was one of the leaders of the anti-sweatshop campaign, who to-gether looked at the world of work from different class, gender, and racial perspectives. These individuals helped articulate a common definition of the sweatshop and its dangers. Theresa Serber Malkiel, an Eastern European Jew-ish immigrant who played a major role in chronicling an important strike of female shirtwaistmakers in 1909, brought the perspective of a former garment maker who later married a wealthy real estate lawyer. Pauline Newman was a garment worker who became a union activist during the 1909 strike and a full-time organizer thereafter, maintaining her relationship with the wealthy leaders of the WTUL. Abraham Bisno was part of the wave of Jewish immi-grants who arrived in the United States in the 1880s and early 1890s. He worked in sweatshops in both New York and Chicago and became an impor-tant leader in the effort to unionize cloakmakers. He was as comfortable in the legislative hearing room as in the union hall.

The fact that these individuals, among many others, were able to cross and obscure lines of difference suggests that their fight against the sweatshop, which united their disparate experiences, spoke to a range of constituencies. For immigrant workers, politicians, reformers, public health advocates, and politicians, the sweatshop encapsulated all the dangers of American indus-trialization. As the United States faced the spread of mass production indus-tries, a new stage of what Price called an "industrial evolution"—a process deeply intertwined with the "history of civilization" itself—the question of work and working conditions invaded a range of social policy issues, from immigra-tion to housing. As Price argued, in 1909 there were in the United States 268,491 "industrial establishments" and uncounted "small domestic workshops" employing 6,615,046 "persons."[11] Many of these "persons" were new immi-grants, and in mass production industries, especially in eastern and midwestern cities, these immigrants came from Southern and Eastern Europe. For an emerging generation of social reformers, journalists, and policy-makers—some of whom would become Price's closest colleagues—the European immigrants who increasingly filled industrial workshops in cities like New York represented something much more ominous than a vaguely discontented proletariat (al-though massive and violent strikes hinted at workers' growing anger). They were also potential carriers of deadly and contagious diseases. Disease might be spread not casually, but in the goods manufactured by immigrant workers and purchased by middle-class consumers.[12]

Immigrant workers were a moral threat as well. Their family life, sexual mores, and work patterns hardly fit the cherished standards of morality outlined in contemporary etiquette books, popular with middle-class readers.[13] A host of critics, from journalists to elected officials, worried about more than the numbers of immigrant women who supported themselves through prostitution or the men who profited from their sex work. They were nervous that the cramped spaces of urban workplaces encouraged flirtation, touching, and perhaps even sex among male and female immigrant workers.[14] The very fact that men and women were working together hinted at moral outrages. Were women in the workforce out of necessity, because of the drunkenness, laziness, or gambling of dissolute husbands? The women who eked out the barest of existences finishing garments in their homes or as low-paid workers in garment sweatshops and the children who were deformed in body and mind from their long hours of labor became symbols of the moral dangers of industrialization. At the same time, observers worried that these children might join what seemed like a growing army of criminals.[15] The Commissioner General of Immigration, Frank Sargent, best captured this sense of moral outrage and fear about immigration and industrial labor in 1905: "Today there is an enormous alien population in our larger cities which is breeding crime and disease. . . . Unless something is done . . . it is my fear and belief that . . . the alien population of the country, or rather cities, will constitute a downright peril."[16]

Sargent's warning evinces a deep and enduring sense of anxiety. This was a concern for the fate of "civilization" itself as much as it was about impending revolution.[17] Worried observers like Sargent looked at the lives and labor of immigrant workers to explain the turmoil of industrialization. Government panels gathered and produced volumes of reports scientifically suggesting how to classify and order European immigrants who seemed foreign in manners, immoral in mores, and deformed in body. Against the backdrop of immigration, such reports defined an increasingly complicated—and contradictory—racial hierarchy, part of what historian Matthew Frye Jacobson calls a fracturing of whiteness. Jacobson argues that the turn of the century witnessed numerous efforts to adapt understandings of race to the reality of European immigration. According to these reports, the European immigrants who found jobs in sweatshops were not part of the same racial group as the inspectors and social reformers who visited their workplaces. More than Jacobson suggests, the conditions of immigrants' work revealed their place within the Progressive Era racial hierarchy.[18] Still, the very fact that some inspectors, like Price, were themselves immigrants attests to the instability and contradictions of racial logic. These government committees saw the categorization of race as intertwined with labor. Thus, the seventeen volumes of the *Reports of the Industrial Commission* (1900), the nineteen volumes of the *Report on the Condition of*

Women and Child Wage Earners in the U.S. (1909), and the forty-two volumes of the *United States Immigration Commission* (1911) linked the economics of industries like ready-made clothing, the conditions of workshops, and the dynamics of industrial disputes to the character of different immigrant groups.[19]

Yet these reports raised even more haunting questions. If the racial characteristics of immigrants could transform the economic conditions of an industry, could the conditions of work alter permanently the character of immigrants? Could Jews, Italians, or other European races improve their status in America? The mutability of racial position was especially evident for European immigrants whose status as a white—but not Anglo-Saxon—race was tacitly and generally acknowledged. Given the right circumstances, the position of these immigrant races could improve; ideally, they might approach the "civilization" of native-born Anglo-Saxons. But, at the same time, under the worst circumstances—like those in the filthiest, most immoral of workshops—immigrants' status could worsen. The debased lives of European immigrant workers suggested that industrialization had set in motion a process of racial degeneration among workers who shared at least a visible whiteness with government officials. Inspectors and journalists worried that the lean, deformed bodies of immigrants proved that immigrants were becoming a debased race. Even worse, they wondered: Were the immoral couplings of the workplace propagating the next generation of a degenerate race?[20]

Still, even the pessimistic Sargent believed that the full danger of European immigrants would only be realized "unless something is done." For Sargent, the solution was to encourage European immigrants to leave eastern cities to find work in the farms of the Midwest. For other critics, the answer lay in immigration restrictions and a tighter scrutiny of new arrivals by immigration officials and medical officers to uncover infected or weak immigrants.[21] For increasingly influential reformers, public health advocates, and factory inspectors, that "something" was effective regulation of industrial production to improve the conditions of labor.[22] Industrial regulation offered safety to workers, but, more important, it might help stabilize a shifting racial hierarchy, prevent disease, and ensure morality. Thus, as Price himself noted, the problems of work, workers, and working conditions moved to the center of political debates: "Factory and labor legislation, industrial relations between capital and labor, improvement of factory conditions and amelioration of the conditions of the large mass of American workers are the burning questions of the day and the most vital problems of the hour."[23]

Anxiety about European immigration and industrialization was not limited to middle- and upper-class policymakers, journalists, and reformers. For native-born workers, European immigrants were a pool of cheap labor that employers could exploit to undermine the position of well-paid skilled artisans. Thus, native-born and older immigrant workers followed each other in testifying before government hearings, blaming new immigrants for falling wages, declining conditions, and, in some cases, the loss of their jobs. In 1892, for example, John B. Lennon, the secretary of the Journeyman Tailor's Union of America, testified before a congressional committee investigating the ready-made garment industry that "immigration has made the conditions worse." In addition to worrying about the jobs of his union's members, Lennon—like the politicians asking him questions—was concerned about disease. "The germs of disease have been carried . . . in the clothing," he testified.[24]

If native-born workers complained about the loss of their jobs and the spread of contagion, European immigrant workers worried about what historian Herbert Gutman has called "the psychic and social costs extracted by American industrial work rules." They worried as well about the physical costs.[25] While massive and often violent strikes in major industrial centers were flare-ups of anger of increasingly desperate immigrant laborers, workers' everyday concern with the effects of work on their bodies and families captured their disillusionment with American industrial labor. The shocking conditions of steerage that immigrants like Price endured on their voyage across the ocean were only a harbinger of what they would encounter in American workshops. As Price wrote, when immigrants made the transition from recent arrivals to industrial workers, they realized that "over their heads constantly, the sword of Damoclean American industry hangs." Immigrants saw themselves as choosing between unemployment and poorly paid jobs in unsafe workplaces. Either way, Price argued, "the worker finds it difficult . . . to keep body and soul together."[26]

Indeed, immigrant workers often described their labor as a process of physical transformation. They described themselves as remade through the monotony and long hours of labor into a "living automatic part of the machine," as Price insisted. As part of their integration into the machinery of the nation, immigrant workers surrendered their health. Images of weakness, hunger, feebleness, and disease filled the rhetoric of immigrant workers.[27] These were the physical scars of class. If, for the first government officials worrying about the tides of immigration, race was etched on immigrant workers' bodies, for immigrants, class was visible in their stooped, diseased frames.

Amid a cacophony of voices worried about the scars of industrialization and immigration, the garment industry emerged as a particular concern. Few industries so clearly showed the effects of European immigration as the ready-to-wear garment industry. Long one of New York's most important and largest industries, garment manufacture, by the 1870s, was based around sizable factories with a workforce composed largely of native-born and relatively as-similated Irish and German immigrant men and women. The arrival of East-ern European Jews beginning in the 1880s, coupled with advances in technology and shifts in fashion that decreased the need for highly trained ar-tisans, dramatically altered the landscape of the garment industry.[28]

Many Jews had worked in clothing manufacture in Europe and gravitated toward garment work upon their arrival in New York. They found low-pay-ing jobs in small workshops, located on the Lower East Side and owned by relatives or acquaintances from the Old Country. Because these small shops demanded little expensive technology and had low labor costs, they easily undercut older, larger factories. As the number of garment shops in New York ballooned, the size of shops decreased. These small shops introduced a new form of manufacture. Whereas previously a garment factory—an "inside shop"—would produce, and sometimes even sell, a complete garment, these new "outside shops" were part of a contracting system. Workers in these shops would complete only an individual task, like sewing hems. In other cases, they might assemble pieces of cloth that were part of bundles of pre-cut garments contracted out by a retailer or manufacturer. Contractors competed heavily and might even subcontract out bundles, placing downward pressure on wages.

The rise of contracting was a frightening development for reformers, inspec-tors, and politicians. It marked the ascendance of an immigrant industry, hard to regulate and often located in the most miserable of workplaces on the Lower East Side. These outside observers were quick to point out that small garment shops looked more like Old World workplaces than large, mechanized Ameri-can factories. And, indeed, the arrival of Jews had made New York an outpost of a global garment industry that depended on a national market for consum-ers, but on transnational migrations for labor. Thus critics of the contracting system denigrated contracting as part of a "foreign industry" imported into the United States by the most miserable of European immigrants. While Ital-ian immigrants, especially in the 1890s and early 1900s, composed an increas-ingly large minority of workers in the New York garment industry, the rise of contracting was firmly associated with Russian and other Eastern European Jews. Even George Price labeled the contractor shop a "Russian shop."[29]

Between 1880 and 1910, for factory inspectors and for the first generation of journalists writing about immigrant industrial labor, the character of Jews as a race comfortable in filth and too physically weak and undisciplined for factory work—more than the logic of an unrestrained "race to the bottom" in wages—explained the "odoriferous, filthy holes" where these immigrants lived and labored.[30] While such an explanation placed the blame for contract-ing squarely on the frail shoulders of Jewish immigrants, it did not make the implications any less frightening. The diseases nurtured in an immigrant industry might be spread into the threads of garments worn by native-born, female, middle-class consumers.

With this looming threat, the garment industry became a primary focus for the first generation of American factory inspectors and the target of many of the nation's first industrial sanitary regulations.[31] Beginning in the 1890s, inspectors related to a host of state and federal government hearings the shock and horror they felt when they entered Lower East Side shops. At the same time, journalists were visiting the Lower East Side in increasing numbers and printing lurid stories of filth and disease in newspapers and popular magazines. Journalists and inspectors cast themselves as explorers visiting a foreign land and returning with details on the lives and labors of a race "filthy in their habits and obstinate in their mode of living."[32] The study of the nation's first anti-sweatshop campaign, thus, contributes to an important literature on factory inspection, protective legislation, and Progressive reform, by identifying the specific languages of race, gender, and class, and the vocabulary of public health and morality used to describe the dangers of immigrant industrial labor.

In the 1890s, in the pages of newspapers and magazines and in government hearing rooms, inspectors, politicians, and journalists coined a term to describe these immigrant contractor shops: sweatshop. While inspectors insisted that the sweatshop was the result of dangerous immigration, they depended on a different sort of migration for their language and strategies, what historian Daniel Rodgers has called the "Atlantic crossings" of Progressive ideas. The very notion of government-enforced sanitary controls was born in Europe and carried over by European-educated American social scientists. And *sweatshop* was defined simultaneously and in similar ways by American and British inspectors and politicians. American observers described the sweatshop as a contractor workshop, often located in workers' tenement apartments that featured the labor of men, women, and children in the most immoral and appalling of surroundings. Drawing on older meanings of sweated labor as physically draining and as immigrant work, the sweatshop and the sweating system—the name given to the contracting system—were directly contrasted with idealized images of "American" factories.[33] Where the factory was sanitary, the sweatshop bred disease. Where the factory hired male workers, the sweating system demanded the labor of men, women, and children. Indeed, in the worst of sweatshops, those that came to be called "homework shops," husbands took on the role of contractor and put their wives to work.

The first government hearings, factory inspections, and journalistic exposés of the sweatshop depended on a particular construction of Jewish immigrants as a debased and degraded race, but capable of improvement. Thus, factory inspections and government hearings were part of a broad policy of social engagement that sought legislative and regulatory solutions to the problems posed by sweatshops. Instead of clamoring for the exclusion or segregation of Jewish immigrants, inspectors, politicians, and journalists ventured regularly into immigrant neighborhoods to support a host of social programs, including gymnasiums and settlement houses, often funded by wealthy German American Jews. These programs held out the possibility of civilizing and Americanizing Jewish immigrants and proved to be a crucial institutional link between immigrant workers and native-born politicians and factory inspectors. Although Chinese and Japanese immigrants and African American migrants, whose fitness for industrial labor was constantly questioned, found themselves forcibly and legally segregated into separate neighborhoods in different American cities, Jewish immigrants in New York were criticized for settling in a "Jewish ghetto." The movement of Jews to other parts of the city—at least to more sanitary immigrant neighborhoods—was hailed as a sign of their Americanization and racial progress.[34]

The very fact that inspectors, politicians, and social reformers sought to engage with immigrant sweatshop workers offered Jews a role in the process of defining the sweatshop and its social dangers, as well as a place in efforts to control and reform the sweating system. Despite linguistic and cultural barriers dividing workers and reformers, Jewish immigrants advanced their own definition of the sweatshop.[35] Less concerned with issues of race or with the fate of middle-class consumers, Jewish immigrants described the sweatshop as a form of class oppression that was obvious in workers' weak and diseased bodies. The poet, immigrant, and sweatshop worker Morris Rosenfeld captured this sense of occupational disease as the visible sign of exploitation in his 1898 poem, "*In Svetshop*" (In the Sweatshop). The poem revolves around his mournful realization that he has been subsumed by labor and reduced to a mere sewing tool. Like Price, he declared, "I am a machine!" But he remained a suffering human. His injured body and the bodies of his fellow workers reflect the trials of work: "I feel my wound, and bitter tears. . . . "[36]

In Yiddishizing a word used by inspectors, immigrants not only held out the potential of alliance with outside observers, but also created a shared past and common experience of work. Different crafts, Eastern European Jewish garment workers insisted, could trace their roots to sweatshops. As the sweatshop, for politicians and inspectors, encapsulated all the dangers of immigrant industrial work, for Jewish workers the sweatshop was a shared experience of pain crucial for the expression of solidarity. In this context, it is also useful to consider Benedict Anderson's idea of "imagined communities." Like the concept of "nation," the sweatshop represented a shared experience for workers who might never "know most of their fellow-members, meet them, or even hear of them, yet in the minds of each lives the image of their communion."[37] Thus, when Jewish immigrants wrote histories of their labor and their experience of immigration and Americanization, they described themselves as a community that had emerged "out of the sweatshop." In later years, women would force their way into the Jewish labor movement, partly by claiming that they, like men, had suffered in the sweatshop.

Male and female Jewish workers' powerful indictment of sweated labor as capitalist oppression seems distant from inspectors' racialized explanations of the sweatshop. Yet the career of George Price suggests that Jewish workers and outside critics could—and did—forge a common definition of the sweatshop that focused on the effects of sweated labor on workers' bodies and families. Both inspectors and workers worried that the sweating system forced married women into the workplace. Inspectors argued that this would lead to a promiscuous workplace, which would encourage decrepit workers to produce another debased generation.

Gender was the key to racial degeneration. For Jewish workers, both men and women, sweatshop-bred disease threatened the sexual division of labor in immigrant families. Partly through their interaction with German Jewish charities, Jewish immigrants, more than other immigrant groups in New York, came to cherish male breadwinning as the key to assimilation and Americanization.[38] A sick male breadwinner could not support his family, forcing married women to return to wage labor. Jewish workers and outside observers came to see the physical effects of sweated labor as a health threat and as a gendered danger. By the second decade of the twentieth century, Jewish workers and reformers realized that alone they could not eradicate the sweatshop. Gender would prove to be the basis of coalition.

Language and Anti-Sweatshop Campaigns

The wave of committee hearings and legislative investigations in the 1880s and 1890s produced laws that empowered factory inspectors to regulate garment production. At the same time, Jewish immigrant garment workers began taking the first tentative steps toward unionization, culminating in 1900 when Jewish workers formed the ILGWU.[39] However, there were simply too few inspectors to visit the hundreds of shops that filled the tenements of the Lower East Side. At the same time, legal precedents blocked the outright prohibition of homework, which was regarded by workers and inspectors alike as the worst form of sweated labor. In the garment trade, workers and inspectors defined homework as the finishing of garments in the home, a task often completed by women. Meanwhile, unions found it difficult to translate the militancy of strikes into stable and enforceable contracts. Even union leaders admitted that immigrant unions espoused confident class radicalism, but struggled to survive at the end of strikes.[40]

In 1910, a strike of male cloakmakers organized in the ILGWU helped consolidate a coalition. The largest strike to date in the garment industry, the strike was settled through the intervention of leading Progressive reformers, like future Supreme Court justice Louis Brandeis. The Protocol of Peace, the agreement ending the strike, led to the creation of the JBSC, with George Price as its leading official. Until 1928, the JBSC set—and unionized workers enforced—sanitary standards. The maintenance of a sexual division of labor was central to these standards. Most important, the JBSC sought to eradicate women's homework by moving garment production away from workers' homes on the Lower East Side. In protecting the health of the male breadwinner, the JBSC might realize Price's vision of the "modern factory."

This examination of the JBSC and its place in an anti-sweatshop movement builds on the history of homework and protective legislation, in particular the work of Eileen Boris. Boris's longer and more national analysis suggests that, in the first half of the twentieth century, anti-homework organizing and legislative efforts sought to protect divisions between the home and workplace. By placing these Progressive Era efforts in the context of an anti-sweatshop campaign, this book argues that the specter of homework also shaped cross-class efforts to define a model and moral workplace. The "modern factory" depended on an ideal of "separate spheres" in which the home was understood by male and female workers, reformers, and inspectors as a reproductive space and the workplace as a productive space.[41] In this context, the connection of homework with the sweatshop—and the subsequent feminization of the sweatshop—raised questions about women's presence in the modern shop.[42]

At the same time, placing women's homework in a discursive binary with men's factory labor shifted the terms of anti-sweatshop labor organizing and anti-sweatshop legislation from class and race, respectively. Together, workers and inspectors came to focus on gender. At the same moment that Jewish workers and their allies were seeking to eradicate sweatshops, they were constructing model factories. Because workers and outside observers represented the sweatshop as a foreign, un-American workplace, the model shop did not dislodge the boss. Male union leaders no longer blamed the wage relationship for the sweatshop. Like vaunted models of American industrialization, shops heralded by immigrant unionists and their allies as model shops featured large workforces, rationalized systems of production (dedicated to the precepts of scientific management espoused by Frederick Winslow Taylor), and strong managers whose prerogatives were assured by industry-wide contracts. In its most ambitious form, the model shop doubled as a tuberculosis sanitorium that offered care primarily to male workers. At the same time, shop managers gave money directly to male worker/patients' families so their wives would not have to return to wage labor.

While the JBSC was the institutional and structural heart of the anti-sweatshop campaign, the coalition depended on a range of cross-class relationships between working-class Jews and outside observers. Most important for the success of the JBSC, male leaders of the ILGWU found allies in inspectors like Price and forged a hybrid form of regulation that depended on inspection for the articulation of policy goals and on unionization for enforcement of those goals. In addition, in a series of strikes between 1909 and 1913—including the famed 1909 "Uprising of the 20,000"—female workers built close alliances with middle- and upper-class members of the WTUL. Female workers' relationship with the WTUL gave them a shield of public, moral respectability that helped them win a place in the ILGWU and bring their workplaces under the purview of the JBSC. Thus, by 1913, the JBSC regulated shops in all the garment trades in which Jews worked in large numbers.

These relationships have often garnered the attention of historians. The Protocol of Peace, for example, has been hailed as the dress rehearsal for the New Deal's tripartite models of industrial relations that brought together unions, government, and liberal businesses. At the same time, historians have described the 1909–13 strikes as a watershed in women's labor history.[43] The ILGWU is regarded as having been at the vanguard of efforts between 1910 and 1930 to solve industrial disputes through cross-class efforts at regulation and reform. Such efforts, labor historians have argued, may have, in certain circumstances, temporarily soothed the tensions of class conflict, but blunted the potential of working-class radicalism.[44] At the same time, the ILGWU is described as a hotbed of socialism and women's labor radicalism. The divergence of findings can be explained by the fact that such interpretations have rarely taken into consideration the cultural distance separating workers and their wealthy allies.

As a corrective, Nan Enstad has examined the relationship between women workers and the WTUL and argues that they had vastly different ideas about the goals of and reasons for activism. Enstad criticizes labor historians for trying to turn working women into exemplary workers, models for their own visions of radicalism. Instead, she suggests, working women forged political subjectivities in frivolous activities. Popular culture—dime novels, movies, fashion—was the cultural resource that women used to construct self-images as strikers. During the 1909 strike, Enstad argues, WTUL leaders, who controlled the distribution and production of publicity, portrayed working women as "ghetto coquettes." She cites WTUL leaders who chided working-class "girls" for choosing obsessions with fashion over real questions of labor politics: wages and conditions. These "girls," in contrast, saw fashion and dress as liberating in itself, and as a motivation for organizing. This was an identity, according to Enstad, that led workers away from the union and away from the WTUL.[45]

Enstad presents an important analysis of working-class popular culture and its relationship to political activism. However, her interpretation is only part of the story. It is largely divorced from the broader political and cultural debates about garment work, race, and immigration. Enstad examines the performance of working-class women's bodies around the issue of fashion. But the dresses that these women proudly and triumphantly wore covered up racialized, ethnic bodies that both workers and reformers saw as scarred by the experience of garment labor. It was around the question of the body—specifically, the proletarian and immigrant body twisted, contorted, and infected by labor—that workers and their critics shared anxieties about the dangers of work, immigration, and industrialization.[46] Workers and outside observers, in the context of unequal power relationships, were able to forge a common definition of the sweatshop and of its social dangers. Moreover, they were able to translate that definition into strategies and structures of resistance, reform, and social change, even in the face of political upheaval, world war, and economic transformation.

In the context of these cross-class conversations, women struggled to win a place in the ILGWU. Enstad notes that women advanced a politically powerful representation of working-class "ladies," largely drawn on popular culture. In fact, female garment workers advanced this idea of ladyhood through a form of cultural negotiation with WTUL leaders. This negotiation involved a process of coalition building in which working women confronted and reconfigured conceptions of workplace seriousness in the context of specific, prevailing languages about garment work. When female garment workers assumed the labels of victim *and* lady, it was a way of claiming a place in the union; they, too, suffered in the sweatshop. Female strikers' efforts to describe their own scars of work were central to their insistence that they shared in a common experience of labor. They were not simply working women, but were women working in sweatshops and, as they sought to represent themselves as both victims and lady strikers, they were responding to and linking discourses about ladyhood and sweated labor. In the process, however, women were acknowledging sexual difference. They rarely challenged directly the workplace sexual division of labor and even tended to claim that they confronted different occupational hazards than men.

Where Enstad measures the cultural distance of class, this book explores coalition building as a linguistic process that reveals the dynamics of power. The relationships that underpinned the anti-sweatshop coalition demanded constant negotiation over the meaning and danger of sweated work. But these were not even and equal negotiations. Still, inspectors, WTUL members, reformers, and policymakers held out to male and female immigrant workers the prospect of immediate and substantial change in working conditions.

Language is understood here not simply as words, but as the meanings given to the circumstances of work, immigration, and family, among other subjects. It involves, significantly, the association of social perils with economic conditions. Those meanings depended on constructions of racial, class, ethnic, and gender difference. As constructions of difference change over time, so, too, is language historically specific.[47] The potential dangers of the sweatshop gained urgency in the context of emerging understandings of germs and contagion. The newly popular—but ill-understood—germ theory of disease arrived in America at around the same time as Jewish immigrants.

Notions of science, medicine, and sanitation helped workers and outside observers read workers' bodies and their physical and medical conditions as evidence that social difference was real.[48] But real did not necessarily mean immutable. The growing alliances across lines of class of anti-sweatshop politics focused more attention at different points in time on particular aspects of difference. As the anti-sweatshop coalition coalesced, gender, more than race or class, became the focus. Workers sought to protect the division of labor in their families by seeking alliances with inspectors and policymakers and, in the process, came to represent the sweatshop as a problem of poor sanitation, not capitalism. Similarly, in seeking the help of workers, inspectors by the 1910s came to blame bad sanitary habits, not workers' racial characteristics, for the sweatshop.

This, then, was the contradiction of anti-sweatshop organizing: it downplayed but never denied certain conceptions of difference only by stressing other notions of difference. It represents an example of what Joan Scott calls the "paradoxes" of feminist politics.[49] Thus, anti-sweatshop organizing depended on the naturalness and desirability of gender difference and worked to preserve it in the home, union, and workplace. In the context of anti-sweatshop organizing, the articulation of sexual difference took many forms, from everyday workplace interaction between men and women to scientific study. As both male and female workers recalled, relations between men and women in the sweatshop were characterized by sexual jokes and physical harassment all aimed at women workers. This sexual harassment was more than a mere torment for women workers. It helped define women as temporary employees who would leave work with marriage and men as permanent workers and breadwinners. Harassment also helped to distinguish between men's and women's work and to define men's work as skilled—in an industry in which few tasks demanded real training. Alliances with public health advocates also helped entrench men and women in different workplace roles. Medical inspections produced putative evidence that men and women experienced work and occupational disease in contrasting ways. Men faced tuberculosis, a disease that undermined their ability to earn a family wage, and women faced disorders that threatened their ability to bear children.

In this way, anti-sweatshop activism depended on, and in turn reinforced, conceptions of sexual difference. Hierarchies of skill, for example, naturalized by the expression of sexual difference, were not only left intact, but also frequently strengthened. This book argues that male and female Eastern European Jewish immigrant workers suffered from a burden of language in their alliances with reformers and inspectors. Not unlike workers in other American industries at the time, male workers and female garment workers came to agree that they naturally had different workplace roles and experiences. The very term *worker* came to have distinct gendered meanings. Worker, in its normative form, came to refer to the male breadwinner, while women claimed instead the title of "women workers." As a result, when men claimed to organize for workers, they almost always advanced ideas about how to protect systems of male breadwinning.

Still, as Scott's analysis suggests, the contradictions of constructions of gender opened up the space for women's activism. Women did seek to organize, not as workers, but as "women workers." They actively engaged middle-class notions of ladyhood to counter male workers' persistent sexual harassment. Scholars have noted the role of masculinity in the construction of skill, but rarely have identified the specific language of interaction—in this case, sexual harassment—used to express and defend masculinity.[50] The expression of masculinity in the sweatshop depended not on the notion of a manly, strong body, but on its contrast with ideals of femininity. Women responded by advancing new definitions of workplace femininity, rather than by challenging masculinity itself. They claimed to be ladies who would leave work with marriage, but still deserved a place in the workplace and the union. Such a strategy, though, left intact constructions of skill and preserved a sexual division of labor.[51] Thus, women confronted the paradox of their organizing. The burden of their language became especially clear when women demanded leadership positions in the union. Women in the ILGWU faced tenacious male resistance—except when they sought programs that would reaffirm ideas about sexual difference, like gynecological care and women's clinics.

The anti-sweatshop coalition that had emerged in the wake of the 1910 strike lasted until 1928, when the alliance collapsed, largely under the burden of the language of anti-sweatshop organizing. Women workers, angry over their exclusion from leadership positions in the ILGWU, set in motion a process that eventually led to the demise of the JBSC and the anti-sweatshop coalition. Unwilling and, probably, unable to challenge dominant gendered ideologies in the ILGWU, women turned to contemporary languages of class radicalism, in particular, Bolshevism, to protest their subordinate positions. This seemingly gender-neutral language called for union democracy and appealed to a range of rank-and-file unionists, men and women. In the end, it empowered a host of male Communist dissidents more than it did female activists.

By the mid–1920s, the ILGWU was embroiled in increasingly bitter and violent factionalism between Communist partisans and those union leaders who espoused socialism, but were tied to anti-sweatshop institutions like the JBSC. Women eventually found themselves drifting to the margins of the opposition movement as male Communists briefly came to lead the union. The Communist leadership, all the while preserving gendered hierarchies, sought to reassert class empowerment as a solution to the sweatshop problem. The sweatshop, both sides argued, had reappeared while the union was preoccupied with its internal battles. In advancing a new strategy, Communist leaders starved the JBSC for funds while leading the union toward a destructive general strike in 1926. In the aftermath of the strike and the bankrupting of the JBSC, reformers, already weakened by larger political shifts away from Progressive reform, backed away from the union and employers openly flouted sanitary regulations. By 1928, as the ILGWU split into two unions— the Communist Needle Trades Workers' Industrial Union and the ILGWU— union leaders on both sides were bemoaning the "return of the sweatshop." The anti-sweatshop coalition could not overcome the burden of language. The hierarchies of the workplace were reproduced in a union that sought, above all, to preserve distinct gender roles, leaving little space for female union leaders. Also, the anti-sweatshop movement could not protect its institutions in the face of class radicalism.

This book links the cultural and social histories of the turn of the twentieth century. It identifies the languages that a host of actors used to express anxiety about industrialization and immigration and examines how these actors employed these languages to mold powerful political institutions. It also suggests how the languages that were used to describe social danger provided scripts of interaction between men and women at work. If the sweatshop was a primary focus of Progressive Era concern, the study of efforts to define and eradicate it can reveal the dynamics of relationships across the lines of class, gender, race, and ethnicity in an era when factory inspectors worried about workers as the vectors of disease, policymakers viewed immigrant groups as distinct and debased races, and male workers saw women as transients who would work only until marriage. It was in the context of these assumptions of difference and realities of inequality that male and female immigrant workers turned to coalitions.

About a century later, this story seems especially pertinent, as a new, now international, anti-sweatshop coalition is emerging. Like its predecessor, this new campaign is a cross-class movement that depends, for its political weight, on the powerful negative connotations of the sweatshop. But the politics of definition that surrounded the first anti-sweatshop campaign can offer an important warning. In defining the moral evils of the sweatshop, the anti-sweatshop coalition that emerged after 1910 depended on conceptions of difference, which ultimately and inherently reinforced social inequality. In the 1910s, George Price and his allies built a potent social movement that, through the combined strength of inspection and unionization, dramatically changed conditions in the United States's largest garment industry center. They could claim to have made "workers well." In the end, though, women workers were complaining about drowning in "a sea of masculinity" and union leaders were worrying about the return of the sweatshop. As a new generation of activists clamors for reform, regulation, and inspection, are they carrying an increasingly heavy burden of language?

Part I

Race, Class, Gender, and Defining the Sweatshop and Modern Shop in Progressive America

Scholars, policymakers, unionists, and workers today describe the sweatshop as a garment workshop characterized by low wages and poor working conditions, the inevitable result of an economic "race to the bottom," unfettered competition fostered by an abundance of cheap labor. When the word "sweatshop" was first used at the turn of the twentieth century, it also described low wages and unclean workplaces. However, the factory inspectors who first coined the word and the Jewish immigrant workers who adopted it did not turn to an economic logic of competition alone to explain the rise of the sweatshop. Initially, at least, inspectors relied on scientific racism and workers used a more emotional and literary language of class to describe its origins. How could race and class simultaneously define the sweatshop and how did these languages help inspectors and workers articulate contrasting ideas about its dangers? How did workers and policymakers reconcile their different definitions of the sweatshop as they forged the first cross-class anti-sweatshop campaign?

Part I explores the language that workers, factory inspectors, policymakers, journalists, and social reformers used to make sense of and to address changes in the New York garment industry. In the 1880s, the garment industry in New York, one of the city's biggest and most visible manufacturing sectors, changed dramatically. As it grew rapidly with a shift from custom to ready-made production (the manufacture of presized garments), the garment industry became centered around small shops, not factories. These small shops were part of a new system of contracting and subcontracting in which numerous contractors, each hiring a few employees, stitched together pre-cut cloth for larger manufacturers and retailers. The rise of these small shops, often located in contractors' tenement apartments, can be explained by changes in fashion, the introduction of new, inexpensive technology, and, most important, the arrival of thousands of Eastern European Jewish immigrants, many of whom came with experience in garment manufacture. By the end of the 1880s, New York industry had become an outpost of a larger transnational garment industry with centers located also in Western Europe and with a workforce composed largely of Eastern European and, later, Southern European immigrants.

While recognizing the role of fashion, technology, and immigration, observers of the garment industry insisted that these factors alone could not account for the rise of the sweatshop. Instead, they argued that the racial characteristics of immigrants explained it. Jewish immigrants arrived in New York poor and the jobs they discovered in contractor shops did little to promote social mobility. But inspectors and journalists saw themselves as explorers visiting the Jewish immigrant neighborhood of the Lower East Side and they described the squalor they found as a reflection of Jewish racial traits, not the result of the low wages in and poor working conditions of the garment shops. Race, more than competition, explained economic changes.

These inspectors saw the sweatshop as a reflection of Jewish racial inferiority and, potentially, as a cause of their racial degradation. For inspectors, the physical decrepitude of immigrants highlighted the threat of the sweatshop to civilization. The threat was manifest in germs that might be passed from filthy immigrants to female consumers. Immigrants, meanwhile, focused less on questions of race, biology, and public health, and more on issues of class. They described themselves as victims of the sweated system. Their victimhood was also concrete. They pointed to their enfeebled, potentially diseased bodies as evidence of their exploitation.

However, inspectors and immigrants did share concerns, in particular about women's labor, particularly in its relationship to occupational disease. Inspectors worried that women's labor alongside men created a promiscuous workplace. The children born from the immoral couplings of the sweatshop would inherit the moral and physical debasement of their parents. Gender, then, was key to immigrants' racial degradation. Immigrants, meanwhile, saw male breadwinning as a key to Americanization and as a marker of assimilation and civilization. Thus, they viewed married women's labor as a danger to immigrants' families and as the inevitable result of the sickness caused by sweated work. The wives of male immigrants would be forced to turn to paid garment labor if their husbands fell ill.

Increasingly, the labor of married women, especially married women's homework, was considered the worst kind of sweated labor by social reformers and male Jewish workers, the latter organized in the International Ladies' Garment Workers' Union (ILGWU). In focusing on homework, immigrant unionists and reformers were able to construct a cross-class anti-sweatshop alliance that focused on specific sweatshop dangers. Questions of race and class moved to the background as immigrants and reformers stressed the gendered disorder created by sweated labor.

To trace the different and shifting languages used to define the sweatshop is to place the changes in the New York garment industry within the larger context of turn-of-the-twentieth-century anxieties about immigration, racial decline, and the public health effects of industrial labor. At the same time, it places anti-sweatshop campaigns in a larger context of burgeoning social reform, factory inspection, public health, and union movements. Explaining the shift in ideas about the threats posed by the sweatshop and the retreat of languages of class and race and the increasing importance of gender helps identify the cultural terms around which workers, inspectors, and policymakers built an enduring anti-sweatshop alliance.

One

Eastern European Jews and the Rise of a Transnational Garment Economy

Eastern European Jewish immigrants arrived in New York in great numbers starting around 1880. Especially in the early years of their migration, many found work in the city's changing garment industry. Paul Novick, a garment worker who later became the editor of the Communist Yiddish daily *Freiheit,* described the neighborhood where fellow Jewish immigrants concentrated as a neighborhood of workers. The immigrants of New York's Lower East Side, the crowded region in the southeast part of Manhattan, were "80 to 90 percent proletarian." He noted as well that many immigrants worked in the neighborhood's small garment workshops.[1]

Novick and his fellow immigrants represented a pool of unskilled and semi-skilled cheap labor. Their desperate need for paid work, their backgrounds as garment workers in unmechanized shops in Europe, pushed them to the city's growing garment industry. They found work with growing numbers of Jewish employers, many of whom they were related to or had known in the old country. Their arrival dramatically altered the contours of the city's industry, integrating it into a transnational garment economy dependent on domestic consumers, but also on migrant workers and employers. This global garment economy stretched from Eastern Europe to the major industrial cities of Western Europe to urban immigrant neighborhoods in America. As Progressive reformers and immigrant workers mourned—albeit in different ways—this global garment economy was characterized by low wages and small workplaces.

In the years of heavy Eastern European Jewish migration to New York, wages declined as large garment manufactories gave way to a byzantine system of contracting and subcontracting. Retailers no longer produced garments but gave work out to contractors. These contractors, many of whom were also immigrant Jews, struggled to earn meager profits in the thousands of minuscule shops that concentrated among the tenement buildings of the Jewish immigrant neighborhood of the Lower East Side. These small contract shops looked very much like the shops where Jews worked in Eastern and Western Europe. The spread of the contracting system hurt immigrant workers the most because contractors and subcontractors took advantage of the glut of workers to cut labor costs. This had the effect of, first, moving the garment industry away from a factory system much cherished by politicians and social reformers and, second, forcing Eastern European Jewish immigrants into extreme poverty. The combined earnings of male workers and their wives might barely equal a subsistence wage.[2]

The arrival of Jews also dramatically altered the ethnic composition of the American garment workforce. While for much of the nineteenth century, the American garment industry was dominated by German and Irish immigrants and their descendants, by the turn of the century, the United States Industrial Commission reported that "the industry . . . is practically in the hands of the Russian Jews."[3] Although other immigrant groups, especially Italians, soon came to find work in the garment industry, Jewish immigrants and their children dominated the industry as both workers and employers until the Great Depression. And, with the rise of garment unions in the twentieth century, they also composed a majority of union leaders and the rank and file.

As the Industrial Commission's report suggests, the arrival of Jews and the subsequent transformation of the garment industry did not go unnoticed by social reformers and policymakers. By the turn of the century, the Lower East Side and its crowded tenements, dank workshops, and impoverished immigrant residents had become the focus of numerous journalistic exposés, government hearings and inspections, and efforts at reform, education, and Americanization. As part of a general transformation in how immigration was analyzed by reformers and policymakers, these frequent visitors to the Lower East Side relied on conceptions of race to describe Jewish immigrants, their homes, and poverty.

Policymakers insisted that Jewish immigrants were a distinct racial group and placed them within a complex hierarchy of races. Racial analysis, these policymakers argued, could give insight into immigrants' inner moral character and state of civilization. Thus, policymakers, journalists, and reformers came to regard the filth and poverty of the Lower East Side as both a reflection of the economic difficulties faced by new arrivals and as negative Jewish racial traits. Drawing on this language of race, these observers complained bitterly about the manners and mores of Eastern European Jewish immigrant workers and accused them of criminality. They also worried that they were carriers of disease and contagion. Jewish immigration, it seemed, was a threat to American civilization, physical vitality, and racial purity.

Yet this racialized interpretation of Jewish immigrant poverty had its dissenters. In particular, German American Jews, older immigrants who, as a group, enjoyed high levels of assimilation and prosperity, protested that Jews composed a religious group, not a distinct race. They worried that the racialization of Jews might threaten their own comfortable economic and social positions. These German Jews spearheaded campaigns of reform, education, and Americanization designed to counter negative depictions of Jewish immigrants. While policymakers and factory inspectors continued to insist that Jews were a distinct race, they generally supported the program of social engagement and reform advocated by German Jews. After all, they tacitly acknowledged Jews as a race potentially capable of adapting to the pressures of industrial labor. Given the flexibility of their racial categories, these policymakers recognized the possibility that Jews could climb the hierarchy of races. Or, if left to face the depredations of poverty alone, they could fall into a lower state of civilization. Thus, Eastern European Jews were the focus of a host of services, reform programs, and legislative initiatives, unlike other immigrants like Asians, whose whiteness was never suggested, whose fitness for industrial labor was constantly in question, and who faced political, legal, and medical isolation and segregation.[4]

From the Garment Industry in Europe to the Garment Industry in America

New York represented a critical destination for Jewish migrants from the Czarist and Austro-Hungarian empires. New York and especially the Lower East Side were important stopping points in the massive migration of Jews from Eastern Europe throughout the world, what the historian Nancy Green calls the "modern Jewish Diaspora." Between 1881 and 1925, 3.5 million Jews departed Eastern European empires. The vast majority of migrants had lived in the Pale of Settlement, the name given to the region of fifteen western Russian provinces and parts of Russian-controlled Poland where Russian imperial authorities allowed Jews to live.[5]

An overwhelming majority of migrants, 2.65 million souls, headed for the United States, with smaller numbers traveling to other North and South American countries, including Canada and Argentina. Others settled in Western Europe, principally England and France. A significant percentage of the Jewish immigrants to the United States and New York entered through processing centers, first at Castle Garden and, after Castle Garden closed in 1891, Ellis Island. From there, many made the short trip across the New York harbor to Manhattan.

By 1914, almost 800,000 Eastern European Jews had settled in New York and, as early as 1900, Jews composed 14 percent of the city's population.[6] Eastern European Jewish immigrants concentrated in particular areas of the city. The Lower East Side became the initial settling point for many of these immigrants. In 1892, 75 percent of New York's Jews lived on the Lower East Side.[7] However, especially in later years, Eastern European Jewish immigrants sought out relatively more comfortable neighborhoods in Harlem, Brownsville in Brooklyn, and the Grand Concourse in the Bronx.[8]

Jewish immigrants migrated to New York intending to leave behind Eastern Europe's troubled empires.[9] Several waves of pogroms in Russia and the failed revolution of 1904 as well as increasing poverty in the face of industrialization all encouraged their permanent migration.[10] Emigration proved a difficult challenge for Jews. Ports of embarkation often lay thousands of miles from their homes and repressive laws restricted travel. Migrants frequently faced difficulties similar to Rose Cohen and her aunt, who were hidden in the back of a haycart and spirited out of a small town in Russia.[11] The nature of and obstacles to the modern Jewish Diaspora also helped determine who migrated. Unlike any other European immigrant group in the United States, Jews arrived in almost equal numbers of men and women.[12]

Eastern European Jews arrived in the United States divided by region and, as time passed, by generation. Although most immigrants spoke Yiddish, dialects varied dramatically based on region and town of origin.[13] Because Eastern European Jewish immigration to New York spanned almost a half century, generational divides added to social, economic, and cultural differences. Older immigrants in New York quickly responded to cultural pressures that put a premium on visual signs of Americanness. As a result, immigrants individually and collectively reconsidered how they dressed, practiced their religion, and organized family life. And, to show their own acculturation, they often denigrated newcomers as "greenhorns." A greenhorn was an immigrant fresh from the old world whose obvious visual characteristics, like their style of dress or a full beard for men or a covered head for women, belied a lack of assimilation.[14]

Despite such initial efforts to look American, many immigrants found themselves working in similar trades and in similar kinds of workplaces as in the old country. The arrival of Eastern European Jews in New York signaled the spread of a transnational garment working class to America. The outpost of the global garment industry that Jewish immigrants helped create in New York sold goods to a domestic market but depended for its competitiveness on relationships and work patterns developed in the Diaspora. The foreignness of workers and the Americanness of consumers were noticed by policymakers. As the Industrial Commission on Immigration concluded in 1901, "the clothing trade leads all others in the United States as an occupation controlled by immigrants."[15]

Garment work was the occupational background for many of the Eastern European Jewish immigrants to New York. Although over 40 percent of Jewish residents in the Pale lived in urban areas, a few immigrants had come from mostly agricultural towns and discovered the industrial world in New York.[16] In 1898, only 2.9 percent of Jewish residents in the Pale of Settlement had agricultural occupations. In contrast, 37.9 percent of Russian Jews worked in industrial jobs and many as tailors. Among Jewish artisans in the Pale of Settlement in 1898, fully 38.7 percent were involved in the manufacture of "wearing apparel."[17] Jewish garment workers in Russia toiled in small, generally unmechanized workshops often owned by Jews. As a United States Consular Report on the garment trade in Russia noted in 1884: "Nearly all the smaller ones (tailor stores) belong to Jews, and the ready-made clothing without exception are owned by the latter (Jews). The hands are also nearly all Jews and Jewesses."[18] The garment industry in the Pale, like the one that would emerge in New York, was based around small shops owned and staffed by Jews.

Garment work was also frequently the occupational background for the many Eastern European Jews who arrived in Western European cities like London, Manchester, Leeds, or Paris, sometimes on their way to America. Many Jewish immigrant garment workers in New York had labored not only in the garment factories in Lodz or Bialystok, but also in London or Paris.[19] As historian David Feldman notes, in 1891, fully 45 percent of Jewish immigrants in London worked as tailors; ten years later that number was 44 percent. As in Eastern Europe, garment manufactories in Western Europe were generally small and unmechanized. One study, conducted in 1889, found that 76 percent of Jewish tailoring workshops in London employed fewer than ten hands and a mere 2 percent hired more than 25.[20]

Thus, many Eastern European Jewish immigrants arrived in the United States and in New York with a background in garment manufacture, although not generally with experience in highly mechanized forms of production. Between 1901 and 1906, of 75,411 Jewish immigrants to the United States who listed their occupation, fully 18,418 claimed to be tailors.[21] Upon their arrival in New York, even those Jewish immigrants without a background in tailoring often looked for work in the needle trades. Eastern European Jewish immigrants, like Bernard Reiskind, often found their first jobs through family members or *landsmen* (immigrants from the same town in Eastern Europe) who had already found jobs in the expanding world of garment manufacture. Reiskind's family, for example, pushed him into garment work: "Two members in the household where my wife and I have temporary living quarters . . . are both employed in the clothing industry. Both of them . . . are outspokenly in favor of my joining the garment industry." He felt that he had little choice of careers: "I have no alternatives but to take the earnest advise [*sic*] of my relatives."[22]

Staying with *landsmen* or with family members sometimes permitted an immigrant a few days rest and the leisure to explore their new surroundings before beginning work. The experiences of two immigrants, Samuel Siegal and Stella Papiroff, were typical. When Siegal first landed in New York, he stayed with Saul Sheifer, a *landsman*, who immediately urged him to shave his beard and purchase a new set of American-style clothing. Then, Sheifer helped him find his first job: carting bundles of clothing for a clothing manufacturer. Similarly, Stella Papiroff enjoyed a few days leisure after she arrived because she found lodging with Elizaveta, a *landsman*. Then she found herself working side by side with Elizaveta.[23]

Adjusting to a new home and finding work were closely intertwined, highlighting the place of the New York garment industry in a transnational world of immigration and ethnicity. Many Jewish employers preferred to hire only relatives or neighbors from Eastern Europe. Jewish employers organized *landsman* shops, which depended on new immigrants for hard work and cheap labor. The tailor Sam Liptzin remembered that Chuneh Miller, the contractor of one such shop, was also the head of the hometown association (*landsmanshaftn*), whose members were his workers. In fact, Miller's shop became known to its employees as "the Society," in reference to the hometown "Society."[24] Only in desperation did Miller ever hire a non-*landsman*, and as soon as a new *landsman* arrived, the stranger was fired. Similarly, the father of the union leader and garment worker Isidore Wisotsky arrived in New York two years before the rest of his family and worked to accumulate enough money to pay for passage for his wife and children. He found a job in a shop owned by a cousin who helped him save money by allowing him to sleep on the floor of the shop.[25]

Not all immigrants arrived in New York with family members or *landsmen* ready to greet and house them and find them jobs. Nonetheless, many still found their way into the needle trades and into the transnational garment economy. Without the immediate support of friends or relatives, such immigrants' need for a job was even more pressing. With numerous Jewish employers and the proximity of shops to immigrants' homes, the needle trades were the most obvious and abundant source of work. Harry Polis, for example, landed in Manhattan in 1906 knowing no one. Most immigrants, he recalled, "had friends who met them and took them into their homes and helped them find a job. . . . The majority of them had pull because of relatives already in the business."[26] With his savings dwindling, Polis asked his landlady where he could find a job in the needle trades. She suggested he look in the want ads in the Yiddish newspapers, like the *Jewish Daily Forward*. He found work in a shop with a Jewish employer and joined a Jewish workforce.[27] Elizabeth Hasanovitz also arrived in New York without friends or relatives and immediately turned to the Yiddish papers to find work. Through an ad, she found a job in a knitted goods shop with a solidly Jewish workforce.[28]

Other workers who could not depend on the help of friends or *landsmen* found work by congregating in open-air labor markets where Jewish agents and employers came to hire Jewish workers. Eastern European Jewish immigrants labeled the largest and most prominent of these markets the *chazer mark*, meaning the "pig market" in Yiddish, perhaps because, as the journalist Jacob Riis put it, one could purchase anything there except pigs.[29] Located in the Hester Street Park in the heart of the Lower East Side, the *chazer mark* became a gathering place for workers, especially recent immigrants. Sam Liptzin remembered his first visit to the *chazer mark*: "Here the workers used to come to 'hire out their hands.' Here the tailors would gather in the hundreds, especially the greenhorns, and wait for the bosses, the contractors, the foremen, and the agents, who come looking for workers. . . . It was here the bosses came to search for cheap labor." A recent immigrant, Liptzin waited only "a few minutes" before he was hired as a baste-puller and a night watchman for a small contract shop on Pike Street on the Lower East Side. Ignorant of both trades, Liptzin was instructed in baste-pulling, but did not even understand the meaning of "night watchman." He fled the darkening shop soon after the other workers left. During the night the unwatched shop was robbed, and the following day Liptzin returned to the *chazer mark*.[30]

Still other immigrants found work at different open-air employment markets. George Price, for example, recalled seeking a job at New York's Battery just across the harbor from Ellis Island: "For several days I made it a practice to stand around the battery and offer myself for some job. . . . People approachd [*sic*] the group in which I stood, asked to examine the hand of applicants for work and selected those whose hands showed some acquaintance with work." Finally, Price unwittingly went to work as a scab. When he found out, he immediately quit the job and returned to the Battery.[31] Other immigrants blessed with more experience in garment work waited to be hired at markets specific to some of the more skilled trades. The cutters market, for example, was located originally at 12th Street and Broadway on the edge of the Lower East Side and by 1916 had moved up Broadway to 25th Street near the present-day garment district.[32]

While religious persecution, political upheaval, and deepening poverty may have encouraged migration, the needle trades acted as an economic bridge from Eastern to Western Europe and from there to America. Many Eastern European Jewish immigrants found themselves in the world of garment work, if only briefly. As Polis quickly observed after his arrival in New York: "It appeared . . . that most of the Jewish immigrants learned the needle trades."[33] His impressions were confirmed by surveys conducted by outside observers seeking to understand the role of Eastern European Jewish immigrants in the garment industry. As early as 1890, a Baron de Hirsch Fund survey of 25,000 Jewish immigrant workers discovered that 12,000 of them labored in garment manufacture. Seven years later, the New York State Office of Factory Inspectors reported that 60 percent of Jewish immigrants worked in the needle trades.[34] Many of those workers not producing garments at the time of these surveys had probably at one time also toiled in garment shops.[35]

Especially given the competitive advantage employers gained from hiring relatives or desperate new arrivals, Eastern European Jewish immigrants quickly became (and remained for nearly a half century) the majority in many of the city's most prominent and largest garment-making crafts, notably women's cloakmaking, waistmaking, dressmaking, raincoatmaking, and whitegoodsmaking. Overall, in 1897 in New York's garment trades, 75 percent of all workers were Jewish and many sought work in shops owned by Jews.[36] Ninety percent of shops on the Lower East Side were owned by Jews. Some of these were German American Jews and, increasingly, many were Eastern European Jewish immigrants.[37] Cloakmaking, in particular, remained an almost homogeneous trade of Eastern European Jewish workers. As late as 1910, almost 90 percent of cloakmakers were Jewish.[38] Of the major crafts, only shirtwaistmaking (the manufacture of separate, lightweight blouses) became ethnically mixed. Fifty-six percent of waistmakers in a 1913 survey were Jewish and 34 percent were Italian.[39]

The arrival of Eastern European Jews helped transform the Lower East Side into the center of the city's growing garment industry. The neighborhood's crowded tenement apartment buildings became honeycombed with small garment workshops. Between 1880 and 1910, the Lower East Side was, at once, New York's most densely populated neighborhood, with over 1,000 people per acre, and the center of garment manufacture, one of the city's most important industries.[40] Nearly 80 percent of the garment industry was located below 14th

Street on the Lower East Side. The needle trades not only provided a bridge for immigrants, but also acted as an economic scaffold for the ethnic Lower East Side. Small garment shops provided familiar work and immigrant workers represented a ready source of labor. As a later report noted: "Once the East Side, South of Houston Street and East of the Bowery, was the garment center, par excellence. Here were located large and small groups of the Cloak and Suit workshops, the location being preferred because the workers in the trade lived in the district."[41]

Fashion, Technology, and the Transformation of New York Garment Manufacture, 1880–1910

The rise of the garment industry in New York was made possible by technological innovations that permitted the inexpensive manufacture of garments, a shift in fashion from custom to ready-made styles, and, most important, a pool of workers so desperate for jobs that they would labor for pitiable wages. Through the labor of Eastern European Jewish immigrants, garment manufacture became one of New York City's largest and most important industries. The city's women's garment shops produced $102,711,604 worth of clothing in 1900, or 64 percent of all women's clothing manufactured in the United States. In comparison, Philadelphia made only $9,452,259 and St. Louis only $2,987,446 worth of clothing.[42]

Around 1800, commercial garment making existed almost solely as a custom trade in which skilled workers made individual garments to order and to measure. However, by the time Jewish immigrants began arriving in New York, the ready-made trade, in which garments were pre-made to standardized sizes, predominated. In 1900, for example, custom manufacturers produced only $14,915,538 of the $123,800,000 worth of women's garments manufactured in New York State.[43] The pace of the transformation from custom to ready-made production varied in the men's and women's trades, suggesting the importance of changes in fashion. The different trends in men's and women's clothing manufacture helped separate the garment trades into two spheres. The needle trades were (and, indeed, remain) loosely divided between men's and women's garments. In men's clothing, the ready-made trade initially emerged during the Civil War.[44] Ready-made production lagged in ladies' garment making, the principal needle trade in New York. The rapidly changing fashions and more ornamented designs of women's clothing hindered the rise of ready made. As late as World War I, millinery, the manufacture of dresses, remained largely a custom trade, although only for the higher end of the market. Still, by the 1880s, women's cloakmaking and shirtwaistmaking were largely readymade trades. The movement of women into the industrial workforce during World War I and the resulting impulse for scaled-down fashions catalyzed the final triumph of ready made in the women's clothing trade.[45] Newly fashionable, looser-fitting women's garments, undergarments, and skirts all lent themselves to standard-ized production.[46]

While fashion surely played a role in the rise of the ready-made trade, mass production was not possible without new technologies. Most important were the sewing machine and cutting knife, invented in 1846 and 1876, respectively.[47] In examining the garment industry in 1859, the *New York Tribune* rightly pre-dicted the death of the sewing needle: "The needle will soon be consigned to oblivion, like the wheel, the loom, and the knitting-needles."[48] While the sew-ing machine permitted rapid manufacture, the cutting knife allowed the cut-ting of multiple pieces of cloth, which would later be machine-sewn into garments. By 1884, cutters could cut cloth piled six inches high.[49] The dual use of the sewing machine and the cutting knife eliminated production bottle-necks. As quickly as garments could be stitched, new cloth could be cut.

In the later half of the nineteenth century and especially after the arrival of Jewish immigrants, inspectors and policymakers noted that the rise of mass production workshops with new technologies diminished the need for skilled workers. With the sewing machine, the honed skills of the tailor became un-necessary. With the cutting knife and the cutting of patterns, the skilled cut-ter was also rendered obsolete. By 1900, a typical shirtwaist shop employed only two to five cutters, and even the cutters, using the long cutting knife, were semi-skilled. They were trained only to cut specific patterns. Factory inspec-tors argued that few tasks actually demanded much instruction, and immi-grants' efforts to define skill became more a way of delineating differences between men's and women's work than a way of marking training and rare talent. Indeed, one report noted that while custom tailoring once needed four to five years to master, tasks that Jewish workers came to label as skilled, like machine operating and pressing, required at most three months of training.[50]

New ways of organizing production further reduced the dependence on skilled workers. Between 1880 and 1900, garment manufacturers introduced the "team" and, later, the "section" systems of labor, which splintered garment work into a myriad of crafts. Garment workers became specialists in one small step in the production of a garment.[51] The sewing and finishing of shirts and shirtwaists, for example, involved twenty to forty different operations, depend-ing on the size of the workshop and the complexity of the style. Specializa-tions ranged from sleeve makers, body makers, sleeve setters, and skirt makers to button setters, collar makers, cuff makers, and machine embroiders—all working side by side in the same factories.[52]

With changes in the form and style of production, garment manufacture became centered around small shops. The sewing machine and cutting knife were generally inexpensive, and with their introduction, the number of garment workplaces proliferated and the size of shops shrank. In the women's clothing industry in New York State, the number of shops increased dramatically from 304 in 1880 to 5,744 in 1890. In 1900, there were 830 shops in the immigrant Lower East Side just making women's cloaks and suits.[53] At the same time, the size and capitalization of shops declined. In 1880, shops averaged fifty workers capitalized on average at $17,606.54; by 1890, shops averaged only eight workers with a capitalization of $2,960.11.[54] Two years later, when the New York Factory Inspectors surveyed 3,836 shops, most shops hired four to twenty-five workers. None employed more than fifty.[55] Federal inspectors also bemoaned the proliferation of small shops. They visited one tenement on the Lower East Side with a small shop on each floor. Each shop had fewer than six workers cramped in a minuscule space: "In each of the foregoing cases . . . a room practically means a space 15 by 20 feet. . . . In almost every case the ceilings were less than 8 foot high."[56] Smaller tenement shops had replaced larger factories.

The move to smaller shops allowed some recent immigrants to become proprietors. Such immigrant shop owners were often as poor as their employees. With only around fifty dollars an immigrant could open a small shop.[57] As one New York State factory inspector noted, all that was needed was to "rent a small room or two in the rear part of an upper floor of a high building, put in a few sewing machines, a stove suitable for heating irons, and then hire a number of men and women to work."[58] Some contractors even made workers rent their own sewing machines and cart them to the shop.[59] At times, immigrants like Yitzchak Yankel Doroshkin became proprietors and, when unlucky, rejoined the ranks of workers. When Doroshkin first arrived in New York, he worked in a dress shop. Later he opened a dress shop with a cousin but soon became a worker again. He remembered that as an owner, he worked alongside his few employees.[60]

The proliferation of such small shops, often owned by immigrants, led to changes in systems of garment production and selling. By 1890, most retailers contracted out "bundles of clothing"—that is, lots of pre-cut garments ready to be assembled. The garment industry soon divided into "inside" and "outside" shops. Inside shops were directly tied to retailers. A handful of inside shops actually oversaw the entire manufacture of a garment from cutting to the final inspection. Most inside shops, however, only bundled pre-cut garments and inspected the final product. Outside contractors bid for bundles of clothing and as the number of potential contractors increased, profit margins shrank. Some contractors in desperate search for profit further contracted out their bundles to subcontractors. In 1892, when a House of Representatives committee began examining conditions in the garment industry, it discovered that one half of all contracted work was further contracted out to subcontractors.[61]

Between 1900 and 1910, further technical advances and the accumulation of capital in the hands of a small number of fortunate proprietors, contractors, and subcontractors again spurred changes in garment production. In a 1911 survey, only 469 of 1,738 shops still relied solely on foot power. The remainder employed electric power. These improvements mandated "a larger and more important kind of manufacturer, with larger capital investments."[62] Still, small shops and systems of contracting characterized much of the garment industry. As late as 1910, only shirtwaist factories regularly hired more than fifty workers.[63] Yet although shirtwaist factories grew, contracting persisted. The Triangle Shirtwaist factory, one of the larger shirtwaist factories, may have hired hundreds of workers but remained dependent on contracting. Within its factory walls, work was given out to inside male subcontractors who hired, fired, and set wage rates for their own largely female employees.[64] In addition, other trades, like cloakmaking, remained housed in small contractor shops. Highly prone to the vicissitudes of season and style, cloakmaking lent itself best to tenement manufacture. In small tenement shops labor was divided between male and female workers, with men claiming the overwhelming majority of skilled and semi-skilled jobs.[65] While shirtwaist shops averaged fifty-two workers, cloakshops averaged twenty-nine. Still, despite the existence of a few larger shirtwaist shops, "the outside contracting method is still all prevalent," mourned one observer in 1911. There was a decline in contracting and an increase in the size of garment workshops throughout the New York needle trades only after 1910 with the rise of garment unions.[66]

New York's factory inspectors noted that the system of contracting and subcontracting depressed wages. The combined earnings of men, women, and their children barely equaled a subsistence wage. Male workers, eager to adapt to the most visible, American cultural ideals about the restriction of married women's labor, still had to depend on the work of their wives and children to augment their salaries.[67] In fact, with increasing numbers of immigrants and the rise of outside contractor and subcontractor shops, wages were actually declining. Between 1883 and 1885 alone, average wages for male workers plummeted from $15 a week to between $6 and $7 a week. At best, dress and cloakmakers might earn $10 a week.

At the same time, both men and women were working longer hours. In the few inside shops that remained in the 1880s, workers labored around sixty hours per week. In contrast, in contractor and subcontractor shops, workers averaged over eighty hours per week, not counting overtime and the hours spent at home finishing the bundles of clothing workers took with them from the shop.[68] Declining wages inevitably meant that male garment workers could not serve as a family's sole means of support, and as contracting spread in the 1880s, garment work became family work.

The Lower East Side, Jewish Poverty, Race, and Progressive Reform

Rapidly declining wages and increasing hours might alone explain the widespread poverty that factory inspectors, journalists, social reformers, and politicians noted among the growing Eastern European Jewish immigrant population of the Lower East Side. These outside observers, though, sought more complex explanations for the persistence, extremes, and character of immigrants' poverty. They turned to contemporary understandings of race and science. By the 1890s, the indigence of immigrants on the Lower East Side had captured public attention.[69] Jewish poverty and the Lower East Side became the focus of frequent journalistic exposés in local newspapers and national magazines. New York newspapers from the *Tribune* to the *New York Times* and major national magazines from the *Nation* to the *Arena* regularly sent reporters to the Lower East Side. Books, like the journalist Jacob Riis's *How the Other Half Lives*, described the poverty of recent immigrants to curious—and frightened—middle-class audiences. These journalists were followed to the Lower East Side by government inspectors and investigators. Theodore Roosevelt, for example, then the chairman of the Police Commission, often accompanied Riis on his visits into New York's poorer areas like the Lower East Side.[70] Reporters, journalists, and politicians all relied on racial explanations of the economics of the needle trades industry and the poverty of immigrant garment workers.

Descriptions of the Lower East Side and Jewish poverty adopted a common narrative about exploration and scientific study. Observers of the Lower East Side cast themselves as visitors to a strange, dangerous neighborhood characterized by powerful odors and appalling conditions. They were explorers of a foreign land, of what one visitor called "a genuine Jewish ghetto" and another labeled "a Russian village."[71] Their goal seemed to be to titillate readers with lurid, even erotic tales of "fish scales and slime," women wearing "a scarcity of clothing," and "children . . . covered with sores." At the same time, they claimed an anthropological role. As one reporter for the *New York Times* concluded, he was a "student of humanity" examining the "daily drudgery and toil of these immigrants."[72]

The narrative of exploration and the shocking, sexualized language suggests how Jewish poverty was examined as much for its details as for the threats that it posed to the rest of the city, the nation, and, specifically, to American racial and physical vitality and civilization. These explorations and anthropological studies of the Lower East Side depended on larger turn-of-the-twentieth-century discourses about race, racial decline, civilization, and public health. Race, in short, provided the cultural vocabulary used to describe Jewish poverty and its social dangers. As the *New York Times* insisted, "The New York ghetto is an inexhaustible mine of interest and information for those who delight in studying the life, manners, and customs of a race which is unique among the races of the globe."[73]

Such journalistic exposés reflected an understanding of immigration, not simply as the arrival of multifarious nationalities, but as the influx of different races. By 1899, the Industrial Commission on Immigration, for example, was classifying immigrants by race, not nationality.[74] According to Progressive Era observers, there was a hierarchy of races. In this complex and changing definition of race, native-born Anglo-Saxons claimed the place at the top, while immigrant races—like "Hebrews"—occupied lower places on the hierarchy, albeit above those races determined to be nonwhite. Most understandings of race recognized three, four, or five main taxonomies of "peoples," including Caucasian, Ethiopian, Mongolian, Malay, and American (meaning American Indians), and, within these taxonomies, large numbers of differentiated races. The United States Immigration Commission in its *Dictionary of Races or Peoples*, for example, identified forty-five distinct races.[75]

The prevailing language of "race," "peoples," and "taxonomies" revealed observers' insistence on the biological and evolutionary roots of race. The hierarchy of races was an evolutionary ladder, and its instability allowed for races to move up or down the hierarchy, depending on their changing state of civilization, especially those European races like Jews that were generally seen as capable of industrial labor. Civilization, then, was understood as a measure of moral and physical conditions.[76] Immigrants' living and working conditions could affect their state of civilization and, thus, their racial position. Consequently, observers worried that the poverty of the Lower East Side would force Jewish immigrants even further down the evolutionary ladder. At the same time, they insisted that the poverty and conditions of the Lower East Side reflected the debased character of the "Hebrew race." As the historian Matthew Frye Jacobson has noted, for Progressive Era observers, physical traits and phenotypes were signs of inner character and morality.[77] Indeed, the Industrial Commission on Immigration concluded that the "new classification of immigrants according to race rather than nationality" best revealed the social "effects of immigration."[78]

Race and racial position, for these explorers of the Lower East Side, was most visible in the bodies of immigrants. And, observers argued, the low racial status of Jews was evident in their characteristic "poor physical condition."[79] The *New York Times* regularly described these "attenuated creatures, clad in old, faded, greasy, often tattered clothing." Or, as one journalist reported about his visit to the *chazer mark*: "Filthy persons and clothing reeking with vermin are seen on every side."[80] Like the *New York Times* reporters, Riis noted the "physical exhaustion" of the "wretchedly poor" Jewish residents of the Lower East Side.[81]

For these repulsed observers, the poor physical condition of immigrant Jews was linked to one of the most widely cited Jewish racial characteristics: a comfort in filth, dirt, and vermin. Jews "seem to prefer to live in dirt," the Industrial Commission on Immigration insisted. Visitors to the Lower East Side claimed to have found ample evidence of this racial trait. The *Tribune* declared that Jewish immigrants were "filthy in their habits and most obstinate in their mode of living," and the *Herald* declared that Eastern European Jewish immigrants were "on social terms with parasitic vermin." One reporter described his horror at Jews' willingness to eat rotten food and cheese. Despite the reek of the cheese, "the long whiskered descendents of Abraham, Isaac, Jacob, and Judah on the East Side would put their fingers in it and then suck them with great and evident relish." This "relish," he insisted, clearly revealed Jews' low racial status. While Jews ate the cheese, the reporter "almost had a spasm from the smell." Their comfort in filth was the reason Jews "cannot be lifted up to [a] higher plane."[82] Legislators used such reasoning to place Jews in a racial hierarchy below French, English, and Irish immigrants.[83]

Indeed, some observers seemed to hint that the experience of immigration and the poverty of the Lower East Side might cause Jews' racial degeneration. One reporter worried that the Polish immigrant Jew had "grown to be looked down upon as a despised one among those of his own race."[84] The Industrial Commission on Immigration similarly worried that "within the last year or two the Hebrews also have shown tendencies to the grosser vices that have never before characterized them." The commission blamed conditions on the "foreign" Lower East Side for "the evils seen to be growing."[85] Others worried that through the process of immigration, the worst of the race had ended up in New York. The *Nation* argued that while "some of this immigration is of excellent character . . . some of it [is] quite the reverse."[86] The labor journalist Eva McDonald Valesh was even less charitable, suggesting that "the very dregs of foreign immigrants always settle in New York."[87] And the Commissioner General of Immigration, Frank Sargent, condemned Jewish immigrants as "decrepit men and women." They were, according to one reporter, "vice-ridden, stolid, bovine parodies of manhood."[88]

For these observers, a lapse in morality among impoverished immigrants was key to their racial and physical decline. Lower East Side poverty, the Industrial Commission concluded, "tends to their physical and moral deterioration." The bad "moral surroundings" of the crowded Lower East Side affected even the "poor Hebrew of quiet family life and moral tradition."[89] Such fears about the degraded character of immigration inevitably focused on "white slavery," a traffic in underage girls and "immoral women" by men of inferior manhood. Thus, when Commissioner Sargent sought to illustrate the "character of immigrants," he pointed to a room of "detained women and girls." When the *Tribune* railed against prostitution as the worst of "the queer features of this foreign district," they pointed out the immoral women as well as the "degraded men." The prevalence of prostitutes and the men who lived off them on the Lower East Side, the reporter insisted, "contaminate their neighbors." Children and neighbors, in return for candy or bribes, became watchers, spies, or agents and were thus "engulfed in the sea of vice."[90]

Anxieties about Jewish racial decline exposed a larger fear about the social dangers of Jewish immigration. Valesh was typical in declaring Jewish immigrants a threat to "civilization."[91] And the threats posed by Jewish immigrants to the civilization of New York were seen as embodied in crime and in diseases that might begin in the Lower East Side and infect the rest of the city. Sargent, for example, declared that the immigration of Jews, among other European immigrant groups, could "poison or at least pollute the very fountainhead of American life and progress." For Sargent, Jews were a significant part of "an enormous alien population in our larger cities which is breeding crime and disease."[92]

Observers also worried about Jews' overrepresentation on police rolls. As a police reporter, Jacob Riis noted that police called the Lower East Side the "crooked ward."[93] Similarly, in 1908, in a widely distributed report, New York City Police Commissioner Theodore Bingham blamed "alien" Jews for many of the city's crime problems. Bingham claimed that while Jews composed only 25 percent of the city's population, they accounted for 50 percent of its criminals.[94] For one *New York Times* reporter, one of the many racial "abominations" of the Jews was their "utter disregard for the law."[95]

While journalists like Riis and city politicians like Bingham viewed Eastern European Jewish immigrants as a threat to public safety, other critics came to see immigrants as a public health concern. They argued that Jews were the carriers of disease and that illness could spread from their squalid neighborhoods to the rest of the city. With a growing fear of communicable diseases after the German scientist Robert Koch announced his germ theory of disease in 1882, public health officials, doctors, and city politicians clamored for increased medical surveys and inspections of new immigrants.[96] Sargent, for example, warned of a plague that could begin among immigrants and engulf the entire East Coast. One journalist worried that, given the lack of cleanliness among Jews, "if the cholera should ever get among these people, they would scatter its germs as a sower does grain."[97] In fact, in 1892, New York City public health officials and politicians blamed Eastern European Jewish immigrants for typhus and cholera epidemics and quarantined boatloads of recently arrived Jews.[98]

The racialized language used to evaluate the social and moral character of Jewish immigrants and the dangers they posed had its detractors. In particular, German American Jews, a previous generation of Jewish immigrants who, as a group, had achieved prosperity, protested "Hebrews" as a racial category. Instead, as the leading German Jewish association B'nai B'rith insisted, Jews were a religious group, not a distinct race.[99] German Jews feared that negative evaluations of Jewish racial standing might threaten their own social standing. At their Nineteenth Annual Convention, for example, the Union of American Hebrew Congregations worried that "if there should grow up in our midst a class of people abnormal and objectionable to our fellow citizens . . . all of us will suffer. . . . The question is largely one of self-preservation."[100]

When German Jewish complaints about the categorization of "Hebrews" as a race fell on deaf ears, German Jews responded by sponsoring countless programs designed to mitigate the effects of poverty and, in the process, instruct immigrants in the manners and mores of civilization.[101] Between 1890 and 1910, German Jews founded a range of educational and medical initiatives and charities. In 1893 alone the United Hebrew Charities, a charity funded by German Jews, spent $116,000 in services for new Eastern European Jewish immigrants.[102]

As B'nai B'rith assured the Industrial Commission on Immigration, German Jewish charities sought to address the specific concerns raised about immigrant Jews' cleanliness, criminality, and health. Even as German Jews insisted that their Eastern European co-religionists were not part of a distinct racial group, they still worked for the "assimilation" and "Americanization" of the "Russian refugees."[103] Thus, in 1891, the wealthy Isidor Straus and Jacob Schiff funded the creation of the Educational Alliance, a large center in the middle of the Lower East Side that offered classes on English literature, hygiene, patriotism, and physical education. The Alliance's leaders sought not to lift Eastern European Jews from the ranks of the working class, but to instruct them in their new roles as American workers. As the Alliance's director, David Blaustein, noted in 1913, the center's aim was to train Eastern European immigrants to accept the "manual work which falls [sic] his lot."[104] At the same time, German American Jews founded institutions from Mount Sinai Hospital to the Hebrew Orphan Asylum that sought to protect the health of Eastern European immigrants.[105] And, in 1908, largely in response to Bingham's report on Jewish criminality, German American Jews organized the New York Kehillah, an experimental association designed after Old World Jewish forms of communal self-government. The Kehillah brought together literally hundreds of charities and institutions charged with the Americanization of Eastern European Jews.[106]

Progressive reformers, public health advocates, and politicians joined German American Jews in their attempts to remake immigrants' lives on the Lower East Side. Jewish immigrants did not face legal social segregation. Instead, observers criticized the creation of a "genuine" ghetto (although it is hard to imagine that such observers encouraged Jewish immigrants to move into their own neighborhoods). They blamed its creation on other immigrant races that "despise them, ridicule them" or on the "exclusiveness of the race itself."[107] Indeed, observers lamented the creation of exclusive "colonies" because they thwarted the potential racial advancement of Jewish immigrants. In contrast to their approach to nonwhite immigrants, observers saluted the movement of Jews throughout the city, especially to cleaner, less crowded working-class neighborhoods. They equated this movement with Jews' assimilation and racial progress. Only "poverty and ignorance" kept Jews on the Lower East Side.[108]

In recognizing Jews' ability for "advancement," observers and critics of Eastern European Jews, like Bingham and Riis, actively engaged themselves in immigrants' lives. While these observers' visits exposed the foreign quarters of the Lower East Side to a worried yet curious audience, they never seemed to lose sight of Jews' perceived ability for social and racial advancement. Instead, visits to immigrants' neighborhoods, in addition to producing lurid exploration narratives, collected evidence to support demands for legislation and reform.

And, these demands were recognized by a host of politicians and social reformers. New York State politicians passed legislation aimed to ease congestion in the Lower East Side tenements much criticized in the popular press. City politicians repaved Lower East Side streets with asphalt to combat filth and the spread of disease.[109] Settlement houses introduced proponents of social reform to the details of Lower East Side immigrants' poverty, and instructed immigrants on hygiene and standards of behavior and manners. The Nurses' Settlement House and its director, Lilian Wald, sought to combat the illnesses they considered rampant on the Lower East Side.[110] By 1908, Wald oversaw a staff of twenty-seven nurses. Her attention to the health problems of immigrants reflected the focus of frequent surveys of living and working conditions carried out by city officials and, later, by the United States Public Health Services.[111]

Journalistic, reform, and political responses to Jewish immigration were shaped by a strange mixture of disgust, fear, curiosity, and even titillation. This mixture was held together by a complex racial vision that described Jews as a degenerate race, but still as a race capable of progress and advancement. Thus, journalists generally advocated and German Jews, reformers, and politicians sought to implement a policy of engagement that sought at once to mitigate the perceived dangers posed by Jewish immigrants and to aid in their progress.

Jewish immigrants' work was central to this policy of engagement and reform. After all, observers noted, if disease was going to spread from the Lower East Side, it would likely be carried in the threads of the garments they manufactured. Garments were the link between the dangerous filth of the Lower East Side and the rest of "civilization." The garment industry seemed to be where the effects of Jewish immigration were most visible and, thus, the small shops that Jews supposedly carried over with them from Europe became reflections of Jewish racial traits: their physical inferiority, peculiar character, and immorality. Jewish garment shops, the incarnation of the transnational garment economy, were cast as the places where Jews became a threat to civilization, where Jewish bodies were further weakened, and where their morals deteriorated. In short, these shops were indicted as both a principal cause and as a symptom of Jewish racial degeneration.

Thus, the garment industry that Jews had come to dominate increasingly became the focus of reform efforts and concern on the part of social reformers, journalists, and German Jews. In describing garment shops simultaneously as a reflection of Jewish racial inferiority and as a cause of their decline, these observers sought to distinguish garment shops from "American" industry. They turned to the term "sweated labor," a description of Jewish immigrants' garment work that stressed its weakening effects on the bodies of workers. It was also a term that had long been associated with the garment labor of immigrants. The "sweatshop," a word born from the racialized language of social reformers and factory inspectors, was a workshop devoid of the supposed civilized character of the American factory. In the sweatshop, workers were weakened in body and mind. Thus, concerns about the public health and moral dangers of immigration became focused on the sweatshop.

Two

"The Great Jewish Métier"

*Factory Inspectors, Jewish Workers, and
Defining the Sweatshop, 1880–1910*

The spread of contractor shops in New York, insisted the United States Industrial Commission on Immigration, was intimately connected to the arrival of Jewish immigrants. "The position of the contractor," the economist John R. Commons testified to the Commission, "is peculiarly that of an organizer and employer of immigrants."[1] Because of the association of garment work with immigrants, especially Eastern European Jews, criticism of changes and conditions in the New York garment industry ran parallel to and often merged with concerns about Jewish poverty on the Lower East Side.

Many of the same journalists, politicians, and inspectors who had explored the streets of the Lower East Side and returned with lurid tales of the foreign quarter also visited the neighborhood's garment contract shops. They found in these shops many of the same signs of racial inferiority and decline as on the Lower East Side's streets. They relied on the same languages of race, with the accompanying fears of disease and racial degeneration, to express concerns about the small garment shops that filled the tenement buildings of the Lower East Side.

These outside observers labeled these shops "sweatshops," a name that drew on centuries-old meanings of "sweated work" as physically exhausting labor. But the exhaustion implied in the meaning of sweatshop took on a new and historically specific racial significance. Physical exhaustion revealed the weak body that factory inspectors believed was emblematic of Jewish racial inferiority. Indeed, inspectors argued that even these shops themselves, with their cramped, dirty quarters and "un-American" ways of organizing production, were the product of Jewish racial characteristics. Race, it seemed, provided an explanation for the economics of the industry.

As definitions of the sweatshop were firmly intertwined with turn-of-the-twentieth-century conceptions of race, efforts to describe the problems posed by the sweatshop were linked to criticisms of immigrant workers. In fact, the narrative of exploration of the Lower East Side that contrasted journalists' disgust and shock with Jewish immigrants' comfort in filth and immorality was reproduced by a host of factory inspectors and journalists as they visited sweatshops. The personal reactions of outside visitors to Lower East Side shops colored testimonies about sweatshops and their dangers. The reports of inspectors and journalists seem to measure and delineate racial differences between workers and outside observers. Inspectors and journalists described the dirty, scantily clad, enfeebled appearance of sweatshop workers as much as they detailed the conditions of factories. In the process, they contrasted their own revulsion and shock to immigrants' apparent acceptance of conditions.

These observers relied on their personal, often sensory responses to the sweatshop, to its smells, sights, and sounds, to deduce the dangers the sweatshop posed to "civilization." As with fears about the threat of Jewish immigrants in general, concerns about effects of sweatshops on civilization focused specifically on the spread of germs. Germs could be bred in the filthy, immoral surroundings of the sweatshop and spread to middle-class consumers. The fear of epidemics, along with concerns about Jewish racial decline, informed factory inspectors and politicians' initial reform and regulation strategies.

While the discourse about sweatshops was expressed in sites like congressional hearings, where immigrants rarely appeared, and in English-language magazines and newspapers, which few immigrants could read, immigrant workers gave their own meanings to the sweatshop. Especially at first, when few factory inspectors spoke Yiddish and few garment workers spoke fluent English, workers and inspectors did interact on the shop floor—if only through the questions workers could understand or through workers' observations of inspectors' methods and reactions. In addition, a few immigrant workers, usually well-respected community or union leaders, testified before government hearings.

Thus, the sweatshop, as a word and as a concept, entered the language of the Lower East Side. Jewish garment workers advanced their own definition of the sweatshop. Like inspectors, Jewish garment workers saw the sweatshop as enfeebling. Immigrants, as well as their German co-religionists, looked around the garment shops and described workers' shrunken chests, stooped backs, and weakened muscles. They also worried about the prevalence of disease, especially tuberculosis, among workers. Unlike inspectors, garment workers placed the blame for their weakened bodies on the conditions of work, not on Jewish racial traits. The enfeebled body of the Jewish immigrant worker emerged because of employers. Where inspectors stressed race as the underlying cause of the sweatshop, workers turned to class and ethnicity. For workers, the sweatshop boss was a "vampire" who drained the lifeblood of immigrant workers, leaving them weak and diseased."

Inspecting the Sweatshop

The journalists who began visiting the Lower East Side beginning in the 1880s were responding to a growing interest in and fear of immigration. Similarly, the inspectors and journalists who entered garment shops reflected an increasing concern about the social effects of industrialization.[2] They worried especially about the labor of immigrants, women, and children. The campaign for factory inspection and workplace regulation in New York gained momentum around the same time as the emergence of a transnational garment industry. Like the garment industry in New York, factory inspection in America was related to developments in Europe. While the United States—New York in particular—had the fastest-growing garment industry in the transatlantic economy, Europe led the way in creating a structure of factory inspection. By the 1880s, France, Germany, and Britain had passed significant pieces of factory legislation, which they further strengthened between 1892 and 1901.[3] This legislation garnered the attention of American progressive social scientists, who imported information about Western European laws and inspection methods. By 1900, most highly industrialized and urbanized American states had created at least the infrastructure of factory inspection.[4]

As in Europe, the garment industry, with its obviously atrocious conditions and high levels of immigrant, female, and child labor, was one of the first and most important targets of inspection. Indeed, European, especially British, and American observers came to share understandings of the sweatshop. The word was used virtually simultaneously on both sides of the Atlantic. At the same moment that German Jews, social reformers, and public health advocates launched initiatives to ameliorate and document Lower East Side conditions, local and national politicians, with the aid of factory inspectors, began widely publicized investigations into the contracting system of garment production. In 1892, a House of Representatives committee held hearings on the contracting system. In 1901, the Industrial Commission on Immigration included details of its hearings on "foreign-born labor in the clothing trade" in its reports. These federal hearings investigated the role of contracting in the erosion of wages and working conditions, the effects of garment labor on workers and their families, and the public health threat of garments manufactured in contractor shops. States like New York that had a sizable garment industry soon followed with their own investigations of immigrants' garment work.[5] These hearings drew the attention of journalists. In addition to printing lurid descriptions of individual reporters' visits to immigrant workplaces, popular magazines and newspapers regularly included details about state and federal efforts to define and reform the sweatshop.

Spurred by such concern, New York passed the Factory Inspection Law in 1886 and substantially revised it in 1892. The law mandated that each worker needed 250 cubic feet of air space and that all tenement garment manufacturers required a permit. The law was to be enforced by a set of factory inspectors with the power to revoke the permits of tenement garment shops. In 1893, the Office of Factory Inspectors proudly reported that "although the act has been in force but about seven months . . . we may safely state that it has proven most salutary in checking the abuses which were daily growing greater in the crowded districts of New York."[6]

The new laws sought to discourage labor in small shops and celebrated the move to more "American" factory buildings.[7] The New York Office of Factory Inspectors in 1893, for example, praised the construction of fifty-nine "modern, well-appointed factory buildings erected upon sites formerly occupied by tenements swarming with people who lived, worked, ate, slept and—all too many—died therein."[8] Yet these boasts were prematurely optimistic. The Office of Factory Inspectors hired too few inspectors to regulate the literally thousands of tiny garment shops, and abuses persisted. In 1900 alone, 1,180 complaints were received about illegal tenement garment manufacture.[9]

Factory inspectors associated the rise of contracting with Eastern European Jewish immigration. When Dr. Annie Daniel, a leading public health advocate and a frequent inspector of Lower East Side shops, described small workshops in her notes for the House of Representatives committee, she first recorded the nationality of the workers. As she wrote in her notes on one contractor shop: "Nationality, Russian Jews; . . . occupation, tailor; . . . number of adult workers, 2; number of child workers, 1; number of rooms, 3; number in family, 7; number of boarders, 15."[10] Inspectors, like Daniel, argued that the needle trades industry in New York was composed of such small workshops, housed in tenement apartments and dependent on the labor of Jewish immigrants. Among journalists, Jacob Riis insisted that the contracting system resulted from "the cutter's long knife and the Polish Jew." New arrivals of Jewish immigrants, he claimed, depressed wages and accelerated the rise of the subcontracting system.

The garment industry, for these investigators, was an immigrant industry and, even more specifically, a Jewish industry. As one factory inspector noted in 1899, "Among the shop workers . . . the Hebrews predominate."[11] The economist Jesse Pope put it even more succinctly when he called the garment industry "the great Jewish métier."[12] These observers viewed the Lower East Side as the center of a foreign industry. In arguing that "the Jew has monopolized the business," Riis noted the location of small shops within the East Side: "You are made fully aware of it before you have traveled the length of a single block in any of these East Side streets, by the whir of a thousand sewing machines."[13]

Defining the Sweatshop

The 1892 House of Representatives hearings advanced a definition of the sweatshop that was reproduced in numerous government and inspectors' reports.[14] First, for the House committee, the sweatshop was a type of workplace, namely, an outside shop owned by a contractor or subcontractor. Sweatshops, the committee argued, sprang up because of the system of contracting and subcontracting in which the onus of production was passed on from a manufacturer to a contractor to a subcontractor and, all too frequently, to a sub-subcontractor. Shop owners' compensation was "sweated" from their employees.[15]

Second, the sweatshop was a set of abominable working conditions. The committee argued that the system of contracting and subcontracting necessarily produced such conditions because contractor shops located work in the home. The location of work in a domestic space suggested the third characteristic of the sweatshop. It was a workplace where wages were so low that male as well as female workers had to work to support their families.[16] Subcontractors and contractors realized their profits by employing men along with their wives and children and by crowding them into a workshop in a tenement apartment. As the House committee wrote in the introduction to their report: "A typical and a most general example . . . is the so-called tenement sweat shop, where the main work room is one of the two larger rooms of the tenement flat, and, overflowing into the adjacent rooms, is made to accommodate from 6 to 15, or even more, 'sweating' employés [sic]—men, women, and children; . . . the flat is the domestic headquarters of the 'sweater.'"[17]

Finally, the sweatshop was an immigrant, and especially a Jewish, workplace. In their testimony to the House committee, factory inspectors and politicians associated the sweatshop and the sweating system with the labor of "green hands, that had just been brought from Castle Garden."[18] Sweatshop employees, argued the committee chairman, John De Witt Warner, "are in the main foreign-born and newly arrived."[19] In particular, inspectors agreed that "Polish and Russian Jews . . . are the most numerous in the 'sweating shops.'" While the committee noted that other immigrants, notably Italians, composed an increasingly large percentage of the sweatshop workforce, it blamed the arrival of Jews for the appearance and proliferation of the sweatshop.[20]

Factory inspectors and politicians were so diligent in reporting the immigrant composition of the garment workforce because they considered "the wide development of the contract system . . . a phase of immigration."[21] The sweatshop was a "foreign method of working" imported into the United States from the "least civilized sections of Europe" by morally and racially suspect Jewish immigrants.[22] Some inspectors and journalists even feared that sweatshops were the result of a shadowy conspiracy to bring immigrants to the Lower East Side to work. As the journalist Eva McDonald Valesh wrote: "Here they toil, under a cunningly devised slavery, until death mercifully sets them free. . . . Their passage here is paid. They are taught the tailoring art in trade schools."[23] In defining the sweatshop as a "foreign" workplace, New York's factory inspectors directly contrasted it to a glorified "American factory" where "you find everything in keeping with the American idea." Where the sweatshop was filthy, the American factory was clean, sanitary, and comfortable. Where the sweatshop featured little technology and hourly wages that led to grueling workdays, the idealized American factory had established hours, weekly or monthly wages, and steam power and machines.[24]

Inspectors argued that the garment industry was located in sweatshops rather than in factories, because of the negative "racial characteristics of the Jew." In explaining the rise of the sweatshop, inspectors looked beyond the simple technology and task system (in which workers completed only a small part of the garment) that made contractor shops more competitive than large factories. Instead, the Industrial Commission argued that Jews were racially unfit for factory production. They were too "individualistic" for the "discipline of the factory." The Industrial Commission suggested that the Jewish worker readily traded the benefits of the American factory for the contractor shop with its "almost complete absence of . . . factory management," because of the Jew's desire to be "his own boss." Piecework proliferated and workdays lengthened "because the Jewish people are peculiarly eager to earn a big day's wages, no matter at what sacrifice." The goal, for these Jews, was not simply to earn money, but to save enough to become an employer themselves. "The Jewish immigrant," the Industrial Commission reasoned, "is not by nature a wage-earner, and he keeps before himself continually the goal of emancipation from hard work."[25]

Some observers even pointed to the weak Jewish body to explain why Jewish immigrants sought work in small contractor shops that lacked the mechanization of large factories. As a "race subject to contempt," the economist Jesse

Pope argued, Eastern European Jews lacked the skills or strength for factory production. They "were the most helpless and inefficient immigrants that have ever entered this country." Yet Jewish immigrants' body type endowed them with a "singular dexterity" that drew them naturally to garment work.[26] Similarly, the New York State Bureau of Labor Statistics and the Industrial Commission both suggested that the Eastern European Jewish body was too physically weak for arduous manual labor and, as a result, immigrants selected "such light occupations as sewing."[27]

Even the word sweatshop reflected these negative images of Jewish weakness and concerns about their continuing physical decline. In choosing "sweat" to describe work in the contractor shop, inspectors were linking criticism of garment labor and of immigrant workers to a language that described certain kinds of work as physically draining. In fact, the association of the words sweat and sweating with difficult, physically challenging, and noisome work stretches back as far as the ninth century. Even in Shakespeare's *Midsummer Night's Dream*, tiresome, exhausting labor becomes "sweat": "The Oxe hath therefore stetch'd his yoake in vaine. The Ploughman lost his sweat."[28] Those inspectors who coined the word sweatshop were also drawing on early-nineteenth-century American and British definitions of immigrant garment work as "sweated." In New York, as historian Christine Stansell has documented, female Irish immigrant women in the 1840s composed a pool of "sweated" homeworkers who completed garments destined for the southern slave or western frontier markets.[29] From the outset, inspectors' choice of the word sweatshop to describe the contractor shop belied their conception of sweatshops as immigrant workplaces that could further enfeeble already weak Jews.

Race, Civilization, and Defining the Sweatshop Danger

For inspectors, race explained the economics of the sweatshop and the spread of contracting. Thus, inspectors, journalists, and social reformers relied on race as they sought to discover and describe the danger of sweatshops. Inspectors claimed to follow contemporary social and medical scientific methods, but such science was profoundly inflected with understandings of race, racial difference, and racial degeneration.[30] As a result, inspectors' reports—like the testimony of politicians and the exposés of journalists—seem to measure inspectors' racial, class, and moral distance from workers. Indeed, New York's factory inspectors had little in common with the immigrants who labored in the garment workshops they visited. Where garment workers were immigrants and large numbers of them were women, New York's factory inspectors were native-born and, until 1890, all male. Inspectors' reports detail their personal reactions and revulsion to sweatshops and to sweatshop workers. In this context, inspectors' reports continued a narrative tradition established by the first journalists who visited the Lower East Side. The reports related explorations of foreign workshops and featured the most lurid images of Jewish racial inferiority.

Inspectors' descriptions of their visits to sweatshops frequently began with their response to the smells and filth of the workshops and to the degraded physical condition of immigrant workers. George McKay, the principal factory inspector for the Lower East Side in the late 1880s and early 1890s, insisted that sweatshops "smell as powerfully and poisonously as the wretched toilers themselves." They are "rarely healthy or clean, while filth and noxious odors are abundant." In one place, he described the smell as "nauseating . . . and the stench abominable."[31] Similarly, John Crowley, secretary of the Anti-Tenement House League, described to the House committee what he claimed was a "typical" Lower East Side sweatshop among the 300 he had inspected. The most noticeable characteristic of the sweatshop was its "terrible stenches . . . [that] would almost knock a horse down." For these inspectors, the stench of the sweatshop alone revealed the racial differences separating inspectors and workers. While Crowley noted that workers seemed content to work in these "filthy and inhuman conditions," he told committee members that "the stench would almost force you down the stairs."[32]

Inspectors blamed the racial traits of immigrants for the filth and smells of the sweatshop.[33] Like critics of the Lower East Side's dirty streets, they highlighted a "Hebrew" comfort in filth. As one inspector wrote: "It does seem to me that they are to blame for the unclean condition in which we find very many of them, as well as the often very filthy condition of the immediate room or rooms in which they work and live. They seem to care nothing about the observance of proper sanitary conditions." Another inspector doubted that Jewish immigrants worried about their "simply vile" surroundings.[34] Annie Daniel simply denigrated Jewish workers as a "dirtier class of people."[35]

If sweatshop conditions already reflected Jews' low racial status, inspectors also worried that they might set in motion a process of racial degeneration. Critics like Eva McDonald Valesh pointed to the weakened body of sweatshop workers as evidence of racial decline. Valesh insisted that Jewish workers' physical weakness was accented by their work in sweatshops: "gaunt figures now and then emerge. . . . All, even to the babies, have that pallid, haggard expression, characteristic of the quarter. Not one of the multitude exceeded the average height, and many fell below it."[36] Jacob Riis, in a similar fashion, noted that Eastern European Jewish workers labored until "mind and muscle give out together."[37] For Riis and Valesh, the Jewish proletarian body was increasingly frail and decrepit with poor muscle structure and a twisted spine.[38]

As one inspector testified to the House committee, immigrant Jews were in danger of becoming "a race enfeebled by the strain of terribly long hours, lack of air, and bad sanitary conditions."[39]

Some inspectors even seemed to cite germs as the medical cause of racial decline, understood as physical and moral deterioration that could be passed down to workers' children. The "exudations from overheated and unclean human bodies," McKay argued, created an "environment laden with such foulness, disease and death as is simply a disgrace to God and man." The evil of *"material* substances in fine, subtle, microscopial forms floating in the air which is already poisoned . . . paralyze . . . vital nerve-centers in the human system, controlling and destroying those very physical organs and activities upon which the unfortunate toiler depends for his very existence." As he struggled to understand the implications of germ theory, McKay suggested that disease might be passed down to immigrants' children, accelerating their own degeneration.[40] At the same time, for McKay, bodily enfeeblement was the outward manifestation of immigrants' moral decline. Work in a "crowded and unhealthy district," he worried, would inevitably lead to "low moral and low intelligence, where the condition of human beings is scarcely above that of animals."[41] Eastern European Jews' "ill-fed and poorly clad bodies," another inspector insisted, left them "unclean in person and degraded in mind." The sweatshop and the poverty it created brought to the surface "their animal disregard of the ordinary decencies of life."[42] The sweatshop sent Jewish immigrants tumbling down the hierarchy of races. "We may see the low level of civilization to which they have been forced," one inspector mourned.[43]

As inspectors sought to define and mitigate the dangers of the sweatshop, they cast themselves as the protectors of civilization itself. Only inspection and laws could prevent sweatshop workers from "being a menace to civilization." Civilizing would not occur without the help of inspectors and reformers. After all, reasoned the Industrial Commission, the "clannishness" of Jewish immigrants meant that they worked only with other Jews and so had "no opportunity . . . of learning from the civilization of other people."[44] Inspectors described themselves as "sweeping back new social evils which follow the ever-coming tides of lower and lower classes of labor every generation."[45]

They were defending "civilization" from very real "evils." The "menace to civilization" of sweatshops was not an abstract threat, but a specific danger of contagion and plague. When inspectors like Daniel described themselves as fighting the "evils of the sweatshop," they were referring specifically to the "contagious" diseases Daniel claimed to have found in every Lower East Side sweatshop she investigated.[46] The same germs that affected immigrants might infect middle-class consumers through the very threads of the clothing they wore.

For this reason McKay and other inspectors believed that the sweatshop posed a significant public health menace. In one report, he argued that "the steam from breath and body, the poison from surrounding putresence [*sic*] and unsanitary plumbing . . . permeates everything present, and it needs only the single bacillus of disease to start into life a horrible death for thousands."[47] In another report, he stated that "the danger from the . . . obnoxious smells that abound therein to those employed is only equaled to that which may be caused by the spread of infectious disease through clothing . . . made up under those conditions."[48]

The fear of an epidemic caused by unclean immigrants was a dominant theme of inspectors' reports, politicians' investigations, and journalists' editorials. For New York factory inspectors, the spread of contagious disease first "among these clothing workers" and then among consumers "is no lightly-drawn possibility, but a matter of the most serious importance."[49] They worried that "the possibility of contagion spreading through infected clothing from these filthy places is very great."[50] Members of the House committee were even concerned that clothing manufactured in sweatshops and brought into their chamber as evidence could be contagious. With obvious disgust, one congressman asked: "Is there any disease in this?" Daniel would have answered affirmatively; she testified, "I consider it dangerous wherever the germs have been carried with the clothing."[51]

Such fears of disease shaped antipathy to Jewish sweatshop workers, middle-class fears of sweatshops, and the first government regulations of sweatshops. The report of the House committee investigating sweatshops declared Jewish sweatshop workers a dangerously unhealthy group who cared little about their poor conditions: "Contagious diseases, which are specially prevalent among these people, thrive along with their work, and even death may distract from their occupation, only the one of the few necessary to dispose of the body."[52] And *Harper's Weekly* reproached the sweating system not simply for its dependence on "foreign immigrants," but also for being "a breeding-nest of disease."[53] Similarly, the Consumers' League of New York, a reformist organization led by middle-class women, urged consumers to reject sweatshop garments, which they claimed would lead to "the spread of infection far and wide."[54] John Crowley perhaps best captured the fears of contagion from sweatshop goods. His short story, "Plague of 1893: The Terrible Scourge of the Tenement House and Reasons for State Control of the Clothing Trade," dramatically envisioned a cholera outbreak spreading from Lower East Side tenement sweatshops throughout New York. To prevent a future "plague," laws are passed to regulate garment production.[55]

The first regulations of sweatshops, like those proposed by Crowley, were designed to protect middle-class consumers, not workers. These laws were bulwarks against the contagion nurtured in the filth of sweatshops and in the bodies of immigrants and passed on to largely female middle-class consumers. As the Industrial Commission admitted: "The legislation . . . has been undertaken not on behalf of the workers, but on behalf of consumers. It is the protection of the public against contagious and infectious disease."[56] And that public was composed of middle- and upper-class female consumers.

Immigrant Bodies at Work

With public health crusades defined as the protection of consumers, inspectors regarded immigrant workers as a hindrance to effective investigation. Immigrants were so obstinate in their habits and so comfortable in the filth of the sweatshop that they undermined efforts to confront the public health threats of the sweatshop. Inspectors believed that immigrants refused to answer their questions. They "take refuge in silence and shrugs of the shoulders, and claim they do not understand what is being said, even by the interpreter."[57] Such criticisms highlight the cultural distance separating workers and inspectors. In entering the shops and demanding answers to probing questions about the conditions and hours of labor, inspectors were forcibly inserting themselves into the complex system of ethnic, family, and community relations that linked workers to their employers. Especially under pressure from their employers, workers might understandably have resorted to "yarns." They were not simply protecting their jobs, but also shielding from the intrusion of the state those networks that workers relied on to find employment and that contractors used to find workers. Immigrant workers hesitated to share their complaints with inspectors, even as amongst themselves they condemned the condition of their labor. In one shop, when workers were asked how long they worked, they responded, "Eight hours." Only under their breath did they acknowledge that it was eight hours both before and after noon.[58]

Yet the racial and class barriers of suspicion that divided workers and inspectors were permeable. Male and female garment workers readily participated in defining the sweatshop, even borrowing the word into Yiddish as *svetshop*.[59] Despite the hostility of inspectors, some Jewish immigrants testified at government hearings, including those held by the House of Representatives. When they testified, workers shared at least part of inspectors' vocabulary. In particular, they focused immediately on the health of workers in contract shops. Bernard Weinstein, a garment worker himself and the secretary of the United Hebrew Trades (a loose coalition of unions composed of Jewish workers), echoed inspectors in describing sweated garment work as physically draining: "We went over to the small dark chamber where the pressers worked, but could not enter because there was no room for us. A few bearded men stood there pressing the kneepants, bathed in sweat."[60] One former worker highlighted the conditions of small contractor shops in labeling them "cockroach" shops; others called them the "moths of Division Street."[61]

Also, like public critics of the sweatshop, Jewish workers noted connections between the arrival of immigrants and the rise of contracting. The House committee reported that immigrants explained the rise of a contracting system by pointing to "the increase in the numbers of those seeking employment, especially greenhorns just come over."[62] Abraham Cahan, an immigrant and the socialist editor of the popular Yiddish newspaper the *Jewish Daily Forward*, blamed immigration in general for sweating. "Curse you, emigration," he declared. "How many lives have you broken, how many brave and mighty have you rubbed out like dust!"[63] Other immigrants pointed to their own search for jobs after their arrival in New York to explain the rise of the sweating system. Beryl Fried, for example, remembered how family connections led her to a cramped, crowded cloakmaking dress shop on the Lower East Side: "My first shop was on Hester Street. Eighteen men and women were crowded into a small dark room."[64]

Jewish immigrants echoed inspectors' concerns about long hours of labor and the horrid conditions of sweatshops located in workers' homes. Abraham Bisno, a cloakmaker who had lived and labored in both New York and Chicago and later became a union official, testified to the House committee that immigrants "work in bedrooms and in shops where there is nothing to breathe."[65] Like inspectors, Bisno compared the sweatshop to the factory. Sweatshops sprang up, Bisno claimed, because in tenement shops that doubled as homes "people can work longer than in a factory." Bisno reported working sixty hours a week—down from the seventy-five hours a week he labored in 1884.[66] Daniel testified in the House hearings that Jewish workers admitted to working "from fourteen to fifteen hours, and sometimes as much as they could endure in two days."

Yet when immigrants like Bisno and Fried described the decline of the factory system and the long hours worked by Jewish immigrants, they pointed to the class relations of an immigrant industry, not to Jewish racial characteristics. As the garment worker and labor leader Morris Feinstone argued: "The products of this forced labor were offered in the open market in competition with 'American' products which were higher in price because native workers commanded higher wages for their labor."[67] For Feinstone, at least, the logic of competition and exploitation, not race, explained the difference between the "American" factory and the immigrant sweatshop. On the whole, Jewish immigrants tended to eschew inspectors' racial explanations. For Jewish workers, their enfeebled bodies revealed the onerous conditions of labor and the unfairness of the system. Immigrants saw the sweatshop as a problem facing working-class Jews, not as a reflection of their racial status. Thus, as workers described the sweatshop and its dangers, they separated ethnicity from race. Workers used visual symbols like clothing, more than supposedly Jewish racial traits like the hooked nose, to identify workers as immigrant Jews. Where inspectors racialized ethnicity and saw race as the explanation for the rise of sweatshops, immigrants described the sweatshop as an ethnic and class problem that was particularly visible in the broken bodies of Jewish workers.[68] So, too, did immigrants describe the filth of the garment sweatshop as a reflection of oppressive management and workplace exploitation, not as a Jewish racial trait. The worker and poet Morris Rosenfeld, for example, blamed his boss for the "damp and murky" sweatshop. He asked how, if his "body is weak from the work's dreadful clutch, . . . can this shirt of mine be kept clean?"[69]

In much the same way German Jews forged links between Eastern European Jews and social reformers seeking to address issues of immigrant poverty, German Jews also helped begin to connect inspectors' and workers' discourses about garment work and its physical effects. Similar to how German Jews sought to protect their own social status by seeking to define Jews as a religious group, not as a distinct—and inferior—race, they used medical investigations of sweatshop workers to try to indict the conditions of work, not race, as the cause of immigrants' enfeeblement. Maurice Fishberg, the chief physician of the United Hebrew Charities, was, perhaps, the most prominent leader in the effort to record the effects of the sweatshop on Eastern European Jewish immigrant bodies. Fishberg was trained not only as a physician, but also as an anthropologist and thus was readily aware of contemporary anthropological understandings of race. Still, he completed medical examinations and bodily measurements in order to trace the enfeebling effects of sweated labor on immigrants' bodies. In a series of articles, Fishberg declared that because of their labor, Jewish immigrants suffered New York City's "lowest 'index of vitality.'"[70]

The Jewish body, he conceded, was weak. Indeed, in his own measurements he discovered that the average girth of Jewish workers' chests was less than half their average height. By comparison, the American norm easily exceeded half. Thus he proclaimed that the Jewish tailor's chest "is not only flat, but also of inferior capacity." Like government factory inspectors, Fishberg described Jewish immigrant workers as physically inferior to native-born Americans. However, Fishberg generally avoided the racialist explanations of inspectors. Instead, he blamed "the cramped attitude of the tailor's body while he is at work

... in conjunction with the defective ventilation of the usual sweatshop." Sweat-shop conditions, he argued, "all conspire to reduce the vitality of the tailor and render his lungs predisposed to infection by the tubercle bacillus."[71]

Immigrants also described themselves as the work-scarred victims of sweat-shops. But where inspectors and German Jewish doctors like Fishberg relied on so-called scientific methods of medical and factory inspection, Jewish im-migrants, both men and women, used their cultural production—art, poetry, literature, and memoirs—to describe their physical trauma. In his memoirs, the cloakmaker Abraham Rosenberg described his fellow sweatshop workers as "pale, overworked shadows."[72] Beryl Fried, also, recalled her fatigue after long hours of work: "During the season there was no time limit. We started working at dawn and stopped at ten or eleven at night. . . . Among themselves the workers often complained, ' . . . there is no more strength left.'"[73] Stella Papiroff, in her autobiography, remembered the physical effects of sweatshop labor on her friend Elizaveta: "In a few months what I worked in the shop I saw why Elizaveta got so thin."[74]

In a particularly graphic image, Rosenberg argued that sweatshops turned hale immigrants into frail proletarians: "The cloak trade still consisted of dark, dirty, overcrowded sweatshops which swallowed healthy immigrants."[75] And, like inspectors, immigrants worried about the prevalence of germs and dis-ease in sweatshops. Abraham Bisno declared that sweatshops "[work] to the destruction of health." He cited the case of his brother, who died after five years labor in a sweatshop. He also insisted that while he paid careful attention to his own health, he would live longer if he "was not to work in such shops."[76] But, unlike inspectors, workers were concerned, not with the health of con-sumers, but with the decline in their own strength. Morris Rosenfeld, the poet and garment worker, came to see the sweatshop as intimately connected with the destruction of his and his fellow workers' bodies. In his oft-cited poem "The Pale Operator," originally published in 1898, Rosenfeld described the "pale op-erator . . . using up his strength." In another poem, "The Tear on the Iron," Rosen-feld describes his own weakness caused by work in the "cold and dark" sweat-shop: "My heart is weak, I groan and cough,—my sick breast scarcely heaves."[77]

Other workers similarly described their bodies or the bodies of workers around them as decimated by sweatshop labor and even as infected with tu-berculosis. The worker and poet Yacob Adler, for example, portrayed one male worker in the sweatshop where he first began working upon his arrival in the United States in 1889: "Weary and shaking,/ every bone breaking,/ home he comes aching,/ home from the shop." The other workers he observed showed symptoms of the ultimate physical indignity of sweatshop labor: tuberculosis, a disease doctors and workers alike insisted was promulgated by exposure to garment work. "Coughing and tearing/ their lungs, they spit blood."[78]

Like inspectors, Jewish workers saw the sweatshop as intertwined with immigration. But the sweatshop preyed upon immigrants; it was not a reflection of their debased nature. Morris Feinstone, for example, stressed the class and ethnic relationships that lay behind the sweatshop: "When these fugitives came to America seeking the promised land, they were taken off the boats by contractors . . . and set to work in subhuman surroundings, for a miserable wage, and under conditions which made protest utterly impossible."[79] Immigrants' artwork, in particular, represented the idea of sweated labor as a threat, not simply to the bodies of workers, but to the bodies of immigrant Jews. Jacob Epstein, a popular artist growing up among garment workers on the Lower East Side, noted the connection between the sweatshop and workers' physical enfeeblement. His drawings of the sweatshop were commentaries on the bodies of Eastern European Jewish immigrants. Like most poets seeking to describe the typical "pale operator," Epstein portrayed only men. He chose to draw the most barren of Jewish male workers, especially those waiting despondently for work at the *chazer mark*.[80]

A "tall, lean, and bearded young man" especially fascinated Epstein, and the lean Jewish garment worker appeared frequently in a series of charcoal sketches he drew for the journalist Hutchins Hapgood's exposé of Jewish proletarian life on the Lower East Side. In the frontispiece for Hapgood's book, he sketched a garment worker staring mournfully out a narrow window at the rooftops of the Lower East Side. The only hint that the garment worker is laboring in a sweatshop is the window and a hastily drawn sewing machine. The "cold and dark" shop and its abominable conditions are revealed only in the worker's deformed body. He stands hunched, his back unnaturally curved as a result of stooping over the sewing machine. His chest is sunken and weak. Careful viewers would easily have recognized such defects as the warning signs of tuberculosis.[81] His abnormally large hands, deformed by long hours of labor, hang limply by his side and hint that garment work has physically altered his body. Like factory inspectors' racially coded representations of garment workers, Epstein's drawing of the "pale operator" clearly identifies the worker as Jewish. But Epstein replaces a racialized ethnicity with a cultural ethnicity. Religious clothing, in particular a yarmulke, much more than physical racial aspects like a Semitic nose, distinguish the worker as Jewish.[82]

The image of the sweatshop worker as a pale, enfeebled Jew and as a victim of work allowed male and female immigrants to illustrate the looming danger of the sweatshop to their immigrant community and families. George Price, a sweatshop worker who later became a doctor and factory inspector, insisted

_____ *Figure 1* _____

Jacob Epstein, "The Spirit of the Ghetto" (frontispiece for Hutchins Hapgood, *The Spirit of the Ghetto: Studies of the Jewish Quarter of New York* [1902; reprint, New York: Schocken, 1965]; image from the collection of the Tamiment-Wagner Labor Archives, New York University). The drawing captures the way Jewish workers talked about their labor in the sweatshop. Epstein alludes to the abominable conditions of labor in the sweatshops, not by drawing a cramped, filthy space, but by focusing on the deformed, obviously Jewish tailor's body. The conditions of work are etched on the male worker's enfeebled frame.

_____ *Figure 2* _____

E. M. Lilien, "At the Sewing Machine" (frontispiece from Morris Rosenfeld, *Songs of Labor* [Boston: Richard Badger, 1914]; image from the collection of the Tamiment-Wagner Labor Archives, New York University). This drawing connects workers' bodily decline and ethnicity with the oppression of the sweatshop. The frail worker is, based on his clothing, obviously Jewish. The half-bat, half–bloated capitalist behind the worker is either the boss or the embodiment of disease—or perhaps both. By depicting a straw from the vampire boss's mouth to the worker's body, Lilien seems to suggest that the sweated system sucks out workers' vitality and injects disease.

that workers understood sweatshop labor and class relations as physically debilitating. Jewish workers, he wrote, described their bosses as capitalist "vam-
pires," sucking out workers' strength.[83] The Jewish graphic artist Ephraim
Moses Lilien depicted this metaphor in a popular print. The print illustrates
Rosenfeld's poem "The Pale Operator" in a 1900 collection of his poems, which
would have been available to immigrants and native-born Americans. In the
print, the tailor labors hunched over his sewing machine while a man, perhaps
his boss, looms behind him. The man is naked and his full hirsute stomach
suggests his plentiful profits. His vampire wings frame the enfeebled tailor.

The suggestion of disease lingers over the picture. The straw or pipe that
stretches from the tailor's neck to the man's hungry mouth implies the debilitating effect of labor. It is not stuck in the worker's neck but emerges as if part
of the worker's damaged flesh. Lilien seems to suggest that the draining of
workers' lifeblood was inherent to the sweated system. Historian Alan Kraut
has also argued that the bejeweled, naked man standing behind the worker
might actually represent tuberculosis germs.[84] As a boss, he drains workers'
blood; as a disease, he infects the worker. Like the poems of Rosenfeld, the
disease suggested by the picture is a threat not to consumers, but only to the
worker. Again, the worker is identifiable as an Eastern European Jew and, once
more, his clothing more than any racial features marks the worker as a Jew.
While the boss—or the embodiment of disease—is depicted naked, draped only
in jewels, the worker is dressed in traditional Jewish garb, including a yarmulke
and prayer shawl.[85]

These images suggest that different understanding of ethnicity and of
Jewishness still separated workers and inspectors. Despite their shared notions
of garment work as physically enfeebling, workers and inspectors had different explanations for the roots and dangers of workers' weakness and disease.
For inspectors, the sweatshop rendered visible Jews' physical inferiority that
belied their low racial status. Physical decline also hinted at the presence of
disease that might be passed on to middle-class consumers. For immigrants,
physical weakness and disease revealed the evils of a system that preyed on
recent immigrants. General concerns about weakness and disease alone, it
seemed, were not enough to create a definition of the sweatshop shared by
workers and inspectors.

Images of work as enfeebling and dangerous appear in male and female immigrants' and inspectors' descriptions of the sweatshop. But immigrants' representations of the typical weakened worker almost universally depicted men,
hinting at uneasiness about women's wage labor. Men's bodies powerfully displayed the depredations of class oppression. They could be transformed into
political emblems. Women's weakened bodies, on the other hand, came to have

other meanings that attested more to the moral dangers of the sweatshop and to the foreignness of Jewish workers. Such gendered meanings of workers' bodies were crucial to the articulation of a common definition of the sweatshop. Immigrant Jews and inspectors were equally concerned about women's work in the sweatshop and the effect of sweated labor on the sexual division of labor within immigrant families. Inspectors worried that men and women working in the close quarters of the sweatshop would lead to sexual promiscuity. This promiscuity was key to the Jews' racial debasement. The physical enfeeblement of immigrant workers might be passed down to the children produced by immoral sexual relations initiated at work. Inspectors also pointed to a breakdown of a sexual division of labor in immigrant families as evidence of the racial debasement of Jews. Immigrants also came to worry about women's labor. Especially through their close relationships to German Jewish social reformers, male and female Eastern European Jews came to see male breadwinning as a mark of civilization and a sign of Americanization.

Thus, despite inspectors' obvious hostility toward immigrant workers and immigrants' distrust of inspectors, the two sides together came to single out Jewish women's homework, the taking of piecework into the home, as the worst example of sweated labor. For inspectors, it was a sign of racial degradation; for workers, it was an emblem of foreignness and social failure. They came to see the homework shop, the ultimate erasure of boundaries between home and work, as the worst kind of sweatshop. Through their concerns about women's labor and the intrusion of work into the home, immigrants and inspectors forged a new, common definition of the sweatshop. Armed with shared understandings, inspectors and workers began to reconsider the public dangers of the sweatshop. Disease came to be seen, not as a sign of weakness or a danger to consumers, but as a threat to the sexual division of labor within immigrant families. If male breadwinners fell ill, their wives might turn to homework. Through this concern about the health of male workers, inspectors and policymakers came to join with workers to urge new regulations aimed not at consumers, but at ensuring the stability of immigrant families through the enforcement of sanitary standards.

Three

"A Race Ignorant, Miserable, and Immoral"

Sweatshop Danger and Labor in the Home, 1890–1910

As outside critics questioned workers' racial status and as Eastern European Jewish immigrants lamented their declining health, both groups came to see the sweatshop as a family problem. They worried that falling wages, debilitating disease, and, most important, the blurred boundaries between the workplace and the home forced married women into the workforce. For social reformers, factory inspectors, and public health officials, levels of women's wage work attested to the immorality of the sweatshop system and contributed to the debased condition of immigrants. Meanwhile, male Eastern European Jewish immigrants, with the tacit and sometimes vocal acceptance of women, declared the preservation of the ideal of the male breadwinner as key to Jews' Americanization and social status. Middle-class social reformers and working-class immigrants shared concerns about the gender disorder of the sweatshop.

Accordingly, workers and outside observers portrayed the homework shop, a sweatshop located in a residential tenement apartment, as the worst kind of sweatshop because it embodied all the dangers sweated work posed for body and family. In the tenement homework shop, the male breadwinner became a sweater, putting his wife and children to work producing garments. Increasingly, inspectors and policymakers came to define homework as a debased form of women's labor and as the worst kind of sweated labor. Homework was the finishing of garments in the home.

By the 1890s, efforts to regulate sweated work became focused especially on women's homework. As the Industrial Commission on Immigration noted, "The . . . 'sweat-shop' legislation of several American States . . . is simply legislation directed against tenement-house work."[1] At the same time as social reform-ers, policymakers, and public health advocates began considering strategies to reform and regulate homework, Eastern European Jewish immigrant work-ers, led by men, began efforts to organize trade unions. They also focused on women's homework. By the turn of the century, as policymakers and inspec-tors began to recognize the difficulty of regulating homework and the impos-sibility of legally abolishing it, the impulse to remove garment work from the home became the foundation for a cross-class alliance of workers and middle- and upper-class policymakers and reformers. This alliance initially included men, but women workers, in alliance with wealthy female reformers, soon de-manded inclusion.

The Gendered Danger of the Sweatshop

At the same time that workers and factory inspectors worried about the effects of sweated work on immigrants' bodies, they also raised concerns about the effects of the "sweated system" on immigrants' families. Factory in-spectors consistently protested the seemingly undifferentiated work of men and women. During their hearings, the House of Representatives committee investigating sweatshops asked witnesses to measure the effects and prevalence of men and women working together.[2] Similarly, journalists lamented the high levels of women's labor. *Harper's Weekly* noted that "while the father is sewing at home, the mother and children are bringing him work to do." In another article, the magazine described how "the proportion of female labor is large."[3]

High rates of women's wage work seemed to confirm critics' suspicions about workers' degraded moral state and low level of civilization. The *Nation's* E. L. Godkin, for example, worried about the "moral evils resulting in the case of women [working]."[4] Similarly, the chairman of the House committee declared that the mixing of male and female workers was a "promiscuous carrying on of the work."[5] The factory inspector George McKay agreed that "so far as mor-als are concerned," the labor of men and women together in the cramped sur-rounding of the sweatshop and tenement was "prompting premature curiosity in young minds, and turning their attention to matters of sexual significance."[6]

For inspectors, like McKay, the immorality engendered by sweatshop la-bor was key to the racial debasement of immigrants. They worried especially that the degraded state of immigrants could become fixed by being passed down from sweatshop workers to the children produced by the promiscuity of the sweatshop. Echoing Lamarckian evolutionary theory, inspectors were concerned that the physical and moral breakdown of immigrant workers would appear in the next generation.[7] As McKay put it, through immoral sexual rela-tions, sweatshop workers would create "a race ignorant, miserable and immoral as themselves."[8] In this fashion, factory inspectors connected fears about the racial degradation of immigrants to concerns about the gendered disorder of the sweatshop. Racial debasement, one inspector testified, would occur with the decline of male breadwinning. Sweatshop work, he argued, "will eventually bring forth ignorant, brutal, unhealthy men and women. This must be when a woman, in addition to the duties of wife and mother is forced to join with her husband as bread-winner." Children were becoming "stunted" because of the "overwork of the parents."[9]

Although Eastern European Jewish immigrants tended to downplay fears of racial decline, both men and women did worry that the sweatshop would undermine what was increasingly a cherished social and cultural ideal: the notion of the male breadwinner. In New York, immigrants recognized the ideal of the male breadwinner as an easily identifiable Victorian-American social standard. The question of women's work represented an important, if not omnipresent, topic for conversation as Eastern European Jews arrived in New York, went to work in garment factories, and sought and received aid from Jewish charities. As Paula Hyman and Nancy Sinkoff both argue, the teaching of proper gender roles lay at the heart of philanthropic programs, like the Clara de Hirsch Home, supported by wealthier Eastern European Jewish immigrants and by older, more established German American Jews.[10]

However, in examining the development of a breadwinner ideal within the New York Eastern European Jewish community, it is important to avoid oversimplified "trickle down" models of the diffusion of cultural values.[11] Eastern European Jewish immigrants did not unquestioningly accept middle-class Victorian beliefs about women's work through their contact with middle-class and German American Jewish philanthropists and reformers. Rather, male and female Eastern European Jewish immigrants and workers advanced ideal models of women's labor that permitted, even encouraged, women's wage work before marriage and allowed different forms of economic productivity, like shopkeeping, after marriage. Sydney Stahl Weinberg, for example, notes how married Jewish women often participated in productive work, albeit in the nonwaged, informal sector. Despite the admonitions and criticisms of social reformers, married Jewish women continued to have important economic roles in the immigrant household as shopkeepers. They also completed housework and provided meals for boarders.[12]

Still, both male and female Jewish immigrants generally discouraged married women's wage labor, especially in the garment industry. As historians of Eastern European Jewish women like Susan Glenn, Kathie Friedman-Kasaba, Riv-Ellen Prell, and Weinberg all note, as a group, Jewish immigrants, male and female, came to value the ideals of the male breadwinner and of marriage as the end of women's participation in garment wage labor.[13] In fact, more than any other immigrant group of garment workers in New York, Eastern European Jewish immigrants generally came to regard married women's wage labor as a symbol of poverty and men's breadwinning as a sign of assimilation and success. In the years after their arrival, they sought to translate gendered cultural ideals into social reality. Thus, as early as 1900, as the observer of the New York garment industry Mabel Hurd Willet documented, while German and Italian women on the Lower East Side might work in garment workshops after their wedding, for many Jewish women marriage meant the end of garment wage work: "Among Jews the situation is radically different. The period of industrial activity of a Jewish woman is normally a short one."[14] Her findings were confirmed by one woman interviewed by Weinberg: "We just didn't let a woman like my mother go to work, even if she wanted to."[15]

As Paula Hyman writes, Eastern European Jewish immigrants' ideal of the male breadwinner also had roots in changing attitudes toward women's work in Europe. While the most religious Jews still believed that women and the broader community should support men's religious study financially, attitudes toward women's wage earning changed dramatically with industrialization, mechanization, and the growing impoverishment of Jews. In the Pale, as Isaac Rubinow documented, Jews' economic status declined as levels of women's employment rose: "The proportion of female . . . labor . . . is seen to be in indirect proportion to the general level of prosperity." Thus, by 1898, in northwestern Russia, women composed 27 percent of factory workers and, in Poland, they represented 21 percent. In addition, Rubinow noted that in small artisan workshops located in workers' homes, Jewish women played significant roles. Numbers of female workers increased as Jewish artisans faced growing economic and political pressure.[16]

Rubinow also suggested that male and female Jewish workers in Eastern Europe came to associate the labor of women with the breakdown of what he called the "proverbial sanctity of the Jewish home."[17] At the same time, as women's work came to signify poverty, the ideal of the husband as the primary family wage earner spread. By the time Jews began migrating to New York in large numbers, as Susan Glenn argues, the stereotype of Jewish women in Eastern Europe providing family livelihood while their husbands devoted themselves to religious study had largely fallen by the wayside.[18] Across the Pale of Settlement, prominent male leaders of the Jewish enlightenment, the *Haskalah,* roundly criticized pious male Jews who avoided wage labor and refused to support their families as the sole breadwinner.[19]

In New York, the social disruption of migration and changing perceptions of the cultural meaning of success solidified male and female Jewish immigrants' understanding of an ideal sexual division of labor. The hardship of life in the industrial Lower East Side forced male immigrants into wage labor, whatever their religious aspirations.[20] In addition, the vigorous efforts of older immigrants and social reformers to instill the breadwinner ethic among male and female Jewish immigrants helped translate the words of *Haskalah* leaders in Eastern Europe into a cultural ideal in America.[21] Early Jewish immigrants to New York carried over and promoted negative attitudes about married women's wage labor and, even with new waves of immigration, they remained firmly tied to conceptions of an appropriate sexual division of labor. Already armed with negative understandings of women's industrial wage work, the earliest Eastern European Jewish immigrants and those who followed them generally accepted the ideal of the male breadwinner, despite married women's continuing economic roles. Thus, as Glenn writes, many male and female Jewish immigrants in New York joined middle-class critics in regarding the labor of married women in New York's garment sweatshops as the humiliating work only of widowed, abandoned, or desperately poor women and as an emblem of workers' foreignness and poverty.[22]

In contrast, male and female Italian immigrants, who composed the other large immigrant group in the New York garment workforce, advanced very different ideas about married women's labor. Married women often continued in wage labor after their marriage. Thus, inspectors sadly remarked on the effects of the married Italian woman "busy plying her needle." The house is left dirty and the children are "neglected and filthy." In addition, the husband, no longer a breadwinner, is "less energetic" in his search for work and spends his money on drink.[23] New York's inspectors similarly viewed Italians as a more hopeless case than Jews: "But the danger [to] the community from [Italian tenement-house workers] is far more sweeping than ever existed in the worst stage of Hebrew sweating."[24] While inspectors lamented the effects of the women's work on Italian families, they cautiously saluted Jewish immigrants' reluctance to allow married women to "work in a shop" as a possible source of Jews' advancement and Americanization.[25] Jews' dedication to the idea of the male breadwinner laid the groundwork for a possible alliance between Jews and social reformers that saw the sweatshop as a Jewish workplace—in which Italians in increasing numbers labored—and increasingly viewed work done by Italian women in their homes as dangerous and exploitative, but not necessarily as "sweated" garment homework.

Inspecting Home and Work

The prevalence of married women's garment labor, in tenement shops or alone at home, became central to how male and female factory inspectors and Jewish workers came to define the dangers of sweated work in similar ways. While inspectors, unlike workers, insisted that sweated work made visible Eastern European Jews' racial inferiority, they shared anxieties with immigrant workers about the dangers of sweated work for immigrants' health and families. Fears about the effects of work on the body and on gendered order came together around concern about the location of garment work in tenement apartments. A coalition of Jewish workers, public health advocates, elected officials, and factory inspectors all insisted that work in cramped, unsafe, and unsanitary tenement apartments and sweatshops not only represented a significant threat to workers' and public health, but also encouraged the immoral labor of married women. When the Consumers' League of New York declared the sweatshop a "menace to the home," it referred to the homes of middle-class consumers who might purchase infected clothing and to the homes and families of working-class immigrants.[26] Increasingly, working- and middle-class critics associated the sweatshop with the dangers tenement homework posed to the sexual division of labor within immigrant families. The worst sweatshop was the homework shop and the most degraded kind of sweated work was women's homework.

The tenement apartments of the Lower East Side had long been the focus of progressive reformers' concern. Starting in the 1870s, social reformers in New York vilified the Lower East Side's tenement apartments as unhealthy, unsafe residences, and as early as 1879, state and city politicians proposed housing and building regulations. Reform laws mandated changes in tenement architecture, introducing the so-called "dumbbell" design. A central ventilating airshaft made each apartment's floor plan look like a dumbbell. Dumbbell tenements included airshafts and common water closets. While the new design certainly improved on the outdoor latrines and airless interiors of older buildings, tenements remained the target of political and public concern. The *American Magazine*, for example, was typical in attacking dumbbell tenements as "great prison-like structures of brick, with narrow doors and windows, cramped passages and steep rickety stairs."[27] New laws passed in 1884, 1887, and 1901 further attempted, albeit largely unsuccessfully, to address sanitary dangers. Despite some slow improvements in ventilation, water closets, and fire safety, the Lower East Side's tenements remained the focus of reform campaigns well into the twentieth century.[28]

One of the principal complaints reformers raised about tenements was that they doubled as dwellings and workshops. Inspectors, social reformers, and health advocates worried about the blending of the industrial and domestic. One inspector was appalled that immigrants "usually eat and sleep in the same room where the work is carried on."[29] New York State factory inspectors also enumerated the dangerous conditions of labor in the dark, cramped quarters of tenement buildings: "The dinginess, squalor and filth surrounding them is abominable."[30] They blamed the intermingling of the industrial and the domestic for such conditions: "In the room . . . used as a kitchen, there was a red-hot stove, two tables, a clothes rack and several piles of goods. A woman was making bread on a table upon which there was a baby's stocking, scraps of cloth, several old tin cans and a small pile of unfinished garments."[31] Thus, the economist Jesse Pope, in his classic study of the early years of Jewish garment manufacture, mourned the "intimate connection of manufacture with the home." "During the busy season," he wrote, "practically all the workers in both inside and outside shops take out work at night."[32]

In conjunction with federal and state investigations of the sweating system, factory inspectors began campaigns in the 1890s to document what they perceived as the insidious social and health effects of locating garment work in residences. "Whole districts in the city of New York are thus being rapidly transformed into small 'factory' centers of the most filthy and wretched character. In these districts what formerly were crowded *dwelling-houses* have become crammed workshops," lamented George McKay.[33] In 1892, when Dr. Annie Daniel first investigated the garment industry in the Lower East Side, she was shocked to discover that immigrants worked, played, and ate all in the same place. Indeed, for Daniel, the blending of industrial and domestic was key to how germs made their way into goods purchased by middle-class consumers: "There is no distinction at all. You may find the work in the bedroom, or you may find it in the kitchen on the table, and people eating; you will find the food and the same clothes on the same table; and you will find the clothes on the same bed with the sick child."[34] The New York State Office of the Factory Inspector similarly declared, "The combination living-room and workshop is a positive menace to the health of the community."[35]

The fears and frustrations expressed by these factory inspections carried over into the popular press. Eva McDonald Valesh, for example, described her visit to a tenement sweatshop and noted the close quarters, dangerous conditions, and health hazards: "The air is stifling. Heaps of clothing lie about on the floor, mixed with rubbish and scraps of food. The clothing on which the family work often serves as covering at night." Valesh blamed the intrusion of manufacturing into a domestic setting for "the foul air and filthy conditions of living." As a result, she reported, "many of the workers are dying . . . from consumption." Like Daniel, she worried that germs "absorbed by clothing" might be passed on to middle-class consumers.[36] For critics like Valesh, the blending of work and home represented a health threat both to workers and to the consuming public.

As Eastern European Jewish immigrants increasingly sought Americanization and assimilation, they came to join factory inspectors in their crusade against garment work in tenement apartments. More than other immigrant groups in New York, Jewish immigrants came to demand a differentiation between home and work. As historian Andrew Heinze suggests, especially after the turn of the century, Jewish immigrants often decorated their apartments with material goods, like pianos, that declared the home as distinct from the workplace and symbolized their rising social status and assimilation.[37] Such emblems of leisure marked immigrants' rise from the time when they struggled to find an economic foothold in New York, when their homes were, at best, purely functional. For newly arrived or for especially impoverished immigrants, a few scraps of wood might even suffice as furniture. As Jennie Matyas remembered her first living quarters in New York: "They were very dark and dingy. For about two years we had no bed to sleep on. The only table that we had was a table my father put together from some pieces of lumber that he got. We had a couple of benches that he made."[38] Looking back on her first home in New York, Rose Cohen similarly remembered it as "a dingy place where the sun never came in. I always felt lonely and a little homesick on coming into it."[39] Poor or new immigrants, especially men, might even sleep in the shop itself to save money. The experience of the father of the future labor leader Isidore Wisotsky was typical. He slept in the shop for two years as he saved money to bring his family over to New York. Yitzchak Yankel Doroshkin also slept in the shop where he found his first job.[40]

Further blurring distinctions between home and work, especially in the 1880s and 1890s, workers, especially men, would often carry work home after the day in the shop was completed. The whole family might work long into the night to supplement their miserable wages.[41] The cloakmaker Abraham Bisno described to the House committee how male Jewish workers, especially the most impoverished, took work home where they could rely on the help of their wives and children: "The manufacturer runs his shop at ten hours a day only, but I, who have a desire to work longer than ten hours, take work home every night. The manufacturer says you can take the work home and produce it at home. He takes it home and he has the use of his wife and children and neighbors."[42]

By the time the House held its hearings on sweated work, some Jewish garment workers, especially male workers like Bisno, joined factory inspectors in criticizing the location of "these sweat shops" in workers' homes. "The nuisance," Bisno complained, "was brought about because the people can work longer than in a factory."[43] For Bisno, with the pressures of subcontracting, the home became, not a site of leisure, but a dangerous workplace. "Sweat shops," he argued, "are shops at home."[44] The cloakmaker Abraham Rosenberg also understood the sweatshop as a workplace in the home: "Most contracting shops were in old tenements on the Lower East Side and the employer and his family lived on the premises. The family wash was set on the pressers' stove to boil."[45]

When these male immigrant workers complained about the "inhuman conditions" of sweatshops, they simultaneously decried the mixing of the industrial and the domestic. The garment worker Samuel Shore noted that in the first years of their migration, Eastern European Jewish immigrants faced "living and struggling in chaotic conditions . . . in the days of the sweatshop." In defining the sweatshop, he focused on the number of hours and the conditions of work: "The hours of labor were frightful, the conditions of employment were oppressive." For Shore, the hours of labor were "frightful" specifically because work and home were intertwined: "The bundle under the table, in the days when this very same bundle often served as a headrest for a worker to catch a few hours sleep and then go on with the task, the moving force in all workers was the desire to get away from it all."[46]

Gendering Jewish Homework

If the sweatshop was invading the home, workers could never escape its dangers. Thus, social reformers, policymakers, inspectors, male workers, and, on occasion, female workers labeled the homework shop, in which the husband served as employer and his wife and children as workers, as the worst kind of sweatshop. In the homework shop the boundaries between the industrial and the domestic disintegrated, conditions deteriorated, and gendered disorder increased. For inspectors, the homework shop accelerated the process of racial decline and, for workers, the homework shop threatened their chance at Americanization. For both groups, the homework shop magnified the health dangers of sweated labor. As John De Witt Warner, chair of the House committee, insisted, "The lot, however, of these 'sweat-shop' workers is luxury compared to those engaged in tenement home work." He traced a hierarchy within the sweated system with homework at the very bottom: "Through the contractor to the 'sweater' and on to the 'home worker,' the steps are steadily downward—of decreasing responsibility, comfort, and compensation." For Warner, the tenement homework shop was the worst kind of sweatshop and the homeworker the most degraded of sweated workers.[47]

New York State's factory inspectors described the homework shop as a sweatshop in which men turned the ideal of the male breadwinner on its head by converting family members into wage earners: "The heads of families form a numerous class of 'sweaters.' They utilize the labor of the members of their families."[48] Breadwinners became sweaters by putting their wives to work.[49] The House committee insisted that male homework subcontractors depended on the labor of their wives and children because they "will work for less wages than those employed in the larger shops and under conditions generally inconsistent with comfort and cleanliness."[50]

For such critics, homeworkers represented the lowest form of sweated worker, not simply because "the poverty of this class is often painfully pitiable," but also because it stood as the basest corruption of the ideal of the male breadwinner. As the House committee mourned, when immigrants were forced to turn to homework, any distinction between home and work disappeared and the degraded state of such workers became especially evident: "No pretense is made of separating the work from the household affairs, if such a term can be used to describe the existence of these people."[51]

For Warner and other factory inspectors, the public health and sanitary dangers of homework were linked to the destruction of a familial division of labor. He insisted that homework, the system where the "head of the family" put his family to work, often led to illness and death.[52] Similarly, the reformer Joseph Lee testified at the House committee hearings on sweated labor that the location of work in homes produced both health and moral dangers: "By introducing outsiders in his home and controverting it into a workroom the occupier has already surrendered the privacy which makes the home sacred; and the results, both sanitary and moral, of the combination of home and factory are worse in degree than in any other class of cases we have been considering."[53] Specifically, the Industrial Commission argued, "the effect on the intelligence and personal initiative of the tailors is also depressing."[54] For the Industrial Commission, the racial decline caused by sweated labor was intimately intertwined with the corruption of male breadwinning.

By the 1890s, factory inspectors and policymakers generally associated homework with the most desperate of workers: newly arrived immigrants and, in particular, struggling married or widowed women. In many ways, this association reflected perception more than it did reality. As historian Eileen Boris notes, few widows could have earned enough through homework to support children, let alone themselves. The association of homework, though, with the most desperate of women suggests the almost paranoid connection of homework with women and with immigrants' racial degeneration.[55] As Warner wrote: "The home-worker is generally a foreigner just arrived and frequently a woman whose husband is dead, sick, or worthless and whose children keep her at home."[56] In addition, as the nineteenth century came to a close and the first government regulations and laws focused on shifting garment production out of tenement apartments and into buildings designed for industrial use, inspectors and policymakers came to restrict their definition of homework to married women's work. In particular, they identified "finishing," the final stitching of garments generally completed at home, as the main type of homework and as a married woman's craft.[57]

Jesse Pope similarly described homework as a form of women's labor distinct from factory work. He did not recognize homeworkers as real workers, a view shared by many other inspectors and workers, which had enormous implications for future workplace organizing and policymaking. Homework was not factory work, and inspectors—and soon male workers and unionists—insisted that it should be regulated differently.[58] For such critics, women homeworkers were, at once, the worst victims of the sweatshop and a symbol of the moral, physical, and racial perils of sweated work. When inspectors, like Lee, pointed out the dangers of sweated work, they focused especially on women's homework. Their representations of female homeworkers tended to highlight their poverty, degraded mental or physical state, and immodesty. One inspector, recalling his visit to a Hester Street tenement homework shop, highlighted the poor health and scant dress of the female workers he observed: "I . . . entered a room on the attic floor. . . . In these cramped quarters were women and four sewing-machines. . . . The women were scantily clad . . . and their pale, abject countenances, as they bent over their work, formed a picture of physical suffering."[59] House committee members even went as far as to suggest that homeworkers were, at worst, "defective in habits or physical or in mental capacity." At best, they asserted, homeworkers were married, foreign women for "whom the death or worthlessness of her husband leaves to support a family, which prevents her leaving her home."[60]

It was around the question of homework that workers, led by male unionists, forged a common language of labor with inspectors and policymakers. Like middle-class observers, workers identified homework as a threat to male breadwinning and as a moral danger. The homework shop was the worst kind of sweatshop and homework was the labor of debased women. As George Price noted with disgust: "A large part of the manufacturing was carried on . . . in kitchens and other rooms of the East Side tenement houses, and not a few of the workers were women. . . . Under these conditions, the so-called sweating system had full sway." "Home work," he mourned, "was rampant."[61] Price worried about the "physical, psychological, and moral deterioration" he associated with sweated homework.[62] And the unionist and garment worker Morris Feinstone blamed "the vicious 'homework' system" for "the steady degradation of whole families."[63] He insisted that when they turned to homework, female immigrants and their families surrendered their "health, moral courage, and at the last even hope of deliverance."[64] Workers, it seemed, had found a language about family deterioration that easily matched inspectors' discourse of racial degeneration.

As historians Susan Glenn and Sydney Stahl Weinberg note, female Jewish immigrants also represented the typical homeworker as a desperate married or widowed female worker. Rose Cohen, for example, described her own diminishing enthusiasm for the New World by focusing on the suffering of her landlady, who took in bundles of garments to be finished to supplement her presser husband's paltry wages. Cohen describes her landlady's physical pain and bodily decline as if to highlight the shame of homework. Cohen's landlady labored in a small room "where she sat a great part of the day finishing . . . big bundles from a shop and rocking the cradle with one foot. . . . She spoke in a whisper scarcely ever lifting weak peering eyes from her work."[65] Such an association of homework with married women's garment manufacture helped refine the cultural meaning of homework. Homework drifted with its feminization into a pernicious nether region between the workplace and the home. It was neither labor in an idealized American factory, nor was it unpaid domestic work. Rose Cohen's pathetic description of her landlady's homework reflects the extent to which many male and female Jewish immigrants vilified women's homework; for them, homework was a public symbol of poverty, not a form of flexible labor that could blend with domestic responsibilities.[66]

Regulating Homework, Organizing Workers, and Restricting Women's Labor

As anxiety about immigration, industrial labor, and disease grew in the 1890s, government officials and labor representatives proposed new regulations of homework. Some factory inspectors and politicians who were apt to blame immigrants for the spread of the sweatshop and homework urged stricter immigration controls.[67] The New York State Office of the Factory Inspector, for example, argued that "Congress can aid very greatly in abating the evils of the sweating system by the passage of more stringent immigration laws."[68] In an argument about immigrants' foreignness and racial difference, another observer argued for a "restriction of immigration" that "will cut off a class of immigrants which tends only to lower the American standard of living."[69]

However, the restriction of immigration was a slow and politically charged process. Indeed, significant restrictions of European immigration would not be passed until 1924. Instead, reformers sought "the restriction . . . of tenement-house work" to counteract "the depressing effects of immigration."[70] Like other efforts at labor and protective legislation, laws to regulate sweated homework were initially proposed "not on behalf of workers, but on behalf of the public." They were concerned, in particular, about "the contagious and infectious diseases which are . . . carried by clothing from tenements to the consumers."[71] In the 1890s, the most widely adopted kind of regulations mirrored the recommendations of the House committee. The committee proposed the licensing and regulation of tenement homework and age restrictions for tenement house workers. In the following months and years, New York, as well as Massachusetts, Pennsylvania, New Jersey, Illinois, Missouri, Michigan, and Ohio, passed laws to regulate tenement manufacture.[72]

The 1892 New York law was revised and strengthened in 1899, 1901, and 1903. The law mandated that tenement house manufacturers have official licenses.[73] Licensing laws, however, had limited success. Between 1892 and 1896, New York's twenty-four factory inspectors investigated 12,054 shops, but brought charges against only 154 shop owners and contractors. In addition, the 115 convictions they won carried little punishment. During this period, inspectors collected a mere $2,500 in fines. On the same day in 1892, for example, Max Goldberg was arrested and paid the small fine of $20 for having employed a fourteen-year-old child, and Morris Saldinger was arrested for manufacturing cloaks in an overcrowded room without a permit. He was also fined $20.[74]

The low cost of fines, the miniscule number of convictions, and simply the paltry number of inspections highlight the relative failure of factory inspection alone as a means to regulate the sweated system. As late as 1903, the New York Bureau of Labor Statistics reported that there remained between 25,000 and 30,000 tenement homeworkers finishing garments. The Bureau also noted that most were women.[75] By the time Eastern European Jewish workers had begun forming powerful unions after 1900, factory inspectors and policymakers were beginning to admit that with only a few inspectors assigned to the crowded Lower East Side, inspection alone could not possibly eradicate sweatshops. As the Industrial Commission concluded, "The strict enforcement of the law . . . since it depends upon the discretion of the inspector, is very difficult to secure."[76]

Thus by the late 1890s and early 1900s, as the Industrial Commission reported, "the excessive evils of tenement-house manufacture, and the difficulties of regulation, have caused a demand . . . for its abolition by legislation."[77] The most far-reaching and ambitious suggestion came from Dr. Daniel. "I believe," she argued, "that the only remedy is prohibition of all tenement-house work, even by members of the family."[78] By 1901, inspectors in New York and Illinois—states with the largest garment industries—advocated state and federal laws for the abolition of homework. Such laws, they argued, would eliminate "the most unsanitary shop" in favor of the "progressive management of the factory."[79] However, despite their pleas for such "radical" legislation, inspectors recognized that laws alone could not abolish homework. Most important, any steps toward prohibiting homework altogether had been declared unconstitutional *in re Jacobs*. In that case, a law prohibiting the manufacture of cigars in tenements was declared unconstitutional because it went beyond the police powers of the state or federal government. No laws simply abolishing homework, therefore, could be considered constitutional.[80]

Representatives of organized labor suggested different ways to reform the sweatshop. Two native-born officers of garment workers' unions who testified before the House committee both rejected inspection as a strategy to regulate tenement homework. Instead, they urged the use of sanitary labels that would appeal to the public's fear of potentially contagious garments produced in sweatshops. As Charles Reichers, the general secretary of the Union of Garment Workers of America (a union of native-born workers that rarely sought to organize Jewish immigrants), told the committee: "I believe that . . . our label would prove to the public that the garment made having our label attached . . . would be made in a large, healthy, airy shop."[81] In their testimony, several male Eastern European Jewish workers also suggested that sanitary labels might encourage consumers to buy safely and fairly made garments, thus protecting their positions as breadwinners. Abram Fells even argued that tags should be placed prominently on the collar of garments.[82]

Eastern European Jewish garment workers also rejected the idea that inspection and legislation alone could solve the sweatshop problem. George Price, for example, described "the inability of state labor legislation to improve conditions and the failure of the state factory administration to curb the 'sweatshop' evil."[83] In their testimony to the House committee, Eastern European Jewish workers pointed to unions as a means to eliminate sweatshops and homework.[84]

In fact, the elimination of the sweatshop and, in particular, the homework system—and the guarantee of a sexual division of labor—became the main priorities of the first Jewish garment unions and of the first wave of male garment workers' strikes. In 1885, male cloakmakers demanded the elimination of "night work," that is, the taking of garments into the home, which the union suggested led to the spread of homework sweatshops.[85] In another strike in 1894, cloakmakers listed their demands in the form of "Ten Commandments." Again, one of their primary demands was that "home work and night work should be abolished."[86] The conditions and pay of men's work could be protected, they argued, through the restriction and, hopefully, the abolition of women's homework and their labor in tenement homework shops.

Despite the high hopes of Bisno, Goldman, and these male cloakmakers, their unions were weak, lacking in both funds and stability. While they might win a strike with one employer, they could not bargain industry-wide contracts that might have had the potential to reshape conditions. As the immigrant worker and trade unionist, Samuel Shore remembered: "And so unions were strong and weak by turns, depending upon the vagaries of the workers. The thought of permanency in organization took a long time to develop."[87] Price similarly remembered that Jewish workers simply lacked the organizational power and experience to eliminate the sweatshop: "While the need for improvement was great and the desire for it not less so, the workers were inexperienced . . . and were unable to effect an efficient organization to fight the evils of the sweat-shop system."[88]

The Eastern European Jewish labor movement slowly gained stability and power after 1900 with the formation of the International Ladies' Garment Workers' Union (ILGWU). Central to the success of the ILGWU was the willingness of its leadership to work in conjunction with factory inspectors and sympathetic government officials. After 1900, Jewish unionists were increasingly ready to participate in public campaigns across what they saw as the lines of class to restrict, control, and, if possible, eliminate homework. Such alliances could offer unions permanency in an industry characterized by many small shops and uneven availability of work. Joining in efforts to regulate the industry and to make workplaces visible to the state assured unions a long-sought-after stability. And it seemed to be the best way of eliminating homework. Like cloakmakers in 1885 and 1894, the ILGWU assaulted the legitimacy and appropriateness of homework. They deprecated homework either as an outgrowth of the tenement sweatshop or as sweated labor itself. As a result, the ILGWU, and its male leaders and rank and file, came to share with factory inspectors a language to describe the sweatshop. In a remarkable echoing of factory inspectors who declared the sweated industry a foreign industry, the ILGWU resolved "that we concentrate all efforts upon the movement for stamping out of the disease-breeding infamous and un-American 'sweating system.'"[89]

After the turn of the century, the ILGWU, initially a union composed almost entirely of men, developed close alliances with factory inspectors, public health advocates, and politicians. As they jointly developed a discourse that represented the sweatshop as the opposite of the modern factory, Jewish trade unionists and factory inspectors developed a cohesive plan to improve sanitary conditions by eradicating homework and eliminating the sweatshop. Together, they advanced the idea that factory inspection could be a form of labor organizing and that trade-union officials should have the right to inspect shop conditions. Homework became the target for male garment workers seeking to distance their wives from the workplace and from garment work in general. Their campaign reached an apex during the watershed 1910 strike of mostly male cloakmakers. In a strike unprecedented in scope and scale, the 1910 strike cemented relationships between the ILGWU and social reformers. This combination of inspection and organizing reinforced the strict segregation of the workplace and the home and promoted a vision of a model workplace. The model shop in the form of a "modern factory" was everything the tenement homework sweatshop was not; it protected workers' health and maintained the ideal of the male breadwinner. As an Illinois inspector quoted by the Industrial Commission put it, the modern factory with effective management and mechanization "was the best hope of doing away with the abuses that are inherent in the sweating system."[90]

Four

Workers Made Well

*Home, Work, Homework, and
the Model Shop, 1910–1930*

In the years after 1910, an alliance between factory inspectors, policymakers, and male Jewish immigrants began to take shape around the issue of women's sweated homework. In 1910, a massive strike of male cloakmakers, organized in the ILGWU, forced employers and policymakers to recognize the strength and vitality of immigrant unions. Factory inspectors, social reformers, and policymakers facilitated the creation of a cross-class anti-sweatshop coalition by encouraging employers to settle with striking workers. At the center of the agreement signed by Jewish garment union leaders and employers was a body empowered to regulate working conditions in the garment industry: the Joint Board of Sanitary Control (JBSC). Women would join this coalition after 1913, but only through alliances with women reformers, and even then in the face of opposition from male unionists.[1]

The JBSC was led and staffed by union leaders and factory inspectors. It regulated initially only cloakmaking, but after women forced their way into the coalition, the JBSC inspected shops in a host of other trades in which female Jewish immigrants worked in large numbers, including dressmaking, shirt-waistmaking, and whitegoodsmaking. The JBSC established a model of industrial regulation that seamlessly blended factory inspection with workplace organizing. At the heart of the JBSC's stated mission was the eradication of women's homework—and this remained its goal even after 1913. Abolishing homework, for the JBSC, remained the key to controlling sweatshops.

The creation and endurance of the JBSC over two decades of labor turmoil in the garment industry was a structural manifestation of the convergence in the ways factory inspectors and workers defined the sweatshop and its dangers. An earlier group of factory inspectors viewed the sweatshop as both a by-product and a cause of Jewish racial degeneration. In contrast, the inspectors of the JBSC—some of whom, in fact, were themselves Jewish immigrants and former garment workers—viewed the conditions of the sweatshop less as a reflection of Jewish comfort in filth than as problems that workers could overcome, if empowered with the aid of sanitary inspectors. Immigrant workers similarly backed away from an emotional language that compared the sweatshop boss to a blood-sucking vampire. Now, the problem was that sweatshops, too often located in immigrants' homes, lacked the conveniences of the idealized factory.

While both workers and inspectors still viewed the sweatshop as a health menace, the focus for inspectors shifted from the health of female middle-class consumers to the health of male breadwinners. In the process, understandings of the dangers of the sweatshop shifted. Languages of race and class receded to the background. In effect, inspectors recognized immigrants' ability to assimilate as well as to improve their health and working conditions, despite older racial notions of a "Hebrew" comfort in filth. Workers—still largely immigrants and their children—for their part cast aside a potentially explosive language of class conflict as they accepted the efficacy of sanitary reform and factory inspection. Supplanting languages of class and race, a language of gender shaped understandings of the sweatshop, its dangers, and strategies to eradicate it. Using the calm rational vocabulary of scientific reform, unionists and inspectors argued that by abolishing women's homework, they were striking at the heart of the sweated system.

According to its leaders and supporters, the success of the JBSC and the anti-sweatshop coalition could be measured in the movement of the garment industry away from the tenement apartments of the Lower East Side to industrial, modern, and mechanized factories located uptown in loft buildings. Thus, the JBSC was recycling an older contrast between the immigrant sweatshop and the American factory. Yet where race had originally shaped this contrast, gender now gave it meaning. In the sweatshop, poor sanitary conditions led to men and women working together, whereas in the modern factory, mechanized production and sanitary control helped maintain male breadwinning. For the JBSC and the ILGWU, the shift in the garment industry uptown was a move from disorderly work and gendered disorder to modern production and an established sexual division of labor within immigrant families.

The gendered contrast between the sweatshop and the factory helped workers and inspectors arrive at a shared vision of a "model shop." In the model shop, the boss remained, but healthy male workers earned a family wage, while enjoying a host of comforts and conveniences. By the 1920s, workers and in-spectors were even building model shops that doubled as tuberculosis sani-tariums. Where the sweatshop enfeebled, the model shop cured. Citing the steady movement of industry uptown, away from the Lower East Side, the JBSC trumpeted its success. In 1913, they claimed that 71 percent of women's cloak and suit shops were located north of Houston Street and the Lower East Side.[2] According to the JBSC, the Lower East Side had become—with the notable exception of the streets populated by Italian immigrants—a residential district.[3] And, two years later, it proudly declared that "no home work is to be found in the industry; sweat-shops have been abolished."[4]

Even as the JBSC was no doubt exaggerating its success, it was sharply nar-rowing its definition of sweated homework to the garment work performed by Jewish women. Despite the thousands of Italians who joined the ILGWU and the Italian women who made up the majority of women who took in piece-work, including garment finishing, the JBSC remained an alliance between Jew-ish workers and inspectors (many of whom were also Jewish). Italians were largely left out of this alliance. Most of the JBSC's publicity was in Yiddish or English, rarely in Italian. And no Italians served as inspectors or on its execu-tive committee. Not surprisingly, the JBSC made no effort to expand its pur-view into those trades, like doll's clothesmaking or artificial flowermaking, where Italians dominated the workforce. Inspectors like Dr. Annie Daniel la-beled these trades homework, but often refrained from calling them sweated homework. They continued to argue, as a result, that regulating this kind of homework could help protect middle-class consumers by controlling the spread of disease, whereas for those trades regulated by the JBSC, the focus was squarely on the stability of the Jewish immigrant family. Efforts to inspect and regulate industries where few Jews labored were never part of the campaign to eradicate the sweatshop.[5]

If the JBSC, in claiming to eradicate the sweatshop, rhetorically separated Italian and Jewish homework, it could not erase the sweatshop from the way immigrant Jewish workers imagined the dangers of the garment industry. While older languages of race and class were less important in determining strategies of inspection and organizing, these more emotional languages be-came central to the way Jewish workers and ILGWU leaders represented the history of garment workers and their union. Jewish workers described them-selves as an immigrant group that had emerged "out of the sweatshop," a lan-guage that sought to confirm their place in American civilization. In much the same way a previous generation of inspectors worried that immigrants' racial status could rise or fall through their experience of sweated work, ILGWU lead-ers insisted that the sweatshop could always return. Its eradication, like Jewish immigrants' Americanization, was never complete. Similarly, the language of class found its place in the ILGWU's self-history that described the anti-sweatshop campaign of inspection and regulation as a "true uprising."

Reforming the Workshop, Eliminating Homework

The demands to eliminate homework and piecework advanced by male cloakmakers during their 1885 and 1894 strikes foreshadowed organizing strategies pushed successfully by the solidly male leadership of the ILGWU during and after the 1910 strike. In both earlier strikes, male cloakmakers argued for a relocation of production away from tenement apartments. Again in 1910, male cloakmakers in the ILGWU sought to reorganize an industry they characterized as a "'sweat-shop' trade."[6] The 1910 strike was a coordinated effort of 75,000 primarily Jewish male garment workers who were struggling to win an institutional role for their union in the shaping of their industry.[7] As a women's shirtwaistmakers' strike that began in 1909 ground to a halt, the ILGWU expanded strike preparations among the cloakmakers in the union's Joint Board of Cloak, Skirt, and Pressers' Unions, the umbrella organization that united different cloakmakers' locals. As early as December 1909, the Joint Board overwhelmingly approved a strike tax of two dollars from every member.[8] In addition, a growing enthusiasm for a general strike rapidly expanded the ranks of the Joint Board. In June 1910, at the ILGWU convention in Boston, several resolutions were presented calling for a general strike.[9] Later that month, the Joint Board conducted a strike vote. Of 19,586 votes cast, 18,771 were in favor of the strike. The strike itself was called on July 7.[10]

The Joint Board sought a solution for what its leaders called the "insanitary [sic] conditions in the trade" by seeking a role for the ILGWU in the organization and regulation of production.[11] Given the focus on the conditions and the location of work, the ILGWU and cloakmaker's union leadership, in negotiations to end the strike, traded a rhetoric of class conflict and the demand for the closed union shop in exchange for preference in hiring for union members, the right to inspect garment factories, and a guarantee that "no work shall be given to employees to be done at their homes."[12] Drawing on the cross-class nature of concerns about the appropriate location of work, the union turned to sympathetic social reformers for aid in settling the strike. On July 27, Meyer London, attorney for the Joint Board, asked the noted judge and leading progressive Louis Brandeis to serve as chairman of a negotiating conference planned for the next day. At the same time, as historian Richard Greenwald argues, the turn to Progressive reformers signaled a shift in control of the union from rank-and-file activists to a centralized male leadership.[13]

Exactly one month later, the Manufacturers' Association and the ILGWU finally reached an agreement, widely called the "Protocol of Peace." Workers won a fifty-hour work week, double pay for overtime, and a wage increase. In addition, while the union retreated from its original demand for the union shop, it accepted Brandeis's idea of the "preferential shop." The "preferential shop" confirmed the right of management to hire and fire but, rather vaguely, insisted that union members be granted preference and set up a board of arbitration to hear grievances. The Protocol of Peace was most specific in its effort to eradicate subcontracting and homework by relocating work away from the tenement apartments of the Lower East Side. To prevent subcontracting, to police working conditions, and to facilitate the movement of industry, the Protocol of Peace established the JBSC, a permanent board of inspectors with the right to survey sanitary conditions in New York's shops and to mandate sanitary and safety improvements.[14]

The formation of the JBSC confirmed an alliance of male workers, organized in the ILGWU, with social reformers and factory inspectors. The JBSC was formed immediately after the signing of the Protocol of Peace, and, based on its first inspections, released its initial report in October 1911. It issued yearly reports until 1928, when it finally disbanded.[15] The JBSC claimed a three-part mission: "Investigation, enforcement, and education."[16] It gathered and analyzed data from annual surveys of garment shops and, under the terms of the protocol, mandated sanitary and fire-control protections. Finally, it undertook a campaign of "propaganda" about workplace health aimed at workers, primarily, but also at employers. Initially, at least, the JBSC focused exclusively on cloakmaking, a trade in which men composed a large majority of shopworkers. It was not until 1913 that the dressmaking, waistmaking, and whitegoodsmaking trades with large female workforces came under the purview of the JBSC.[17]

The JBSC and Inspection as Organizing

The JBSC created "a machinery of enforcement" that united an enduring alliance of Eastern European Jewish immigrant workers, employers, union representatives, reformers, and public health advocates. It brought together the principal players of the cloakmakers' strike, Meyer London and Julius Cohen, the attorney for the manufacturers' association, as well as inspectors and public health advocates like Lillian Wald, the founder of the Nurses' Settlement House. The JBSC also employed three investigators to conduct shop visits.[18] The JBSC emerged as a coalition between workers and reformers as both the ILGWU and the Progressive public health movement reached the apex of their political and cultural strength. The JBSC also enjoyed the support— or, at least, the tolerance—of important employers who were content to have inspection drive out smaller shops with lower operating costs.[19]

The coalition between workers, reformers, and inspectors that was embodied in the JBSC depended on a shift in the language used to define the sweatshop. For inspectors, inclusion in the JBSC meant retreating from a definition of the sweatshop as a reflection of Jewish racial inferiority. Workers, meanwhile, largely abandoned a language of class that compared the sweatshop boss to a vampire. In turning to a gendered language that focused on the effects of garment work on male breadwinners, this cross-class coalition prioritized the reform of working conditions. They came to describe the sweatshop as a correctable problem of poor management. As the JBSC explained in 1911: "The real menace to the health of workers . . . lies not in the nature of the industry itself or the capitalist system of production, but the defective sanitary conditions of the shops: not in the peculiar character of the work, but . . . in the lack of cleanliness, and in the absence of needed comforts and conveniences."[20]

Having retreated from a language of class, the ILGWU came to advance a vision of factory inspection as organizing and as the best way of eradicating homework. As the 1910 strike came to a close, the ILGWU vowed to "start an agitation forthwith for an increasing vigilance of factory inspectors and for the ultimate abolition of home work."[21] Inspection was crucial to transforming unhealthy working conditions. Thus, in 1928, when the ILGWU's Education Department offered a course about the unions' history, it celebrated the role of "intellectuals," principally health professionals, in helping the union counter the sweatshop and eliminate women's homework.[22]

Similarly, having gradually replaced the focus on race with gendered concerns, factory inspectors transformed their understanding of the health dangers of sweated work. Where earlier inspectors saw the sanitary problems of the sweatshop as a threat to middle-class consumers, the JBSC's inspectors were more concerned with the effect of poor conditions on workers.[23] At the same time, JBSC inspectors advanced a different attitude toward unions. When the House of Representatives first held hearings on the "sweated system," inspectors and policymakers categorically rejected labor organizing, however friendly to the state, as a means of controlling sanitary conditions.[24] With the growing strength of the ILGWU, inspectors became convinced of the necessity of workers' activism in inspection. Inspectors recognized workers' ability "to organize for the improvement of their conditions," as Meyer London put it.[25]

The alliance between workers and reformers in the JBSC served to blur distinctions between trade union and reformist discourses around health, gender, and the effects of work. The expanding connections between unionization and inspection were especially evident in the careers of the most active functionaries and officials of the JBSC: its inspectors and its executive committee chairman. Many of the JBSC's most active leaders had backgrounds that bridged the reform and trade union movements. Their experience appeared to help consolidate workers' and reformers' sometimes divergent understandings of the sweatshop and its dangers. Although the chemist and welfare advocate William J. Schieffelin was elected the chairman of the board, much of the daily work and responsibilities fell to the chairman of the executive committee, Dr. George M. Price.

Perhaps more than any other JBSC official, Price embodied the alliance of labor unionists and reformists. Price immigrated to the United States from the Pale of Settlement in 1882 and, like so many other Eastern European Jewish immigrants, became a garment worker. By 1893, he had begun a long career in social reform and social work within his own community of Eastern European Jewish immigrants. He published an early history of Russian Jews in America before earning a medical degree and joining the burgeoning campaign for public health.[26] In 1901, Price founded a "School of Sanitation" to train factory and tenement inspectors. In the same year, he published the *Handbook on Sanitation: A Manual of Theoretical and Practical Sanitation,* a text offering methods of sanitary inspection, including of garment sweatshops and immigrant tenements. At the same time, Price maintained a deep political and cultural connection to Eastern European Jewish immigrant garment workers and their unions. He remained a strong advocate for labor unions and an ally of the ILGWU.[27]

In addition to Price, the JBSC's inspectors also reflected this alliance of unionism and factory inspection. Of the three original inspectors, John T. Turner had served as a professional factory inspector for twenty years, A. J. Rosenblatt brought a perspective hardened from years as a cloakmaker, and Rose Blank had worked with garment labor unions after graduating from the New York School of Philanthropy.[28]

The JBSC, then, was at once a new form of factory inspection and a new type of labor organizing that garnered support from both the trade union movement and reformers. The JBSC combined frequent inspections with outreach to and education of workers. It created powerful proletarian shop floor structures that reinforced the right of workers to regulate workplace conditions and helped ILGWU leaders define clear boundaries between the garment workplace and immigrants' homes. The JBSC's inspections served to establish the workshop, as opposed to the home, as the site of men's labor and as a legitimate, even perfectible, workplace.[29]

The JBSC defined a strict hierarchy of shops based on conditions and proximity to homes. It conducted annual surveys of garment shops, detailing conditions on the shop floor. In 1911, between January 16 and February 23, for example, the inspectors visited 8 shops a day and 1,243 of the 1,549 shops of which the JBSC was aware. The JBSC used the results of factory inspections to classify shops as "A," "B," "C," or "D." "A" shops had "fully complied with all the state and municipal laws as well as with our own standards" and were located in industrial buildings. "B" shops were plagued by "minor sanitary defects and . . . would be regarded as free from violations of the labor code by the state factory inspectors." Yet the JBSC claimed stiffer standards. "C" shops were often housed in tenement apartments and contained minor violations but also fire hazards, including narrow aisles and obstructed exits. Finally, "D" shops were those in tenement apartments that included major "structural sanitary defects" like foot power instead of electric power, which was seen as less physically debilitating, and insufficient or improper toilets. In 1914, the JBSC discovered 948 "A" shops, 1,045 "B" shops, 476 "C" shops, and 53 "D" shops.[30] The JBSC could mandate changes or even close a shop. By the end of July 1911, the JBSC found 823 "defective shops," of which 740 "made improvements and complied with our orders." It also "removed" twenty-nine of the most abominable shops.[31]

The board interceded in disputes between workers and bosses by inspecting shops where workers reported sanitary abuses. From May through July 1911, the JBSC responded to seventy-five such complaints.[32] Sometimes, the JBSC simply recommended closing the shop. In one tenement shop, investigated after a complaint, the JBSC discovered overflowing toilets, a trash-filled rear yard, dirty windows, unpainted walls, and unsafe fire escapes. The inspector determined the shop located in a tenement apartment "not a fit place to work. I therefore recommend that this shop be vacated." The shop was subsequently closed and the owner moved from the Lower East Side to a larger, cleaner industrial building.[33] At other times, the JBSC even called "sanitary strikes," ordering workers to quit work until abuses were corrected or factories moved. The board inspected a shop on December 17, 1910, found it "unfit for working purposes," and therefore authorized a sanitary strike "while these conditions prevail."[34] In 1913, the JBSC authorized twenty-seven sanitary strikes, actions that united inspection and rank-and-file support for sanitary control.[35]

The JBSC sought not only to inspect workplace conditions, but also to educate Jewish workers especially about sanitation. It directed an extensive education campaign intended, as the JBSC suggested in 1911, "to make workers . . . respect sanitary laws."[36] George Price wrote updates on the JBSC and on workers' health in the *Neue Post,* the Yiddish cloakmakers' newspaper. The JBSC contributed articles to newspapers and journals commonly read by garment workers, including *The Daily Trade Record, Women's Wear, Gleicheit, The Message,* and the ILGWU's official journals, *The Ladies' Garment Worker* and

Justice.[37] The JBSC widely distributed regular bulletins and leaflets on issues of workers' health, including bulletins on "Safe and Sanitary Shops" and on industrial disease. In 1916, for example, the JBSC passed out 100,000 copies of the "Workers' Health Bulletin."[38]

In addition, it sponsored a series of well-attended lunchtime talks and longer evening lectures in local public schools. In 1912 alone, George Price on numerous occasions delivered three different lectures: "Factory Sanitation," "Industrial Conditions in the State of New York," and "Industrial Poisons." In addition, the anti-homework reformer Florence Kelley spoke on "Factory Legislation"; Abraham Bisno, an official in the Cloakmakers' Joint Board, on "Factory Education"; and Dr. Henry Moskowitz on "Factory Co-Operation." A common theme of these lectures was a condemnation of the tenement homework shop and praise for the "factory" as the only site of work that could be effectively regulated.[39]

The JBSC created a system of inspection that advanced a vision of the workplace as a potentially sanitary space. Sanitation could be measured by the distance separating a garment workplace from tenement homes and by the absence of married women's labor. In a retreat from an earlier racialist language that cast the poor conditions of the sweatshop as a reflection of Jews' comfort in filth, the JBSC argued that only workers, already extensively educated by the JBSC, could fully compel bosses to comply with sanitary regulations. The board, for example, criticized state labor laws, which depended solely on thirty-seven factory inspectors to protect all the workers in New York City with its 40,000 workplaces.

For the JBSC, filthy workplaces were the result of poor management, not workers' racial traits. Thus, the JBSC exhorted workers to "*demand* better sanitary conditions" and sought "to make them unwilling to work under any other conditions."[40] One of the board's bulletins in 1911, for example, empowered workers to inspect their own workplaces and to "demand cleanliness from your employers." Sanitary control, the board suggested, was the duty of organized union workers as much as it was of paid inspectors: *"The preservation of health is the most important consideration of the worker.* Therefore, join in securing *safe and sanitary shops,* in order that your life may be prolonged and your health preserved."[41] Thus, the JBSC encouraged workers to organize sanitary shop committees, headed by a sanitary chairman. Such committees either confronted bosses directly about sanitary abuses or brought complaints to the board. By 1912, the JBSC had succeeded in organizing 398 committees. In connecting the preservation of health with "sanitary shops," the JBSC suggested that workers should demand to work only in factories, not in tenement homes.[42]

Homework, Gender, and the "Sanitary Millennium"

The blending of factory inspection and organizing in the JBSC was centered around Jewish workers, inspectors, and reformers' gendered discourse about homework and the location of labor. The reform of the workplace, the site of male breadwinning, as encouraged by the JBSC in its bulletins, speeches, and shop meetings, depended rhetorically and strategically on eradicating homework and tenement homework sweatshops. The vision of the workplace articulated through the structure of the JBSC by garment workers, and originally by male cloakmakers, reinforced gendered divisions between home and workplace. The JBSC and its assessment of workplaces as "A," "B," "C," or "D" shops created a hierarchy shaped by the idea that a workshop, distinct from a home, represented the only legitimate site for labor.

When the JBSC first inspected the Lower East Side's "dirty and neglected" shops, they discovered that Jewish workers were not comfortable in filth, but "complained of these conditions."[43] In investigating these "small overcrowded, ill-lighted, badly ventilated, unsafe and unsanitary workshops," the JBSC blamed the prevalence of tenement apartment work: "Home work was the order of the day . . . ; the East Side was full of so-called sweatshops."[44] JBSC's inspectors viewed the location of labor in workers' tenement apartments and homework as essential elements in their definition of the sweatshop: "In the early 80's . . . [a] very large part of the work was done in tenement houses, in the so-called sweat-shops, in the homes of the workers, by contractors, subcontractors and sub-sub-contractors."[45]

The JBSC also blamed homework for the spread of germs. One of the first goals of the JBSC when it began work in 1911 was to remove bedding from factories, a common feature in small sweatshops and homework shops: "In the old buildings of the congested districts, an added danger is the presence of bedding in the shops. Here, there is not only fertile ground for bacterial growth, but also propagation of vermin."[46] In 1913, one board inspector again complained about workers sleeping in shops: "In some of the shops, evidence of their use as sleeping-rooms was found."[47]

To reform the sweatshop and its sanitary dangers, the JBSC sought to abolish women's sweated homework. As it claimed in 1914: "To insure proper sanitary rules and regulations . . . to abolish tenement house, home work and sweat-shop work . . . these were some of the problems which confronted the Joint Board of Sanitary Control at the inception."[48] Sanitary progress could be measured by the movement of the garment industry from the "little dingy sweat-shops of the East Side" to "light airy and comfortable" factory buildings along Fifth Avenue.[49] While the board presented the East Side as synonymous with sweated homework, it saluted Fifth Avenue factory loft buildings as

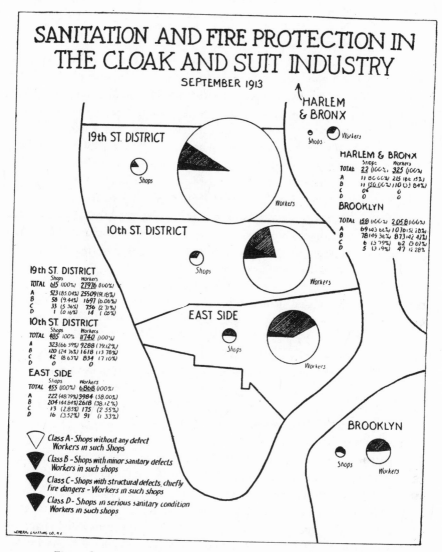

_____ *Figure 3* _____

Pie-chart illustrating the movement of the garment industry uptown (from *Five Years' Work and Progress of the Joint Board of Sanitary Control in the Cloak, Suit and Skirt and the Dress and Waist Industries: An Experiment in Industrial Self-Control* [New York: Joint Board of Sanitary Control, October 31, 1915], 5; image from General Research Division, The New York Public Library, Astor, Lenox and Tolden Foundations). The map captures the JBSC's sense of progress in the ladies' garment industry. The pie graphs laid over the map of Manhattan highlight the movement uptown, implying an improvement in conditions. It also suggests a new focus on scientific, rational reform among inspectors and workers and a departure from older ways of talking about sweatshop dangers.

sanitary progress. As the JBSC happily noted in 1915, "in the so-called Fifth Avenue District . . . the sanitary care, comforts and cleanliness of the shops have improved a hundredfold and the gain in health of the workers has been considerable."[50] One map printed in the board's third annual report illustrated the way it associated the movement of industry away from East Side residential buildings to Fifth Avenue lofts with the general improvement in conditions. With pie charts counterpoised over a map of the city, the JBSC captured the increasing size of the industry north of Tenth Street. For the JBSC, the move separated workplace and home and helped control the sweated system. At the same time, the seemingly objective and dispassionate use of maps, figures, and data showed the convergence of the JBSC's rhetoric with broader Progressive Era scientific, rational languages of reform. It also suggests a retreat from earlier lurid descriptions of Jewish racial character and from workers' emotional, pathetic appeals to class empowerment.[51]

Still, despite this move toward a language of scientific reform, the JBSC recycled and reformulated factory inspectors' older comparison between the dangerous, promiscuous, foreign sweatshop and the healthy American factory. Now, the JBSC compared the Lower East Side sweatshop with the "modern factory," as George Price called it. Where earlier comparisons depended largely on race, the JBSC's contrast relied on gender and geography. For the JBSC, the Lower East Side sweatshop was a site of men and women's work. The persistence of sweatshops was blamed on women's homework, whereas the modern shop was a site of male breadwinning.[52]

A close examination of the JBSC's presentation of photographs in its annual reports reveals a sense of progress toward modernity. Gender, more than race or ethnicity, seems to be the concern of the JBSC and the measure of modernity. The JBSC used dramatic and carefully posed photographs in its literature to highlight the dangers of tenement work and the progress represented by loft factories. Especially in its earliest reports, the JBSC contrasted images of "modern" shops with photographs of Lower East Side tenement shops. Images of modern shops often relied on a panoramic view photographed from above workers' heads. Such a perspective seemed to highlight a rational order of many workers doing the same task in a large, spacious room. While women certainly worked in these shops, photographs generally only depicted men, as if to highlight how sanitary reform protected the male breadwinner. Older shops, in contrast, were photographed from close range and frequently emphasized the disorder and debris of sweatshop floors. These photographs appeared to picture especially the crowded conditions, dangerous clutter, and men and women laboring side by side.

The photographs also present a revealing contrast to images and descrip-

_____ *Figure 4* _____
"Shop on East Fourth Street" (from *A General Survey of the Sanitary Conditions of the Shops in the Cloak Industry* [New York: Joint Board of Sanitary Control, 1911], 9; image from the collection of the Tamiment-Wagner Labor Archives, New York University). Mention of the tenement garment shop's location in the photograph's original caption seems sufficient to explain the danger, mess, and illegitimacy of the shops.

tions of sweatshops of a previous generation of inspectors and immigrant workers. In these older descriptions, the worker was the focus, as inspectors gazed at the workers' degraded racial condition and workers recognized the symptoms of bodily decline and disease. In the JBSC's photographs, the focus is more on shop conditions than on workers' bodies. Images of workers are too small to allow a real inspection of their bodies. Only gender is visible, as workers are pictured in their workplace surroundings.

A 1911 photograph of an older Lower East Side shop is representative. The photograph caption simply lists the shop's location as if to label it a remnant of an earlier era of sweated work on the Lower East Side. The shop is immediately identifiable as a converted tenement flat. The photograph aims toward the windows at the far end of the tenement shop, highlighting the poor ventilation. The photograph reveals which sanitary violation it appears to condemn. It focuses on a floor littered with trash and scraps of cloth. The suggestion of health danger from bacteria harbored in the refuse looms large. Not only is the shop arranged irrationally within cramped quarters, but also workers labor uncomfortably. They either stand or sit on benches without backs.[53]

The JBSC paired this photograph with a photograph of a "Modern Shop with Many Windows" several pages later. The caption itself seems to project a sense of progress. Through its focus on the shop's rational organization and size, the photograph stresses its modernity, and, thus, its perceived benefits. The photograph was taken from far above workers' heads at an angle that accentuates the tremendous length of the shop by aiming toward the large, bright windows. The workshop is arranged in long rows of tables. The shop boasts electric power for efficiency (although the JBSC recommended that the lights be shaded) and chairs, not benches, for safety and comfort. In addition, underscoring the idea of protecting the site of men's work, this "modern shop" depicts only male workers, despite the fact that some women worked in the shop.[54] Rationality, sanitation, and gendered order, true to the JBSC's mission, are intertwined. At the same time, questions of race are relegated to the background, as it is impossible to look at the workers' bodies closely enough to

_____ Figure 5 _____

"Modern Shop with Many Windows" (from *A General Survey of the Sanitary Conditions of the Shops in the Cloak Industry* [New York: Joint Board of Sanitary Control, 1911], 25; image from the collection of the Tamiment-Wagner Labor Archives, New York University). The JBSC praised this new loft factory for its modernity. The composition of the photograph captures the sense of spaciousness, rationality, modernity, progress, and ultimately sanitary safety.

discern the tell-tale signs of physical or racial degeneration. Instead, the two photographs focus on the conditions of work and, in that context, reveal the gendered disorder of the tenement shop and the order of the modern factory.

The gendered nature of the JBSC's presentation of the vision of a sanitary shop is even more apparent in a comparative presentation of photographs in the same report. For the JBSC and the ILGWU, modernity could be measured by the safety, efficiency, and sanitation of the site of men's work. The JBSC defined sanitary progress as the eradication of tenement work and women's homework. The top photograph's caption cites only the shop's location on the Lower East Side. The JBSC seems to insist that, in itself, the spatial location of the shop in a converted tenement on the Lower East Side explains the poor, cramped conditions and implied gendered disorder. Male and female workers stand together in a crowded, poorly organized shop. There are no windows or ventilation. The photograph below lauds the shop as a "Modern Shop." The gendered confusion has disappeared. Again, in picturing a "modern" workplace, the JBSC presents an entirely male workforce. Work appears to be efficiently organized at safe, comfortable tables all perpendicular to large windows. Once more, the photograph is taken from above workers' heads to underscore the shop's spaciousness, and workers are pictured only in the context of the shop. They are not the principal focus of the photographs.[55]

Languages of race receded when inspectors presumed the ability of Jewish workers, through their union, to confront issues of health and filth. Meanwhile, gender was critical to conversations about progress toward a model garment factory. What becomes apparent in this reading of photographs is the extent to which the JBSC advanced the image of the masculinized "union" sanitary shop as an ideal workplace, in which male workers and bosses achieved a common goal of sanitary protection. It was not a shop where workers controlled the means of production. Thus, the ILGWU and the JBSC together blamed sweated work and the sweatshop, not the nature of garment work itself, for deforming workers' bodies and assaulting the male living wage.

For George Price, the modern shop offered benefits to employers and workers. It promised efficiency in exchange for a sexual division of labor and improved conditions. In the specific context of the garment industry, the modern model shop enjoyed limited competition because smaller shops could not meet minimum sanitary standards. In the model shop, the boss remained while unions and factory inspectors sheltered workers.[56] This definition of the model shop was echoed by workers like Yitzchak Yankel Doroshkin, who remembered one dress shop on 265 West 36th Street, far removed from the Lower East Side, as a "perfect model of a union shop." Gone was the vampire, the bloodsucking boss of an earlier generation. Instead, Doroshkin praised the

——————— *Figure 6*———————

6. "Shop on Greene Street" and "Machine Room of a Large Modern Shop" (from *A General Survey of the Sanitary Conditions of the Shops in the Cloak Industry* [New York: Joint Board of Sanitary Control, 1911], 28; image from the collection of the Tamiment-Wagner Labor Archives, New York University). The JBSC used such comparisons of tenement and modern shops to depict progress toward a model shop. Filth is compared to order, confusion to rationality, and labor in homes to work in modern shops. Note also the sense of gendered disorder as men and women labor together in the Greene Street photograph and the all-male order in the photograph of the modern shop. Ethnicity and race are also obscured; only signs of sexual differences are visible.

"easy-going tolerant" boss and the cordial relations between the boss and the union shop chairman that fostered sanitary control.[57] Significantly, Doroshkin described this shop housed in an industrial loft and run by a boss who tolerated a union, rather than the cooperative shop where he had worked before, as a model shop.[58] For Doroshkin, the bodily protection offered by the union through the JBSC, not an alteration of the system of production, was the foundation for an ideal workplace. Such a representation of the model shop, grounded in the politics of factory inspection, public health reform, and labor-management cooperation, focused on the safeguarding of Jewish immigrants' bodies and, especially, male breadwinners' bodies. The model shop maintained gendered ideals of work by preventing the need for women's homework. It helped men recover their health and earn a living, family wage. The model shop could even reform and cure workers.[59]

In the JBSC's language of organizing and reform, the model shop appeared not only as a concrete, achievable goal, but also as an emblem of the ILGWU's potential to relocate the workplace, protect workers' health, and preserve the ideal of the male breadwinner. The JBSC and male workers in their vision of the ideal workplace seemed to value the protection of the male breadwinner and sanitary reform over a revision of the wage relationship. The monthly bulletin of the JBSC even included advertisements for safety and sanitary products that promised to help employers as much as employees. One ad for a ventilating system urged: "Speed Them Up With Fresh Air." The bulletin also featured a column, aptly named "Model Shops," that listed concrete examples of shops that were "aiming at 'super-model' shops." One column, for example, listed luncheon facilities (with "'unsurpassed' coffee") at one shop and white aprons given to all workers at another shop.[60]

Even after 1913, when the JBSC began inspecting shops where women worked in large numbers, the JBSC remained dedicated to protecting male workers' ability to earn a family wage—if only to prevent wives from returning to wage labor or to homework. The JBSC described the workshop as a space where men worked throughout their lives: "Here he spends two-thirds of his waking hours from childhood to old age." Thus, the JBSC claimed that it protected the rights and abilities of male workers to earn living, family wages by ensuring their health and safety. "Living wages, hours of labor that do not cause fatigue and safe and sanitary shops," the JBSC declared in 1915, "are the three cardinal rights of the worker."[61]

After several years of factory inspections, the JBSC and the ILGWU began advocating experimental workshops that doubled as hospitals and sanitariums. The JBSC first suggested a curing workshop in 1914 based on the idea that work, if organized appropriately, could cure rather than debilitate the male breadwinning worker. It could safeguard his ability to earn a family wage: "There is urgent necessity for the organization and establishment of an ideal *open air workshop* where [consumptive] workers could be sent and where their work could be done under medical supervision . . . and at the same time not endanger their health by their work or confinement within the workshop."[62]

The JBSC's call for an open air workshop was part of a larger effort among public health advocates and Jewish social reformers to combine the methods of the sanitarium with well-organized labor as a way of combating working-class tuberculosis. In 1922, W. I. Hamilton, the industrial research secretary of the National Tuberculosis Association, echoed the opinion of many doctors in urging a rationalized, scientific organization of the workplace that emphasized the role of doctors and health experts: "Too many tuberculous people are being advised to abandon their jobs. . . . The employee is fortunate who can work in a plant under the supervision of an industrial physician."[63] Workers infected with tuberculosis and convalescing in the Denver sanitarium of the Jewish Consumptive Relief Society (JCRS) and their doctors also encouraged labor as a cure. Like the JBSC, the JCRS was supported by an alliance of middle-class reformers, German Jews, and Eastern European Jewish immigrant workers. Also, like the JBSC, the JCRS sought to protect the ability of male workers to earn a family wage. In *Hatikvah*, a magazine published by patients and their doctors at the sanitarium, a sarcastic letter ridiculed a male patient who denied his role as breadwinner and longed to linger happily in the sanitarium: "WORK AND I HAVE NEVER AGREED, AS I HAVE ALWAYS HATED IT. . . . THE MERE MENTION OF THAT ODIOUS WORD 'WORK' IS ENOUGH TO MAKE ME THOROUGHLY SICK."[64]

The JCRS, like the JBSC, sought to construct a curing workplace. In 1923, the JCRS started an Industrial Rehabilitation Department and a bookbinding factory. In 1927, the shop, proudly proclaimed by the JCRS as a "new model shop," expanded and began providing jobs for ex-patients as well.[65] Like the "modern shops" lauded by the JBSC, the JCRS's shop boasted rational, scientific organization in a large, airy room ventilated by large windows.[66] The open-air cure, it seemed, had arrived in the workplace.

In New York, the United Hebrew Charities helped build the most ambitious experimental shop. Through its chief physician, Maurice Fishberg, the United Hebrew Charities had long been concerned with the effects of garment labor on Eastern European Jewish workers' bodies and families. In 1915, the Charities founded the Altro Works, a garment factory that doubled as a tuberculosis sanitarium. As the open air cure was imported to the garment factory, the Altro Works realized the JBSC's dream of a curing workplace for male breadwinners. The Altro Works started with 24 workers—all male—and at its peak employed 135 tubercular Jewish workers, most of whom previously had been garment workers. The Altro Works produced garments for sale to hospitals and, during World War I, even won a Navy contract.[67]

The Altro Works sought to create a curing workplace that contrasted with debilitating sweatshops not only in its work conditions, but also in the composition of its workforce. Its managers described tuberculosis as a "family problem" because a male breadwinner's illness could undermine his family's well-being.[68] They worried about the effect on the "pride and self-respect" of male workers if "during a husband's absence the wife and children have had to assume added responsibilities which they are loath to relinquish." As part of their program of care for breadwinner patient/workers, they offered monetary aid to families so as to preserve and protect the sexual division of labor.[69] In fact, when the Altro Works boasted of success, they cited cases like that of Morris Seltzer, an operator who returned to "his old trade, earning enough to support his family and to keep himself in good physical condition."[70]

Reflective of the ILGWU's retreat from languages of class in its strategies of workplace reform, the Altro Works retained the position of boss, although as its director, Edward Hochhauser, claimed, the doctor had become the boss. Housed in a loft building and later in its own two-story factory, the Altro Works had a carefully arranged shop floor designed to realize the standards suggested by the JBSC. Its slogan captured the connection between well-organized work and a sanitary factory where "garments are well made . . . and patients made well."[71] In its publicity, the Altro Works celebrated its spacious workrooms, large windows, sanitary precautions, and concern for male workers. One photograph in its twenty-third anniversary report seemed to link hygienic shop floor conditions and gendered order. The photograph is aimed not at workers, but between worktables toward towering, shining windows. The orderly arrangement of the workroom is underscored by its spaciousness. The aisle between worktables is expansive and the loft ceiling dwarfs the sitting workers. Also, like the JBSC's photographs, all the workers shown are men. In this ideal workplace, the photograph appears to suggest, the sick male worker could keep his place as the family wage earner. The photograph links gendered order, hard work, rationality, and curing.[72]

The Altro Works stands as the ultimate example of the model shop and, in this context, completed the rhetorical axis between feminized homework and sweatshops, on the one hand, and the masculinized experimental curing shop on the other. This axis coalesced especially after 1910 as primarily male Jewish workers and their unions, in close correspondence and collaboration with reformers, inspectors, and health experts, constructed an image of a model shop based on the idea that a workplace distant from the home represented the only appropriate site of labor. Their political conception of an ideal shop

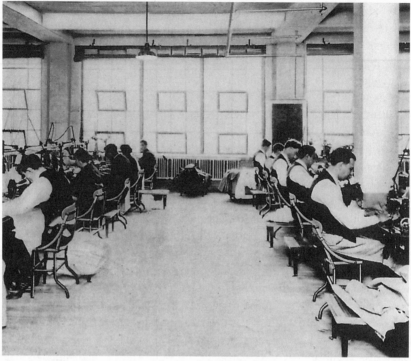

_____ *Figure 7* _____

"Sewing Room" (from *Report of the Committee for the Care of the Jewish Tuberculous, 1913–1936* [New York, 1937], 38; image from the collection of the Tamiment-Wagner Labor Archives, New York University). This picture of the Altro Works's main sewing room aims toward wide-open windows, thereby stressing the sanitary modernity of the workroom. The orderliness of the shop is reflected in the gendered order of the all-male workforce. As a model shop, the Altro Works sought to care for sick male bread-winners.

floor emerged from the process of hardening boundaries between home and work. As the Jewish home became ideally a site of consumption, Jewish workers came to celebrate the shift in industry uptown. The home was to be distinct from the workplace, an oasis from garment work. Thus, the U.S. Bureau of Labor noted approvingly that "no matter how great the poverty, the Hebrew men seldom allow the women of their family to do the [clothing] work at home."[73] The more distinct these boundaries, the faster workers could attain what the JBSC called a "sanitary millennium," a time when garment labor did not render workers diseased and deformed, but where the male family wage was protected, workers were made well, and married women were kept out of wage garment labor.[74]

The Sweatshop in Workers' Self-History

Definitions of the sweatshop and representations of Jewish immigrant sweatshop workers shifted dramatically with the creation of the JBSC. Where a previous generation of factory inspectors described Jewish immigrants and their sweatshops as a threat to civilization, the JBSC saluted cloakmakers as the "pace-makers" of "civilization."[75] Still, echoes of older definitions of the sweatshop as a reflection of workers' racial position persisted, paradoxically, in Jewish immigrants' self-representation as a people who had emerged from the sweatshop. The idea of progress suggested by the idea of a "sanitary millennium" was the foundation for histories of the garment labor movement presented by Jewish workers and unionists. It was central to what they claimed as their advancement toward Americanization and respectability. In the years after 1910, when Jewish garment workers and trade unionists synthesized a history of the needle trades, they described an emergence from the sweatshop. The unionist and former waistmaker Pauline Newman, for example, described Jewish immigrant workers after 1910 "as a group of people who had just emerged from the sweatshop with all its implications."[76]

The structure of ILGWU that emerged out of the cloakmakers' strike concentrated power in the hands of a few male leaders, permitting close and, at least until the late 1920s, stable relationships with reformers and inspectors. These ties helped encourage union leaders to advance a language of rationality and science. Still, when talking about their history, Eastern European Jewish immigrant garment workers and union leaders in their organizing rhetoric remembered and recycled an earlier language of Jewish immigrants as the class victims of the sweatshop. Thus, Meyer London, the popular Jewish socialist with close ties to the labor movement, proclaimed to the 1914 ILGWU convention that the sweatshop was a shared Jewish workers' heritage: "And down under our very noses people slaved in the sweat-shops! The word 'sweat-shop' was inseparable from the word 'tailor.' Jewish industries were supposed to be sweat-shop industries."[77] Leaders, like London, cast unions as protectors of Jewish victims. As leaders of the Cloakmakers' Union of the ILGWU insisted: "The history of the Cloakmakers' Union is a history of fighting . . . for the elimination of the pest-holes used for 'factories.'"[78]

Workers described the 1910 strike as a victory against the sweatshop. The memoirs of cloakmaker Abraham Rosenberg, which trace the history of the trade and the Cloakmakers' Union from the beginnings of Eastern European Jewish migration to the 1910 strike, is essentially a history of the struggle against the sweatshop. Cloakmakers went on strike in 1910, Rosenberg insisted, because they "had been victimized far too long by the vicious 'sweating system.'"[79] The strike itself "was more than just a strike—it was a true uprising, a revolt of the cloakmakers against inhuman conditions which existed in the trade at that time. That historical moment, when the strike was called, marked the last hours of the chaos and slavery which characterized the cloak shops."[80] The Cloakmakers' Union also proudly described the 1910 strike as a victory against the sweatshop: "It took years, many years to slay this many-headed hydra in the cloak industry. The collective will of the workers, the united strength of the Union has, nevertheless, carried the day."[81]

However, like understandings of racial progress as reversible, Jewish workers continued to worry that the sanitary progress achieved by the JBSC could be reversed. Thus, the sweatshop remained a persistent discursive focus within the Eastern European Jewish labor movement. It was a looming danger for immigrant garment workers and a justification for the cross-class alliance that had created the JBSC. When leaders of the ILGWU, long after 1910, expressed concern about changes in the garment industry, they consistently worried about the return of the sweatshop. The Cloakmakers' Union's image of the sweatshop as a "many-headed hydra" is illustrative. After all, one of the heads of the hydra was immortal and could always grow back. The sweatshop, like the hydra, could always return. Even Rosenberg in all his optimism warned his fellow unionists that the sweatshop might return if they became lax in their vigilance: "The light of unity will shine on the path we tread as long as our members maintain their level of understanding and militancy and use their organization to protect their interests."[82] In fact, in 1921 the president of the ILGWU, Benjamin Schlesinger, publicly accused manufacturers of reintroducing the "sweat-shop in the garment trades" in their effort to move from weekly wages to piecework. Piecework, he argued, would result in "the return of chaos, that pell-mell rush, and that overworking of defenseless operatives which existed in the cloak industry."[83]

The ILGWU also described new kinds of shops with exploitative conditions as sweatshops. When the ILGWU called a strike in July 1922 to banish the "corporation shop" (a small shop, similar to the contractor shop, in which workers were expected to contribute to the shop's start-up capital), union leaders again raised the threat of the sweatshop. Each cloakmaker received a circular with the screaming headline: "The Sweat Shop and 'Corporation Shop' in the Cloak Industry Must Go!" Workers must remain vigilant, ILGWU leaders insisted, because of the persistence of the sweatshop: "So long as the "sweat-shop . . . exist[s], our workers are not secure with their bread and butter."[84]

At moments of increased agitation and labor-management conflict, the ILGWU accused bosses of reintroducing the sweatshop, in a rhetorical return to an earlier language of class. During a 1926 cloakmakers' general strike, when the ILGWU appealed to the American Federation of Labor (AFL) for support, the union once again referred to efforts of employers to resurrect the sweatshop. As Morris Sigman, the president of the ILGWU, wrote to William Green, the AFL president: "[The Cloakmakers] are fighting against the threatened revival of the notorious sweat shop system which in the past has disgraced the industry and kept the workers in a condition of indescribable misery and oppression."[85]

Finally, and perhaps most alarming to union leaders, the ILGWU came to worry that the sweatshop could even enter loft buildings, if the union's power waned. When the 1926 strike ended in the union's defeat, ILGWU leaders worried that the sweatshop had crept inside "modern shop" buildings. Loft buildings, they argued, could appear like "modern shops," but without the protections of sanitary control and strong unions, conditions might deteriorate, occupational disease might spread, and married women might have to return to wage labor. Thus, in the aftermath of the strike, at the same time that the ILGWU lamented the spread of shops in the rear rooms of tenements, they also worried about the proliferation of sweatshops in loft buildings: "The sweatshop, of course, need not be understood [as] the . . . kitchen production of twenty-five years ago. The present-day sweat shop has sprouted out in . . . big loft buildings which have the outward appearance of decent shops but in which conditions of labor are such that the majority of workers employed in them find it impossible to make even a meager living."[86] The sweatshop, then, remained a central part of the organizing language of the Eastern European Jewish immigrant labor movement. When Sigman referred to the "condition of indescribable misery and oppression," and when Schlesinger warned of a "return of chaos," they were relying on explicit and widely understood meanings of the sweatshop as a dangerous workshop whose conditions posed a threat to workers' bodies and to an established and cherished sexual division of labor.

The way male cloakmakers, their union leaders, and their middle-class allies represented the sanitary shop as a site of male breadwinning implicitly raised questions about women's potential roles on the shop floor and in the labor movement. In the experimental model shop women were physically absent, and in pictures of the sanitary shop women were represented as absent. The model shop became associated with men's labor, an association cemented by its contrast with the feminized sweatshop. Did women have a legitimate place on the shop floor and, if so, what roles could they claim in the labor movement? How did women force their way into the anti-sweatshop coalition and, when they did, why did the JBSC's priorities remain so constant?

The firmly entrenched meanings of the sweatshop meant that even as the location of work and architecture of the shop floor was changing, women still faced questions about their legitimacy as workers. Women's wage labor still hinted at sweated work. Thus, as women demanded roles in the labor movement, they found themselves constrained by ideals of men as lifelong workers and breadwinners and of women as temporary workers whose wage-earning lives would end with marriage. While the Eastern European Jewish immigrant labor movement largely succeeded in ameliorating the harsh conditions of garment sweatshops, the discursive links between the sweatshop, homework, and women's labor continued to shape workers' organizing. Women's efforts to claim a place on the shop floor and in the labor movement in the face of this restrictive language are the focus of the next section.

Part II

Women and Gender in the Sweatshop and in the Anti-Sweatshop Campaign

The anti-sweatshop coalition that took shape after the 1910 strike originally united male Jewish cloakmakers with public health advocates and factory inspectors. They constructed a program of sanitary reform and control that helped remake the landscape of the New York garment industry. In those trades where Jews worked in large numbers, factories, located in loft buildings, generally replaced small shops and homework. Behind this vision of a "sanitary millennium" was a desire to protect the health and position of the family breadwinner.

In a series of strikes in 1909 and 1913, female Jewish workers pushed their way into the cross-class coalition. By 1913, the same inspection and sanitary control committees also oversaw those trades like waist and dress-making, where women composed the majority of workers. Winning a place in anti-sweatshop campaigns was a struggle for women. In fact, these strikes were aimed as much at male workers and unionists as at employers. Female workers were confronting understandings that lay behind concern for the male breadwinner, specifically that men were normative workers and that women were temporary employees who would leave work with marriage.

The gendering of the title of worker assigned men the role of family wage earner and women the role of transients and future mothers. The focus on protecting the male breadwinner that dominated campaigns against the sweatshop inherently called into question women's legitimacy as workers and as trade unionists. Eastern European Jewish immigrant men sought to create and maintain ideals about male breadwinning in a garment industry in which women did, in fact, compose a significant minority of the overall workforce, and in some trades, an overwhelming majority. Complicating even further the gendered confusion of the garment industry, technological and fashion changes disrupted understandings of skill. Men claimed the ability to define certain jobs as skilled and better paid, maintained a monopoly on those trades, and enforced ideals about male breadwinning by calling into question women's legitimacy as workers. Through sexual taunting, harassment, and physical abuse, male workers highlighted connections between women's future roles as mothers and wives and their present status as temporary wage earners.

Thus, female strikers in 1909 and 1913 were fighting for a place in the union and its anti-sweatshop coalition. Like male cloakmakers, they forged cross-class alliances. Female workers turned to the Women's Trade Union League (WTUL), an organization led mostly by middle- and upper-class women that sought to encourage women's participation in unions. To be sure, a cultural gulf separated working-class women and their WTUL allies. WTUL activists, who were the primary leaders of the strikes, cast female Jewish workers as "shop girls" and "girl strikers," while female strikers described themselves as "women workers." Yet together, WTUL leaders and female strikers negotiated a shared language that represented working women both as ladies, deserving of respect, and as physical victims of the sweatshop. This language fit women into an ongoing discourse about health and the sweatshop, suggesting women's legitimacy as workers. Yet it also recast harassment, not as an expression of masculinity, but as an assault on working-class ladyhood carried out only by foremen and bosses, not by male workers. So, too, did this language implicitly recognize sexual difference by affirming that women, despite their place in the union, would still leave work with marriage.

In claiming status not as workers, but as women workers and as ladies, women effectively ceded to men normative status as workers and left unchallenged the singular importance of marriage. Thus, when women sought roles within the Jewish labor movement, they worked within the confines of ingrained understandings of sexual difference. Women were most successful in claiming a voice in labor organizing in campaigns for health care. Women advanced ideas that they needed forms of treatment different from those of men in ways that reinforced understandings of difference. Relying on the medical inspections of public health officials, male and female Jewish labor leaders came to argue that women and men faced different occupational diseases that belied their contrasting workplace roles. For men, doctors and unionists worried about tuberculosis, a disease that might threaten men's roles as breadwinners, whereas for women, they were concerned about reproductive disorders. The health treatments advanced by the Jewish labor movement as a way of reversing the effects of the sweatshop protected men as breadwinners and women as future mothers.

Because of the endurance of conceptions of sexual difference, women had little success in claiming access to positions of union leadership. In keeping with ideas of women as temporary workers, male union leaders represented female workers as novice unionists. Female workers resented their subordinate place within the union, but their protest was constrained by their own construction of the women worker. They advanced plans for new leadership positions that could be held by women and rarely sought access to positions held by men. When they criticized the structure of the International Ladies' Garment Workers' Union (ILGWU), they employed contemporary languages of empowerment of class, not of gender, in particular, Communism. The words and language of Communism proved effective in creating a rank-and-file dissident movement, but male Communists led the movement, not women.

The rise of opposition within the ILGWU set in motion a process that led to the demise of the anti-sweatshop coalition. Under the cover of factionalism, employers were increasingly thwarting sanitary regulations. The Communists, who by 1926 had replaced the old ILGWU leadership, reasserted languages of class in the fight against sweatshops. They proposed a general strike, not the strengthening of inspection. A failed general strike in 1926 not only led to the fall of the Communist leadership, but also bankrupted the structures charged with the enforcement of sanitary regulations. The strike also led to violent factionalism between the ILGWU, with its old leaders back at the helm, and a breakaway Communist union, the Needle Trades Workers' Industrial Union (NTWIU). This factionalism, seen by its partisans as an expression of manly unionism, further restricted women's participation in the movement and sundered ties with inspectors. At the height of anti-Communist hysteria and with the overall decline of Progressivism, inspectors were unwilling to make alliances with Communist unionists.

Thus, after 1926 as the institutions of the anti-sweatshop coalition were withering away, male NTWIU and ILGWU leaders were accusing each other of bringing back the sweatshop. But neither side challenged the definition of the sweatshop or advanced alternative strategies of anti-sweatshop organizing that might have expanded women's potential roles on the shop floor and in the union. At the same time, women were again complaining about the weighty masculinity of the union.

Five

Gaunt Men, Gaunt Wives

Femininity, Masculinity, and the
Worker Question, 1880–1909

I n 1910, at the same moment that the Joint Board of Sanitary Control (JBSC) was being organized, the poet and immigrant worker Morris
Rosenfeld sought to describe the garment workplace in his poem "The Sweatshop." It was, he wrote, a room in a tenement building on the "corner of pain
and anguish." Even in choosing as a title a word first used by inspectors,
Rosenfeld takes on the viewpoints of both workers and inspectors. The poem
leads the visitor/reader into the tenement, past a tavern and upstairs to a small
"Bible room" where immigrants lament their "exile." Finally, the visitor/reader
climbs to the third floor to the sweatshop. The visitor is cast, first, as the exploring inspector examining the filth, dirt, and disease: "rarely washed, rarely
swept—rottenness and mud are mixed here." Then, the visitor takes on the
role of the workers and feels the pain of their labor. They have "torn spirits
and broken bodies." The poem ends by indicting the "master" of the shop, who
struts around like a "Czar," for the conditions and the broken bodies of workers.

In placing the reader in the role of worker and inspector, Rosenfeld reveals
two different claims about the dangers of the sweatshop. A closer read, though,
suggests another lurking danger: the fear of a promiscuous workplace where
men and women work together. The workforce, Rosenfeld makes sure to point
out, is composed of "gaunt men, gaunt women." Furthermore, Rosenfeld reveals the marital status of the women. He uses the Yiddish word *"vaiber"*
(wives) rather than the word *maidlekh* (girls). For inspectors and workers, this
workplace included all that was dangerous about the sweatshop. For inspectors, men and women were working in close and dirty quarters. For workers,

the sexual division of labor had collapsed; these were wives at work. For Rosenfeld, female workers were not simply women. In the context of fears about the breakdown of a sexual division of labor in immigrant families, they were defined by their marital status.[1]

As an anti-sweatshop campaign coalition was uniting around a comparison between the sweatshop, where men and women worked together, and the modern factory with its male breadwinning workforce, the normative worker was cast as a male Jewish immigrant. Men's legitimacy on the shop floor was beyond question. Women's workplace legitimacy, in contrast, was contested. Their labor was linked inexorably to the dangers of the sweatshop. Yet the image of the model shop—the modern factory and the opposite of the sweatshop— was based on a fundamental contradiction. It pictured a solidly male workforce, but, as historians of Jewish women and labor note, women composed an important part of the garment workforce and their wages were critical to their families' welfare.

Historians also write that women tended to work for fewer years than their male counterparts. Most Jewish women left the garment shops soon after marriage.[2] Thus, male workers described women as laboring only temporarily as they searched for husbands.[3] Male and female workers and reformers' efforts to find a common definition of the sweatshop rested on concerns about the unnaturalness and immorality of women's labor and on ideals of family breadwinning. Between 1880 and 1910, emerging discourses that associated the dangers of the sweatshop with women's labors called into question women's shop floor status and limited their access to trade union membership.

Women's marital status, as Rosenfeld's poem suggests, was forcibly removed from the private realm and politicized. Sex, sexuality, and sexual relations, men argued, defined women's position in the workshop. Sexuality, consequently, was a major part of workplace life for men and women, as scholars of Jewish women have noted. They have identified high levels of sexual harassment and sexual banter, but have rarely explored how this sexualized atmosphere served to restrict who could claim the mantle of a real worker.[4] As the legal scholar Katherine Franke has argued, sexual harassment is more than a torment for women. It is "a tool or instrument of gender regulation." Sexual harassment in the sweatshop was crucial in the definition and policing of what Franke calls "hetero-patriarchal gender norms in the workplace."[5] The sexuality of the garment sweatshop helped delineate the boundaries of sexual difference through the gendering of the title "worker." This confirmed the workplace as a manly space even before the JBSC worked to realize a model shop with its male workforce. Men's sexual conversations, jokes, and predation marginalized women at a time when immigrant workers, inspectors, and reformers were first defining the sweatshop.[6] At the same time, the sexuality of the workplace realized the worst fears of reformers about the sweatshop as a promiscuous workplace.

The contradiction between the model shop ideal of a breadwinning workplace and the reality of women's labor opened up a space for women's organizing. At the same moment that the structure of the anti-sweatshop coalition was taking shape, women were challenging the sexuality of the workplace and the notions of women's work that it protected.[7] While the 1910 strike helped male cloakmakers claim victory over the sweatshop, women workers used strikes in 1909 and 1913 to challenge conceptions of who could be a real, legitimate worker. Women, especially active and ambitious female trade unionists, came to challenge depictions of women workers as sexualized transients in the workplace. They claimed sexual respectability in describing themselves as "women workers" and as "ladies." In creating images of sexually respectable, class-conscious workers and strikers, women claimed a place in organizing and in the anti-sweatshop coalition. At the same time, women carefully noted the scars of work on their bodies. Occupational disease, as it offered male workers a battle cry for organizing, could give women the legitimacy they craved. Like male workers, they suffered in the workplace.

Yet in representing the "woman worker" as a "lady" and as a sweatshop victim, female Jewish trade unionists also expressly accepted certain articulations of sexual difference. Men and women, they acknowledged, still experienced garment work differently. While Jewish women workers may have defended their sexual respectability using contemporary notions of ladyhood, they still generally recognized the singular importance of marriage in defining how long women could remain in garment shops and in garment workers' unions.[8]

Like male cloakmakers, female Jewish workers forged cross-class alliances in their organizing. Most prominently, female Jewish garment workers received the support of the Women's Trade Union League (WTUL), an organization funded and run by wealthy women who supported the union organizing of female workers. As the historian Nancy Schrom Dye has written, the unionization of female garment workers was a particularly important project for WTUL leaders, like its president, Mary Dreier.[9] Through the strikes of 1913, the WTUL played a crucial role in Jewish women's union organizing. Not only did the WTUL provide institutional and monetary support for their organizing, but also the WTUL's leaders garnered public support for their cause by joining Jewish rank and file on picket lines.

Yet their help came at a cost. In the strikes of 1909 and 1913, WTUL leaders served as the mouthpiece for Eastern European Jewish women's organizing, carefully shaping public representations of what they called "girl strikers" and "women workers." Indeed, as historian Nan Enstad points out, WTUL officials prepared most of the public statements in the press by female Eastern European Jewish strikers in 1909 and 1913. WTUL leaders wrote articles describing the lives of working Jewish immigrants, planned meetings between workers and wealthy potential supporters, and pleaded their case in front of politicians, judges, and male trade union officials. The voices of Eastern European Jewish immigrant women appear in these sources, however distorted and faint, as the subjects and interviews of stories, articles, and presentations. Nonetheless, their presence as mediated voices and as subjects still helped determine the focus of publicity and public representation. It was through this cross-class alliance that female Jewish strikers challenged representations of female workers that denied their legitimacy on the shop floor. They did so by publicly accepting notions of gender difference.[10]

The Social Construction of Skill and Workplace Masculinity

In the 1870s and early 1880s, when Eastern European Jewish immigrants began arriving in New York, men dominated only a few garment crafts. Within the largely Irish and German workforce of the garment industry at the time, male workers controlled only two of the principal trades. Both these trades, custom tailoring and skilled cutting, were declining segments of the industry. Women composed the bulk of the garment workforce, especially in the expanding readymade delicate garment trades, like waistmaking, dressmaking, kimonomaking, undergarmentmaking, and women's cloak and suitmaking. They even controlled a number of skilled occupations.[11]

The arrival of Jewish immigrants helped transform the gendered identification of certain garment trades and skills. As historian Susan Glenn has noted, changes in the sexual division of labor accompanied Jewish immigration.[12] According to the observer of the turn-of-the-century clothing trade Mabel Hurd Willet, the arrival of Jews was "to a large extent responsible for the restriction of women's work in New York City."[13] Eastern European Jewish male immigrants slowly seized control of certain readymade trades, like women's cloakmaking. Of 45,199 women's cloakmakers surveyed in 1911, 36,941 were men.[14]

The rising numbers of male workers, especially in important crafts like cloakmaking, helped foster a new sexual division of labor as well as new hierarchies of skill and pay. Even though women still represented at least a sizable minority in all the garment crafts, a strict sexual division of labor emerged by 1900. With new technologies and methods of production, male Jewish workers solidified a monopoly over highly paid trades that both male and female Jewish garment workers came to consider as skilled or semiskilled.[15] As the turn-of-the-century economist Jesse Pope noted: "With the later development of the industry, however, the employment of women cutters rapidly declined till at the close of the period now under consideration they had completely disappeared. . . . The less-skilled tailoring work, such as button-hole making, felling and basting came to be the principal function of female labor."[16] Among Jewish cloakmakers, one survey found a strict gendered divide as men controlled well-paying skilled trades. Women were relegated to poorly remunerated unskilled tasks: "There are very few women among the operators, none among the cutters, and hardly any among the pressers. Most of the women are employed in basting, finishing, and button-hole-making."[17] Even in trades still largely controlled by women, like dress and waistmaking, men also came to dominate the well-paying skilled tasks.[18]

How did Jewish men come to claim hegemony in an industry where the sexual division of labor had not been predetermined before their arrival and where skill had evolving meanings as the processes and technology of production changed?[19] Eastern European Jewish immigrant garment workers did not inherit definitions of skill and a sexual division of labor, nor did they possess or acquire upon their arrival time-honored craft traditions that could confirm manliness or gendered authority. At the same time, male garment workers could not rely on notions of muscular masculinity to claim dominance in the workplace.[20] Male workers' representation of the sick, enfeebled worker's body undercut ideas of a muscular masculinity.

Instead, male Jewish workers grounded masculinity in sexual relations on the garment shop floor. They claimed the workplace as a manly space and confirmed workplace masculinity, not by focusing on the strength of the male worker's body, but by representing female workers as transients. "Jewish men," Mabel Hurd Willet claimed, "are not inclined to regard the work of women as worthy of serious attention."[21] They highlighted female sexuality to prove and maintain women's impermanent status as workers. Often in collusion with bosses, male workers created a workplace atmosphere so rife with sexual innuendo and harassment that women found themselves marginalized on the shop floor and in the first efforts to organize unions.[22] Male workers were able to exploit sexuality and conceptions of gender difference to define skill and, thus, to claim choice jobs. Gender largely determined hierarchies of wages and skill, first in the sweatshop and then in the model factory.

Marriage and Women's Workplace Legitimacy

Male Jewish workers' identity as legitimate workers and not as recent immigrant usurpers of women's garment jobs depended on the social construction of female Jewish workers as illegitimate or, at least, as temporary workers.

In fact, Jewish women did not labor long past marriage. In 1911, the Senate Immigration Committee reported that only 8 percent of married immigrant Jewish women worked outside the home.[23] As a result, male garment workers tended to be significantly older than their female counterparts. A 1915 survey of predominantly Jewish, foreign-born shirtmakers found that nearly half the female workforce was under twenty-one years old, compared to under 20 percent for the male workforce. Not surprisingly, while 50 percent of the male workers were married, 83 percent of the female workers were single.[24] A 1914 survey of about 3,000 male and female garment workers from a number of trades found that the average age of male workers was 32.36 years, compared to 22.86 for women.[25]

Female Jewish workers recorded mixed emotions about leaving garment wage work after their wedding. For some, marriage represented an opportunity to escape the physical trials of garment work. As Clara Lemlich, the socialist union activist and prominent leader of the 1909 waistmaker strike, pointed out: "Almost all women . . . work under long hours and miserable conditions, they lost their hopes. Their only way to leave the factory is marriage."[26] One popular song heard in garment factories also confirmed some women's conception of marriage as an escape from garment labor: "And all I do is sew and sew and sew/ May God help me and my love come soon/ That I may leave this work and go."[27] This was exactly how one 1909 writer to the *Jewish Daily Forward* remembered her life as a waistmaker. She described marriage as the only escape from the "dreary shop." "Like all shopgirls," she wrote, "I hoped and waited for deliverance through a good match."[28] Yet sometimes, Jewish women wanted to stay in the shops, enjoying the money and the company of other women. Fannie Shapiro, for instance, left work reluctantly and only at the insistence of her husband: "I hated to leave. After I was making such nice money, I hated to leave. My husband pestered me."[29]

In fact, the economist Jesse Pope recognized among Jewish male immigrants a general prejudice "against the labor of women."[30] It became a measure of manly success for male workers like Ephraim Wagner to keep their wives at home. "As soon as I was able to earn six to seven dollars a week," he remembered, "I did not let my wife go into a shop, but stay at home."[31] One survivor of the 1911 Triangle Shirtwaist Factory fire recalled how her fiancé had associated their marriage with her leaving work. After their marriage, he told her, "you'll be a housewife and never go to work in the shop again."[32] Other male workers recorded embarrassment when misfortune forced their wives back to garment shops. Michael Gold remembered his father's feelings of humiliation when illness prevented him from working and his wife sought a job.[33] Such male workers sought desperately to prevent their wives from having to return to the shops. Mabel Hurd Willet noticed that male Jewish workers, far more than any other group of immigrant garment workers in New York, might pursue extraordinary measures so as to keep their wives at home: "The Jewish man is unwilling to have his wife go out to the shop or factory to work and will toil to an unlimited extent himself rather than permit this degradation."[34]

Women's presence in garment factories, in short, seems to have depended largely on their marital status, a nexus between work and sexual position that men could exploit to maintain social control on the shop floor. The way that men tended to see female workers as temporary because of marital status suggests an effort to adapt the ideal of "separate spheres" to the reality of women's paid labor. The focus on the reproductive in a site of industrial productivity divided the workplace into ideologically separate spheres of so-called legitimate and temporary workers, between shop girls and male breadwinners. If women were married and thus sexually active, men presumed, they had little right to a place at the workbench. Conversely, if women did labor in the shops, men assumed that they were chaste, looking to marry and quit their jobs.[35]

Thus, male workers often described female workers as mere transients. Men's representations of female workers as temporary can be discerned in the writing of Eastern European Jewish men describing women's experience in the workplace. A short story by Abraham Cahan, the editor of the popular Yiddish newspaper the *Jewish Daily Forward*, is a good example. "A Sweatshop Romance" takes place in a small "cockroach" shop, a sweatshop in the heart of the Jewish Lower East Side, whose standardized setting serves to universalize the story. Four employees crowd into the tiny shop: Heyman, the operator; Meyer, the presser; David, the baster; and the one woman, Beile, the finisher. Beile, not surprisingly, labors in the only unskilled job. The story revolves around whom Beile would marry; for Cahan, a single woman in a shop of men automatically becomes the target of romantic interest. Cahan begins the story by describing David thinking about the physical appearances of the other workers in the shop. He contemplates Heyman's "chunky nose." Beile is the object of David's sexual desire (despite her also imperfect nose): "And a strong impulse seized him to throw himself on those lips and to kiss them, which he did mentally, and which shot an electric current through his whole frame."[36]

But Beile is already openly courted by Heyman: "His attentions to her were an open secret. He did not go out of his way to conceal them." Heyman places a public claim on Beile by escorting her home after work, taking her to balls, and addressing her openly with the diminutive, endearing form of address, "Beilinke." However, their romance suffers as Heyman is profoundly stingy, often failing to take Beile out or to bring her gifts. Nonetheless, marriage seems imminent until Beile refuses to run an errand for the boss and is threatened with firing. Only David springs to her defense and they are both fired. David, however, is rewarded with an engagement with the female co-worker he has secretly desired. Cahan depicts Beile as a docile shop girl. Even her refusal to run the boss's errand comes at David's insistence. She patiently waits for marriage. If she did not marry Heyman, surely she would marry someone else in the shop.[37]

As a thinly veiled allegory, "A Sweatshop Romance" connects sexual prowess, the acceptance of appropriate gender workplace roles, and class consciousness. Heyman, the stingy worker whose courtship was lacking, also lacks the fortitude to defend a fellow worker and oppose the boss. David, on the other hand, is ultimately sexually fulfilled after he protects the female worker and opposes the boss. Beile, meanwhile, acquiesces to her role as an unskilled, lower-paid worker and as the object of desire. She passively acknowledges attentions from two workers and readily accepts the idea of marriage. The hint of her future lies in the character of Meyer's wife, who does not appear; after all, she no longer works in the shop. Her only mention in the story is an offhand reference to her bringing Meyer's dinner to him at his workbench.[38]

Cahan's story seems to suggest that women's transience, guaranteed by marriage, might transform the promiscuous sweatshop criticized by inspectors into an ordered workplace with a class-conscious workforce. For inspectors, the sweatshop featured unnatural sexual mingling, and for Jewish women, the sweatshop was a site for courtship, whether they sought it or not. One immigrant women remembered that as "a single girl" she went to work in a garment shop "as is usual." Naturally, she recalled, "boys began to court me."[39] For Cahan, a virtuous woman, like Beile, accepted male attentions and traded treats for promises of marriage. Conversely, a female worker who resisted marriage could be publicly derided as loose. One worker, Stella Papiroff, recalled the nasty rumors about her friend Elizaveta, who accepted gifts from a male worker but resisted offers of marriage.[40] Thus, one observer of the garment trades claimed that female Jewish workers considered themselves temporary workers whose primary identity lay outside the shop: "When the Jewish girl enters the shop she, as well as her parents, regards the work as a temporary makeshift, bridging over the period intervening before her marriage.... Their work is by no means their primary interest."[41]

Sexualizing the Workplace

Male workers protected their representations of women's work by persistently reminding women of their temporary presence on the shop floor through harassment and sexual predation. As the former waistmaker and unionist Pauline Newman remembered, in all "the cloak factories and all other shops in the city of New York . . . every one of the men will talk to the girls, take advantage of them."[42] Male workers and bosses both seemed to have participated in harassment. In fact, for female workers, the line between male bosses and fellow workers was often blurred as women, especially in the dress and waistmaking trades, often worked as helpers hired by male skilled workers. Jennie Matyas, for example, found her first job in a dress factory but was hired by "another worker" who set her wages.[43] A male worker who hired women helpers inside the Triangle Shirtwaist factory even started the 1909 shirtwaistmakers' strike. The male worker in a conflict with the Triangle's owner appealed to his female employees as a "fellow worker." They joined him and walked out.[44]

Male workers' and bosses' sexual jokes rendered the workplace a sexualized space. Male workers recalled that "genito-urinary jokes" were often aimed directly or indirectly at the few female workers.[45] Sam Liptzin recalled one incident in a shop where male workers and the boss collaborated on an elaborate sexual practical joke on a pious young female worker. The male workers called her Pesha the *Rebbetsin* (rabbi's wife), highlighting her desire to be married. The boss pinched and touched Pesha and "drove her to tears," forcing her to drop her thimble. The boss grabbed the thimble and put it on her finger while reciting the Hebrew invocation of marriage, *haray at mekudeshes lee b'taba'as zu k'das Moshe v'Yisroel* ("Behold, you are sanctified to me with this ring according to the laws of Moses and Israel"). His joke delighted the male workers, who immediately broke a light bulb, as in the traditional conclusion of the marriage ceremony, and shouted, "*Mazl tov.*" Pesha burst into tears, fearful that she was now married.[46]

When male workers like Liptzin recalled the sexualized atmosphere of the workplace, they consistently referred to the effects on women, seemingly in recognition of how sexual banter helped generate a hierarchy of social control. As Liptzin recalled: "The result was that many of the men became coarsened and their language inside the shop verged on the pornographic. For a woman . . . there was no greater torment than to work in the midst of this vulgarity." Benjamin Kapp also noticed that male workers aimed their sexual jokes at women, creating an oppressive sexualized atmosphere: "A few were addicted to salacious bantering and indecent ribaldry at every opportunity as at lunchtime or at the failure of electric power. . . . All this in the hearing capacity of the finisher girls."[47]

Sometimes sexual jokes descended into open physical contact or demands for sexual favors. Lazarus Marcovitz recalled that one worker in his shop, called by fellow workers "Loony" Berger, often walked over to women and tickled them. Berger even explained that his tickling helped keep him sane in the sweatshop: "If I would not act the way I do I certainly would become loony."[48] Similarly, Rose Cohen's boss requested that she visit him privately at home to receive her wages, and when she arrived he demanded she sit on his lap.[49] Another worker, who identified herself only as Rosie, remembered that her boss demanded that she eat dinner and spend the night with him at a "swell hotel."[50] Sadie Frowne also received this kind of unwanted attention from her fellow male workers: "When they passed me they would touch my hair and talk about my eyes and my red cheeks, and make jokes."[51]

Male and female workers recognized that direct resistance to the sexualization of the workplace was difficult, if not impossible. Sam Liptzin recalled how difficult it was for women to "muster up the courage to put an ordinary worker in his place" and nearly impossible to challenge a boss.[52] A well-known strike of whitegoodsmakers was one of female workers' few collective efforts to resist directly the physical attentions of male workers and bosses. The strike, dubbed the "orphan strike," was called to protest the "laying on of the hands" of the subcontractor. The subcontractor explained his pinching of "girls" as a "fatherly attitude." Female workers went on strike demanding to be treated, instead, as "orphans."[53] Yet the fame of the orphan strike seems to highlight its uniqueness. More typical were the experiences of Rosie and an anonymous writer to the *Jewish Daily Forward*. Rosie and her fellow female workers formed what they called "The Young Ladies' Educational Society" to resist their boss's "freshness." In the end, however, she was forced to confront her boss's sexual demands on her own. Similarly, the anonymous writer to the *Jewish Daily Forward*, who signed her letter as "A Shopgirl," complained that fellow female workers were afraid "to be witnesses" against the "vulgar advances" of a male worker. She was left to face his advances alone.[54]

More often than not, such women felt badgered and bothered, marginalized into silence at their workbench. Rose Cohen, for example, described herself as huddled at her sewing table and remembered that the first phrase she learned in English was "Keep your hands off, please."[55] When she refused to sit on her boss's lap, she was immediately fired; on another occasion, the only possible response to the sexual taunting of a male worker was to cry out and flee the shop. Her sister, however, preferred to hang her head and pretend "not to hear" rather than lose her position.[56] "A Shopgirl" could not ignore the advances of the male worker. She wrote that she ran home "as if the Devil were after me." She was left without a job.[57] Quitting a job represented one of the few ways for women to escape the sexualized atmosphere of work—an act that ceded to male workers effective control of quotidian shop floor life. Pesha, for example, never returned to the shop, where she was so taunted by the workers and the boss.[58] Rosie also quit the shop where her boss had demanded sexual favors and found work at a new shop. Yet her old employer contacted her new boss, who then discharged her, leaving her without work.[59] Sadie Frowne's harassment was only relieved when a male worker, identified as Henry, threatened to fight her tormentors. However, she was not entirely freed from sexualized attention. Henry soon began courting her; walking her home from the shop, he "makes love" to her. Even Henry viewed Frowne as a sexually available single woman.[60]

The uncomfortable atmosphere of the shops, dependent as it was on a sexualized construction of femininity, minimized the ability of women either to participate in the everyday life of the shops or to challenge hierarchies of skill and pay.[61] Women's relationships with male workers determined their workplace positions as much as their employment relationships with bosses, an idea that Sam Liptzin seemed to recognize in his recollections of the workplace: "Life in the sweat-shop was miserable enough for the men, but for the women it was a thousand times worse."[62] Women often recorded feelings of being separated from other workers and from the life of the shop. Cohen sensed the quiet embarrassment of female workers when she arrived at her first job: "The men were so close to me on each side I felt the heat of their bodies and could not prevent myself from shrinking away. . . . One made a joke, the other laughed and the girls bent their heads low over their work."[63]

Jokes and harassment did more than make life miserable for women. Rather, the sexualized hierarchy of the shop floor was reproduced in hierarchies of skill and pay.[64] Female workers earned significantly less than their male counterparts in the same trades. In a 1902 survey, men's wages in the dressmaking trade ranged from $10.24 to $15.35 compared to $5.86 to $8.46 for women. Similarly, among cloakmakers, men's wages averaged $15.35 compared to $8.46 for women. For the skilled tasks, men commanded wages of over $24 per week.[65] Both male workers' protection of gendered boundaries of skill and the machinations of bosses helped maintain the lower wages of women. Skill, as recent feminist historians have pointed out, is not an inherent label, but is largely determined by gendered claims. This was especially the case in garment work, where pressing or cutting, considered skilled trades by female and male workers, did not demand significantly more training than finishing or stitching, women's trades that both viewed as unskilled.[66] Rather, the construction of skill represented the cornerstone of male workers' efforts to define the masculinized garment workplace. As they controlled the manners and daily activity of the shop, they also came to define skilled tasks as the realm of permanent male workers. Male Jewish workers' ability to tie definitions of skill to questions of shop floor permanence rested in large measure on assertions of different work identities for male and female Jewish workers, specifically, that women workers were transients waiting for the sexual fulfillment of marriage.[67]

As more Eastern European Jewish immigrants arrived in New York, the sexual division of labor became increasingly entrenched. A 1902 survey of shirt-waist and cloak shops revealed that men entirely monopolized the skilled craft of cutting, while women were relegated to unskilled tasks.[68] And male work-ers responded to the few women's efforts to win skilled jobs angrily, violently, and collectively. As Sam Liptzin remembered, men jealously guarded their claims to the best-paying jobs that they claimed demanded skill. In his shop, as in many smaller cloakmaking shops, "there was an unwritten law in the sweatshop that women were not to become machine-operators," he noted; "they did only certain operations—making buttonholes, sewing on buttons, basting linings, and other handwork—but machine-operation was reserved for men." (In larger shirtwaist factories, especially by the 1910s, some women did work on machines.)[69] In one cloak shop, male workers became furious when they heard rumors about women running machines. Such an affront, they reasoned, threatened not only men's wages, but also their ability to control the manners and mores of the shop. As one presser angrily exclaimed: "If we keep quiet about it, they'll become pressers and operators too! We won't be able to drop our suspenders or take off our shirts." Manly prerogative in a sexually inte-grated space would be shattered. In another shop, when the boss hired a fe-male relative as a pocketmaker, a well-paid, supposedly skilled trade claimed by men, male workers responded bitterly. They sabotaged her work and smudged oil on her coat. Her acceptance of lower wages would not mollify the men. They eventually went on strike "with a warning to the boss that they would refuse to work as long as a woman ran a machine."[70]

Actions like this strike reinforced the association of certain trades with skill and masculinity. Male workers called upon notions of sexual difference to natu-ralize gendered workplace hierarchies. Thus, the cutter Louis Panken insisted that women were not discriminated against in the cutting industry. Instead, he argued, cutting was simply a "man's trade."[71]

Similarly, as Mabel Hurd Willet noted, male workers cited notions of female transience when they sought to restrict women's involvement in organizing. She argued that male unionists did not consider women as potential unionists: "The East-side Jewish tailor refuses to regard the industrial activity of the Jew-ish girls as worthy of serious attention, and thinks it is hopeless to expect women employees to be unionists."[72] Thus, Rose Cohen recalled how men alone enjoyed the benefits of a union, like a longer lunch break. The men in her shop, all members of a union, left the shop for lunch or ate leisurely, read-ing a paper. The "girls," meanwhile, "ate hurriedly, and sat down to work at once."[73] Lazarus Marcowitz noted that men in his shop deliberately avoided including women in their efforts to organize. "They are only temporary workers in the trade," the men protested. "After working a few years, they get married and leave the shops. Why should we have them in the union and have to fight for them?"[74]

Women Strikers in a Men's Union, 1909–1913

When Jewish women in collaboration with the WTUL did seek to organize, they were forced to challenge men's constructions of femininity. Their 1909 and 1913 strikes included not only obvious confrontations with bosses, but also more subtle struggles with Jewish male workers and male union leaders.[75] In calling theirs a "women's strike" (despite some male participation), Eastern European Jewish immigrant women were asserting their legitimacy as workers who deserved a place on the shop floor and, therefore, in the unions. Yet where other women workers in different industries confronted constructions of masculinity to guarantee their privileges as workers and unionists, female Jewish garment workers initiated a challenge to certain male constructions of femininity.[76] In particular, through their association with middle- and upper-class women whose sexual respectability was virtually beyond question, female garment workers depended on notions of ladyhood and on the dangers of sweated work to demand different treatment at work.

In 1909 and again in 1913, tens of thousands of female Jewish strikers and unionists supported by the WTUL and other wealthy female sympathizers challenged men's resistance in order to secure the place of Eastern European Jewish immigrant women in the workshop. The dramatic waistmakers strike of 1909–1910, often called the "Uprising of the Twenty Thousand," was a model for Eastern European Jewish organizing as the first in a series of across-trade general strikes. Leaders and rank and file during the 1913 strikes of white-goodsmakers as well as of waistmakers consciously modeled their efforts after the Uprising.[77]

The 1909 strike began in the fall with independent stoppages at three waist factories: Leiserson's, Rosen Brothers, and the Triangle Waist Company. On November 22, the strike spread to the remainder of the waist industry. A general strike was declared at a lengthy meeting held at the Cooper Union, a meeting hall in a college near the Lower East Side. The strike dragged on through the winter as close to thirty thousand female workers joined the picket lines. Individual shop owners settled, but no general industry agreement was reached because employers were unwilling to accede to demands for the closed union shop. By February 1910, the union leadership declared the strike over, although thirteen shops remained without a contract.[78] Despite its mixed economic results, the strike represents a turning point not only in women's garment organizing, but also in the history of the Jewish labor movement as a whole. An unprecedented number of workers reinvigorated the previously small, ineffective shirtwaistmaker's Local 25 of the ILGWU, setting the stage for a series of general strikes throughout the needle trades in the coming years.[79]

In particular, as Rose Schneiderman, a former waistmaker and one of the lead organizers of the 1913 strikes, noted, the 1909 general strike had an enormous impact in the whitegoods trades, where the ILGWU had chartered Local 62 only in March 1909. Schneiderman remembered that rank-and-file women in the whitegoods trades were immediately committed to organizing for a general strike. "The girls would say," she claimed, "'We never can organize our trade until we do what the shirt waist makers did. We must have a general strike. . . . ' For four years this was the persistent demand of the girls."[80] By 1913, Local 62 felt ready to call a general strike meeting. Like the similar meeting in 1909, the meeting was held at Cooper Union. The next morning the predominantly Jewish and female rank and file launched a strike that would last five weeks. In the same year, waistmakers began another general strike to secure some of the gains that had eluded them four years earlier. In particular, they sought to be included in the new anti-sweatshop coalition, anchored by the JBSC.[81]

Especially in 1909, the male leadership of the ILGWU initially discouraged the idea of a general strike. Both the ILGWU president John Dyche and AFL president Samuel Gompers resisted approving the waistmakers' strike, doubting that young girls, as they understood Jewish female workers, could effectively organize. Indeed, as the strike progressed, they comically derided striking women as "our fiery girls" (*fabrente maydlakh*).[82] Even the first Cooper Union meeting had paternalistic overtones as male union leaders, like Gompers, offered a tepid mixture of sympathy and caution. "There is the time and the opportunity," he warned assembled waistmakers at the Cooper Union; "do not enter into hostility but when you can't get the manufacturers to give you what you want. . . . If you strike be cool, calm, collected." Gompers, like other male leaders, seemed to doubt the resolve and discipline of the "working girls."[83]

In fact, it was only through the intervention of Clara Lemlich, an Eastern European Jewish immigrant who was among the strikers, that the meeting actually discussed the general strike. Lemlich interrupted yet another well-known but discouraging male leader and cried, "I have listened to all the speakers. I would not have further patience for talk, as I am one of those who feels and suffers from the things pictured."[84] The frustration of the largely female audience seems evident in Lemlich's enthusiastic reception. Her speech may have thrilled the audience, but also surely represented an affront to the male leadership of Local 25 and the invited speakers. It was also a claim to workplace legitimacy, perhaps aimed at male workers and unionists who regarded her labor as merely temporary. She, too, suffered in the sweatshop.

It may have been the intervention of an immigrant worker that provided the spark for an open vote on the issue of the general strike in 1909, but the direction of the strike immediately passed to the WTUL. The WTUL's leaders included wealthy women like Mary Dreier as well as a few former workers like Leonora O'Reilly and Rose Schneiderman. Together, such leaders directed picketing, helped male ILGWU officers conduct negotiations, organized union strike halls, and coordinated relief efforts. In the 1913 strikes, probably as a result of the success of women in 1909 and a growing reluctance of the WTUL to organize immigrant women, Eastern European Jewish immigrant women did rise to a few positions of prominence. They served as picket captains and strike hall chairladies. Nonetheless, much of the overall direction of the strike again fell to elite and maternalist WTUL activists and to male and paternalist ILGWU leaders, like Local 62 chairman Samuel Shore.[85]

Girl Strikers, Women Workers, Ladies, and Sweatshop Victims

Most important, in 1909 and again in 1913, the WTUL and other female sympathizers claimed nearly complete control over strike publicity. They wrote articles for the WTUL magazine, *Life and Labor*, and contributed articles to the socialist *New York Call*, the *Jewish Daily Forward*, popular magazines with middle-class readership like *McClure's*, and to widely distributed New York newspapers like the *Evening Journal*.[86] In addition, especially in 1909, the WTUL carefully controlled the public appearances of strikers. They prepared rules and regulations for rank-and-file picketers that stressed trade union discipline and ladylike decorum. In both strikes, they arranged meetings with potential public supporters, especially wealthy women.

Even at such meetings, Eastern European Jewish immigrants served more as physical, visual models for the effects of garment work than as spokespersons for their cause. Their damaged and frail bodies—although, as Enstad argues, not their comportment—served as emblems for their seriousness as strikers and workers. On December 5, 1909, for example, wealthy female members of the Political Equality Association heard Leonora O'Reilly, Rose Pastor Stokes, and Dr. Anna Shaw explain the issues of the strike and glimpsed strikers, but did not hear from them. Ten days later a committee of "society ladies" provided a luncheon for ten strikers but heard speeches from Dreier, Schneiderman, and Mary McDowell. Clara Lemlich was the only striker who spoke.[87] In a similar fashion, the WTUL often publicized the arrest of their middle-class members on the picket line more than the police harassment of rank-and-file strikers. During the 1909 strike, the WTUL used the arrest of Dreier, for example, to demand that the city investigate the actions of the police.[88]

Still, workers' voices did pierce the barriers set up by WTUL leaders. While numerous female workers had the opportunity to recount their experiences, they had to do so in articles prepared by WTUL leaders who conducted interviews of workers and wrote the stories. In 1909, the WTUL presented Clara Lemlich, the heroine of the Cooper Union meeting, as the symbolic voice of the strikers. Thus, in an article in the *Evening Journal*, Lemlich explained the reasons for the strike to an interviewer.[89] In addition, Sue Ainslie Clark and Edith Wyatt presented the life stories of "shirtwaist-makers" for *McClure's Magazine*, and Sarah Comstock interviewed strikers for *Collier's*. In both cases, the authors offered their own commentary on the strikers.[90] Similarly, Martha Bensley Bruere interviewed whitegoodsmakers in 1913 for *Life and Labor*. In another article on the 1913 strikes, the magazine presented annotated versions of "girl's stories."[91] Their insistence on labeling female strikers as "girls," despite the fact that most were in their late teens or twenties, seemed to acknowledge men's representations of female workers as transients—when they grew up, they would leave the shop. It also worked to silence strikers. They were but girls, incapable of speaking beyond their own personal experiences.

Such a representation of strikers as "girls" was in tension with WTUL efforts to cast strikers as serious. In many ways, WTUL leaders even sought to cast women's demands as similar to those advanced by men. Without denying the overall primacy of the male breadwinner, strike publicity highlighted the familial importance of women's wages. Rose Schneiderman and Leonora O'Reilly, in their article "The Bitter Cry of Factory Girls," quoted a striker who claimed that she worked "to earn money to bring my people here" and another who worked to support her sick father.[92] Similarly, Sue Ainslie Clark and Edith Wyatt described and quoted shirtwaist strikers about their budgets to prove the importance of their wages in supporting families and in bringing over family members from Russia. Sarah Comstock also focused on the familial importance of the wages of "working girls." Comstock negotiated tensions between images of female strikers as girls and as serious wage earners (but not family breadwinners) by suggesting that the experience of conflict made girls into unionists; they grew up. She related her conversation with a striker in 1909 and described how when the issues of wages came up, "instantly there was a transformation. From a Ghetto Coquette the child passed in the twinkling of an eye to an orator." The striker told how her wages helped support her mother and her grandfather. Comstock was typical in the way she used strikers' voices as well as her own middle-class interpretations and commentary to argue for the seriousness and earnestness of the strikers. In focusing on the familial importance of women's wages, WTUL leaders subtly countered notions of women's work as merely temporary or women's wages as simply pin money. However, they also ignored female workers' concerns about sexual harassment.[93]

Female workers would not completely follow the script. Instead, women workers sought to use strike publicity to talk, albeit in a mediated fashion, about workplace sexuality. WTUL leaders' commentary on and editing of strikers' words served to present a particular representation of "girl strikers." Even so, it allowed some Eastern European Jewish immigrant women to present to a large audience their experiences at work. And, they used the opportunity to speak about the sexualized atmosphere of New York's garment shops. "The Bitter Cry of Factory Girls," featuring stories on strikers in 1913, is indicative. Luckily, the notes that O'Reilly and Schneiderman used to prepare the article remain and provide a glimpse at the process of negotiation between workers and their allies over the representation of women's work. O'Reilly and Schneiderman interviewed around forty strikers for the article, using prepared questions that focused on whom strikers were supporting with their wages, seemingly in an effort to depict the seriousness of strikers' concerns. Strikers used the interviews to present an image of the woman worker, a worker who was also a lady. In an article promising "girls' stories," they appropriated a middle-class language of morality, gender, and ladyhood to describe themselves as women workers.[94] In their answers workers rarely followed the scripted questions and commented in particular on sexual harassment on the shop floor. One striker was typical in demanding "to be treated like ladies, with the union behind us, they wouldn't dare use the same language to us."[95] The published article addressed many more issues, most notably workplace harassment, than O'Reilly and Schneiderman had originally intended. Still, the final edits were theirs.[96]

In creating strike publicity, the language used to talk about and vilify the sexualization of the sweatshop workplace was circumscribed. Harassment was cast primarily as an affront to ladyhood. While historian Nan Enstad argues that working women created their own version of "working-class" ladyhood through their reading of popular culture, in fact this notion of ladyhood was articulated through a process of negotiation with WTUL leaders.[97] It was a shared, cross-class language that capitalized on the unquestioned respectability of WTUL leaders, but rhetorically separated harassment from the construction of skill and workplace hierarchy. This conception of harassment as a threat to working-class ladies, rather than a cornerstone of workplace hierarchy, may have garnered sympathy among a middle-class audience reading the WTUL's English-language publicity, but it did not help women workers confront inequalities of skill and pay. Indeed, this language tended to recast harassment as something committed only by "foremen who insult and abuse girls beyond endurance," as Rose Pastor Stokes declared, not by fellow male workers and union comrades.[98]

Bosses typically exported the sexualized atmosphere of the workshop to the picket line. They employed known prostitutes to harass strikers and to suggest comparisons of strikers to prostitutes. But as much as bosses and their allies among the police tried to depict strikers as sexual miscreants, striking workers and their allies proposed alternative views of strikers' sexuality by publicly decrying their appearance at the night court alongside prostitutes. One striker, Yetta Ruth, complained that police had equated her with the prostitutes and another wondered whether "it is worse to be a streetwalker."[99] They also disparaged the prostitutes they met in jail.[100] In 1913, one seventeen-year-old striker in an interview with O'Reilly and Schneiderman related her anger about an officer who told her that she "could make an easier living on Fourteenth street," a known red-light district. To highlight the humiliating comparison, in the published article, her quote is printed in bold letters.[101] Clark and Wyatt also tried to disassociate strikers from prostitutes by quoting one arrested worker's response to her night in jail alongside prostitutes: "It was dreadful! There were three other women in the cell—some of them horrid women that came off the street. . . . The horrid women laughed and screamed and said terrible words." In efforts to distinguish female workers from prostitutes, the image of the "ghetto coquette" gave way to that of the "lady" striker.[102]

In casting harassment as a question of respect, not workplace skill, complaints about harassment could confirm strikers' status as ladies, but not as workers. To claim positions as legitimate workers, female workers and their WTUL allies turned to prevailing languages about sweatshop work, health, and the immigrant body. Martha Bensley Bruere pointed out that waistmakers were "the youngest, the most ignorant, the poorest and most unskilled group of women workers who have ever struck in this country." Even as she pointed out their age, Bruere insisted that women workers carried the physical scars of work, just like male workers. The socialist *New York Call*, in a special edition published to support the shirtwaist strikers, sought to capture this image of enfeebled immigrant women workers in a cartoon. The cartoon presents workers in an exaggerated state of decline. It admonishes wealthy women that their quest for bargains and fine dress caused the enfeeblement of their shirtwaistmaking sisters they should have been supporting. While wealthy women are shown in good health with lavish clothing and hats, shirtwaist-

_____ *Figure 8* _____

"Two Phases of Yuletide, 1909" (from the *New York Call*, December 24, 1909). This cartoon was typical in the way it presented female workers as physically decrepit and young. It was partially in their enfeebled bodies that workers and their middle-class leaders claimed to find workplace legitimacy. The cartoon is also emblematic of the cross-class dialogue that was integral to the direction of the 1909 and 1913 strikes.

makers are depicted in poor clothing with hunched backs. Their poor dress covered their enfeebled bodies, which, in turn, seemed to confirm their status as real workers. In this context, bodily decline signaled workplace legitimacy.[103] The cartoon reverses older ideas about the relationship between the sweatshop and middle-class consumers. Once workers were held responsible for the spread of disease to middle-class consumers. In the cartoon, working-class frailty is now blamed on middle-class spending habits.

O'Reilly, Schneiderman, and the workers they interviewed also appeared to suggest that women's legitimacy as workers was etched on their bodies. O'Reilly and Schneiderman quoted one eighteen-year-old worker and striker who claimed that she "went to bed" directly after work to maintain her strength. Thus, when the striker explained the need for a union "in back of us to keep us strong," she was referring most immediately to physical strength.[104] It was in the context of the effects of work on female immigrants' bodies that workers and strike leaders like Clara Lemlich complained about shop floor conditions. "The shops are unsanitary," she explained, "that's the word that is generally used, but there ought to be a worse one used." In pointing out the effect of such conditions on their bodies, strikers and their leaders seemed to be forcefully inserting their experiences into the prevailing discourse on the work and the health of legitimate workers. In suggesting that the word "unsanitary" was used by others, namely inspectors, Lemlich seems to demand a place in emerging efforts to define and solve the problems of sweatshop conditions.[105]

Despite such claims to workplace legitimacy based on physical weakness, female strikers and their leaders remained conscious of sexual difference and the male breadwinner ideal. For women, the discourse around health and the body may have helped them claim legitimacy as women workers, but it did not allow them to claim workplace permanency. Indeed, this language even admitted women's transience. Publicity continued to stress strikers' youth, not simply as an appeal for sympathy, but as a gesture to women's shop floor impermanence. Clark and Wyatt's description of the striker Natalya Urusova was typical: "She is little, looking hardly more than twelve years old, with a pale, sensitive face . . . and the gentlest voice in the world, a voice still thrilled with the light inflections of a child." Her paleness confirmed her legitimacy as sweatshop worker—she, too, suffered—while her youth hints that she would soon grow up, marry, and leave the shop.

This claim to workplace legitimacy, qualified by an acknowledgment of the importance of marriage, becomes especially apparent in a close examination of one lengthy document, Theresa Serber Malkiel's *Diary of a Shirtwaist Striker*. Malkiel encapsulated in her own experience the cross-class alliance of the WTUL and Eastern European Jewish immigrant women. She arrived in the United States in 1891 from Eastern Europe. After finding work in a garment shop that manufactured cloaks, she became involved in the fledgling Jewish union, the Infant Cloakmakers' Union of New York. She also became enmeshed in the city's socialist factionalism, first joining the Socialist Labor Party and then quitting to join the Socialist Party. In the Socialist Party, she met her future husband, Leon A. Malkiel, a lawyer who had accumulated a fair fortune in real estate. Like so many of her female co-workers, marriage signaled the end of her stay in the shops, but for Malkiel marriage also meant an entrance into a world of privilege. She lived at the dividing line between the striking shop girls and their wealthy allies in the WTUL.[106]

Malkiel became increasingly active in the Socialist Party and was especially vocal about women's roles as wives, workers, and socialists. She wrote a series of pamphlets that concentrated on the relationship between women's factory work and marriage and drew on her own experience as a shop girl. Women's limited tenure as workers, she claimed, made women responsible for lowering men's wages. "Working-girls" who were waiting for marriage, she suggested, would accept lower wages. After all, Malkiel continued: "The wheel of life turns until it reaches the man you are about to marry."[107] Malkiel insisted that women accepted lower wages because they understood themselves as temporary workers. In her only lengthy work, *The Diary of a Shirtwaist Striker*, Malkiel combined arguments about women's shop floor legitimacy with pronouncements about how marriage should signal the end of women's wage-earning lives. It represented a negotiated middle ground between workers and WTUL leaders.

The Diary of a Shirtwaist Striker first appeared in 1910, only three months after the strike's conclusion, as a serial in the *New York Call*. It was published later that year in book form.[108] *The Diary* drew on Malkiel's close involvement with the strike and with the strikers through a fictionalized account of the shirtwaist strike in the words of "Mary," interestingly not a Jewish immigrant, but "a free-born American." As the historian Françoise Basch argues, the choice of a non-Jewish (or, even, non-immigrant) heroine allowed Malkiel the opportunity to comment on "noble Jew girls," their experiences, thought, and organizing strategies.[109]

The plot of *The Diary* pointedly counterpoises Mary's relationships with her fiancé, Jim, and her father alongside her increasing strike activity. By centering the question of Mary's impending marriage, *The Diary* openly assaults the idea of the transient shop girl as unserious. Malkiel initially portrays Mary as the kind of "ghetto girl" criticized by Sarah Comstock. Her first thought is to treat the strike as a joke all the while contemplating Jim's reaction: "Ha, ha, ha! That's a joke. By Jove, it is. I'm a striker. I wonder what Jim'll have to say to this?"[110] Mary, her self-image as a transient confirmed by her constant thoughts of Jim, sees no need for a union for women: "What in the world do I want with a union? My mother and grandmother have gone through life without belonging to one and I guess I, too, can get along without it."[111]

Embedded in the "I guess" lies Mary's growing recognition that "this strike is a more serious business than I thought."[112] Her changing emotions echo the WTUL's thinly veiled criticisms of the worker-coquette. At the same time,

Mary's changing opinions also reflected women workers' discontent with workplace sexuality. The "ghetto girl," Mary claims, saw the workplace as nothing more than a place to find a husband: "We think it nothing but a place of entertainment and therefore try to dance through it."[113] With such a critique, Mary challenges the idea that marriage and sexual flirtation were at the center of working women's identity. As if to mark her political epiphany, Mary quarrels with Jim. Their uneven marriage, dependent as it was on her leaving work and obeying her husband, is now in doubt.

Malkiel uses Mary's observations of Jewish strikers to present an alternate image of working women as sexually respectable female workers. They were, for Malkiel, women workers, distinct from men perhaps, but still legitimate workers. Like much of the strike publicity, Mary cites examples of Jewish working girls whose meager wages supported whole families: "Here Rose is the supporter of the family ever since her father died three years ago, leaving five children, herself the oldest."[114] Mary proclaims Rose a real worker because she contributes to the family income: "Talk about martyrs, I guess Rose is the real stuff."[115] At the same time and, again, echoing strike publicity, Malkiel affirms the sexual respectability of striking women through Mary's condemnation of prostitutes disrupting the picket line. Mary describes one striker, Sarah, as in tears over being called a prostitute. Mary becomes irate. Working women's quiet shop floor behavior, for Mary, clearly confirmed them as the opposite of "street women": "Why, she has always been the quietest and most refined girl in the workroom."[116] When Mary herself is arrested, her loudest protests are over being locked in a cell together with prostitutes.[117] For Mary, echoing the words of the middle-class supporters of the strike and of other female workers, diligent factory work for the purpose of earning money to support families, as well as self-sacrificing striking, confirmed the respectability of the Jewish working woman: "It makes me real mad, when they try to tell us that it ain't lady-like to go out on strike. Why don't they say it ain't lady-like to go out into the factories and work from morn until night . . . till we get to see nothing but work and the machine before us." At the same time, in talking about the arduous work, she links claims to ladyhood to languages of sweatshop danger.[118]

Through the cantankerous relationship between Mary and her discouraging father, Malkiel captures the struggle of Jewish women to claim legitimacy within the union and on the shop floor. Mary's father is a dedicated unionist himself but forbids Mary—unsuccessfully—from participating in picketing: "And my pa, a good union man, has the courage to say it ain't a girl's place to belong to a union!"[119] For Mary, claiming a place in the union meant reformulating workplace sexuality, denouncing, in particular, sexual harassment. Mary criticizes her mother's domestic docility and, as she becomes increasingly active in the strike, she questions not simply men's treatment of women but, more specifically, men's constructions of femininity and their social effects: "I wonder what a man means when he'd want you to be a woman? If to believe in everything that's right, to sorrow for the needy, to help the weak, to censure the wicked, to refuse being stepped upon, used and abused, means not being a woman, then I don't want to be a woman."[120] Malkiel recognized that Jewish female workers' self-conception as respectable female strikers and legitimate workers potentially undermined the social significance of marriage. Indeed, Mary breaks off her engagement. "To tell the truth, I was never so sure that a working girl gained so very much by getting married. I always felt that us girls do it more because we can't help ourselves. But I've been cured."[121]

Yet, in the end, Malkiel, like other female workers and WTUL leaders, carefully argued that the women's newfound work identities did not entirely reverse the significance of marriage in women's working lives. As Jim comes to recognize the justice of the strike, he and Mary reconcile. The book concludes with the strike settled and Jim arriving at Mary's apartment with the signed marriage license in hand. Jim even joins Mary on a picket line shift. Malkiel asserted that marriage should still signal the end of women's wage-earning careers. Only the hierarchical dynamic of marriage, not the hierarchy of the workplace, had to change. Mary informs Jim that in marriage she desired equality, not paternalistic care. In the end, she remained willing to abandon the factory: "I'd want to mind our home and take care of our children, or in short, I explained to him that I'd want to be a partner to the game."[122]

Shop Girl to Working Woman

In the fictional life of one worker, Malkiel's text portrayed Jewish women's collective effort to transform the shop girl persona from a sexually available transient into a respectable working woman and striker. In the years during and after the Uprising and the 1913 strikes, female unionists repeatedly pressed the idea of respectable female worker, often claiming the title "working woman" and rejecting "shop girl." As Lemlich herself suggested, one of the primary successes of the strike was separating the idea of workplace transience from questions of seriousness or legitimacy as workers and as unionists: "They used to say that you couldn't even organize women . . . they were 'temporary' workers. Well, we showed them!"[123] Fannia Cohn, similarly, in looking back on the strike that marked the beginning of her own lifelong career with the ILGWU, described the Uprising as a coming-of-age for female workers. In her writing, Cohn signaled the discursive transformation in representations of female employees that she and other female unionists pushed so fervently during the strike. At the beginning of her description of the strike in her un-published history of the ILGWU, she portrayed female workers as "mere girls," but by the end of the description, she called them "working women."[124]

For Lemlich and Cohn, the claim to legitimacy on the shop floor inherent in the rejection of the notion of the "ghetto girl" and "shop girl" also became a claim to roles for women in the ILGWU. "The strikers," Cohn insisted, "dem-onstrated a fearlessness and a readiness to fight that was heretofore not sus-pected in women. They gained confidence in their own power as women and workers."[125] When Cohn praised another strike of female waistmakers in 1919, she again referred to workers' discipline. Women unionists, she argued, were serious unionists, not ghetto girls: "But these young children act like grown-up mature people, and the more I come in touch with the various committees who are carrying on the general strike, the more I am convinced of this."[126] Thus, when female unionists demanded places for women in the ILGWU, they berated male garment workers for still treating female workers as the kind of shop girls criticized by the WTUL. Soon after the conclusion of the Uprising, one female organizer declared: "If men would build a strong and solid defense against low wages, they will have to treat the girls not as children . . . but as women, who must take their places along with men on the fighting line."[127]

Still, female unionists' efforts to shift representations of female workers had limited application. It left untouched and, seemingly, beyond question notions of sexual difference and the hierarchies of skill protected by such notions. Jewish women workers rarely sought entrance into the ranks of better-paying jobs. They never collectively forced or demanded a significant rethinking of gendered definitions of skill. In addition, like Malkiel, most female workers and unionists still recognized that marriage signaled the end of women's shop floor careers. Finally, with all its limitations, women's assault on constructions of femininity may have emphasized women's respectable roles in the workplace, but did not guarantee women leadership positions in trade unions.

The few women who sought full-time positions as trade unionists contin-ued to battle the ongoing sexualized association of women's work with mar-riage. Most of these women remained single, recognizing that they could not combine marriage and union organizing. The leading Jewish female organiz-ers of the ILGWU before 1930, among them Rose Schneiderman, Pauline Newman, and Fannia Cohn, never married. In an immigrant community where norms of heterosocial and heterosexual behavior still governed workplace gen-der interactions, their sexuality sometimes became the subject of ridicule and discussion. Harassment served to protect gendered hierarchies in the union, in much the same way that it had on the shop floor. Pauline Newman often found her sexuality in question. John Dyche, the ILGWU's secretary, for example, once asked Newman: "Why do you wear a skirt? . . . Getting to be respectable, Paul?"[128] Thus she reported: "I do not feel at home with them anymore." Newman's and other female organizers' decision to forgo marriage probably emerged partially from their own choice and partially because in the face of hostility from male unionists it would have been difficult to maintain legitimacy as a married union organizer. In this context, many preferred the comfort and camaraderie of other female organizers. Many, it seemed, sought loving and enduring same-sex relationships.[129] Nonetheless, as Schneiderman wrote, women organizers generally acknowledged that their decisions to work as full-time organizers virtually erased the possibility of marriage.[130]

For female organizers like Newman and Schneiderman, the idea of dedicating a lifetime to work and unionizing meant stepping outside of the heterosocial world of the Jewish garment workplace. Perhaps, for this reason, as historian Annelise Orleck notes, Pauline Newman dressed in a consciously nonfeminine manner, with short hair and tweed jackets.[131] The resignation of trade unionists like Schneiderman to the elusiveness of marriage alongside Malkiel's careful reaffirmation of women's duty to marry suggests the durability of images of Jewish women workers as temporary and of standards of heterosocial and heterosexual relationships.[132] Female Jewish trade unionists, like Schneiderman, realized that their ability to coexist alongside male union leaders demanded public affirmations of sexual chastity and open rejections of heterosexual interactions. They rejected the institution, which, even in its most benign form, would drag them out of the workplace and, thus, out of labor organizing.[133]

In her autobiography, the organizer Elizabeth Hasanovitz highlights the difficulty female Jewish unionists faced in trying to separate personal sexuality and union activity. She seems to have been unable to claim a role as a union activist and, at the same time, to acknowledge sexual or romantic desire. Hasanovitz presents herself as the consummate female trade unionist, serving as a shop chairlady, even several times sacrificing her job for the sake of the union. Her dedication to the union is underscored, indeed, confirmed, by her conscious downplaying of her sexuality. Even as female workers struggled to claim the title "working women" in place of the "shop girl," she refuses to acknowledge herself as a woman, describing herself as a pale girl who always looked abnormally young for her age, too youthful for romance.[134] At the same time, she consistently describes herself as ill, as if to show her seriousness as a worker. To emphasize her shop floor legitimacy, she echoes WTUL leaders and criticizes some of her fellow female workers for acting like "ghetto girls" and ignoring unions and focusing on "fellers" and "swells."[135] Whether or not this self-portrait reflected physical reality and her real behavior, it served to minimize her sexuality. Rhetorically, Hasanovitz's autobiography connects her loyal ties to the union with her continual rejection of sexual relationships. She rebuffs the crude sexual advances of bosses and fellow workers and the court-ship of fellow unionists.

The tension in Hasanovitz's autobiography between her identity as a unionist and as a romantic or sexual woman suggests the way the discourse around female worker's femininity and sexuality after the 1909 and 1913 strikes was increasingly linked to disputes over women's trade union roles. One short story by the respected worker-poet Abraham Reisin that appeared in the ILGWU's monthly magazine, *The Ladies' Garment Worker*, captured both the partial ac-ceptance of women's own construction of femininity and men's fears of creep-ing disorder. In his story "Equal Rights," sexual order is reversed. Not only does the woman worker, Ida, refuse treats or gifts from men, but also her sexual favors depend on her workplace gains. She demands that her boyfriend Harry wait until she earns $15 a week, a salary commanded only by skilled workers and unheard of for women. Ida challenges the hierarchies and the role of mar-riage in ordering workplace and sexual relationships between men and women; she even calls "wife" "an ugly word." And, in the end, when Ida remarkably earns her desired salary and offers to treat Harry, he is emasculated, fright-ened, and insulted.

While Harry's resistance is quietly criticized, the warning clearly emerges: at the moment that women refocus their identities as individual ambitious work-ers, rather than as mothers and wives, or, more generally, as sexual beings, they begin to challenge manliness itself. Harry finds the sanctum of male skill and high pay in the workplace and treating outside of the workplace penetrated by his industrious girlfriend. With her ultimate success, the relationship is doomed and sexual relations become impossible.[136] Reisin seems ambivalent about the potential of equal gender rights.

Reisin's ambivalence offers an insight into the paradoxical legacy of the 1909 and 1913 strikes that is the subject of the final two chapters. Women forced their way into the anti-sweatshop coalition through the strength of their strikes and by aligning themselves with efforts to cure occupational disease. If only because of the large numbers of female workers and because of their concen-tration in certain segments of the ILGWU, women forced male unionists and public health officials to accept programs to address women's specific concerns and needs. While this fact testifies to the collective strength of female rank and file after 1909 and 1913, their success depended heavily on their public acceptance of and support for the ideal of the male breadwinner. Thus, this gendered ideal remained at the heart of efforts to combat and defeat the sweatshop and to realize the model shop. In fact, male and female workers' oft-shared conceptions of sexual differences and ideals about the gendered division of labor were to become the foundation of the Jewish labor movement's curative initiatives in the 1910s and 1920s.

Six

Inspecting Bodies

*Sexual Difference and Strategies
of Organizing, 1910–1930*

As the 1909 waistmakers' strike edged toward its conclusion, the male leadership of the ILGWU appealed to the union's male membership to recognize female waistmakers as employees who faced many of the same challenges and indignities suffered by male workers, namely poor wages and declining health. "Remember the shirt-waist girl," they implored. They cited the success and bravery of female strikers on the picket lines. Their appeal seemed to afford women strikers a place in the union and a legitimacy on the shop floor by promising them the benefits of union organizing, particularly in the area of "health and welfare."[1]

As the general strikes of 1909–13 ended, the potential of union organizing seemed limitless to the ILGWU's leaders and the rank and file. The membership of the ILGWU and other segments of the New York Jewish labor movement swelled during and immediately after the strikes. The ILGWU, sometimes in alliance with the Arbeter Ring (Workmen's Circle [AR]), a socialist mutual benefit society, sought to use its large membership to advance ideas about how to care for workers damaged by years of labor in sweatshops. The initial definition of the sweatshop had intimately linked occupational disease with sweated work, and so curing sick workers became the primary organizing goal of the ILGWU and the Jewish immigrant labor movement. It was a way to combat and defeat the sweatshop. As the ILGWU loudly promised shirtwaistmakers: "THE UNION IS ON THE JOB EVERY HOUR OF EVERY WORKING DAY TO SEE THAT THE HEALTH AND WELFARE OF ITS MEMBERS ARE PROPERLY LOOKED AFTER."[2] Most prominently, the AR joined the ILGWU in developing extensive plans to protect the health of workers. Their programs were remarkably similar and intermingled in numerous ways. Not only did ILGWU and AR leaders respond to the same discussions about public health and sanitary reform, but also they even shared resources. The ILGWU, for example, regularly sent its most dangerously consumptive workers to the AR's sanitarium.

As the ILGWU's appeal suggests, women's voices and health concerns were recognized in these organizing strategies primarily because women's participation in the union continued to depend heavily on conceptions and articulations of sexual difference. After all, understandings of the sweatshop connected occupational disease with the breakdown of the family and the gendered division of labor. In the ILGWU, more than in the AR, women organized collectively to demand medical plans that recognized what they deemed their particular needs.[3] Because women did not use health programs to demand access to union power or to challenge ideas of appropriate gender roles, their demands were, for the most part, accepted by the ILGWU's male leaders. Women still described themselves as different kinds of workers whose experiences diverged because of their temporary roles on the shop floor. Men's and women's shared belief that they experienced work in different ways led the AR and the ILGWU to represent the effects of sweatshop labor on male and female bodies differently. In Jewish proletarian associations' medical view, the ill effects of labor undermined workers' ability to perform their assumed primary functions: for men, earning a family wage, for women, leaving the workplace and raising a family. Their words became part of contemporary discourses about public health and sanitary reform.[4]

In their campaigns to protect workers' health that emerged as part of campaigns to reverse the effects of sweated work and to realize the model shop, the ILGWU and the AR came to rely on the language and expertise of public health officials and advocates of occupational safety. With their help, the leadership of the ILGWU and the AR undertook a program of medical inspections and examinations of the bodies of their members not only to discover levels of disease, but also to find the evidence of sexual difference. With the authority of science and medicine, their results confirmed ideals of a sexual division of labor. They claimed to have uncovered experimental evidence that men and women experienced work in different ways.[5]

When male and female workers and their unions, with the help of public health advocates and government officials, examined their bodies, they uncovered different injuries and illnesses. In male bodies, they uncovered the telltale signs of tuberculosis—a disease they believed would hamper men's ability to labor and to provide for their families. Among women, they found injuries that affected women's reproductive abilities. Thus, when the ILGWU and the

AR sought to cure men, they concentrated heavily on the prevention and treatment of tuberculosis, whereas for women, they focused on reproductive issues. The Jewish workers' movement, its male leadership, female unionists, and rank and file, through their alliance with the public health movement, insisted that women's temporary status in the workplace was inscribed on their bodies. As they identified different bodily ailments for men and women, male and female Jewish workers contemplated contrasting strategies of curing. Yet because their strategies depended on and preserved ideas of sexual difference, they managed to forge compromises. In the way they represented their labor, women and men's efforts to confront the very real problem of sweatshop-induced occupational disease served as well to solidify ideas, generally held by both women and men, of sexual difference. And difference, it seemed, translated into inequality.

New Power and New Visions of Curing

The second decade of the twentieth century proved a watershed for Jewish immigrants' proletarian societies and trade unions. More than ever before, Jewish workers came to depend on such associations for care, rehabilitation, and relaxation. The strikes that paralyzed nearly every branch of the ladies' garment industry at different times between 1909 and 1913 institutionalized the ILGWU as a permanent part of New York's industry and as a critical part of cross-class efforts to regulate and eradicate sweatshops. The AR also thrived with an expanding and newly invigorated membership. New legal licensing by the state of New York allowed the association to offer expanded services, guaranteeing the AR an important place in the Jewish immigrant community. For much of the 1910s and early 1920s, an era in which Jewish immigrants and their descendants formed the majority of New York's garment workforce, the ILGWU and the AR thrived and their leaders enjoyed a relatively unchallenged tenure. Both associations easily recognized their new power and initiated intense conversations about ways to refigure garment work. In the context of campaigns for workplace regulation and sanitary control, their planning inevitably turned to new possibilities, programs, and ways to protect the health of garment workers.[6]

The strikes transformed the nature of Eastern European Jewish garment unionism. Previously, the ILGWU and its predecessor unions languished, too weak and too transient to win victories apart from shorter hours and slightly higher wages. As Paul Novick, a former garment worker and the editor of the Yiddish Communist paper *Freiheit*, noted, Jewish garment unions in the earlier years of Eastern European Jewish migration lacked the stability to organize for broader issues outside the confines of a single shop: "So it began about in the eighties and then in the nineties as the unions began to form. . . . The union would fall apart and then . . . again a strike, again a union."[7] Abraham Rosenberg, an early leader in efforts to organize cloakmakers, also recognized that the first unions concentrated on signing up workers already on strike. After a small pay raise, sometimes negotiated over "a barrel of beer," settled the strikes, the unions often collapsed.[8] Earlier immigrant workers organized garment unions in only a handful of shops, and their efforts were crippled by seasonal shifts in the workload, which made it difficult for the unions to maintain a presence.

While workers in these years may have promoted a discourse that decried the effects of work on their bodies, their small unions could hardly advance plans that promoted proletarian health care. In 1905, the economist Jesse Pope even went as far as to claim that "the influence of the union upon conditions in the industry was practically nil."[9] As Meyer London, one of the most astute observers and leaders of the Jewish garment labor movement, mourned, speaking of the years before 1910: "We had unions some time ago—they existed on paper. . . . We talked about a social revolution and had a 70-hour week!"[10]

In contrast, after the strikes of 1909–13, female and male rank and file and their male leadership sought a broader role for the ILGWU in the remaking and rehabilitation of workers' bodies. The "social revolution" would be acted out on workers' bodies, not on the shop floor; workers' health would reflect the strength of the labor movement. The leadership readily encouraged and the membership accepted new proposals, like a union-owned resort, worker education programs, and benefit funds. Members also considered other, perhaps more ambitious proposals, like union-owned factories, a workers' university, and cooperative, communal housing.[11] Although most such suggestions fell by the wayside, their very proposal testifies to the extent to which the ILGWU's established leadership and growing membership enthusiastically sought to wield union power. But, as in their reliance on the Joint Board of Sanitary Control (JBSC), union leaders sought to exercise power in the context of cross-class alliances with a range of Progressive reformers, from government inspectors to public health advocates. Labor leaders, through their commitment to the anti-sweatshop coalition, came to measure success by the ability to care for workers, rather than to remake the wage relationship of the garment industry.

The AR also experienced enormous expansion around the same time as the ILGWU. Like the ILGWU, the AR experimented with new kinds of services and extended the programs it already offered. Increasingly, the AR sought to remake garment work by offering physical care to its members. The AR benefited from Eastern European Jewish immigrants' turn to collective action and general strikes. Between 1908 and 1910, the AR doubled its membership from 19,324 to 38,866 members. By 1925, the society's membership had ballooned to 84,791.[12] Jewish immigrants flocked to join the AR after 1905 when New York finally granted the AR a charter as an insurance provider. Within a few years, the society was able to increase payments to sick and debilitated workers and extend its life insurance coverage.[13]

The AR's leaders and activists recognized the possibilities inherent in expanded membership. Bolstered by the growth in membership and by the influx of notable Eastern European Jewish socialists and revolutionaries after the failed Russian revolution of 1905, a new ambitious generation of AR leaders demanded a rapid expansion in the activities of the society. They encouraged the formation of Yiddish schools for children, an expanded educational department, lectures, and political choruses in order to strengthen participation in the AR's health and curing programs.[14] Yitzchak Yankel Doroshkin, a rank-and-file member of the AR, remembered, for example, the "Sunday morning forums at Clinton Street, in a room which held 500 people. The hall was always fully packed. . . . We organized a speaker's class . . . and many cultural activities."[15] As the AR expanded such activities, the heart of its program remained the maintenance of its members' health. The new leadership understood even the new cultural programs as secondary to the health benefits, insurance, and other physical protections offered by the AR.[16]

As the AR's and the ILGWU's leaders introduced a spectrum of new programs, they continued to represent garment work as hazardous to body and family. As the AR declared: "It is our lot to live in a highly industrialized society. . . . The human body is subjected to stress and strains . . . in industry."[17] An overriding focus on the health of workers is evident in the wide array of strategies proposed in both the ILGWU and the AR. As the ILGWU announced in 1915, the union sought to exercise its new power in order to safeguard the health of its members: "Since the aim of the Union is to enter fully into the lives of its members and make them feel its benign influence . . . it is manifestly wrong to . . . leave them to chance to the tender mercies of charity when they fall into sickness."[18] Care for ill workers became the union's essential priority, even superseding direct class conflict. "The point of view that a trade union has only one purpose—the economic fight against the employer—is very much outdated," the ILGWU's official paper declared in 1924. "It stands to reason that when workers are sick . . . the union should come to their assistance."[19]

Similarly, the AR as a proletarian association aimed to reverse the ill effects of work. As the society reaffirmed at its 1922 convention: "An ever increasing number of workers . . . are beginning to realize that through their united effort . . . it is possible to alleviate and to avoid many of the evils which fall to the lot of workers and their families in times of illness."[20] In addition to providing insurance, the AR introduced other kinds of health protections, ranging from a sanitarium for tubercular members to health clinics to more generous sickness benefit payments.

Like the ILGWU, the AR highlighted physical care as the unifying core of its mission. The image of the enfeebled, sick worker that first appeared in the 1880s and 1890s remained an emblem of the need for the AR, as an illustration in the AR's 1910 yearly report dramatically highlighted. The drawing, simply labeled *"hilf"* (help), depicts an angel counseling an obviously sick and tubercular proletarian male patient (although the patient's ethnicity, unlike earlier images, is no longer obvious). The patient, whose naked, sunken, weakened chest forms the center of the drawing, raises himself with effort from his bed. His eyes follow the fingers of the angel to an image of the AR's tuberculosis sanitarium in Liberty, New York. The angel seems to symbolize the AR's ideological purpose. In her right hand she displays a copy of the AR's charter. The image seems to suggest that in light of the new strength of the AR, this male proletarian victim of garment work could be restored to vigor and, it is hoped, returned to his place at the shop bench.[21]

In the same way that the decrepitude of sweatshop workers' bodies reflected the horrors of the sweatshop, the health and vim of male union workers could prove the potency of trade unions and proletarian associations. The AR, for example, demonstrated its success in an image of three generations of men: a healthy, chubby baby; a lean, growing adolescent; and a muscular young man. The older man especially seems to have shed the racialized weak body described in earlier inspectors' descriptions of suffering sweatshop workers and the ethnic labels of immigrant workers' cultural images and pictures. Clad in stylish, athletic garb, the immigrant worker as a healthy man appears to claim his Americanness and what the ILGWU's official historian called "industrial citizenship."[22] The man holds aloft a wreath with a ribbon proclaiming the size and strength of the AR: "134 Cities, 435 Branches, 36,000 Members." The body of the man, in particular, seems to embody the numerical, social, and ideological strength of the society and to reflect the goals of the AR. Thus, the caption of the picture states simply: *"Fereinigung"* (Association).[23] Muscular strength signaled collective strength and social inclusion.

As the rank and file and leadership of the ILGWU and the AR placed the health of its workers at the center of their efforts to utilize new-found strength, the curing of workers emerged as central to the reform of sweated work. Jewish workers, like Harry Golden, came to see health care as politicized. Golden remembered that his doctor included the words "Join the union" on every prescription he wrote.[24] The AR similarly recast *"klasn kampf"* (class conflict) as

_____ *Figure 9* _____

"Hilf" [Help] (from "Der Arbeiter Ring Sovenir Den Tsenten Ierlicher Konvenshion Gevidmet" [1910], YIVO, Bund Archives, Workman's Circle Collection RG #1400, 33). The angel, holding the Arbeter Ring's charter and gesturing to its sanitarium, embodies the ideological goals of the AR to cure its members. The tubercular patient is a male worker with a sunken chest.

_____ _Figure 10_ _____

"Fereinigung" [Association] (from""Der Arbeiter Ring Sovenir Den Tsenten Ierlicher Konvenshion Gevidmet" [1910], YIVO, Bund Archives, Workman's Circle Collection, RG #1400, 1). The Arbeter Ring depicted its desire and ability to care for its members throughout their lives in this allegorical drawing. The strong physique of the older male represents the success of the AR.

the building of effective sickness benefit funds. The strength of the working class was embodied in the health of the male worker. Even in the first line of its "Declaration of Principles," written in 1901 and reconfirmed at its annual conventions, the AR plainly cited sickness caused by toil as the fundamental reason for the society's creation: "The constant want and frequent illness which particularly afflict the workers, have led us to band together in the Workmen's Circle."[25]

This focus on health care and curing ran parallel to efforts at factory inspection. The relative vigor or feebleness of the proletarian body attested to the effectiveness of anti-sweatshop regulation and, more broadly, to the strength of the labor movement. Similarly, weak bodies justified union organizing. Thus, when the ILGWU issued a call in awkward verse to male members of Local 6, the union of embroidery workers, it cited workers' physical decline as the justification for organizing. With a strong union there would be no need for direct confrontation with manufacturers: "Come, listen to my plea—we must be preparing, for our health is wearing;/ With your assistance there will be no resistance by the bosses' association to plans of negotiation."[26] At the same time, ILGWU leaders echoed female strikers in pointing to women's weak bodies to justify their inclusion in unions: "The girls' thin and poorly nourished bodies . . . testified at what cost to themselves . . . they were working."[27]

With the proletarian movement on the ascent, workers' bodies could be strong, strengthened in body and mind. Even on the masthead of its official journal, the ILGWU listed "longer life" alongside "higher wages" as the benefits of unionization.[28] Similarly, the AR rested on "the conviction that the wage earner's lot might be one of everlasting well-being and good health, if the working class were . . . a power in society and exhorted an effective influence in shaping the conditions of work and pay."[29] Thus, when Baruch Charney Vladek, the socialist editor of the *Jewish Daily Forward* and a close ally of the ILGWU and the AR, was asked to list what he would include in organized labor's pavilion at the 1936 World's Fair, he listed a scale model of the AR's Liberty Sanitarium for consumptive workers alongside reproductions of sweatshops. The juxtaposition, he seemed to suggest, would demonstrate the ability of the trade union movement to shield physically its members from the ravages of sweated work.[30] At the same time, it is important to note the gendered implications of Vladek's comparison. Women and men labored together in sweatshops, much to the chagrin of unionists and social reformers. But, as will be seen, the Liberty Sanitarium, based on understandings of tuberculosis as a disease that threatened male breadwinners, treated men almost exclusively.

Gendering the Workers' Body and the
Representation of Occupational Illness

Workers' health and the curing of Jewish workers' occupational diseases lay at the heart of the AR's and the ILGWU's organizing plans after 1909. But neither organization immediately selected a single strategy. Rather, male and female members proposed different plans for organizing around issues of health. As male and female Jewish workers and unionists advanced different ideas about what it meant to be a worker, they espoused dramatically different strategies. The study of how they selected or rejected particular plans demands an exploration of how workers examined their own bodies. In conjunction with public health officials, male and female workers and unionists claimed to have discovered not only evidence of labor's hazards, but also manifestations of sexual difference. Women generally agreed that they were different kinds of victims of the sweatshop than men.[31] Inspections served to codify, in seeming medical fact, men's and women's different physical experiences at work and men's preeminence on the shop floor.[32]

The centrality assigned here to the process of inspecting female and male workers' bodies draws on recent feminist texts that examine the gendered nature of scientific discourse in confirming sexual difference. Such studies foreground the study of the subjectivity of bodies. The body must be understood, not just as flesh and blood, but also as a subject of social anxiety and discussion. Bodies are inscribed with and, indeed, produced by the historical conditions of social order.[33] The cultural representation of male and female Jewish workers' bodies as decrepit cannot be separated from the diagnosed prevalence of disease among garment workers or from the languages of public health and germs used to uncover illness. After all, for workers and inspectors, the diseases uncovered through examinations confirmed their shared beliefs about the dangers of garment work and the physical reality of sexual difference. In fact, neurasthenia, an alleged nerve ailment described as rampant among Eastern European Jewish workers (as well as middle- and upper-class women) has since been reevaluated by doctors and historians as an imaginary disease grounded in the era's ideologies of gender and class.[34] Medical inspections imbued with scientific authority the gendered social order of the workplace that left women in subordinate positions on the shop floor and in unions.[35]

The way that male and female Eastern European Jewish workers inspected their bodies and discovered connections between work, disease, and sexual difference depended heavily on a Progressive Era language of public health, hygiene, and germ theory.[36] In the years after 1909, workers and their allies used ideas about the causes of proletarian illness and physical weakness to support a number of causes. Male workers and inspectors employed such images to justify the regulation of the garment industry. Women workers and the WTUL used them to confirm their seriousness and legitimacy as workers.

Medical inspections, therefore, were naturally a cross-class project that could support these different aims. Although Jewish proletarian associations had long sought to comprehend the baleful effects of labor on their own—the AR, for example, conducted annual surveys of causes of death among its members in order to trace the levels of work-related trauma—their most systematic surveys were conducted with the help of public health officials.[37] Beginning in 1913, soon after the signing of protocols in the waist and whitegood trades, the ILGWU, in association with the United States Public Health Services (PHS) and the Manufacturers' Association in the cloakmaking branch of the industry, conducted a thorough survey of male and female, mostly Jewish garment workers in order to understand the harmful effects of garment work.[38] With the cooperation, encouragement, and assistance of the ILGWU, the PHS inspected about 3,000 garment workers, over 90 percent of whom were Jewish, including 2,000 males and 1,000 females. Inspections took place at the offices of the JBSC.[39]

The survey they produced proved crucial for the union, providing much of the evidence of the physical effects of work that it used for more than a decade to encourage health programs and sanitary reform. The survey, in short, used the language of science to prove what Jewish garment workers and their allies had long insisted: proletarian, immigrant bodies displayed the ill effects of garment labor.[40] The PHS survey acted as the cornerstone for the ILGWU's ongoing inspections. Between 1911 and 1924, the ILGWU conducted inspections of 50,000 garment workers and compiled records to present a detailed picture of male and female garment workers' health.[41] Inspection work filtered throughout the ILGWU, and by the end of the decade several important locals, like the large Locals 1 and 10, conducted health inspections of their members.[42]

The PHS inspections can be understood as active processes that brought together workers, policymakers, doctors, and bosses. Through inspection, they all sought to prove links between work, disease, and gender. The process of inspection—the act of deciding on and agreeing to inspections, the selection of human subjects, the physical act of examination, and the interpretation and later use of data—became a form of public performance that connected the medical visions of policymakers to the proletarian concerns of Eastern European Jewish immigrants. Even before the publication of results, the scale of inspections confirmed the perception of the physical dangers of garment work and of the diseased condition of Jewish immigrant workers. The exchange between doctors and worker/patients allowed garment workers to voice physical complaints and to have those complaints recognized and named scientifically. During the examinations, "each person was . . . asked to state any complaints."[43] In the PHS survey, 69.7 percent of garment workers (men and women in about equal numbers) reported specific physical problems. Most listed more than one.[44] At the same time, the inspections uncovered different patterns of illness among male and female Jewish garment workers that men and women insisted confirmed presupposed understandings of sexual difference.[45]

The process of inspection, heightened in its significance by the growing social authority of doctors, was both influenced by and verified gendered preconceptions about men and women's contrasting relationships to garment labor. In particular, the way that male and female Jewish workers, unions, and inspectors described the effects of work on women's bodies reveals a shared belief between Jewish men and women that they represented different kinds of workers. Jewish women's temporary status was reflected in the complaints they made and their proposals for reform. The PHS recognized the importance of women's temporary status when they claimed that women's garment work was "provisional only, the expectation of marriage and the establishment of a home being always in the background." As a result, the PHS argued, women had different "physique," complaints, and general health than their male counterparts.[46] Indeed, inspectors regarded male bodies as the point of reference. Men's bodies were the normative bodies of "workers" and women's were the exception. Perhaps this was part of the reason that the PHS examined twice as many men as women. Thus, inspectors described women's injuries as different from men's and not men's injuries as different from women's.

In describing men's bodies as the norm, the PHS seemed to suggest that women's temporary status as factory garment workers was inscribed on the body. Union inspectors also noted unique damage caused to the female body. ILGWU inspectors pointed out that women suffered from garment work in different ways: "It is probable that women suffer more from the effect of the stooping posture, the whir and noise of the machines and the eye strain than men workers." George Price, the director of the JBSC, also argued that women suffered more than men from the long hours of sitting and sewing.[47] In particular, they raised special concern about damage that work caused to sexual organs. As the ILGWU worried: "The effect of constant work or machine sewing upon the pelvic organs is also probably an important factor . . . in the many pelvic complaints from which they are known to suffer."[48] Jewish women themselves worried about the effects of work on their reproductive functions. In the PHS survey, women's most common complaint concerned menstruation, especially dysmenorrhea (painful menstruation). Fully one-fifth of female

garment workers complained of dysmenorrhea.[49] Women's dual and competing identities as transient workers and "shop girls" waiting for marriage and
childbirth were etched on their bodies. Accordingly, women workers complained of and health inspectors diagnosed sexual impediments.

In contrast, when the PHS inspected male workers' bodies, they generally
uncovered illnesses that diminished their ability to labor and to provide for families. The PHS cited tuberculosis as "undoubtedly the most important disease
among garment workers," even though only 3.11 percent of men and 0.9 percent of women had the disease. The special significance, they suggested, lay
in the fact that the illness undermined men's ability to work. Male Jewish workers worried especially about contracting tuberculosis. In fact, the PHS noted
that it probably diagnosed inordinately high levels of infection because of the
number of workers, especially men, who actively sought inspections because
they feared the disease.[50] Coughing, among the tell-tale signs of tuberculosis,
was one of the most common complaints of male workers. In a notable contrast, almost 11 percent of male workers, but only 2.1 percent of female workers, complained of coughs.[51]

If individual male workers used the survey to authenticate their own fears
about tubercular infection, the Jewish labor movement also employed the survey as evidence for their argument that men's roles as breadwinners made
them more vulnerable to tuberculosis than women. The mostly male leadership of both the ILGWU and the AR anguished about their male members contracting tuberculosis. The union and the association regarded consumption as
a festering disease that reduced or obliterated men's ability to labor, and both
groups considered tuberculosis a male disease. If the diseases the ILGWU worried about for women were pelvic and menstrual disorders, the danger that
faced men, they argued, was tuberculosis. Almost a decade after the survey's
publication, the ILGWU still quoted it in their official journal to support their
representation of tuberculosis as a men's disease and as a threat to male breadwinners: "Men, in much greater proportion than women, are at work outside
the home—physical, laborious work is more their lot."[52]

Male leaders of the AR and the ILGWU insisted that men's and women's
different ailments resulted from their different relationships to work. Men's
lifetime of labor and providing for families, in contrast to women's limited stay
in garment shops before marriage, rendered men especially susceptible to consumption. After all, the AR declared, consumption emerged only after years of
labor: "Tuberculosis is a chronic disease. The seeds sown in childhood may
not bear fruit . . . until adult life. The disease may be latent (asleep) for many
years before it 'wakes up' and becomes discoverable."[53] Men's permanence
as wage workers and their labor in potentially poor conditions was reflected

in their high rate of tuberculosis, as the ILGWU insisted: "Tuberculosis is unduly prevalent among garment workers, especially among males. Factors influencing that great prevalence . . . are apparently their greater average age, longer time in the industry, the high percentage of males with families dependent upon them, thus leading to self-denial on the part of the breadwinner . . . to earn high wages for themselves and their families."[54]

When the leadership of the ILGWU and the AR, as well as the health inspectors working with the union, examined male workers, they primarily sought to pinpoint the signs of consumption that might hamper men's ability to labor and to provide for their families. They noted male workers' stooped, pale, and emaciated physique and worried about the onslaught of tuberculosis, especially given the stress of earning a family wage. The pressure of providing for families, they argued, pushed male workers beyond their physical capabilities and helped bring latent consumption to the surface. The PHS suggested that higher tuberculosis rates for men partially resulted from the "unusual exertion" of male workers to provide for "others dependent upon them."[55] The family wage represented, the PHS suggested, "in the case of males . . . an added element of overstrain which in itself would predispose to acquiring tuberculous infection by diminishing vital resistance."[56] Men alone faced particular work responsibilities that made them vulnerable to the workers' disease, the "proletarishe krankheit" (proletarian sickness).

As they argued that disease had gendered roots, male and female workers and union leaders worried that it could disrupt the sexual division of labor. This, then, was the scientific basis for the notion that garment work and sweatshop labor was a "family problem." Tuberculosis, the ILGWU and the AR worried, threatened men's ability to earn a family wage, whereas women's illness hampered their ability to bear children. If male workers contracted tuberculosis, they might be unable to return to jobs and to provide for their families. As the ILGWU claimed: "The worker's efficiency is lowered when suffering from an incipient disease . . . [and] while efficiency is lowered the disease spreads and becomes aggravated."[57] Tuberculosis proved so immediately debilitating that it prevented male workers from being productive enough to earn a family wage. For both male and female garment workers and unionists, the body came to display men's and women's different relationship to and understandings of labor.

The "Organization of Happiness" and the Curing Debate

PHS inspectors claimed to have found the evidence of gender-specific occupational disease. The results of their inspections influenced how male and female Jewish workers arrived at contrasting ideas about how to cure occupational diseases caused by work in sweatshops. Male workers and leaders generally advanced plans that sought to protect men's ability to labor and to earn a family wage. They celebrated the ability of the workers' movement to rehabilitate male workers so that they could return to work, whether as a result of the AR's health insurance, sickness benefits, and sanitarium or the ILGWU's tuberculosis and sickness relief funds. In turn, women argued for a broader vision of curing. However, their plans remained constrained by their acceptance of difference that assigned them subordinate roles on the shop floor. They sought to cure the female proletarian body with an eye not simply to returning an invalid to work, but to forging enduring ties between workers and their unions. Such connections, they insisted, should not be sundered when women left the workplace. Rather, efforts at curing should aim at proletarians, male or female, whether current or former workers. Male workers, in contrast, when they described a curative role for the workers' movement, generally meant protections that men could rely on when the family wage was threatened. In the end, men and women reached a tenuous compromise. Male workers and leaders of the ILGWU encouraged some (but certainly not all) women's efforts to create a broad curative program for the union.[58]

Again, as in the debate over women's ability to claim the benefits of the title "worker," women workers generally acknowledged the social reality that they would only work in the factory until marriage. As much as their male counterparts, female Jewish workers and trade union organizers appeared to recognize publicly their impermanence as garment workers. Even after the shirtwaistmakers' Local 25 emerged from the strikes of 1909 as the biggest local in the ILWGU, its male leaders, female organizers, and female rank and file noted the overwhelming turnover as a result of marriage: "Thus the working population changes every few years. After working three of four seasons some of them may leave the industry to get married."[59] Female organizers and activists in Local 25 also claimed that women left work with marriage while men remained at the workbench: "It should be remembered that men, even when they marry, come to work the very next day. . . . For girls, however, particularly Jewish girls, the marriage license is an automatic withdrawal from the union. In plain words, when a girl marries she replaces shop work by housework."[60] While Local 25's female activists were the strongest advocates in the Jewish labor movement for health care for women, they hardly seemed to challenge the gendered medical view of female workers' bodies as suffering from diseases centered around reproduction. Jewish women did not claim equality with men either as workers or as sweatshop victims. Rather, in acknowledging sexual difference, they struggled to create institutions that would serve what they considered their particular needs and would treat their specific illnesses. They, too, suffered, but in different ways.[61]

In recognizing that women's experience of garment wage work differed dramatically from men's, Local 25's female organizers argued for health care strategies that extended far beyond the workplace to address illnesses that might threaten female proletarians' domestic roles after leaving wage labor. Such strategies, they suggested, not only would help women survive their years and seasons in garment work healthy enough to bear and raise children, but also would allow female former garment workers the tangible benefits of the workers' movement. One female organizer argued that women had dual identities as workers and future mothers: "She is not only a woman, but a worker in the shop. She belongs to the female sex, but she is also a proletarian. Womenhood, motherhood, machine . . . this is the trinity which controls the fate of the working girl."[62] In acknowledging female workers' futures as mothers, she insisted that as workers, mothers, and industrial victims, women needed special kinds of care.

Women workers, especially those concentrated in Local 25, sought curing strategies with goals less concrete than simply returning workers to the shop floor. Rather, they sought a broad range of services designed to combat the work-related stresses and illnesses of female wage earners as well as the diseases of female former workers. They demanded care for when they became mothers and protection of their reproductive abilities while still workers. According to a report in the ILGWU's official journal, after the strikes of 1909 and 1913, Local 25 was "seething with life and unrest" as its members advanced many different strategies of organizing around health care.[63] Members urged cooperative housing, communal living, holiday resorts, and leisure activities, including worker-owned libraries. The underlying goals of these disparate programs were rest, recuperation, and education for female workers. Even plans and programs not immediately medical were frequently presented as central to the protection of body and health. In effect, Local 25's organizing strategy recognized the continuum of its members' lives from the workplace to the home and argued, therefore, that the union had a duty to safeguard women's health in their roles as workers and mothers: "And for the woman of the working class there remain in addition to all the questions of education, of recreation, of health the eternal problem of womanhood and motherhood. We are concerned, therefore, not only with the 'conquest of bread' but with the organization of happiness."[64]

The "organization of happiness" in Local 25 was a jubilant proclamation of social power. Female workers described the involvement of the union in all elements of women's lives during and after their years of labor as a way to counteract broadly the deleterious physical effects of garment labor. As Fannia Cohn, one of the leading architects of Local 25's broader plans of health, recalled, women's visions of curing often focused on the recreational: "We considered play as important . . . for health. Our mottoes became 'Playing, Thinking, and Acting' and 'Develop Mind and Body.' We wanted to stimulate in our people a healthy, hearty response to life."[65] Women's efforts to "develop mind and body" and to achieve the "organization of happiness" remained grounded in understandings of sexual difference. Female unionists like Cohn urged special methods to cure women's illnesses beyond the shop floor. Thus, Local 25 planned a series of outings for its members, for example, as a way to counteract the effects of "sedentary occupations, like those of the needle trades where the blood has little chance to circulate and vital organs are cramped."[66]

Some of Local 25's most ambitious projects never progressed. The idea of cooperative housing, among others, did not advance beyond rudimentary experimentation.[67] Others were successful enough that, ironically, they were seized from the local and placed under the control of the international. In 1918, Local 25 purchased a sylvan resort to rest the battered bodies of workers and their families, a place where, as one worker noted, "jaded worn-out bodies and spirits are renovated, rebuilt and recharged with energy and vitality."[68] The resort, formerly the Forest Park Hotel, was renamed Unity House and became the central element of Local 25's broad vision of curing not just obviously ill workers, but all "exploited workers" and their families.[69] As the Local's president told vacationers at Unity House, the resort realized a "long cherished hope . . . that the union might someday have a big farm where members could . . . build up their strength." One visitor also celebrated the resort as an experiment in trade union organizing beyond caring for workers in the shops: "Members of Local No. 25 may well rejoice in this for it indicates that their summer home is what they want it to be—not merely a better summer boarding house in one of the beautiful spots in the world, but an experiment, an example of what an organization can do towards solving problems other than those of hours and wages."[70]

Unity House received frequent public mention from the ILGWU's male leadership. Regular reports on activities filled the pages of *Justice*, the ILGWU's official newspaper. Soon after the resort's opening, the ILGWU General Executive Board asked Local 25 to open the doors to all international members and their families, and by 1922 the international itself, rather than the local, ran Unity House.[71] The board praised it as "one of the healthiest signs of the vitality and strength of our organization."[72] Yet when the predominantly male members of the board praised the "vitality and strength" fostered by Unity

House, they generally referred only to how it benefited the union, not to the resort's curative value. The male leadership seemed to view the resort largely as a recreational resort for workers and their families and never accepted it as a means to protect workers' bodies. Recreation for such male leaders remained distinct from health care. As the leadership editorialized: "We are proud that our Union has been the first Union in America to start social . . . activities."[73]

Still, if the male leadership of the ILGWU did not recognize the curative value of Unity House, the union as well as the AR came to promote significant protections for female workers beyond the shop floor. As the ILGWU and the AR moved from decentralized curing initiatives, run by locals in the ILGWU and by branches in the AR, to centralized health centers, they both expanded the scope of health protections. Specifically, they introduced comprehensive gynecological care and women's clinics, suggesting the profound impact of women's particular visions of curing. This was most evident in the ILGWU where women, organized in Local 25, proved especially vocal.

Gendering Work, Gendering Curing

As women moved into the ILGWU in large numbers after 1909, they were able to advance understandings of what it meant to rehabilitate workers' bodies. Far more than in the AR, ILGWU women claimed a significant role in shaping the organizational response to the ill effects of garment work. While the AR focused largely on protecting the family wage and the health of male breadwinners, the ILGWU created a dual system of health care. The union simultaneously sought to protect men's efforts to earn a family wage and to recognize women's broader vision of curing former and current workers and their families.

Sickness benefit funds represented the first examples of protections for the male wage earner. The AR took the lead in providing such medical benefits. From its initial founding, sickness benefit funds lay at the heart of the AR's vision of socialism based on practical services, and its members consistently pushed the association to provide more generous support. At the 1908 convention, for example, one New York City branch proposed that members receive benefits after only one day's sickness. However, despite this long ideological commitment to sickness benefit funds, the AR developed its programs mostly after 1910. In 1906, only 804 members applied for benefits. In contrast, in 1911, in response to 5,145 claims, the AR paid out $118,770.[74]

The ILGWU, especially its male-dominated locals, followed the lead of the AR in setting up sickness benefit funds, especially for members suffering from tuberculosis, the men's disease. Morris Sigman, soon to be a president of the international but then the manager of Local 35, was one officer who called for some form of sickness benefits for male workers. "Men with pale and emaciated faces, infected with consumption," he recalled, "would come to the office [of Local 35] and beg and cry for help."[75] As early as 1913, majority-male Locals 35 (pressers), 9 (finishers and tailors), and 23 (skirtmakers) had all started sickness and consumption relief funds. Between 1913 and 1922, Local 35 alone distributed $19,672 in benefits, principally to consumptive members.[76]

The sickness and tuberculosis benefit funds of both the AR and the ILGWU depended heavily on a discourse of protecting the male breadwinning wage. Their aim was to return male workers as quickly as possible to their jobs. When the male leadership of the ILGWU described the funds as a "worker's mainstay in life," they generally referred to the safeguarding of men's roles as breadwinners. The ILGWU's General Executive Board declared that when a male worker fell ill, the union must assume the role of breadwinner, if only to preclude the possibility of wives having to return to garment labor: "The union . . . must make it possible for him to come to the union whenever he is in trouble and distress and leave in its hand the fortunes and destiny of his wife and children."[77] Similarly, the official historian of the AR recalled the advantages to sick male members when the association paid tuberculosis and sickness benefits directly to their families: "The knowledge that his dependents are not left wholly without support . . . contributes no little to the patients' peace of mind."[78] In effect, the union was formalizing a shop floor custom in which male workers would work more hours and give the extra wages to the wife of a male coworker ill with tuberculosis.[79]

As a result, when the male leadership of the ILGWU and the AR planned sickness and tuberculosis benefit funds, they focused primarily and sometimes exclusively on male workers. In an extreme example, in 1918, when the ILGWU leadership urged the international's convention to adopt a unionwide sickness and death fund, they proposed it only for male members. Women would benefit only as the wives and widows of male workers. Upon a male worker's death, "widows . . . should be immediately and without delay paid."[80] Similarly, in 1910 when the AR finally opened its long anticipated sanitarium in Liberty, New York, it initially offered care only to male Jewish consumptive workers.[81] Soon after the sanitarium's opening, a female garment worker stricken with consumption flabbergasted the AR and the sanitarium directors by applying for care. Not a single bed had been set aside for female patients.[82] The sanitarium quickly reorganized their bed arrangement and admitted the female patient. Nonetheless, the number of female patients cared for at the Liberty Sanitarium remained strikingly low.[83] In 1911 the sanitarium sheltered 123 men but only 9 women and two years later it provided care for 104 men and only 4 women.[84]

At the same time, the AR provided benefits to family members of male sanitarium patients so wives would not have to return to labor.[85]

Locals dominated by women tended to shy away from sickness and consumption benefit funds, as they ceded to the union the position of breadwinner. In fact, at the same time that Local 25 founded Unity House and experimented with cooperative living, it postponed starting a sickness fund for lack of interest and money.[86] A gendered compromise around curing that blended certain elements of women's visions of curing with protections of men's roles as breadwinners emerged when the ILGWU, and to a lesser extent the AR, moved to create centralized programs of curing, health care, and health education. These programs emphasized health clinics, not sickness benefit funds.

In accepting conceptions of sexual difference that seemed to confirm men's roles as breadwinners, women were able to win a range of health protections when the AR and the ILGWU founded clinics for their members. This was especially true in the ILGWU, where women were collectively stronger. Nonetheless, similar elements did appear in the AR's organizing strategies. After all, male workers generally came to recognize that women suffered for their labor, albeit in different ways than men. By 1920, the discourse around curing occupational diseases shifted perceptibly as both the ILGWU and the AR began offering a wider range of medical treatments. In 1919, the AR began providing basic medical care when it founded its Medical Department, which catered to worker members as well as to their families. In the first year alone, its doctors conducted 60,000 visits, and by 1922 the department opened a permanent clinic on Irving Place in lower Manhattan.[87] In a similar fashion, the ILGWU united the largest local's sickness funds when it opened its own health clinic, the Union Health Center, in late 1920.[88]

The AR's Medical Department and, to a greater extent, the ILGWU's Union Health Center represented significant compromises between the different visions of curing advanced by male and female organizers, local leaders, and workers. With the opening of medical clinics, the AR and ILGWU consciously created forms of care based on gendered perceptions of work. Accordingly, returning men to the workplace remained a central objective. The Union Health Center offered frequent talks about preventing illness on the shop floor, such as a presentation about the "daily dozen," a set of exercises for garment workers.[89] Tuberculosis, the men's disease, still represented a particular concern. In 1922 alone, the center hosted several weeklong programs with exhibits and talks. In addition, the center's doctors conducted intensive medical examinations to alert workers to the danger of consumption, to screen potential consumptives, and to discuss treatments.[90]

Concern about tuberculosis victims remained tied to the protection of the family wage. One talk even promised workers that "if [tuberculosis] is caught early enough . . . the patient should be able to return to industry and continue to support his family."[91] The Health Center published stories boasting about helping workers recover enough to return to labor. In the pages of the ILGWU's official newspaper, the center celebrated the story of a "short, wizened little man . . . with [a] wife" whose illness prevented him from working. Through the efforts of the Health Center, "he had gained 17 pounds in weight, looked stronger, healthier, and happier." The natural order of industry and family was restored when the newly reinvigorated worker immediately sought employment again.[92]

Although a primary role of the Union Health Center and the Medical Department remained to provide care for male workers in order to return them quickly and healthy to the shop floor, they also offered a more expansive vision of curing for families and for married women no longer laboring in the factory. In 1924, for example, the Union Health Center sought to expand its services beyond male workers, proclaiming the "need of extending our service to the members of the families, to the children and wives of the members of our organization."[93] The ILGWU and AR presented this vision by recognizing what the Union Health Center labeled "diseases of women." Both the Union Health Center and the Medical Department started women's and gynecological clinics. Such clinics formed the core of the Union Health Center's and Medical Department's wider vision of curing and a major part of the care given to female workers. Indeed, in 1924, 746 of the 6,429 examinations given at the Union Health Center were gynecological exams.[94] In reference to the need for gynecological examinations and, perhaps in a subtle reminder, to the expectation that they were seeking a husband, the center exhorted women: "WOMEN WORKERS, TAKE STOCK OF YOUR PHYSICAL ASSETS AND LIABILITIES NOW."[95] Thus, the ILGWU's women's clinic urged "women workers" to "have their body overhauled."[96] In an illustrative example of the widening of the discourse around curing occupational ailments, the Union Health Center and later the Medical Department expanded their public talks to include presentations about health and hygiene in the home. At its popular Friday night lecture series, the Union Health Center presented talks about "Married Life," "Health and the Child," and "Indoors and Outdoors," alongside those about "Labor and Health."[97]

The introduction of women's clinics focusing in particular on women's reproductive concerns, within centers that concentrated as well on the prevalence of tuberculosis, reflected gendered representations of men's and women's proletarian bodies. It was this reiteration of sexual difference that facilitated the inclusion of broader visions of curing, even in the AR where the voices of female workers reverberated more quietly than in the ILGWU. The Union Health Center and Medical Department were able to smooth distinctions between life in and beyond the shop floor by identifying women workers as the link to a proletarian world beyond the shop walls. After all, the Union Health Center suggested, women would soon leave the workplace to raise families. Thus, in the same place and clinic where the center treated women workers, they also cared for mothers, babies, and children.[98]

"The Interdependence of Health and a Strong Trade Union"

About twenty years after the founding of the Union Health Center, Fannia Cohn recalled its significance in bringing health care to male and female garment workers. For Cohn, a garment worker turned union official, the Union Health Center was a crucial institution in reversing the effects of sweated work. After all, she declared, "Many physical illnesses have their source in an unjust economic system." For unionists like Cohn, curing programs were a primary achievement of a trade union movement that through the struggle against the sweatshop had come to recognize the "interdependence of health and a strong trade union."[99] The Union Health Center best represented the primacy of health care in the organizing strategy of the Eastern European Jewish immigrant labor movement in its motto: "IN SANITATION AND HEALTH AS WELL AS IN ECONOMICS, THE SALVATION OF THE WORKERS DEPENDS ON THE WORKING CLASS ITSELF."[100] Other Jewish workers and leaders also praised the structures of curing created between 1909 and 1920 as major milestones of the Jewish workers' movement. Joseph Weinberg, the AR's president, celebrated the Liberty Sanitarium: "The heart is filled with joy and enthusiasm when we remember that all this is the creation of Jewish workingmen."[101] Pauline Newman, the garment worker who became an organizer and, later, worked at the Union Health Center, praised the ILGWU for its "achievements . . . in the field of sanitation and health" and cited the "phenomenal" success of the Union Health Center in caring for "the health of the workers."[102]

The pride of these labor leaders reflected their understandings of unions as associations that should counteract the overall dangerous effects of sweated work on health and family all the while reinforcing the gender roles of men and women. Workers and unionists, like Newman or Cohn, boasted that they had helped build a trade union whose success could be measured by looking at the bodies of its members. Health care cured the sweatshop victim. Curing programs represented the goals of the mainstream of the Eastern European Jewish immigrant labor movement, and it was in this context that women were most successful in having their roles as workers recognized by male workers and unionists. Women were able to insert themselves into conversations about health care for two reasons. First, they bowed to dominant languages about sexual difference within anti-sweatshop campaigns and acknowledged their impermanence as wage workers. Second, especially in Local 25, they enjoyed strength in numbers.

Women were not able, however, to convert numbers into official positions of union leadership. Still, they tried. At the same time that women advanced programs for curing women's occupational diseases, they began collectively to demand positions of union leadership and to face the harsh opposition of male unionists. Yet women were hindered in their efforts by their own language of opposition, a language that constantly ran up against representations of women wage earners as temporary. The final chapter examines the political and cultural limits of women's organizing by exploring their failed efforts to gain leadership positions within the ILGWU before and after World War I. Their efforts starkly revealed the limits and contradiction of the anti-sweatshop coalition: it concentrated power in the hands of a few male leaders in order to preserve relations with inspectors and government officials. At the same time, it left women little room—or words—to complain about their circumstances. The institutions of the anti-sweatshop coalition, it turned out, could not withstand the crisis unleashed by women's revolt.

Seven

"Swallowed Up in a Sea of Masculinity"

Factionalism and Gender Struggles in the ILGWU, 1909–1934

On July 10, 1925, male and female predominantly Jewish garment workers filled Yankee Stadium. They had not come to watch a cloakmaker turned catcher or an operator turned outfielder. Rather, their mass attendance at a rally in the stadium was a powerful public cry for union democracy and rank-and-file participation in the ILGWU. The Communist-led opposition within the union organized the gathering and argued that the 40,000 garment workers at the Yankee Stadium rally proved the extent of rank-and-file ire toward the ILGWU's anti-Communist leadership and their practice of centralized control and decision making.[1] One garment worker iterated the concerns about the established leadership that led him and other workers to attend the rally; the old leadership of the ILGWU "never worked for them."[2] The ILGWU leadership, socialist in sympathy but eager to maintain the cross-class ties that supported anti-sweatshop efforts, questioned the attendance figures and even hinted that thousands of non-garment Communist workers swelled the numbers at the stadium. The rank-and-file movement, they derided, represented little more than a mirage created by a few Communist insurgents doing the bidding of Moscow.[3]

The movement of disgruntled Jewish trade unionists who gathered in Yankee Stadium had been growing for more than a decade, although its leaders had not always been Communists. The movement developed as much out of female workers' frustration with their subordinate roles in the ILGWU and in its anti-sweatshop efforts as it did out of fascination with the Bolshevik Revolution.[4] Indeed, long before Lenin became a familiar name to New York's Jewish garment workers, female unionists were voicing the first rumblings of rank-and-file discontent, as they sought to translate the sense of legitimacy they claimed as unionists and women workers in the mass general strikes of 1909 and 1913 into real leadership positions. Communism provided female and, later, male rank-and-file unionists with a powerful language they could use to critique the structure of the immigrant Jewish labor movement and the anti-sweat-shop coalition. They turned to languages of class empowerment for more than its radicalism. Given women's acknowledgment of notions of sexual difference, class, not gender, seemed the most effective language of revolt.

The first factional opposition in the ILGWU emerged, not after 1918, but before World War I, and was a women's, not a Communist, opposition. While women began voicing anger at their subordinate roles in the ILGWU after 1913, the Communist opposition did not emerge until the early 1920s. It slowly gained strength until 1925, when Communist leaders were elected to most of the major positions in New York City ILGWU locals. At the same time, Communists were enjoying a growing influence in the Arbeter Ring (Workmen's Circle).

Nowhere, though, was the struggle over Communism more pointed and violent than in the ILGWU, and nowhere were the effects of this struggle on the anti-sweatshop coalition more visible than in the ILGWU. Communist strength declined in the union quickly after a 1926 cloakmakers' strike that ended in defeat. Socialist unionists who opposed the Communists used the disastrous results of the strike to reclaim local officerships. Communists, however, did not surrender quietly. By 1927, they formed a breakaway union, the Needle Trades Workers Industrial Union, which battled the ILGWU for members. The struggles between the two unions often took the form of street brawls between paid gangsters. In the shadow of factional violence, working conditions declined and, by the end of the period, leaders from the rival unions were bemoaning the return of the sweatshop.[5]

That the descent into violent factionalism came at the same time that union leaders were admitting that sweatshops were returning to the industry is not coincidental. The rise of opposition movements in the 1910s and 1920s starkly revealed the restrictions and contradictions of the language that had sustained anti-sweatshop movements after 1910. The primacy of that gendered language of health, sanitation, and family had helped union leaders build strong ties with a range of powerful Progressive reformers, but had also hardened gendered inequality in the garment workplace and in garment unions. The focus on effective regulation had helped ensconce a few male leaders who might have espoused socialism, but shied away from a confrontational language of class conflict. A stable, centralized leadership could best guarantee standards of sanitation and, for these leaders, curing workers' bodies, not direct conflict with employers, was the most effective form of class struggle. By the late 1910s, with a changing workforce and an evolving industry, the ILGWU had many members, but its leaders had few devoted followers. As women and, later, also men struggled to voice their frustration, they found that they could not change the union and leave in place the institutions of the anti-sweatshop coalition. In fact, one of the earliest victims of factionalism was the Joint Board of Sanitary Control (JBSC).

The ILGWU has rightly been described as one of the few unions at this time to organize female workers. But women's enduring sense of sexual difference helped circumscribe the vocabulary they would use to demand active union leadership roles.[6] In the 1910s, women rhetorically sought roles in their union as female unionists, not simply as unionists. The conviction that women were temporary employees and that men were the normative workers was the foundation for a manly culture of unionism within the ILGWU. Even in the largely female Local 25, the top positions remained claimed by men.

Women expressed frustration at men's domination of the union and its masculinized atmosphere, but they rarely employed a language of gender equity to challenge men's monopoly on established union officer positions. Female Jewish garment workers tended instead to suggest new forms of unionism that demanded new types of leadership roles. Women, they claimed, could appropriately fill such positions. Women created an alternative community within the union that spawned non-traditional leadership opportunities. If women did not become local business managers, they organized lectures, shop floor clubs, and gatherings.[7] Long before the October Revolution in Russia began spawning legions of sympathizers in the United States, female rank-and-file trade unionists had begun demanding access to power, albeit in a form that seemed appropriate for women.[8]

Paradoxically, however, women's efforts to foster a safe space for themselves in the ILGWU still cultivated the seeds of revolt, especially in the politically charged years after World War I. They offered an implicit and sometimes explicit critique of a union leadership structure whose anti-sweatshop policies of sanitary control and reform tended to consolidate power in the hands of a few male officers. When women attacked the leadership structure of the ILGWU, they increasingly relied on a new language of class, not gender, empowerment. In employing contemporary languages of class radicalism, in particular Bolshevism, female dissidents argued that all rank-and-file workers, not simply women, needed broader access to union leadership. This was a new language of class power that contrasted with earlier languages of class, born in the sweatshop of the 1880s and 1890s that cast workers, not as the vanguard of revolution, but as victims of vampire bosses.

Visions of gender empowerment were profoundly limited by the persistence of ideas about sexual difference. In contrast, the possibilities of Bolshevism seemed limitless. In the immediate aftermath of World War I, the United States simmered with class conflict as general strikes paralyzed major industries and industrial centers. At the center of these disputes were Communist partisans. With the model of the Bolshevik Revolution fresh in the minds of workers who had immigrated from Russia, Communism might have seemed to offer more than alliances with reformers, especially at a time when the influence of Progressivism was ebbing.

Unfortunately, in the end, calls for union democracy and rank-and-file control worked to open up the potential for men's participation in union leadership while still restricting women's access. Representations of female workers as novice unionists and transients who should not serve as union officers remained unchallenged. Communist leaders, most of whom were also men, tended to distance their movement from the earlier women's opposition. The way the Communists interpreted and preformed democracy—the acting out of massive rank-and-file participation through large rallies—actually served to restrict further women's access to leadership roles. So, too, did increasingly violent factionalism, with its dependence on gangsters, limit women's participation. Indeed, for some male trade unionists and factional partisans, the violence of factionalism was a manly ritual.

Women recognized how their concerns had become lost and diluted within the world of factional strife. By the end of the period of factionalism, female trade unionists were again complaining about their limited role in the ILGWU's leadership structure. The persistence of their concerns across two decades suggests that women recognized that the left-right split had cloaked gendered concerns about women's roles in Jewish garment trade unions. At the same time, their protests suggest the inability of the leaders of the ILGWU to transcend or reexamine ideas of sexual difference, ideals of a sexual division of labor, and the manly, hierarchical structure of the union, all the while maintaining a cross-class anti-sweatshop coalition. As the union descended into factionalism, weakened reformers distanced themselves from the union and reinvigorated employers took the opportunity to move their factories out of New York. Those that stayed openly ignored sanitary regulations. As leaders on both sides of the factional split sought to make sense of a labor movement in decline and a coalition in shambles, they described a return of the sweatshop.[9]

From Female Worker to Female Unionist, 1909–1913

With the exception of the 1910 cloakmakers' strike, the ILGWU's major strikes in New York between 1909 and 1913 involved mostly female workers. As women vigorously advanced the cultural construct of the "woman worker," male rank-and-file and male ILGWU leaders increasingly admitted that female workers had a place in the union's ranks. They did not, however, offer women equal roles with men. Male union leaders reiterated their beliefs that women experienced work differently from men. They refused to acknowledge women simply as workers, but, in a manipulation of the language women used to gain access to unions in the first place, paternalistically labeled them "our women workers."[10] For male leaders, "our women workers" were mere novices who needed lessons and training to become disciplined, class-conscious unionists, in the model of the normative male worker. Through this linguistic isolation and marginalization of women workers, the union's male leadership outlined the circumscribed rank-and-file roles they considered appropriate for women.

During the strikes of 1909 and 1913, female workers in Local 25 as well as in other largely female trades, notably whitegoodsmaking, had flexed their newfound muscles to win industry-wide contracts that guaranteed them a place in the anti-sweatshop movement. The Dress and Waist Manufacturers' Association capitulated in the 1913 strike of female waistmakers by signing a contract that established a Protocol of Peace modeled after the one signed two years earlier in the principally male cloak industry.[11] In the same year, women wrapper, kimono, and housedress workers, organized in Locals 41 and 62, launched a general strike. This time, the victory did not come as easily for 12,000 female strikers. They struggled not only against powerful manufacturers' associations, but also against male local leaders who urged a weak settlement. Female rank and file rejected the first strike settlement by a two-thirds majority and the strike continued.[12] Within a month, the manufacturers' associations, as in the dress and waist industry, also agreed to an industry-wide Protocol of Peace that brought the trade under the purview of the JBSC.

Thus, women established themselves as a sizable block in the ILGWU and revitalized those locals where women composed the majority of members. The 1909 strike, for instance, transformed Local 25, the shirtwaistmakers' local. Before the strike, Local 25 sadly reported that it had fallen into a "precarious condition owing to loss of strikes and general crisis."[13] With the strike's conclusion, Local 25 emerged as one of the ILGWU's strongest locals, with over 10,000 members. By the end of the strike, Local 62 alone had grown to include 15,000 to 20,000 members.[14] As a whole, the 1913 strikes ushered almost 50,000 mostly female members into the ILGWU.[15]

The audacity as much as the material success of these strikes focused the international's attention on Locals 25, 41, and 62, and especially on their female rank and file. The international celebrated the victories of the women's locals and of female workers, especially waist and dressmakers. The ILGWU's official journal, for example, regularly carried items and reports about Local 25 and its activities.[16] As early as 1911, ILGWU leaders warned male workers to treat women as legitimate workers and fellow unionists, but, at the same time, they seemed to recognize sympathetically men's discomfort with the idea of women workers: "When will our men learn that the time has gone by when there was any chance of getting the women out of the trade? . . . It is not only justice but wisdom to accord women the same dignified consideration the men demand from each other."[17]

Despite such pleas, male union leaders still isolated female members as a separate group from men with different concerns, contrasting patterns of organizing, and fewer opportunities to advance to positions of power and prestige. Understandings of sexual difference pervaded male union leaders' mixed praise of female strikers. For example, starting in 1913, *The Ladies' Garment Worker*, then the ILGWU's official newspaper, carried a column dedicated to "Our Women Workers." The column offered trade union news aimed at female members and commentary on how and why to organize women. However, while the column proved useful to women workers in promoting their legitimacy as union members (often it was even written by female unionists), it still portrayed women unionists as novices in need of training and education.[18]

In the column and elsewhere, the ILGWU's male leadership roundly praised new female members, but in a fashion that belied their belief that women were immature trade unionists. They characterized women's organizing successes as efforts to learn to be workers and unionists. One column in the *Ladies' Garment Worker*, for instance, celebrated the women workers who "learned the importance and necessity of standing together."[19] Similarly, a poem by Max Danish, the business manager of Local 41, praised the "girls of all races, ages" who participated in the strikes of 1913. He saluted their bravery as strikers and seemingly acknowledged their roles as legitimate workers: "They who have dearly bought/ The right to collectively sell Labor and muscle and brain,/ Showed a wondering world they have not fought in vain." He couched his praise in descriptions of how women workers had learned trade union methods. Illustrating how such representations of female workers as novices served to protect the union's gendered hierarchy, he also offered a quiet reminder to women not to stray from their appropriate role in the union as rank and file: "They who've marched to the battle, . . . / Learned to stay in the ranks,— women of sixty, sixteen."[20]

Danish's combination of praise for female unionists he considered novices and subtle statements of women's correct union roles captures the way the male leaders welcomed women into the union. They belittled women's skills as unionists and insisted they remain as rank and file. Particularly illuminating is the ILGWU's use of fiction as propaganda to acknowledge women as workers (itself a shift in language from the years before 1909) and as trade unionists. At the same time, these didactic stories cautioned women to accept the union's structure and gendered hierarchy.

The union's official newspapers often printed stories that portrayed women strikers as novice unionists whose appropriate roles were as rank and file. One short story, plainly entitled "At the Shirt Waist Factory," appeared shortly after the 1909 strike and offered a combination of exhortation and maternalism in a parable about women's need to organize. It suggested that many women needed to be taught necessary trade union discipline. The story relates the efforts of Edna, an active shop floor leader, who teaches Beatrice, "a dressy" fellow worker absorbed in "fairy tales and dream books," the value of collective action. Edna threatens the factory manager that unless the factory hires another checker (the male foreman who punched the women's timecards), none of the women would pay late fines. The threats pay off as the next morning another checker appears. Edna urges Beatrice and the other women to "take up a collection of common sense among yourselves" and to depend on shop floor collective force rather than on dreams.[21] Echoing wealthy women's and Women's Trade Union League (WTUL) leaders' criticism of women workers as ghetto girls, the author describes Beatrice as a young girl distracted from the union by the temptations of fiction and fashion but who could learn the benefits of unionism. Edna, in contrast, is portrayed as a loyal union member who does not seek a leadership position beyond that of rank-and-file activist.[22]

Another story that appeared immediately after the successes of 1913 abandons the maternalism of "At the Shirt Waist Factory," but still reflects male workers' ambivalence toward female unionism. In "Mr. Skinner Climbs Down: A Story of a Girl's Strike and Its Success," no equivalents of Beatrice remain. In this ideal world of female unionism, the "girls" have become disciplined female trade unionists with legitimate shop floor concerns. Having learned the skills of organizing, they recognize their particular role in the union. The strike at Mr. Skinner's shop begins after Mr. Skinner insists that Molly work overtime. She refuses the overtime and Skinner tells her not to come back in the morning. The "girls" immediately realize their duty to a fellow worker and walk out with Molly. Molly, in turn, reluctantly acknowledges her duty as a shop floor leader: "But then she remembered that she had started the fight; she had made herself a leader, and she must be strong and fight on." Molly and her co-workers quickly join the union and, with the help of a male union leader, organize pickets. The girls' discipline is rewarded, first, when the union promises help and, second, when Skinner backs down and promises the end of overtime. The benefits of union appear as Molly tells her co-workers: "We've got this much now, and God knows what we'll get next."[23]

It was a successful "girls' strike" because class-conscious female workers accepted the leadership of male unionists. "Mr. Skinner Backs Down" seemed to portray women's activism as restricted to their own shop floor, and female leadership—like women's wage work—as temporary and born of necessity. Molly and her co-workers depend on the services of a male union official. The lesson seems to be that the union with its male leaders would help women when they organized in their own shop. However, many of the female workers empowered by the 1909–13 uprisings began advancing demands for female organizers. They insisted that the legitimacy they gained on the picket line should be translated into positions above the level of shop floor, rank-and-file leadership. The Mollys of the ILGWU, it appeared, wanted enduring power.

The Women's Opposition, 1914–1918

Some women who joined the ILGWU during the strikes of 1909 and 1913 formed a core of increasingly restless activists. Pauline Newman, for instance, echoed male leaders in characterizing the 1913 strikes as learning experiences for women workers, but she still insisted that the female strikers had become unionists capable of independent organizing. They did not need the paternalist leadership of male unionists or the maternalist guidance of the WTUL. As Newman editorialized in the pages of the *Ladies' Garment Worker*: "With what enthusiasm they took up the first lessons of the class struggle! Picketing, getting arrested, remaining nights in jail, arguing with their employers. . . . They had learned in the past five weeks to do their own thinking, thereby realizing their own power and to use it for themselves and their class."[24]

The core of female unionists that emerged especially during the 1913 strikes was concentrated in the three major women's locals, the shirtwaistmakers' Local 25, the wrapper and kimonomakers' Local 41, and the whitegoodsmakers' Local 62. Fannia Cohn and Pauline Newman worked as organizers in both the shirtwaist and whitegoods strikes. In Local 41 alone, they were joined by other women, such as Gussie Powsner, B. Spanier, Pauline Gerlman, and Pauline Berman. These women would remain active after the strikes. Gerlman became one of the few female members of Local 25's executive board and, later, emerged as a leader of the Communist opposition. Berman remained active in Local 41 throughout the 1920s, serving as shop chairlady, one of the few elected positions women held.[25] Female workers cited the strikes as the moment they became active in the union. Sarah Borenstein, for example, had been a quiet member of Local 25 for almost three years before the strike. During the strike, she proudly recalled, she served as a chairlady of one of the twenty strike halls. In her oral history, she proudly listed her extensive duties: nightly meetings, daily reports to the international, and ensuring that particular shops remained on strike.[26] Jennie Matyas also became active during the 1913 strike and sought to continue her leadership role after its conclusion: "When the strike was on, I was a member of the general strike committee. When the strike was over, I was a member of the executive committee of my local, and the grievance committee. When I finally did find a job, I was elected a shop steward."[27]

Even during the strikes, such female leaders and rank-and-file members vocally and sometimes physically protested the heavy-handed tactics of the male international leadership and, to a lesser extent, the outside advocacy of the WTUL. Especially in Local 62, rank-and-file women and the new cadre of leaders wrested control of their strike from male leaders at the crucial moment when male leaders presented an agreement with management. Women formed an effective caucus that defeated the proposed settlement of the whitegoods strike pushed by the male ILGWU and female WTUL leadership.[28] Garment worker Mary Goff Shuster, for example, remembered that women protested when they learned that the proposed contract did not contain provisions for shop chairlady, one of the few leadership positions open to women. They even physically assaulted their male leaders. Female strikers defeated a settlement and continued the strike in order to preserve a structure of women's rank-and-file leadership, as Shuster recalled: "We raised the devil in the halls, and we appealed to the members not to vote for it, to endorse it. . . . A few of our girls went up and they were pinching the leaders. They were pushing them and shouting at them. . . . At the big Webster Hall meeting, a few thousand people . . . voted against the agreement. And extended the strike from four weeks to six, and finally got our demands."[29]

At the same time that women workers resisted the direction of male union leaders, they also began rejecting the maternalism of the WTUL that stressed public virtue and depended on middle- and upper-class leadership. In the 1913 strikes, the female rank and file started to distance itself from WTUL leaders and organizers, most of whom were wealthy women, like J. Pierpont Morgan's daughter Anne. To be sure, the WTUL's maternalist leadership style continued to set much of the strategies of the 1913 strikes.[30] WTUL leaders, like Gertrude Barnum, served as organizers, and again the WTUL used its leaders' social status to garner middle-class public support and aid. Even Theodore Roosevelt associated himself with the strikers' cause.[31]

The WTUL's maternalism persisted in its depiction of the strikers as "tender charges of our boasted civilization" or as "young maidens, at the very loveliest age," as Barnum called them.[32] In the 1909 strike, female workers tended to describe themselves as "ladies." In 1913, activists portrayed the strikes as moments of growing up and coming of age as class-conscious workers. Jennie Matyas directly rejected the image of the strike as a strike of girls, declaring instead that during the strike she adopted the adult task of union activism: "Instantly, I began to see myself as a grown-up who would have to change the world for . . . the generations that would come after us."[33] Similarly, even as Pauline Newman saluted the "great amount of assistance that came from the Women's Trade Union League," she described the whitegoods strike as the moment that the female rank and file assumed roles as class-conscious workers and ILGWU members: "But . . . they have gladly accepted the urging invitation to join the school of solidarity—the Union."[34] Emblematic of the way that women rank-and-file trade unionists seized the initiative from their wealthier allies, the WTUL leadership announced in early 1914 that, rather than act as organizers themselves, they would start classes to train working-class female organizers.[35] Indeed, as Annelise Orleck notes, during and after the 1913 strikes, the WTUL was moving away from organizing immigrant "girls" to focus instead on native-born women.[36]

As they began pushing away from the WTUL, women workers insisted that they desired full inclusion and leadership positions of their own in ILGWU locals. Pauline Newman, for example, declared the need for female unionists willing and able to represent the union to other female workers: "We need speakers. We need girls who should be able to give expression to what they feel and think. . . . Why should not the locals of the International have a band of girl agitators? We need them."[37] At the same time, Newman included a subtle suggestion to rank-and-file women workers that they press male local leaders to increase efforts to organize women: "Get together your committee; if your local has no committee, see to it that they elect or appoint one. . . . Approach all the unorganized girls and urge them to join your organization."[38]

Female unionists like Newman soon confronted male leaders' continuing resistance to women's organizing. Despite the paeans of male ILGWU officials to the courage of new rank-and-file female unionists, male leaders seemed to pay little attention to organizing female workers. For some female activists, initial enthusiasm with the ILGWU gave way to discouragement and resignation. Rose Schneiderman, in fact, literally resigned, leaving the ILGWU to work full-time for the WTUL. Pauline Newman frequently expressed dissatisfaction with the international's commitment to organizing women. In a letter to Schneiderman, for example, Newman complained that the "international does not give a hang whether a local lives or dies." Similarly, she felt that the male leaders of the union would not listen to her complaints: "I can't expect any justice of the ignorant, stupid and conservative fools."[39]

Fannia Cohn echoed Newman when she sadly proclaimed that the ILGWU faced a "woman question."[40] Even those locals dominated numerically by women remained controlled by male leaders who generated and protected a masculinist atmosphere that, as one female organizer lamented, rendered female rank and file "apathetic and indifferent to the Union."[41] Thus, Cohn worried that because of the masculine nature of the union, "Women developed a decided feeling of inferiority which has not left them."[42] Newman put it even more dramatically. Women union members, she insisted, felt "swallowed up in a sea of masculinity."[43]

For workers and trade unionists like Cohn and Newman, the "woman problem" was the virtual drowning of women in a union culture still controlled by men. The sexualized atmosphere of the older sweatshop reemerged within the union and, again, it centered around women's temporary position as workers and their future as wives, not wage workers. Jennie Matyas, for instance, recalled that Benjamin Schlesinger, the union's president, denigrated waistmakers like herself as ignorant unionists whose primary role should be motherhood, not union leadership. "What do you women know of the economics of an industry?" she remembered that the president told them. "You'd better go home and have babies."[44] Newman similarly described Schlesinger as uninterested in women as trade unionists, only as sexual beings. As she recalled: "I think he was interested in women as women. I'm quite sure he was not interested in the intellect of women."[45] Cohn felt that other male leaders shared Schlesinger's prejudices. Male leaders, she argued, "naturally enough, have the same attitude towards women as men in every other walk of life."[46]

Female workers and the few female trade union leaders sought to create a physical space within the ILGWU safe for women, distanced from the overriding masculine culture. In the immediate aftermath of the conflict between male leaders and the female rank and file during the 1913 strikes, some women even proposed separate locals for women.[47] For one worker, women's locals would help the female rank and file overcome the weighty masculinity of the traditional local and permit women a louder, freer voice and access to tangible power. "Apart from the fact that the men necessarily bring into the meetings too much of distasteful masculinity, too much for many of the girls to stand, at any rate," she argued, "the women in their branches would have a better chance to assert themselves . . . and to govern themselves."[48]

Other female activists believed that they could create new kinds of leadership positions that would expand rank-and-file participation and provide new roles for women within the gender-mixed local. Female activists invented an alternative leadership structure that effectively ceded traditional leadership positions to men. As early as 1914, women leaders in Local 25, especially Cohn, promoted the lectures and activities of an "Educational Club" to facilitate the active participation of female rank and file. The Educational Club offered immensely popular concerts and lectures on topics ranging from politics to union history to literature. As the club proudly reported after one lecture: "The Friday night popular lectures . . . are proving a success. The attendance is large, and the interest, both in the lectures and the splendid musical programs that precede them, is very keen."[49] As they reported to the international's 1918 convention, the women leaders of the Educational Club carefully positioned education as the natural desire of "women and girls with a deep craving for literature and poetry."[50] This feminization of education programs insulated the Educational Club as a female space, free from the masculine culture of the union meeting and distinct from the other workings of the union.

Cohn and other leaders envisioned the Educational Club as space to articulate frustration with their roles in the union. For Cohn, education programs helped women replace their "inferiority feeling" with a "consciousness of power."[51] At the same time, female workers described education as a form of women's trade unionism. Jennie Matyas, for example, recognized the drive for education as a women's campaign: "It was under the influence mostly of the 'girls.' . . . The 'girls' in Local 25 . . . got it through the International."[52] In a paradox of women's activism, these leaders, in pushing for education programs, both acknowledged that men and women experienced trade union life in different ways and conceded that women could not hold the same leadership positions as men. For Cohn, female workers were drawn to the union and to union leadership positions when "we discuss something beside [sic] trade matters."[53]

From a Women's to a Communist Opposition, 1917–1921

Cohn recognized that given the tension between the frustrated female rank and file and male leaders over the masculinized culture of the union, the creation of a safe space for women still hinted at revolt. As women ceded traditional leadership positions to men, they still suggested that women workers, in some fashion, deserved a place in the leadership of the union. In fact, workers' education proved the only way in which some women, like Cohn, won a spot on the union's General Executive Board (GEB). Indeed, male officials adopted education programs as a valued part of the union, but, in many ways, effectively limited their potential as a secure place for female workers. The Workers' Education Program was wrenched from the untrustworthy grasp of Local 25 in the late 1910s and forcibly tamed by its adoption and inclusion into the union hierarchy. Nonetheless, the impulse that led to the introduction of education programs generated other associations of female workers between 1917 and 1921.[54]

During and immediately after World War I, women's activism in Local 25 became increasingly confrontational. In 1917, rank-and-file women in Local 25 organized the "Current Events Committee," a committee, like the Education Club, nominally dedicated to open discussion of politics and literature.[55] After a brief waistmaker strike that achieved mixed results in 1919, female dissidents in Local 25 abandoned the cover of seemingly benign educational activities and formed oppositional groups. They founded a number of short-lived, but progressively more outspoken "societies" and "workers' councils." In June 1919 one of the most prominent of such groups, the Workers' Council, boasted of an imposing meeting of 320 delegates representing shops with 14,000 mostly female workers.[56] Later in 1919, dissidents within Local 25 unified the rebellious spirits that had fostered the Current Events Committee and the Workers' Council. Borrowing ideas of shop floor rank-and-file empowerment from English and Soviet unionists, Local 25's opposition built on the success of the Workers' Council to form the Shop Delegate League. The Shop Delegate League actually assumed a number of different names, including the Shop Delegate Propaganda Committee.[57]

The move to align themselves with international radical politics must have seemed like a natural move in the heady atmosphere of 1919, with a strike wave crippling many industrial cities. Women were placing themselves at the vanguard of American and international labor radicalism. They were also appealing to a union that, at least on paper, espoused socialism, some of whose leaders had experienced the first waves of revolution in Russia. In this sense, women were seeking ways of moving away from the margins of the ILGWU. They were, it seemed, using a new activist interpretation of class to make an end-run around restrictive understandings of women's roles as workers and unionists.

In the process, these groups irrevocably altered conversations about the meaning of trade union membership. While they hesitated to criticize openly the gendered hierarchy of the ILGWU and its anti-sweatshop activities, they launched harsh attacks on its political compromises. Cohn noted the expanding targets of women's criticism: "In 1917 a group of members in the waist and dressmakers' Local Union 25 organized a Current Events Committee with the aim of denouncing the leaders of the Union as too conservative." Cohn also recognized how the rise of a female opposition was linked to the emergence of an American left that drew its inspiration from European radicalism and the Bolshevik Revolution. "Soon the committee ceased to exist," she wrote, "but the radicals in the union in 1919 formed a Workers' Council."[58] If the pioneering Current Events Committee claimed that it met only to discuss current political issues, the later Workers' Council and the Shop Delegate League shed all pretense of education and offered pointed indictments of local and international leadership.

The Current Events Committee, the Workers' Council, and the Shop Delegate League were women's dissident groups, insofar as their members were largely women. They were not, however, self-consciously gendered revolts. Jennie Matyas recalled the women of Local 25 as the "more active" members, and Charles Zimmerman, then a new male member of Local 25 and later a leader of the Communist faction, remembered the early dissidents as "women particularly."[59] Thus, when the Shop Delegate League ran candidates for election in Local 25, all twenty-one of its nominees were women.[60] The large numbers of women and the remarkable goal of trying to elect women to union officer positions notwithstanding, class more than gender was the language of dissent. The Current Events Committee, the Workers' Council, and the Shop Delegate League all blamed union leaders for being "too conservative," not for having excluded women.

This language evolved between 1917, with the Current Events Committee, and 1919, with the Shop Delegate League; as it became more confrontational, its vocabulary became ever more gender-neutral. Female dissidents voiced complaints about their subordinate roles by appealing to broader concerns about a lack of democracy and authoritarian control. The rhetoric of rank-and-file empowerment replaced any language of gendered dissent. In 1918, for example, when the male local leadership expelled two Current Events Committee members for criticizing international officers, the committee responded with a bellicose challenge to the rank and file of the union and the local, the "members of the International Ladies' Garment Workers' Union in general and the Ladies' Dress and Waistmakers' Union in particular." The committee addressed itself to rank-and-file members without any special appeal to women: "The case concerns you, and you only; you alone are interested . . . to see that your officials busy themselves with more important things than petty intriguing to harm and eliminate their opponents."[61] Significantly, in sharpening appeals for union democracy, the committee's female leaders shifted to the background questions of women's leadership. For the committee, concerns about "free speech, the right to criticize," and "tyranny in Your Union" replaced discontent with the manly, oppressive atmosphere in the union.[62]

"Rank and file" now referred to women as well as to men. Even Pauline Newman, one of the most outspoken proponents of opening up the ranks of union leadership to women (and not a friend of Bolshevism), rephrased her rhetoric to complain about a general alienation of the rank-and-file from union officials: "The rank-and-file . . . look upon the union not as a vehicle for the realization of their self-interest but as something remote, run by paid officers."[63]

Accordingly, the "Workers' Council of the Waist and Dress Industry" attacked the structure of leadership that concentrated power in the hands of a few. But "few" no longer carried a stated gendered tag. "We have the wrong form of organization," the council complained in a broadside, "which give[s] a small group of officials authority over workers, instead of placing all power where it belongs."[64]

As this language deemphasized gender inequalities in the union, it raised the issue of working-class empowerment, a potentially powerful gambit in an era of militancy. Women might find allies in discontented but radicalized men. And they could put to the test union leaders' stated dedication to socialism; nearly all the ILGWU's conventions still endorsed resolutions espousing socialism. A reading of the Workers' Council's publicity and broadsides suggests that as the vehemence and strength of the council grew, pleas for greater access for women to union leadership positions gave way to demands for rank-and-file direction of the local. A conference of the Workers' Council in May 1919 shunted aside the question of women's access to power, debating instead the potential shape of a democratic council of representatives from each shop. The council called for all workers to assert power collectively in the shops and even disrupted executive board meetings of Local 25: "Keep the power where it belongs,—in the hands of workers. . . . *Act for yourself* in the shops in such a manner as you yourself think best."[65] Similarly, the Shop Delegate League challenged the basic structure of local leadership. In the league's stated plans, power was to shift from local leaders to the heads of shop floor rank-and-file committees.[66] The league called for an assembly with delegates elected from each shop. This assembly would, in turn, elect an Executive Council, effectively superseding the international's GEB.[67]

In laying out the intricate architecture for democracy, complaints about the "sea of masculinity" were muted. The choice of language about democracy in many ways seemed natural. In the context of a union dependent on ideas of sexual difference, democracy with its apparent gender neutrality and contemporary political urgency might have appeared a more powerful language of protest than claims about women's legitimacy as trade unionists. After all, the language of democracy emanated from its immediate connection with class radicalism and revolution. The issue of women's legitimacy might have seemed less urgent in a post-suffrage era. Council and league supporters and leaders insisted their demands were shaped by contemporary revolutionary class radicalism, not by the feminism of the coalition of women workers and the WTUL that supported strikers in 1909 and 1913. As one of the principal leaders of the Communist opposition, Charles Zimmerman, remembered, the growth of dissidence in Local 25 dovetailed with the Russian Revolution. He recognized that political alignment and class politics became a cover for disputes between female rank and file and male leaders: "I was always impressed when I came to meetings in the beginning the discussion that took place. A group of young girls discussing . . . Marxism . . . and it were [*sic*] some of the men who opposed them or attacked them for being Marxist students"—not for stepping out of the ranks as women.[68]

As the intensity of disputes over Bolshevism increased, such meetings of female dissidents centered around discussions of radicalism and revolution, not of women's place in the union. As Jennie Matyas recalled, "They were encouraging revolution against the union itself and against the union leadership."[69] As the Communist Party leadership itself later recognized, a language of revolution grounded in the success of Russian Bolsheviks proved especially attractive to Eastern European Jewish immigrants and, surely, helped turn ILGWU dissidents from gender-based to class-based concerns. In fact, as the party leadership wrote, some dissidents, including some of the men who joined the first waves of female activists, had participated in or supported earlier Russian rebellions: "The revolutionary wave of 1917, as a result of the Bolshevik ascendancy . . . had a tremendous effect on the needle trade workers of this country, most of whom had received their revolutionary training in Russia."[70]

Thus, the Workers' Council and the Shop Delegate League especially pushed an agenda that was increasingly phrased in the language of Bolshevism. The Workers' Council's written plan even began with a reprint of the first paragraphs of the Soviet constitution.[71] The council and later the league described their work as a dress rehearsal for the coming revolution and cited the success of shop delegate systems in Soviet Russia: "It is already in successful operation in Russia. . . . The time has come to put our industry in line with the march of progress and prepare ourselves for the final struggle for industrial freedom."[72] The league boasted in 1920 that it sought to make the ILGWU "a really revolutionary organization, expressing the will of its members."[73]

Those members of Local 25 involved in the growing dissident faction generally saw their protests as involving women, but voicing class-based revolutionary protest.[74] One female supporter was typical in remembering the Shop Delegate League, not as a women's revolt, but as a revolt of women led by men. It was, she recalled, "eighty percent women [with] male leadership."[75] One of these male leaders, Charles Zimmerman, similarly recognized the disproportionate participation of women: "A large number of those who participated particularly among the dressmakers were women. The largest number among the dressmakers were women and many of them were active." But he vehemently denied that leftist protest reflected anger over women's subordinate place in the union.[76] Increasingly, female and male league supporters seemed to portray the left faction as a militant group willing to struggle for rank-and-file empowerment. The left "wanted to fight," as one male worker put it.[77] Another male worker recalled: "Bread and Butter. The left wing was fighting for it."[78] Neither worker described the league as an organization struggling for women workers.

Although female activists relied on languages of class opposition, they could not escape representations of female unionists as excitable, novice, and temporary unionists. Against the dissident left-wing faction stood mostly male anti-Communist international and local leaders. They loudly described the Current Events Committee and later dissident associations as the voice of women's rank-and-file discontent and rebellion. They habitually pointed out the roots of the new left faction in the older women's opposition and highlighted the large numbers of women supporters of the left. Gendered revolt, it seemed, was less threatening and less legitimate than class opposition. The ILGWU's official historian, Louis Levine, echoed the voice of male leaders when he described the committee as an "organized and persistent effort to 'rejuvenate'" the local by getting rid of "old" male leaders and officers. He noted that the rank and file regarded such leaders as "too practical" and "conservative."[79] The male leadership often couched their attacks on the league and later on the Communists in dismissals of women as intemperate trade unionists. By describing leftist activism as a gendered revolt, rather than as a class protest, such leaders seemed to be trying to diminish the left's appeal and to deny its seriousness. Communism, they argued, claimed such success in the ILGWU because of the number of "excitable and emotional" women who lacked the effectiveness of "class conscious" and "deliberate and balanced" men.[80] In these attacks, the ILGWU's male leadership seemed to be linking representations of left unionists to images of women as novice trade unionists. The established male leadership blamed the success of the left rank-and-file movement on inexperienced, excitable, female unionists: "The demagogue in the labor union, so it would seem, has a more fertile field for his machination in those locals where the woman element is large."[81] Thus, when male leaders first tried to eradicate the rebellion, they focused exclusively on Local 25. The male leadership argued that Local 25's rank and file revolted because "it is a local composed almost wholly of girls."[82]

The international responded to Local 25's opposition forcefully with a campaign of discouragement aimed at female activists. As early as 1915, the *Ladies' Garment Worker* discontinued the "Our Women's Workers" column. When international president Benjamin Schlesinger attacked the idea of individual local newspapers, he singled out Local 25's the *Message*, a voice of the growing women's opposition.[83] Attacks increased by 1918 when the international lashed out at the Current Events Committee. Local leaders expelled commit-tee members who dared openly criticize the international.[84] In the face of such repression, the committee disintegrated. Later, as the committee's supporters coalesced once more in the Workers' Council and the Shop Delegate League, the ILGWU's male leadership canceled local elections. As the league com-plained: *"They postponed the elections when they saw that all of the 21 candi-dates of the Shop Delegate Propaganda Committee would be elected."*[85]

Finally, during the winter of 1920–21, the ILGWU leadership sought to break up the large and influential Local 25 itself. The local, it claimed, was plagued by a rebellion that could be eliminated by quarantining female waistmakers and dressmakers in smaller locals. Two years later, as if to further mute women's voices, the leadership forced the remnants of Local 25, now divided into Locals 25 and 22, to merge with (and be submerged in) the solidly male cloakmakers' unions.[86] The international made half-hearted arguments that dividing Local 25 into two new locals would better promote democracy. Rank-and-file dissidents, however, understood the breakup as an effort to disable the opposition. As the dissident's Shop Delegate League claimed in a broad-side: "In order to save their soft jobs they . . . divided Local No. 25."[87] In fact, even the international's leaders quietly acknowledged the role of factionalism in its decision to dismantle the local.[88] Other observers argued, though, that the international simply sought to eliminate any concentration of female work-ers. As the left-leaning manager of the Waist and Dress Makers' Unions, Julius Hochman, noted: "We must not lose sight of the fact that we are primarily a women's organization."[89]

The Culture of Factionalism: The Gender-Neutral Language of Class and Democracy, 1921–1926

Opposition to the (male) leadership of the international by the 1920s was no longer restricted to the female rank and file. Male workers joined the ranks of the left's dissent. At the same time, some women abandoned the op-position because of what they considered a discomforting language of class radicalism. Jennie Matyas, for instance, remembered that she and other women broke with the opposition following its association with Communists: "I ran away . . . and a lot of my colleagues felt as I did."[90] In fact, in some ways the language of Communism seemed to appeal more to the male rank and file than to the female. First, the initial forms of the women's opposition and even the Workers' Council and the Shop Delegate League grew out of women's recog-nition that they experienced work and trade unions differently from men and needed only to create an alternative structure of leadership, more open to women. The Communist left, however, increasingly sought to capture established leadership positions and, indicative of persistent gendered ideologies, when they were successful, they filled positions with men. Second, Communists' pleas for democracy came to refer to the general relationship of the rank-and-file to leadership, not to female members' particularly subordinate positions.[91]

Some women joined Matyas in leaving the opposition movement and even in leaving the union. In fact, the female membership in the union declined precipitously from about 75 percent of the international's membership before 1920 to almost 39 percent by 1924 while the ILGWU's overall membership remained fairly constant.[92] Even the ILGWU's GEB recognized that the union was lax in organizing women. The GEB in 1928 admitted that while the industry's workforce was 70 percent female, 58 percent of the union was male.[93] Meanwhile, between 1921 and 1923, branches of the Shop Delegate League appeared in other locals, including in the locals formed from the breakup of Local 25. As the league grew, conversations about whether women could create an alternative structure of leadership gave way to broader, less obviously gendered struggles over who would control the union. In fact, in some of the more heavily male locals, like Local 9, the struggle pitted men against men.[94] With the spread of the rank-and-file opposition movement throughout the union, Communists and their supporters used a language of international revolution to talk about local issues.[95] They adopted and adapted the rhetoric of rank-and-file power that fueled the women's opposition, denuding it of its gendered appeal.[96]

The women and increasingly large numbers of men in the left replaced women's gendered alternative structure of power with a rank-and-file movement increasingly linked both structurally and linguistically to Communism. Yet leaders like Charles Zimmerman continued to cite the roots of the left faction in the distinctly gendered revolts in Local 25.[97] Zimmerman, for example, asserted that the Communists' success in Locals 22 and 25 depended on a "radical element" of "young girls": "When the Communists came in, they cashed in on this sentiment that existed all the time. It was there all the time."[98] Another leftist leader, Rose Wortis, speaking at the Yankee Stadium rally, also traced the origins of the left to the efforts of the female "dressmakers who fought the officialdom" in 1917.[99]

By 1923, in the aftermath of the breakup of Local 25, the league was moving ever closer to the Workers (Communist) Party. Many members of the league joined the Trade Union Educational League (TUEL), the trade union branch of the American Communist movement. As historian Edward Johanningsmeier notes, because of its practices and strategies, the TUEL in the ILGWU could not avoid accusations of dual unionism. Indeed, after 1923, the opposition sought not simply to change ILGWU policy, but also to seize control of important locals.[100] The transformation in strategies of opposition that occurred as the left moved closer to the Communists becomes apparent through an examination of the way that the left and right in the ILGWU acted out factionalism in public, what can be called the performance of factionalism.[101]

Factionalism changed dramatically in 1923 as the Communists in the ILGWU no longer tried to create an alternative structure of power, but attempted to seize established positions of power. In the process, individual male leaders, like Charles Zimmerman and Louis Hyman, came to represent the left. With the support of the male and female rank and file, they urged campaigns to seize local officer positions. As a letter from the left leadership of Local 22 explained: "The ten thousand members who packed four halls last week demonstrated their loyalty to us and the cause for which we are fighting; and they instructed us to lead this struggle against this corrupt machine which has gotten control of our union."[102] The left's opposition seemed to rely on such public demonstrations of rank-and-file support to confirm the legitimacy of Communist leaders. The strength of the message of the left rested on the ability of the Communist-led opposition to assemble male and female bodies, as at the Yankee Stadium rally.[103]

Factionalism, by late 1923 and early 1924, had become a struggle over which male individuals would hold traditional officer positions. Led by President Morris Sigman, the ILGWU's established leaders launched a vigorous campaign to rid itself of the TUEL. In August 1923, the ILGWU's GEB threatened TUEL members with expulsion unless they resigned from the TUEL.[104] But what the GEB hoped would be individual decisions about whether or not to remain in the ILGWU became public struggles within the international's largest locals. By the end of the year, the TUEL leaders in the ILGWU had mobilized male and female supporters to disrupt Executive Board meetings of Locals 1, 9, 10, and 22. In this way, the TUEL leaders suggested, the rank and file acted out their power over their officers. As one league supporter remembered: "The right-wing leadership couldn't do things they do [sic] before, because they know there was somebody outside watching them."[105] Even hearings about the expulsion of individual league supporters became occasions for public mobilizations. Rank-and-file ire paralyzed Locals 1, 9, and 22 after the expulsions of league leaders.[106]

By 1925, Sigman's assault seemed to have backfired. After walking out of the international's 1925 convention and winning overwhelming victories in local elections, Communists controlled virtually all officer positions in the Joint Board of the Cloak, Skirt, Dress, and Reefer Makers' Unions (the Joint Board controlling policy for most of the local unions in New York City). In June 1925, the international leadership tried again and ordered the expulsion of the Communist officers of the principal locals in the Joint Board, Locals 2, 9, and 22. In what appears to have been an effort to minimize opposition, the international's leaders ordered raids of the locals' offices in the middle of the night. Their ploy failed as the Communist leadership rallied numerous supporters to guard, in particular, the offices of Local 22 and formed a defense organization, the Joint Action Committee (JAC).[107] The international leadership was reduced to pleading with the rank and file to ignore Communist "lies" about union democracy and local self-determination. They accused the Communists of faking the large turnouts at earlier shop delegate meetings.[108] Later in July, the Communists launched their largest public defense of ousted local leaders with the rally at Yankee Stadium.[109] By September, the international leadership had backed down and proposed new elections in the locals and in the Joint Board, virtually assuring Communist victories.[110] The JAC, with its tactics of defending a few individuals, concentrated the rank-and-file movement around a small number of male leaders. Even Workers (Communist) Party leaders noted and criticized how the Communist partisans in the ILGWU had changed the rhetorical terrain of struggle, casting opposition as a defense of a few (male) leaders who sought to occupy traditional officer positions.[111]

As the Communists came to power in the ILGWU, questions loomed: could class mobilization, still dependent on gendered hierarchy, offer an alternative means of controlling sweatshops? Under the shadow of factionalism, many employers were seeking to avoid the most stringent union and sanitary regulations. Even the union's embattled socialist leadership bemoaned a "revival" of the sweating system.[112] The Communist leadership offered class power in the form of a general strike, more than strict regulation, as a solution. By early 1926, the newly installed Communist male leadership steadily moved the union toward a confrontation with industry bosses. In that year, a strike of mostly male cloakmakers proved a turning point in the factional struggle among Jewish workers in the ILGWU, further reducing the potential role of women. At the same time, the Communist leadership drained funds from the Union Health Center and the JBSC to fund the strike. The strike began on July 2, 1926, with a massive display of public rank-and-file support for a strike. Twenty-five thousand cloakmakers gathered at Madison Square Garden and voted unanimously to authorize a strike, which was immediately called by the Communist leadership of the Joint Board.[113] The strike also began with the tepid support of a cowed, but still anti-Communist, international leadership.[114] By November, however, with the strike dragging on and relief funds running low, rank-and-file support for left-wing Joint Board leaders ebbed.[115]

The international's right-wing socialist leadership capitalized on rank-and-file dissatisfaction with the running of the strike by launching an assault on the Communist Joint Board leadership. An editorial in the ILGWU's *Justice* the week after the proposed agreement demanded: "Who Led the Cloakmakers' Strike?" In distancing the right-wing international leadership from the bad fortunes of the strike, the editorial blamed the Communists: "The cloak makers know how President Sigman was defeated for chairmanship of the general strike committee, and how every other experienced and capable workers or leaders [*sic*] who did not bear a Communist label had been sidetracked in favor of Communists."[116] The Communists, the international leadership insisted, had failed, and on December 17, the ILGWU's General Executive Board, dominated by the socialist right, successfully seized control of the Joint Board offices. The international's leadership settled the strike quickly through quiet and rapid negotiations that implicitly repudiated the public performances of rank-and-file participation championed by the Communist left.[117]

The Manliness of Violence and the Twilight of an Anti-Sweatshop Campaign, 1926–1934

After the failure of the 1926 cloakmakers' strike and the subsequent decline in rank-and-file oppositional fervor, Communists and the international leadership performed factionalism in increasingly violent ways. As the pendulum of power shifted perceptibly away from the Communists, factionalism came to be acted out by small numbers of male, paid, professional partisans and "gangsters." The significance of this transformation in the everyday culture of opposition lies not only in the way it symbolized the general decline of the left opposition, but also in how violent factionalism removed women from debates over union structure.

Vestiges of the language of women's opposition seemed to evaporate as male Communist leaders increasingly complained more about violence propagated by the right than about the lack of democracy. The everyday performance of factionalism became a limited display, public only by its location on streets and in workplaces. Initially, the Communists attempted to defend their claims to Joint Board leadership positions through appeals to rank-and-file supporters. However, a Madison Square Garden rally in early 1927, which the Communists had hoped would equal the success of the earlier Yankee Stadium event, proved an ill-attended failure. Unlike the 1925 defense of Communist leaders, few workers arrived to defend the Joint Board offices from seizure.[118] As a way of weeding out remaining left-wing supporters, the ascendant international leadership forced all members of the union to reapply for admission.[119]

Factionalism, however, did not disappear with the ouster of left-wing leaders from the ILGWU. Rather, the ILGWU split into two competing and combating unions, the right-wing ILGWU and the Communist Needle Trades

Workers' Industrial Union (NTWIU). The two unions competed violently for members between 1926 and 1934, when the Industrial Union finally rejoined the ILGWU during the Popular Front years of reconciliation.[120] The ILGWU and the NTWIU contested the split, as one worker put it, "shop-by-shop by force."[121]

In an earlier period when the left leadership was able to set the terms of factional struggle, they turned to a mass public that included women, but did not acknowledge their particular concerns. When their power receded, the public disappeared and they joined right leaders in adopting a more restrictive script of violence and gangsterism. In the aftermath of the strike, the right and left traded accusations of gangsterism. The Communists were reduced to indicting Sigman himself for hiring strong arms: "Sigman is the father of gangsterism in the International Garment Workers Union. . . . He is an expert in employing strong arm men and in keeping up his rule with their force. And still he has the nerve to come out with statements about the gangsterism of the lefts in the needle trades!" Indeed, Sigman accused the "lefts" of "gangsterism" in a 1927 circular letter distributed to all union members: "Through their irresponsible tactics and their methods of stupid and brutal violence they . . . have fostered gangsterism, terrorism and scabbism within the ranks of the cloakmakers."[122] One male left supporter remembered that after the 1926 strike gangsters became a constant, dangerous presence at union meetings. He recalled that he was "very lucky that they didn't kill me."[123]

The shift toward gangsterism especially restricted the ability of female workers, whether supporters of the Communists or of the international leadership, even to participate in, not to mention set the terms of, factionalism. If the public performance of factionalism immediately before the 1926 strike at least permitted women to take part in the opposition, the gangsterism that followed the strike depended on strictly defined gender roles. As gangsters consolidated their positions in the two Jewish garment unions, women in the left had limited assignments. They organized "fainting brigades" whose antics helped instigate factional battles carried out by gangsters or, less frequently, by male trade unionists. Fainting would be the signal that led to a brawl. Isidore Wisotsky, a strident supporter of the right, recalled one incident involving the fainting brigades. At a meeting organized by the right, a woman pretended to faint, which Wisotsky considered "a communist trick, to break up the meeting." The faint promulgated an open brawl and Wisotsky proudly remembered attacking a "bloody Bolshevick [*sic*]" and sending him "rolling down the steps of the balcony."[124]

The "fainting brigades" can be read as gendered performance. Such tactics signaled the removal—the fainting away—of women from factionalism. The very act of fainting represented a dropping out of the action of factionalism. The feigned sleep in itself seemed to cede to men alone active roles in the violence of factionalism. In effect, the rise of the professional gangster had reestablished the union, both in its left- and right-wing variants, as a solidly masculinized space, gendered masculine by its restrictions and regulations about who could participate in factionalism. For male workers, like Wisotsky, gangsterism seemed to be a display of manly trade unionism. Wisotsky described his participation in the violence of the years between 1926 and 1934 as "becoming a *mench*."[125]

Female trade unionists came to recognize their failure to claim leadership roles in the Jewish trade union movement. Starting in 1927, in the aftermath of the split and as factionalism became embroiled in violence, a series of articles appeared in *Justice* that eerily recalled the complaints of earlier female trade unionists. Fannia Cohn lamented women's "inferiority" in the ILGWU. She urged women to resist the attacks of male unionists and to seize active roles in local unions: "Women . . . must not be over-sensitive to men's criticism of feminine attitudes. They should rather let men complain of women's intrusion than have women kick against men for preventing them from taking their proper place in the labor movement."[126] At the same time, Cohn acknowledged the failure of past efforts of women to organize collectively to strengthen female workers' roles in the union.

In repeating complaints of a decade before, Cohn recognized the meandering development of the women's opposition. By the Great Depression, factionalism had ended up in a morass of violence and gangsterism. "Democracy," a word tossed around blithely by the left opposition, claimed intricate gendered meanings. In its supposed gender neutrality, the democratic revolt systematically came to exclude women. Female voices, always few, but often particularly eloquent and vocal, now became lost in the cacophony.

Communism, however, did not simply steamroll the women's revolt. To be sure, the male leadership of the left was generally unconcerned with women's plight and denied the primacy of gendered discontent, but female trade unionists bore some responsibility too. Their belief that as women workers they experienced work and thus unions differently from men was grounded in the very definition of the sweatshop and in the original articulation of its dangers. This conception of appropriate female work roles made women generally unwilling or unable either to challenge the image of female unionists as novices or to seek the leadership positions long claimed by men. Thus, they raised the idea of alternative structures of leadership and, when that failed, they rightly complained about the lack of democracy. Class empowerment in the form of Communism provided a language of dissent that was comfortably gender-neutral insofar as it allowed women and men to leave intact conceptions of sexual difference and ideals of a sexual division of labor. Thus, as the American economy and the New York garment industry stood on the brink of the economic collapse and upheaval of the Great Depression, the limitations of the political and cultural discourse around the sweatshop were clearly revealed. The union that was Eastern European Jewish immigrants' contribution to the anti-sweatshop movement had become factionalized. In the turmoil, women's voices were muted.

The violence of factionalism, which helped maintain gendered inequality within the Jewish garment labor movement, in the end also helped accelerate the disintegration of the anti-sweatshop campaign. After 1926, leaders of both the NTWIU and the ILGWU admitted that conditions in the garment industry had deteriorated. Again, they turned to the word "sweatshop" to describe the problems of the industry. As the ILGWU's membership sank to the lowest level since 1910, hundreds of small contracting shops, what both ILGWU and NTWIU leaders denigrated as "sweatshops," spread throughout the industry.[127] Thus, the ILGWU bemoaned the fact that "there still are in New York scores upon scores of cloak shops and shoplets where men and women are toiling under sweat-shop conditions," and the NTWIU mourned the return of "sweat shops of the past."[128] Meanwhile, the system designed to combat the physical effects of the sweatshop, which Jewish labor activists had helped construct over the course of two decades, was rapidly falling apart. The ILGWU announced to its 1928 convention that the JBSC, the cornerstone of the campaign for sanitary regulation, could no longer investigate all the shops of the industry because of a lack of personnel and funds. The Union Health Center, the institution that the ILGWU praised as crucial to "the prevention of occupational disease with which the needles trades were afflicted, especially the scourge of tuberculosis," also complained of a lack of money. At the height of factionalist violence in September 1927, the Union Health Center appealed to the ILGWU's remaining rank and file for $25,000 in aid.[129]

For the cross-class coalition, the assertion of a confrontational language of class conflict and the strategy of a general strike—not inspection—could not have come at a worse time. With postwar anti-"red" hysteria still reverberating, inspectors were loath to maintain relationships with openly Communist unionists. This was especially true at a moment when political support for factory legislation and inspection was rapidly ebbing. Inspectors could not and would not have struggled to preserve the JBSC and the infrastructure of reform in the face of new, expressly radical language or organizing. Thus, by the Great Depression, the right was blaming the left for bankrupting the JBSC and the Union Health Center, and the left was attacking the right for cynically using these institutions to protect the power of a few. But neither side challenged the goal of replacing sweatshops with model union shops, even as the structures of anti-sweatshop regulation were collapsing. Gender inequality and the focus on the sweatshop and its effects on the body and family, it seemed, had survived the turmoil of factionalism. The NTWIU, like the ILGWU, called on dressmakers to join its ranks to win healthy working conditions and to defeat the sweatshop. The Communist union implored its members: "There is only one way you can improve your conditions. There is only one way how you can turn your sweat shop in which you are slaving into a union shop where you can earn a decent livelihood. That is to organize yourselves in the shops and fight for union conditions."[130]

Conclusion

"Our Marching Orders . . . Advance toward the Goal of Industrial Decency"

Measuring the Burden of Language

By 1927, as the ILGWU split into two warring camps, the Eastern European Jewish labor movement tottered on the brink of failure and extinction. In an era when gangsters often carried out the work of organizing, union density among Eastern European Jewish garment workers declined precipitously. Factionalism had taken its toll not only in membership totals of the ILGWU, but also in the organizing zeal of the workers that remained. As three local officers reported to the union's 1928 convention: "The factional struggle with the Communists has sapped the vitality of our leadership, has divided our membership into hostile groups, has created a condition of disharmony in our Union and has almost completely undermined the morale of our members."[1]

The ILGWU's General Executive Board (GEB) a year later also noted the "apathy, indifference and hopelessness" of the remaining rank and file. With the rise of violent factionalism, the GEB mourned that the rank and file had "apparently lost all hope of a better day."[2] Perhaps the bankruptcy of the principal structures of the anti-sweatshop coalition contributed to rank-and-file "apathy." Only the arrival of New Deal labor legislation later in the 1930s would rescue New York's garment labor movement from total obscurity and resurrect a cross-class campaign against the sweatshop. By then Eastern European Jewish immigrants and their descendants had begun their long march out of the garment shops and, indeed, out of the blue collar industrial working class and into what they increasingly described as the middle class.[3]

The instability of the Eastern European Jewish immigrant labor movement and the concurrent collapse of the anti-sweatshop coalition in the late 1920s and early 1930s were not simply the results of the missteps, misdeeds, and mistakes of individual union leaders or factory inspectors. In a politically contentious era with Progressivism on a fast retreat, the burden of language became too heavy. Workers and inspectors faced the political limits of their definition of the sweatshop. For them, the sweatshop was a threat to health. And they believed that men and women experienced sweatshop work and thus occupational disease in different and unequal ways. Out of this understanding of the sweatshop emerged a coalitional anti-sweatshop movement that sought a gendered and medicalized solution to the sweatshop problem.

Thus, the anti-sweatshop movement in its rejection of racialized economics and of overt class conflict came to depend heavily on the protection of workers' health and the rehabilitation of injured or diseased workers with the aim of maintaining separate workplace roles for men and women. The Joint Board of Sanitary Control (JBSC) mandated sanitary regulations in the site of male breadwinning: workplaces in industrial buildings. The JBSC also sought to eradicate married women's homework. Sanitary reform, on the one hand, and the abolition of homework, on the other, strove to protect men's roles as breadwinners and to prevent married women's garment wage labor. Similarly, the health programs launched by the ILGWU through its Union Health Center and the Arbeter Ring (Workmen's Circle) through its Medical Department and sanitarium also sought to safeguard men's ability to earn the family wage and women's capacity to bear and raise healthy children. Health care was tied to immigrants' and their allies' desire for gendered order, an order that would help confirm immigrants' Americanization and assimilation. The focus on combating occupational disease and the way this focus was tied to anxiety about the sexual division of labor served to tie the labor movement to middle-class social reform and public health movements. It also concentrated power in the hands of a few male union leaders. These trends discouraged the expression of class power while forcing women into subordinate positions on the shop floor and in the labor movement.

An examination of two JBSC documents illuminates how immigrants' and their allies' representation of the evils of the sweatshop worked to naturalize sexual difference, while denying class difference in ways that profoundly restricted the scope and goals of organizing. The first document issued in 1912 toward the end of the ILGWU's major period of strike activity announced plans for intensive organizing around issues of sanitation and health. The second document, distributed in 1914 at the height of Jewish workers' efforts to combat the sweatshop and to relocate garment production from the Lower East Side to the garment district, details the structure of the JBSC.

The first document listed the union and the JBSC's organizing goals. In January 1912, one year before women strikers forced the JBSC to inspect shops where women worked in large numbers, the JBSC issued its organizational goals for the coming year: "Our marching orders for 1912 are 'Forward! Advance toward the Goal of Industrial Decency.'"[4] This short, bombastic phrase encapsulates Jewish workers and inspectors' understandings of sweated garment work as physically hazardous. The phrase is the last line in the "New Year's Greeting" from the JBSC addressed to "Co-Workers in the Cloak and Suit Industry." Many, if not most, cloak and suit makers, predominantly Jewish male workers, would have received the greeting at work. The JBSC's "Bulletins" were regularly distributed on the shop floor by JBSC employees and by activist workers and unionists.

In the "Greeting," the JBSC promised to rid the industry of sweatshops and to reverse the ill-effects of sweated work through the "active desire" of workers to enforce regulations. The "Greeting" also promised a medical inspection of 1,500 workers "for the purpose of determining if possible the effect of their work upon their health . . . as a basis to recommend necessary changes in working conditions."[5] The dangers of the sweatshop, the JBSC argued, could be read from workers' bodies, from their abnormalities and defects.

In the struggle against the sweatshop, the JBSC promised, not revolution or a challenge to the employment relationships of the industry, but the "humanizing of modern industrial processes." Indeed, the JBSC scoffed at the idea that the sanitary dangers of the garment industry could be combated through revolution: "When overcrowded, badly ventilated, and ill-lighted shops are not exceptional but normal conditions in an industry, it is too much to expect a sudden revolution." Instead, at the height of the ILGWU's power, the union implored male cloakmakers through a JBSC bulletin to "advance toward the goal of industrial decency."[6] And, "industrial decency" had specific meanings that spoke directly to garment workers' positions as immigrants hoping for Americanization and struggling against negative depictions of racial Jewishness. In the 1880s and 1890s, Jewish immigrant workers felt the sting of critics labeling them a debased and degenerating race. Now, the JBSC saluted unionized garment workers as "pioneers in a virgin field of civilization."[7]

The "Bulletin" aimed to "enlighten" workers about the "meaning of decent sanitary conditions in the shops," that is, to explain their vision of "civilization." In the years that followed the "Greeting," it became especially clear that the "meaning" of sanitary reform was deeply embedded in the maintenance and policing of gender roles, even as the JBSC's jurisdiction came to cover the Dress and Waist industries in which women composed a majority of the workforce. For the JBSC and its officials, men were breadwinners and women were temporary workers and future wives and mothers.

The second document explained how the JBSC's structure was designed to eradicate the sweatshop. In a May 1914 issue of the "Bulletin," the JBSC provided workers with a simple chart explaining its "Organization, Functions and Methods of Work." The JBSC was divided into four divisions: Sanitary, Medical, Fire Drills, and Education. The three largest divisions, Sanitary, Medical, and Education, directly worked to maintain separate gender roles through the regulation of the site of work, the inspection of bodies, and the education of workers in their perceived distinct roles.[8]

The Sanitary Division, led by sanitary inspectors, divided the industry into hierarchies of shops, with homework shops, where married women labored, at the very bottom. Such shops faced monthly and bimonthly inspections and their owners were encouraged either through "personal suasion" or through "sanitary strikes" to move production to industrial loft buildings. This goal of eradicating the homework sweatshop had a particular effect on women; the JBSC considered the homework shop as the worst kind of sweatshop not only because of its truly awful conditions, but also because of cultural prohibitions that discouraged married women's wage labor. Similarly, the restriction, as opposed to regulation, of married women's labor further entrenched representations of single female workers working in a range of factories as mere transients who would leave wage work with marriage.[9]

Similarly, the Medical Division, led by medical examiners, focused heavily on identifying and caring for tubercular workers. From the outset, examiners cast tuberculosis as a men's disease by focusing their efforts on the "Pressers' Local," an exclusively Jewish, male, and skilled ILGWU local. The division promised the "examination of applicants to the Pressers' Local," the "examination of sick members of the Pressers' Local," and the "supervision of tuberculosis benefit of Pressers' Local [sic]." With its overriding focus on caring for male tubercular workers, the JBSC foreshadowed the work of the United States Public Health Services, whose inspections would serve to confirm the gender-specificity of occupational disease and to provide the supposed medical evidence of men's and women's different workplace roles. In fact, in the same issue of the "Bulletin," the JBSC announced the start of the Public Health Services inspections and invited men and women to come to their offices "for the purpose of being examined."[10] Even the earlier "Greeting" contained hints that the JBSC saw men and women as facing different occupational diseases. The JBSC promised medical inspections not simply of workers, but of employees in gender-specific trades. They intended to examine "five hundred pressers" and "five hundred operators," most of whom were men, as well as "five hundred finishers," most of whom were women. The identification of trades with their tacit gendered labels as an important scientific variable to be measured revealed how a socially constructed and gendered hierarchy of skill was protected and naturalized in medical examinations.

Finally, the "Division of Education," through the efforts of lecturers, sought to instill proper sanitary practices in workers. Talks, delivered in shops and in the meetings of union locals, often depended on ideas of separate working roles for women and men. On the one hand, the JBSC offered presentations on workplace health and the prevention of tuberculosis that offered Jewish male workers strategies to protect their health in their roles as breadwinners. On the other hand, it also gave lectures explicitly aimed toward women about caring for children and on sanitation in the home. Men and women, lecturers suggested, should learn different sanitary practices even as they often worked in the same factories.[11]

Thus, while the JBSC's initial marching orders in the 1912 "Greeting" made no mention of men or women, only "co-workers," the JBSC's structure depended on gender, and its practices affected men and women in profoundly different ways. While men enjoyed protection as breadwinners and benefited from an array of safety and sanitary reforms, women faced the steady restriction of their productive roles, as homework shops were gradually eradicated. In addition, through its publicity and "propaganda," all of which worked to explain the JBSC's understanding of "decency," single female workers also found their labor rendered invisible. As noted earlier, photographs of "modern shops" distributed by the JBSC's Division of Education tended only to depict workplaces with male workers. Ten years after the "Greeting," the director of the JBSC, George Price, proudly announced that "the industry as a whole has rid itself of the 'sweat-shop' stigma, and may claim that 'the sanitary conditions under the jurisdiction of the Joint Board of Sanitary Control are immeasurably better.'" Yet men and women experienced sanitary improvements and the JBSC's jurisdiction in contrasting ways.[12]

Still, if Price claimed that the JBSC had rid the industry of sweatshops, the idea, if not the stigma, of the sweatshop remained paramount in Eastern European Jewish immigrant workers' discourse around work and organizing. The period of factionalism in the 1920s did little to undermine gendered representations of the sweatshop and, in fact, served to confirm the continuing centrality of the image of the sweatshop in discussions and debates about work and organizing. If the Needle Trades Workers' Industrial Union (NTWIU) and the ILGWU could agree on one thing, it was the definition of the sweatshop. The two unions accused one another of facilitating the return of sweatshop conditions. In 1927, the NTWIU excoriated the ILGWU's leadership for allowing the return of the sweatshop in exchange for political power: "The class collaboration policy of the International Ladies Garment Workers . . . has brought sweat shop conditions . . . in the entire needle industry."[13] According to the left, coalitional politics had brought back the sweatshop. The ILGWU's anti-Communist leaders, meanwhile, blamed left leaders for allowing bosses to ignore sanitary regulations, thus permitting the return of the sweatshop. At the union's 1929 convention, the ILGWU's GEB mourned the "return of the sweat shop on an extended scale in the cloak industry." The GEB blamed Communist leaders for the lack of enforcement of sanitary regulations: "These shops frankly owed their existence to the fact that they were able to violate wholesale all union work-terms."[14] For the right, class radicalism, at the expense of reform, had allowed the sweatshop's return. ILGWU leaders pointed out that the JBSC was facing a financial crisis because of the poor management and politics of the left: "The Joint Board [of Sanitary Control] has had to reduce its staff considerably, although its task has greatly increased, because of the growth of substandard shops during and after the strike [of 1926], many of which were housed in basements, stores, and in the rear of houses."[15]

Still, both sides believed that the sweatshop embodied specific dangers to health and family. References to "sweat shop conditions" underscore the stability of definitions of the sweatshop. The sweatshop still meant cramped quarters, occupational disease, low pay, and the breakdown of a sexual division of labor. Accusations about the return of the sweatshop were also a public admission of failure for both sets of union leaders. If the sweatshop was returning—and both sides seemed to concede that it was—then the labor movement had failed in its stated goal of eradicating the sweatshop.

For the JBSC in 1912, the Jewish labor movement was advancing to "decency," and, for Price, in 1922, it had rid the industry of sweatshops. In contrast, according to left and right partisans in the late 1920s, the sweatshop had returned. The stark contrast between these perspectives suggests, first, how the sweatshop remained a constant focus of organizing and, second, how immigrant labor leaders saw the garment industry as always on the verge of returning to gendered disorder and occupational disease. Such leaders, it seemed, did not see their movement as a juggernaut, but as an advance from sweatshop to model shop whose progress could at any moment be halted. For leaders on the right, the anti-sweatshop movement could not survive the weakening of the ILGWU and the end of the Progressive moment—if only because it lacked the strength of numbers or the enforcement of inspectors to realize the "modern factory."

Workers and unionists had built a cross-class movement that depended on a common definition of the sweatshop and on a shared goal of an ideal workplace. That language of labor, the discourse that ascribed particular cultural meanings to the sweatshop, shaped the priorities and strategies of organizing for two decades. It also depended in large measure on images of victimhood. Workers and their allies pointed to diseased and enfeebled proletarian bodies as evidence of the depredations of sweated labor. This embodiment of victimhood, that is, the idea that the problems and evils of the sweatshop could be read visually from the bodies of workers, placed women in an awkward position. Initially, inspectors and workers read the working-class body in different ways. For workers, their bodies bore the scars of class exploitation; for inspectors, workers' bodies revealed their inferior racial status. In forging alliances, workers—led by male unionists—and inspectors exchanged these languages for a shared language of gender. While women forced their way into the anti-sweatshop coalition partly by pointing out the scars of work on their own bodies, they could not deny supposed scientific evidence that workplace disease revealed men and women's contrasting workplace roles. Only men could claim the title of real workers. At best, women could claim to be "women workers," a title that acknowledged their shop floor impermanence and future roles as wives and mothers.

The model garment shop where workers were "made well" also depended on notions of sexual difference and, paradoxically, on the unnaturalness of class difference. The boss remained on this idealized shop floor while women went home. Men could receive care in their roles as breadwinners, even in the workplace. Women could receive care in resorts or women's clinics that helped bridge their lives as workers and then as mothers. In the end, the language of victimhood, strengthened by the medical evidence of disease, worked to reinforce structures of inequality within the labor movement and on the shop floor, as male workers seized upon women's acknowledged transience to depict women as novice unionists who could not and should not hold positions of union leadership or skilled jobs. And while women challenged such negative representations, their own acceptance of difference limited the kinds of resistance to which they had access. They turned to a language of class radicalism at a moment of what might have seemed like impending worldwide revolution. Class difference, they seemed to say, was as real as sexual difference. They helped set in motion a process in which literally thousands of rank-and-file workers—men and women—voiced frustration with union leaders too much tied to the politics of coalition. Could shop committees and a democratic union represent an alternative way of replacing the sweatshop with a "modern factory"? On the eve of the Great Depression, the only consensus that remained between male and female workers, Communists and socialists, workers and inspectors, was the sad recognition that the sweatshop had returned to the New York garment industry.

Epilogue

Anti-Sweatshop Campaigns in a New Century

Sweatshop remains a powerful word. It still evokes images of cramped, dirty, and dangerous workplaces. While the United States General Accounting Office (GAO) defines the sweatshop unemotionally as a workplace "that violates more than one federal or state labor law governing minimum wage and overtime, child labor, industrial homework, occupational safety and health, workers compensation, or industry regulation," the popular American image of the sweatshop is more lurid.[1] Even the most ardent defenders of capitalism and globalization will not defend the sweatshop. Nicholas Kristof and Sheryl WuDunn, for example, celebrants of the global economy, could only muster "two cheers for sweatshops" in a recent article in the *New York Times Magazine*.[2] Even there, though, they recognized that the sweatshop is "dirty and dangerous."

So, too, do Kristof and WuDunn recognize that the sweatshop is a central element of the global economy. They describe it as the "price of development" for countries like Taiwan, South Korea, and Cambodia. The GAO, meanwhile, confirmed the "return of the sweatshop" to the globalized American economy. The GAO estimated that 2,000 of 6,000 garment shops in New York City were sweatshops. The situation was even worse in other major garment centers in the United States. According to the GAO, 4,500 of 5,000 shops in Los Angeles were sweatshops, 400 of 500 in Miami, and 50 of 180 in El Paso.[3] At the same time, the sweatshop has returned to the American discourse about industry, economy, class, immigration, and consumerism. The raid on a sweatshop in El Monte, California, in 1995, where seventy-two Thai immigrants worked in slavery, captured public attention and became the subject of a major Smithsonian Institute exhibition. Revelations about Kathie Lee Gifford and her company's use of sweatshop labor to sew her clothing line also focused public attention on the prevalence of sweatshops.[4]

About a century after the word "sweatshop" was first used in the United States, it reverberates in popular television shows, newspapers, and shopping malls. As journalist Liza Featherstone writes: "In malls nationwide, it's no longer unusual to overhear shoppers in front of a Gap store debating whether to go inside. 'I've heard they use sweatshop labor,' one will say.'"[5] History is central to the evocative power of the sweatshop. The Smithsonian, for example, placed the El Monte sweatshop in a timeline that stretched back to the 1820s. Andrew Ross, in his book *No Sweat*, the first in a growing number of works in "sweatshop studies," counterpoises pictures of the early-twentieth-century sweatshops with more recent photos. The *New York Daily News*, in a recent four-day investigation of the city's sweatshops, compared the locked doors of the New Elim shop in the Garment District to those in the Triangle Shirtwaist factory. The Triangle factory was the site of a 1911 fire that killed 147 workers. (Interestingly, the grim shadow of the Triangle factory looms large in the contemporary discourse about sweatshops. Yet, at the turn of the century, its location in a loft building might have earned it the title of modern shop!)[6] The attention to history suggests that today's sweatshop is a step back in time to a more brutal age. Meanwhile, placing the sweatshop of today alongside, for example, the Triangle factory also strengthens the association of sweated work with women, immigrants, and non-Americans.

Concern about the sweatshop——1996 has been called the "summer of the sweatshop"—reflects a growing anxiety in the First World about the effects of economic globalization, among them immigration. The global "race to the bottom" in labor costs has led to the proliferation of small, low-wage workplaces. That these shops become known as sweatshops reflects growing social anxiety about globalization and its effects.[7] Attention to the sweatshop also testifies to the success of a new activist movement in the United States and in Europe that uses a word coined in the West. They rely on the word "sweatshop" and the moral repugnance it evokes to cobble together a transnational movement protesting conditions in Third World or immigrant workplaces. The sweatshop has been cast as the common experience of labor in the global factory.[8]

As historian Eileen Boris has noted, unionists and liberal activists responded to deregulatory urges of the Reagan Administration by warning of a "return of the sweatshop." By the 1990s, increased immigration, the rise of neo-liberal economics in the form of trade agreements like the North American Free Trade

Agreement (NAFTA), the decline in the strength of American garment trade unions, and the almost complete breakdown of government regulation and enforcement all helped spur a new anti-sweatshop activism. In 1990, the National Labor Committee (NLC), an independent organization concerned with labor rights in the developing world, adopted sweated labor as their primary concern. In the immediate aftermath of the El Monte raid, Sweatshop Watch was formed in California. And, in 1998, college student activists formed the United Students Against Sweatshops (USAS). Europe has also witnessed a major surge of activism with groups like the Clean Clothes Campaign, Women Working Worldwide, and Labour Behind the Label.[9]

In the United States, student activism continues to be the driving force behind the anti-sweatshop movement. USAS is part of the biggest manifestation of student activism since anti-apartheid demonstrations. Anti-sweatshop activism has appeared in the "usual suspects" schools like the University of Wisconsin and the University of Michigan, as well as in typically conservative colleges like Virginia Commonwealth University. USAS has forced universities to demand certain codes of conduct from firms that contract to make university-licensed goods—hats, T-shirts, and other clothing bearing university logos. In the face of student activism, including lengthy building takeovers, major universities have withdrawn from the Fair Labor Association (FLA), a Clinton-administration sponsored self-monitoring group. Instead, activists have supported the Workers' Rights Consortium (WRC), an independent monitoring group soundly rejected by major manufacturers like Nike.

The larger anti-sweatshop movement has forced large companies to sign agreements allowing for independent monitoring. Most notably, in 1995, American activists, led by the NLC, began a campaign to highlight abuses at Mandarin International, an El Salvadoran company that sewed garments for the Gap, J. C. Penney, Eddie Bauer, and other American name brands. Teenagers worked for pitiable wages, and bathroom breaks were carefully controlled. Female workers were forced to take birth control pills (a nefarious reversal of early-twentieth-century concerns about female garment workers and motherhood). Also, the company fired many union activists. The NLC led a corporate campaign that focused attention on the Gap and that appealed to the sympathy of American consumers by bringing a few Mandarin workers to the United States for a speaking tour. By the end of the year—in Brooklyn, New York, not in San Marcos, El Salvador, where Mandarin is located—an agreement was signed by the Gap that allowed for independent monitoring of labor conditions in its Central American contractor shops.[10] More ominously, while anti-sweat activism has put companies on notice that working conditions at their contractor shops will be revealed to western consumers, it has also spurred companies to launch massive campaigns to convince consumers that activists are exaggerating. Nike, most prominently, has begun a website, www.nikebiz.com, and a program, "Transparency 101" (clearly aimed at the collegiate audience), that combine happy images of life in shops making Nike goods with criticism of anti-sweatshop activists.[11]

The Mandarin agreement and www.nikebiz.com suggest that the First World consumer is at the heart of contemporary struggles over the sweatshop. The new anti-sweatshop movement has been most successful in revealing to the First World both conditions in the Third World and in workplaces in the First World where immigrants from the Third World labor. As the sociologist Ethel Brooks points out: "U.S.-based (white, elite) activists, protected by laws and geography, are able to mobilize U.S.-based consumers with access to 'disposable' income to boycott goods from high-profile retailers in support of labor rights of Third world and immigrant (women) garment workers."[12] Thus, the NLC used the high profile of Kathie Lee Gifford to highlight conditions at sweatshops in Honduras and Manhattan where Kathie Lee clothing was made for Wal-Mart.[13] Unionists and activists urge consumers to "shop 'sweat free.'"[14]

Activists and workers are again looking at each other across lines of difference. And, once more, activists present their findings using narratives of exploration and travel. They record their shock and horror at the conditions of Third World women workers. Where turn-of-the-century observers spoke to government hearings and printed lurid articles, today's activists have traveled to sweatshops and created websites complete with pictures and first-person descriptions of their reactions. Charles Kernaghan, the director of the NLC, contributed to the *No Sweat* collection, and his presentation is revealing. Immediately, the reader is greeted by a large, dramatic photo of Kernaghan. His long coat, hat, and tie contrast with the tropical background. He is clearly an ousider. Kernaghan leans against a rock while talking on a cordless phone; the technology of the First World meets the nature of the Third. To capture the sense of exploration, the photo's caption reads: "Charlie Kernaghan: 'Sweat Detective.'" The photo complements an open letter from Kernaghan to Michael Eisner, the chief executive officer of Walt Disney, reprinted several pages later. Written in the first person, the letter describes Kernaghan's visit to Haiti, where he met workers at N. S. Mart, a sweatshop making Walt Disney clothing.

As the narrative of exploration recalls the first investigations of sweatshops in New York, so, too, do many of the notions of the dangers of the sweatshop. Kernaghan, for example, begins his narrative by focusing on an individual, and presumably representative, worker: a single mother with four children. Most obviously, the bodies of her children speak to the breakdown of the family caused by the sweatshop. One child has malaria and another has dysentery.

At work, Kernaghan reports: "Sexual harassment is common." The workplace is also dangerously dirty and rats "are everywhere."[15] The *Daily News* series also reveals how workers' bodies, more than their voices, come to speak about the dangers of the sweatshop. The drama of the series is augmented by large pictures of Asian workers, mostly women and presumably immigrants, sleeping exhausted on bundles of garments in filthy and disorganized shops. Like critics a century ago, is the *Daily News* lamenting that the workplace has become a home?[16]

Workers' bodies, in particular, hint at filth, disease, and foreignness. As the *Daily News* wrote: "Within New York's illegal clothing workforce, which is mostly Chinese, there exists a slavelike subclass: men and women smuggled here by so-called snakeheads, then put to work in factories as indentured servants." Again, the sweatshop is portrayed as a foreign workplace, imported into the country on the tired backs of the most desperate—and, in this case, illegal—immigrants.[17] However, many activists define the sweatshop danger not with a language of germs, contagious disease, and public health, but with a discourse of citizenship, rights, and democracy. Thus, student protesters hold signs declaring "this is what democracy looks like" and the NLC indicted the N. S. Mart sweatshop for its assault on rights: "The most fundamental human and workers' rights of the N. S. Mart employees are being violated on a daily basis."[18]

The language of rights, not germs, is immediately more amenable to organizing campaigns that are genuinely friendly to workers—as opposed to efforts in the 1880s and 1890s that seemed to blame workers for the conditions of the sweatshop. Partly for this reason, the sweatshop has come to refer to more than a garment workplace. It is now used to describe shoe factories, electronic data entry firms, even restaurants.[19] The broadening of the definition of the sweatshop is supported by the principal union in the American garment industry, the Union of Needletrades, Industrial, and Textile Employees (UNITE) (the union formed from a merger of the ILGWU and the Amalgamated Clothing and Textile Workers' Union, the main union in the men's garment trade). UNITE is a mere shadow of the former ILGWU. Global competition has devastated the union, which has dwindled in size and strength. UNITE has chosen to expand beyond the garment industry, organizing a host of workers, especially immigrants, in low-paid industries. Union leaders such as UNITE president Bruce Raynor have transformed the organization into a union of sweatshop workers. For Raynor, "supermarket and restaurant delivery workers, servers at catered parties, cabdrivers, child-care providers, home health care workers and apartment cleaners" are "workers in service-sector sweatshops." He employs the word "sweatshop" to evoke images of "mistreatment and abuse."[20]

The widening description of the sweatshop has allowed the anti-sweatshop movement to focus on issues and workers beyond the garment industry. The National Mobilization Against Sweatshops and the Chinese Staff and Workers Association, for example, criticized the Dong Khanh restaurant in New York's Chinatown as a "sweatshop." Despite several name changes, the restaurant "remains Chinatown's most notorious sweatshop," implying long worker hours, harassment, and poor working conditions. The charge is especially forceful by the implicit comparison between the restaurant and the garment shops that fill Chinatown.[21] Again, the activists rely on a language of rights to attack the restaurant. The National Mobilization Against Sweatshops declared that it is "aimed at fundamentally transforming the sweatshop system according to the needs and human rights of working people."

Yet even as such campaigns stress a language of rights, they still continue to depend on meanings of the sweatshop as an immigrant workplace, often characterized by high levels of women's labor. Anti-sweatshop activists have regularly brought sweatshop workers, especially from Central America, to the United States to speak at college campuses and union conventions. In much the same way that Women's Trade Union League leaders created publicity during the 1909–13 strikes, activists give the larger analysis while women workers of color from the Third World provide first-person narratives to American audiences. Such "testimonials" bring the reality of sweated labor to American consumers, but also they provide the visual evidence that connects the sweatshop to female, immigrant, and Third World labor.[22]

The close and persistent connection between feminized sweated labor and Third World and immigrant labor mirrors a century-old binary that saw the sweatshop as the opposite of the American factory. Today, despite its omnipresence in the United States, the sweatshop is cast as an "illegal, alien" workplace or as a stage of production for countries that are not as far along as the United States or Western Europe in their development. Such a representation of sweated labor shapes how the First World (embodied in white, middle-class consumers) comes to see sweatshop workers.

One view is articulated by Kristof and WuDunn. They see sweatshops in Southeast Asia as "a clear sign of the industrial revolution that is beginning to reshape Asia." As such, American consumers and Asian sweatshop workers cannot understand each other. Americans focus on dangerous conditions, harassment, disease, and long hours of labor, but Asian workers actually want to work that hard, according to Kristof and WuDunn. Indeed, they contend that one Cambodian woman they met would have taken a job in a sweatshop in order to afford a mosquito net to protect her children from malaria. Now, it seems, the sweatshop cures disease. To stress the distance separating consumers and workers, Kristof and WuDunn begin their article by describing the food eaten by Thai villagers: "a huge green mango leaf filled with rice, fish paste and fried beetles. It was a hearty breakfast, if one didn't mind the odd antenna left sticking in one's teeth." Like the reporter criticizing Lower East Side Jews for eating smelly cheese, Kristof and WuDunn present a racist image that presumes the disgust of Western readers. Of course, even as the authors argue that westerners cannot understand the culture and material wants of Asian workers, they still speak for the Cambodian worker in claiming that she would have taken a sweatshop job.[23]

The other view is more immediately sympathetic and less obviously racist. As Ethel Brooks argues, sweatshop workers become emblems of the problems of globalization. They are cast as sweatshop victims. Thus, the *Daily News* ran a large, close-up photograph of a sleeping sweatshop worker to begin their series. The sleeping worker with closed eyes does not speak to the viewer, nor does the series record the voices of workers. Rather, the reader is transformed into a voyeur, looking at workers' bodies and hearing only the voices of employers, activists, unionists, and government officials. In a similar fashion, the repeated testimony of workers in anti-sweatshop campaigns aimed at western consumers transforms workers into victims. As Brooks argues: "In transnational campaigns against sweatshops . . . tactics have relied upon the circulation of stories of abuses, visions of factories and women's bodies."[24] Thus, Kernaghan testified about workers making Kathie Lee clothing for Wal-Mart: "What a profound difference it would make in the lives of tens of thousands of poor, struggling families if Kathie Lee and Wal-Mart stated publicly that never again would Kathie Lee clothing be made by exploited children or by women whose basic rights are violated."[25]

Such a strategy, Brooks suggests, also reserves for activists the ability to define the danger of the sweatshop. Still, Brooks perhaps overestimates the extent to which this silences workers. After all, Jewish women's negotiation with their wealthier allies during the 1909–13 strikes over the meaning of sweatshop victimhood helped working women to claim a place in garment unions and immigrant women. They shifted meanings of the sweatshop, even as their role in the production of strike publicity was limited. Nonetheless, Brooks and an increasing number of activists correctly point out the limits of the language of contemporary anti-sweatshop organizing. The relentless focus on the sweatshop casts it as an excess, not as symptomatic, of neo-liberal globalization.

Pioneering activists and scholars, like Andrew Ross, hoped that anti-sweatshop activism would reveal the broader structural inequalities behind the sweatshop. In fact, for some, as Ross laments, there is a "tendency to see sweatshops, however defined, as an especially abhorrent species of labor and therefore in a moral class of their own." Therefore, one can attack the sweatshop, but accept legal, low-wage labor. And one can criticize a company like the Gap for its use of sweated labor, but ignore the global inequalities fostered by neo-liberal capitalism. As Liza Featherstone asks, is the anti-corporatism of anti-sweatshop activism a cover for anti-capitalism or just an effort to soften its edges?

In fact, the focus on the sweatshop as the worst kind of workplace allows for an easy escape for corporations. They can make small improvements, like those Nike boasts about in its "Transparency 101" campaign. Not only does this blunt the force of consumer-oriented activism, but it also obscures the real problems of work as defined by workers themselves. As Brooks points out, when the *New York Times* returned to Mandarin (now renamed Charter) in 2001, they pointed out the improvements. The comforts, conveniences, and "unsurpassed coffee" of a century ago have returned; workers take "coffee breaks and lunch on an outdoor terrace cafeteria. Bathrooms are unlocked, the factory is breezy and clean, and employees can complain to a board of independent monitors if they feel abused." The low wages are ignored, and there is no effort to gauge the complex hierarchies of power between workers and contractors, contractors and corporations, and between male and female, adult and child workers, fostered by global production.[26]

The example of Mandarin points out another burden of language of anti-sweatshop activism. In much the same way that a century ago the drive for and definition of a model shop increasingly focused on legislation and inspection, contemporary campaigns have again come to stress regulation and monitoring, not by workers but by independent bodies. Even as USAS activists have rallied to support union campaigns as part of a growing recognition of the problems of older anti-sweatshop strategies, the answer to the sweatshop still seems to be "enforcement, enforcement, enforcement," as the *Daily News* editorialized. The drive for monitoring directs activism toward a particular vision of a model shop, as imagined largely by activists. Does this specific, detailed vision of an alternative to the sweatshop ignore—even discourage—local forms of resistance, especially hidden, everyday kinds of resistance that are the main "weapons of the weak"?

As anthropologist Aihwa Ong has written, mass and seemingly spontaneous visions and fainting spells among Malaysian workers represent a way for otherwise powerless workers to negotiate the rigors of industrial production. Is there a way for the movement to recognize such resistance, to help transform what anthropologist James Scott calls a "hidden transcript" of resistance into a "saturnalia of power"?[27] It is not hard to imagine that, like workers a hundred years ago, today's sweatshop workers will come to wonder about their place in the movement and to criticize the prevailing alternative to the sweatshop.

The focus on monitoring puts the power for change in the hands of consumers, more than it does in the hands of workers. Corporate campaigns, boycotts, even "sweat-free" shopping might solve the most egregious problems of the sweatshop, but they leave in place the global inequality of wealth and local inequalities within families, communities, and nations.

As the sweatshop has moved to the center of political discourse and has catalyzed the reemergence of a labor left in the First World, it is useful to compare two anti-sweatshop movements at the turn of the twentieth and twenty-first centuries. The language to define the danger of the sweatshop has shifted dramatically, from public health to rights, a change that works to place the blame for the sweatshop squarely on the broad shoulders of corporations. At the same time, the definition of the sweatshop has expanded. It is no longer a contractor garment shop located in a tenement apartment building. Indeed, even the definition of the sweatshop in history has changed. Once hailed as a modern shop, the Triangle Factory building is now cast as a sweatshop. However, the focus on regulation and "comforts and conveniences" remains.

Workers and activists have both begun to examine the burden of the language of their campaigns. Activists have challenged their own representations of sweatshop workers and questioned the focus on monitoring. Workers have demanded a greater leadership role in the movement, demanding more support for unionization campaigns. As part of this process, it seems useful to revisit the definition of the sweatshop itself. What are the dangers of the sweatshop? Is "enforcement, enforcement, enforcement" a solution even if, as historian Xiaolan Bao points out, the sweatshop is deeply intertwined not simply with class inequality but with family and ethnicity?[28] Does the idea of the sweatshop as the worst form of global capitalism cement the role of the Third World as a site of production and the First World as a site of consumption? And finally, does the notion of the sweatshop as a feminized and immigrant or Third World workplace serve to naturalize conceptions of gender, racial, and ethnic difference and obscure the inequalities these conceptions perpetuate? The anti-sweatshop movement is a vibrant form of activism, and "sweatshop" is a powerful word. Its initial definition a century ago helped to consolidate an alliance that changed the landscape of an industry, but left women "awash in a sea of masculinity" and male and female workers wondering about their place in the union. Perhaps the image of Jewish female unionists in 1930 once again calling out for real inclusion in the ILGWU can serve as a historical reminder for critics, unionists, and workers once again struggling against the sweatshop and its "mistreatment and abuse."

Notes

Introduction The Language and the Limits of Anti-Sweatshop Organizing

1. George Price, untitled autobiographical sketch, undated, YIVO Institute for Jewish Research, George M. Price Papers, RG #213, 1.
2. See, for example, George Price, *Administration of Labor Laws and Factory Inspection in Certain European Countries* (Washington, D.C.: Government Printing Office, 1914); George Price, *Handbook on Sanitation: A Manual of Theoretical and Practical Sanitation: For Students and Physicians* (New York: J. Wiley & Sons, 1901, 1913); George Price, *Hygiene and Public Health* (Philadelphia: Lea & Febiger, 1910).
3. The Garment Trade Authority, "Joint Board of Sanitary Control Made Enduring Contribution to Welfare of the Ready-To-Wear Industry," YIVO; George M. Price Papers, RG #213, 49.
4. Price, autobiographical sketch, 7.
5. George M. Price, *The Russian Jews in America* (St. Petersburg, Russia, 1893), trans. Leo Shpall, reprinted from the *Publication of the American Jewish Historical Society* 48 (September-December 1958): 50–51.
6. George Price, *The Modern Factory* (Brooklyn: The Scientific Press, 1914), v.
7. Price, *Russian Jews in America*, 54.
8. Emphasis in the original. Price set out this vision of the model shop in *Modern Factory*, esp. 67.
9. Ibid., 42, 56.
10. Ibid., 56.
11. Ibid., 1.
12. Howard Markel, *Quarantine!: East European Jewish Immigrants and the New York City Epidemics of 1892* (Baltimore: Johns Hopkins University Press, 1997), 13–40; Alan Kraut, *Silent Travelers: Germs, Genes, and the "Immigrant Menace"* (New York: Basic Books, 1994), 136–165; Deborah Dwork, "Health Conditions of Immigrant Jews on the Lower East Side of New York, 1880–1914," *Medical History* 25 (January 1981): 1–40.

13. Karen Halttunen, *Confidence Men and Painted Women: A Study of Middle-Class Culture in America, 1830–1870* (New Haven: Yale University Press, 1982).

14. Kathy Peiss, *Cheap Amusements: Working Women and Leisure in Turn-of-the-Century New York* (Philadelphia: Temple University Press, 1986); Ruth Rosen, *The Lost Sisterhood: Prostitution in America, 1900–1918* (Baltimore: Johns Hopkins University Press, 1982); Barbara Meil Hobson, *Uneasy Virtue: The Politics of Prostitution and the American Reform Tradition* (New York: Basic Books, 1987); Ruth M. Alexander, *The "Girl Problem": Female Sexual Delinquency in New York, 1900–1930* (Ithaca, N.Y.: Cornell University Press, 1995), 1–68.

15. Eileen Boris, *Home to Work: Motherhood and the Politics of Industrial Homework in the United States* (Cambridge: Cambridge University Press, 1994), 1–200; Alice Kessler-Harris, *A Women's Wage: Historical Meanings and Social Consequences* (Lexington: University Press of Kentucky, 1990); Kathryn Kish Sklar, *Florence Kelley and the Nation's Work: The Rise of Women's Political Culture, 1830–1900* (New Haven: Yale University Press, 1995).

16. "Are We Facing an Immigration Peril?" *New York Times*, January 29, 1905; John Higham, *Strangers in the Land: Patterns of American Nativism, 1860–1925* (1955; reprint, New Brunswick, N.J.: Rutgers University Press, 1992), 35–67.

17. Gail Bederman, *Manliness and Civilization: A Cultural History of Gender and Race in the United States, 1880–1917* (Chicago: University of Chicago Press, 1995); T. Jackson Lears, *No Place of Grace: Antimodernism and the Transformation of American Culture 1880–1920* (Chicago: University of Chicago Press, 1981), 3–47; Nell Irvin Painter, *Standing at Armageddon: The United States, 1877–1919* (New York: W. W. Norton & Company, 1987), 1–71.

18. James R. Barrett and David Roediger, "Inbetween Peoples: Race, Nationality, and the 'New Immigrant' Working Class," *Journal of American Ethnic History* 3 (Spring 1997): 3–44; Matthew Frye Jacobson, *Whiteness of a Different Color: European Immigrants and the Alchemy of Race* (Cambridge, Mass.: Harvard University Press, 1998), esp. 39–90, 137–200.

19. Matthew Guterl, *The Color of Race in America, 1900–1940* (Cambridge, Mass.: Harvard University Press, 2001).

20. Mark Pittenger, "A World of Difference: Constructing the Underclass in Progressive America," *American Quarterly* 49 (March 1997): 26–65.

21. Markel, *Quarantine!*, 135–182; Kraut, *Silent Travelers*, 50–77; Elizabeth Yew, "Medical Inspection of Immigrants at Ellis Island, 1891–1924," *Bulletin of the New York Academy of Medicine* 56 (1980): 488–510.

22. David Rosner and Gerald Markowitz, "The Early Movement for Occupational Safety and Health, 1900–1917," in *Sickness and Health in America: Readings in the History of Medicine and Public Health*, ed. Judith Walzer Leavitt and Ronald L. Numbers (Madison: University of Wisconsin Press, 1985), 507–524; Judith Walzer Leavitt, *The Healthiest City: Milwaukee and the Politics of Health Reform* (Princeton: Princeton University Press, 1982); Fitzhugh Mullan, *Plagues and Politics: The Story of the United States Public Health Service* (New York: Basic Books, 1989); John Duffy, *The Sanitarians: A History of American Public Health* (Urbana: University of Illinois Press, 1990); John Duffy, *A History of Public Health in New York City*, 2 vols. (New York: Russell Sage Foundation, 1974); Alice Kessler-Harris and Jane Lewis, eds., *Protecting Women: Labor Legislation in Europe, the United States, and*

Australia, 1880–1920 (Urbana: University of Illinois Press, 1995); Leon Fink, *Progressive Intellectuals and the Dilemmas of Democratic Commitment* (Cambridge, Mass.: Harvard University Press, 1999).

23. Price, *Modern Factory*, v.
24. "Reports of the Industrial Commission on Immigration" (Washington, D.C.: Government Printing Office, 1901), 15: xvi–xvii; David Montgomery, *The Fall of the House of Labor: The Workplace, the State, and American Labor Activism, 1865–1925* (Cambridge: Cambridge University Press, 1987), 70–82; Gwendolyn Mink, *Old Labor and New Immigrants in American Political Development* (Ithaca, N.Y.: Cornell University Press, 1986).
25. Herbert Gutman, *Work, Culture, and Society in Industrializing America* (New York: Vintage Books, 1977), 3–78.
26. Price, *The Russian Jews in America*, 52–53.
27. Daniel T. Rodgers, *The Industrial Work Ethic in America, 1850–1920* (Chicago: University of Chicago Press, 1974), 153–181; Laura Hapke, *Labor's Text: The Worker in American Fiction* (New Brunswick, N.J.: Rutgers University Press, 2001), 91–166.
28. Wendy Gamber, *The Female Economy: The Millinery and Dressmaking Trades, 1860–1930* (Urbana: University of Illinois Press, 1997), Christine Stansell, "The Origins of the Sweatshop: Women and Early Industrialization in New York City," in *Working-Class America: Essays on Labor, Community, and American Society*, ed. Michael H. Frisch and Daniel J. Walkowitz (Urbana: University of Illinois Press, 1983), 78–103; Nancy Green, *Ready-to-Wear and Ready-to-Work: A Century of Industry and Immigrants in Paris and New York* (Durham, N.C.: Duke University Press, 1997).
29. Price, *The Russian Jews in America*, 52.
30. Ibid., 53.
31. Boris, *Home to Work*, 49–80.
32. *New York Tribune*, September 4, 1882. On narratives of exploration in visits to working-class and immigrant neighborhoods, see Pittenger, "A World of Difference"; Toby Higbie, "Crossing Boundaries: Tramp Ethnographers and Narratives of Class in Progressive Era America," *Social Science History* 21 (Winter 1997): 559–592.
33. Green, *Ready-to-Wear and Ready-to-Work*, 137–160; N. N. Feltes, "Misery or the Production of Misery: Defining Sweated Labour in 1890," *Social History* 17 (October 1992): 441–452; Sheila Blackburn, "'Princesses and Sweated-Wage Slaves Go Well Together': Images of British Sweated Workers, 1843–1914," *International Labor and Working-Class History* 61 (Spring 2002): 24–44.
34. Nayan Shah, *Contagious Divides: Epidemics and Race in San Francisco's Chinatown* (Berkeley: University of California Press, 2001).
35. The sweatshop was associated with Jews primarily. Americanization campaigns were also aimed more at Jews than other groups, largely because Eastern European Jews were the reform focus of older, prosperous German Jewish immigrants and their descendents. There were no groups that acted as institutional bridges for Italians, the other major immigrant group working in the garment industry. See Kathie Friedman-Kasaba, *Memories of Migration: Gender, Ethnicity, and Work in the Lives of Jewish and Italian Women, 1870–1924* (Albany: State University of New York Press, 1996); Elizabeth Ewen, *Immigrant Women in the Land of Dollar: Life and*

Culture on the Lower East Side, 1890–1925 (New York: Monthly Review Press, 1977).

36. Morris Rosenfeld, *Songs from the Ghetto*, trans. Leo Wiener (Boston: Small, Maynard and Co., 1900), 3–7.

37. Benedict Anderson, *Imagined Communities* (1983; London: Verso, 1991), 1–7. See Elias Tcherikower, *Geshikte fun der Yidisher Arbeter-Bavegung in di Fareynikte Shtatn, I* (New York: YIVO, 1943), 254–308.

38. Naomi Cohen, *Encounter with Emancipation: German Jews in the United States, 1830–1914* (Philadelphia: Jewish Publication Society of America, 1984); Hasia Diner, *A Time for Gathering: The Second Migration, 1820–1880* (Baltimore: Johns Hopkins University Press, 1992); Arthur Goren, *New York Jews and the Quest for Community: The Kehillah Experiment, 1908–1922* (New York: Columbia University Press, 1970); Paula E. Hyman, *Gender and Assimilation in Modern Jewish History: The Roles and Representation of Women* (Seattle: University of Washington Press, 1995), 93–133; Nancy B. Sinkoff, "Education for 'Proper' Jewish Womanhood: A Case Study in Domesticity and Vocational Training, 1897–1926," *American Jewish History* 77 (June 1988): 572–599; Miriam Cohen, *Workshop to Office: Two Generations of Italian Women in New York City, 1900–1950* (Ithaca, N.Y.: Cornell University Press, 1993).

39. The ILGWU was the most important union in the garment industry in New York, where the ladies' garment trade was the most important industry. For case studies of other garment unions and of other garment centers in the United States, see Jo Ann Argersinger, *Making the Amalgamated: Gender, Ethnicity, and Class in the Baltimore Clothing Industry, 1899–1939* (Baltimore: Johns Hopkins University Press, 1999); Steve Fraser, *Labor Will Rule: Sidney Hillman and the Rise of American Labor* (Ithaca, N.Y.: Cornell University Press, 1991); Ruth Frager, *Sweatshop Strife: Class, Ethnicity, and Gender in the Jewish Labour Movement in Toronto, 1900– 1939* (Toronto: University of Toronto Press, 1992).

40. Boris, *Home to Work*, 49–80; Hadassa Kosak, *Cultures of Opposition: Jewish Immigrant Workers, New York City, 1881–1905* (Albany: State University of New York Press, 2000), 107–129.

41. Jewish workers' effort to define the boundaries of the workplace offer a commentary on the principal paradigms of American labor history: the community and industry/workplace studies. Labor historians have often assumed that home and work represent universal categories. The patterns of Jewish labor organizing suggest that home and work represent spaces whose specific historical meanings are the result of constructed social boundaries. See Elizabeth Faue, *Community of Suffering and Struggle: Women, Men, and the Labor Movement in Minneapolis, 1915– 1945* (Chapel Hill: University of North Carolina Press, 1991), 1–20.

42. Boris, *Home to Work*.

43. Anson Rabinbach, *The Human Motor: Energy, Fatigue, and the Origins of Modernity* (New York: Basic Books, 1990).

44. Steve Fraser, "Dress Rehearsal for the New Deal: Shop-Floor Insurgents, Political Elites, and Industrial Democracy in the Amalgamated Clothing Workers," in Frisch and Walkowitz, *Working-Class America: Essays on Labor, Community, and American Society*, 212–255; Richard Greenwald, "Bargaining for Industrial Democracy?: Labor, the State, and the New Industrial Relations in Progressive Era New York"

(Ph.D. diss., New York University, 1998); Maxine Schwartz Seller, "The Uprising of the Twenty Thousand: Sex, Class, and Ethnicity in the Shirtwaist Makers' Strike of 1909," in *"Struggle a Hard Battle": Essays on Working Class Immigrants*, ed. Dirk Hoerder (DeKalb: Northern Illinois University Press, 1986), 254–279; Ann Schofield, "The Uprising of the 20,000: The Making of a Labor Legend," in *A Needle, a Bobbin, a Strike: Women Needleworkers in America*, ed. Joan M. Jensen and Sue Davidson (Philadelphia: Temple University Press, 1984), 167–182.

45. Nan Enstad, *Ladies of Labor, Girls of Adventure: Working Women, Popular Culture, and Labor Politics at the Turn of the Twentieth Century* (New York: Columbia University Press, 1999), esp. 84–160.

46. Enstad's efforts to trace the distance between workers and outside observers reflects a broader cultural and political historiography of the period that argues that expressions of anxiety about industrialization and immigration rarely crossed class lines. Lears, *No Place of Grace*; Bederman, *Manliness and Civilization*; Painter, *Standing at Armageddon*; Dorothy Ross, *The Origins of American Social Science* (Cambridge: Cambridge University Press, 1991); James Kloppenberg, *Uncertain Victory: Social Democracy and Progressivism in European and American Thought, 1870–1920* (Oxford: Oxford University Press, 1986).

47. This book uses methods of the linguistic turn to address structural questions about production and organizing. See Joan Wallach Scott, "On Language, Gender, and Working-Class History," in *Gender and the Politics of History* (New York: Columbia University Press, 1988), 53–67; Kathleen Canning, "Feminist History after the Linguistic Turn: Historicizing Discourse and Experience," *Signs* 19 (Winter 1994): 369–403; Kathleen Canning, *Languages of Labor and Gender: Female Factory Work in Germany, 1850–1914* (Ithaca, N.Y.: Cornell University Press, 1996).

48. Judith Butler, *Gender Trouble: Feminism and the Subversion of Identity* (1989; New York: Routledge, 1999); Judith Butler, *Bodies That Matter: On the Discursive Limits of "Sex"* (New York: Routledge, 1993); Elizabeth Grosz, *Volatile Bodies: Toward a Corporeal Feminism* (Bloomington: Indiana University Press, 1994); Katherine Ott, *Fevered Lives: Tuberculosis in American Culture since 1870* (Cambridge: Harvard University Press, 1996); Nancy Tomes, *The Gospel of Germs: Men, Women, and the Microbe in American Life* (Cambridge: Harvard University Press, 1999).

49. Joan Wallach Scott, *Only Paradoxes to Offer: French Feminists and the Rights of Man* (Cambridge: Harvard University Press, 1996), esp. ix–18.

50. Katherine Franke, "What's Wrong with Sexual Harassment," *Stanford Law Review* 49 (1997): 691–772, argues that harassment works to maintain gender norms in the workplace. Annelise Orleck, *Common Sense and a Little Fire: Women and Working-Class Politics in the United States, 1900–1965* (Chapel Hill: University of North Carolina Press, 1995), 31–120, examines the relationship between working-class activists and wealthy supporters.

51. This book argues that skill, particularly in the context of an industry that featured flexible production like the garment industry, was socially constructed. On the social construction of skill, see Anne Phillips and Barbara Taylor, "Sex and Skill: Notes Towards a Feminist Economics" in *Feminism and History*, ed. Joan Wallach Scott (New York: Oxford University Press, 1996), 317–330; Ileen DeVault, "'To Sit among Men': Skill, Gender, and Craft Unionism in the Early American Federation of Labor," in *Labor Histories: Class, Politics, and the Working-Class Experience*, ed. Eric

Arneson, Julie Greene, and Bruce Laurie (Urbana: University of Illinois Press, 1998), 259–283.

One Eastern European Jews and the Rise of a Transnational Garment Economy

1. Interview with Paul Novick, YIVO Institute for Jewish Research, Irving Howe Papers, RG #570, Box 1, 10.
2. Irving Howe and Hadassa Kosak both describe the effect of Eastern European Jewish immigration on the garment industry in New York and detail the declining wages and the spread of the contracting system. Irving Howe, *World of Our Fathers: The Journey of the East European Jews to America and the Life They Found and Made* (New York: Harcourt Brace Jovanovich, 1976), 148–168; Hadassa Kosak, *Cultures of Opposition: Jewish Immigrant Workers, New York City, 1881–1905* (Albany: State University of New York Press, 2000), 74–80. Jo Ann Argersinger traces a similar narrative in her study of garment work and Jewish labor organizing in Baltimore. Jo Ann Argersinger, *Making the Amalgamated: Gender, Ethnicity, and Class in the Baltimore Clothing Industry, 1899–1939* (Baltimore: Johns Hopkins University Press, 1999), 8–27.
3. "Reports of the Industrial Commission on Immigration," Volume 15 (Washington, D.C.: Government Printing Office, 1901), xxvi.
4. For the way Jews and other European immigrants were differentiated from non-European races based on their ability to adapt to industrial labor, see John R. Commons, *Races and Immigrants in America* (New York: Macmillan Co., 1907). Jews were still regarded as the carriers of disease. Indeed, as Howard Markel notes, whole boatloads of Jews were blamed for epidemics in New York in 1892 and quarantined. There were also calls for restrictions of European and Jewish immigration for medical reasons. But the Lower East Side was never itself physically or legally cordoned off from the rest of the city. Howard Markel, *Quarantine!: East European Jewish Immigrants and the New York City Epidemics of 1892* (Baltimore: Johns Hopkins University Press, 1997). This last point is crucial and, in many ways, is the key to the history of garment industry and of Jewish labor organizing. Unlike other immigrants in these years, in particular, Latino/a and Asian immigrants who faced extreme ghettoization and segregation, Eastern European Jewish immigrants were viewed by older immigrant groups and by politicians and policymakers as immigrants who could be, at least partially, integrated into American industrial life. George Sanchez, in a recent review of the literature on immigration and race, notes the decision to segregate or engage immigrant groups is crucial to the history of immigrants' working lives, social status, and resistance. George J. Sanchez, "Race, Nation, and Culture in Recent Immigration Studies" *Journal of American Ethnic History* 18 (Summer 1999): 6–84. For a comparison with an immigrant group that was forcefully segregated, see Nayan Shah, *Contagious Divides: Epidemics and Race in San Francisco's Chinatown* (Berkeley: University of California Press, 2001).
5. Nancy L. Green, "The Modern Jewish Diaspora: Eastern European Jews in New York, London, and Paris," in *European Migrants: Global and Local Perspectives*, ed. Dirk Hoerder and Leslie Page Moch (Boston: Northeastern University Press, 1996),

263–281; Samuel Joseph, *Jewish Immigration to the United States from 1881 to 1910* (New York: Arno, 1969). The Pale of Settlement—the land set aside for Jews in the Russian empire—is often pictured in studies of American Jewry as static, unchanging, and even idyllic. For the oft-cited example of this image, see Mark Zbrowski and Elizabeth Herzog, *Life Is with People: The Jewish Little Town of Eastern Europe* (1952; reprint, New York: Schocken Books, 1995). In fact, life in the Pale cannot be captured in the restrictive image of the *shtetl*, the small Jewish town. The Pale changed dramatically between 1880 and 1925, affected by industrialization, revolution, the arrival of socialism, war, anti-Semitism, and by the growing trend of emigration. For more nuanced social histories of the Pale, see Isaac Levitats, *The Jewish Community in Russia, 1844–1917* (Jerusalem: Posner and Sons, 1981); Salo Baron, *The Russian Jew under the Tsars and Soviets* (New York: Macmillan, 1964); Deborah Dash Moore, ed., *East European Jews in Two Worlds: Studies from the YIVO Annual* (Evanston: Northwestern University Press; YIVO Institute for Jewish Research, 1990).

6. Green, "Modern Jewish Diaspora," 268–269.
7. Gerald Sorin, *A Time for Building: The Third Migration, 1880–1920* (Baltimore: Johns Hopkins University Press, 1992), 70.
8. Jeffrey Gurock, *When Harlem Was Jewish, 1870–1930* (New York: Columbia University Press, 1979); Deborah Dash Moore, *At Home in America: Second Generation New York Jews* (New York: Columbia University Press, 1981). The ability of Jewish immigrants to move out of the Lower East Side and spread throughout the city highlights the way in which Jewish immigrants were not legally segregated. For a larger social history of European immigration, see John Bodnar, *The Transplanted: A History of Immigrants in Urban America* (Bloomington: Indiana University Press, 1985), 1–56.
9. Immigration and labor historians have often noted the exceptional nature of Jewish immigration, pointing out that unlike other immigrant groups, Jews saw immigration as permanent. Nell Irvin Painter, *Standing at Armageddon: The United States, 1877–1919* (New York: W. W. Norton, 1987), xxxi–xxxiv; Herbert Gutman, *Work, Culture, and Society in Industrializing America* (New York: Vintage Books, 1977), 3–78; Joseph, *Jewish Immigration to the United States from 1881–1910*, 139. Even Jonathan D. Sarna in his study of the return migration that did exist notes that statistics of returns suggest that for most Eastern European Jewish immigrants, their immigration was permanent. Jonathan D. Sarna, "The Myth of No Return: Jewish Return Migration to Eastern Europe, 1881–1914," *American Jewish History* (December 1981): 256–268. Italian immigrants, in contrast to Jews, often engaged in a triangular and often seasonal migration from Italy to the factories of the United States to the harvests of Argentina and then back to Italy. The fact that Jews saw their migration as permanent suggests why Jews, more than other groups, embraced relationships with older immigrants and social reformers. Donna R. Gabaccia and Fraser M. Ottanelli, eds., *Italian Workers of the World: Labor Migration and the Formation of Multiethnic States* (Urbana: University of Illinois Press, 2001).
10. Simon Kuznets, "Immigration of Russian Jews to the United States: Background and Structure," *Perspectives in American History* 9 (1975): 35–123; Lloyd P. Gartner, "Jewish Migrants en Route from Europe to North America," *Jewish History* 1 (Fall

1986): 49–66; Bodnar, *Transplanted*, 53–54; Thomas Kessner, *The Golden Door: Italian and Jewish Immigrant Mobility in New York City, 1880–1915* (New York: Oxford University Press, 1977), 33–53.

11. Rose Cohen, *Out of the Shadow: A Russian Jewish Girlhood on the Lower East Side* (1918; reprint, Ithaca, N.Y.: Cornell University Press, 1995), 41–65; Howe, *World of Our Fathers*, 26–63.

12. Kosak, *Cultures of Opposition*, 85; Bodnar, *Transplanted*, 20. For two studies of the demography of European migration and of women's roles in this movement, see Walter Nugent, "Demographic Aspects of European Migration Worldwide," and Donna Gabaccia, "Women of the Mass Migrations: From Minority to Majority, 1820–1930," in Hoerder and Moch, *European Migrants*, 70–111.

13. Regional difference was visible even in New York. Moses Rischin points out that different streets on the Lower East Side were identified with different Jewish immigrant groups. Hungarians lived just above Houston Street, Rumanians from Chrystie Street to Allen Street, and Galicians between Houston and Broome Streets. Moses Rischin, *The Promised City: New York's Jews, 1870–1914* (New York: Corinth, 1964), 78.

14. On relations between older immigrants and new arrivals, see Howe, *World of Our Fathers*, 119–255.

15. "Report of the Industrial Commission on Immigration," 316. Nancy L. Green, *Ready-to-Wear and Ready-to-Work: A Century of Industry and Immigrants in Paris and New York* (Durham, N.C.: Duke University Press, 1997), 188–204.

16. Kuznets, "Immigration of Russian Jews to the United States," 71.

17. Isaac Max Rubinow, "Economic Condition of the Jews in Russia," *Bulletin of U.S. Bureau of Labor* 15 (1907): 500–501, 521–522. On Jewish garment work in Eastern Europe, see Ezra Mendelsohn, *Class Struggle in the Pale: The Formative Years of the Jewish Workers' Movement in Tsarist Russia* (Cambridge: Cambridge University Press, 1970), 1–27: Yoav Peled, *Class and Ethnicity in the Pale: The Political Economy of Jewish Workers' Nationalism in Late Imperial Russia* (New York: St. Martin's Press, 1989).

18. Cited in Jesse Pope, *The Clothing Industry in New York* (Columbia: E. W. Stephens Publishing Company, 1905), 49.

19. On immigration between New York and London and comparative studies on work in London and New York, see Andrew S. Reutlinger, "Reflections on the Anglo-American Jewish Experience: Immigrants, Workers, and Entrepreneurs in New York and London, 1870–1914," *American Jewish Historical Quarterly* (June 1977): 473–484; Selma Berral, *East Side/East End: Eastern-European Jews in London and New York, 1870–1920* (Westport, Conn.: Praeger, 1994). For a comparative study of the needle trades in New York and Paris, see Green, *Ready-to-Wear and Ready-to-Work*.

20. David Feldman, *Englishmen and Jews: Social Relations and Political Culture, 1840–1914* (New Haven: Yale University Press, 1994), 163–164. See also Joseph Buckman, *Immigrants and the Class Struggle: The Jewish Immigrant in Leeds, 1880–1914* (Manchester: Manchester University Press, 1983).

21. Rubinow, "Economic Condition of the Jews in Russia," 503–504. Tailoring was far and away the largest category of employment.

22. Bernard D. Reiskind, *In Two Worlds*, undated, YIVO, American Jewish Autobiographies (AJA), RG #102, #358, 245; Kosak, *Cultures of Opposition*, 69–74. For a his-

tory of searching for work, see Walter Licht, *Getting Work: Philadelphia, 1840–1950* (Cambridge: Harvard University Press, 1992).

23. Samuel Siegal, unpublished autobiography, YIVO, AJA, #281a, 110; Stella Seligson Papiroff, *With Open Eyes*, undated, YIVO, AJA, #368, 20–32; Andrew Heinze, *Adapting to Abundance: Jewish Immigrants, Mass Consumption, and the Search for American Identity* (New York: Columbia University Press, 1990), 45–46.

24. Sam Liptzin, *Tales of a Tailor: Humor and Tragedy in the Struggles of the Early Immigrants against the Sweatshop*, trans. Max Rosenfeld (New York: Prompt Press, 1965), 67–70. For a fictional account of the *landsman* shop see the novelette *Uncle Moses* by the popular Yiddish author and playwright Sholem Asch. Asch, *Three Novels: Uncle Moses, Chaim Lederer's Return, Judge Not*, trans. Elsa Krauch (New York: G. P. Putnam's Sons, 1938). On the important cultural role of the hometown associations both in finding jobs for new immigrants and in easing the transition to the United States, see Elias Tcherikower, *The Early Jewish Labor Movement in the United States*, trans. and rev. by Aaron Antonovsky (New York: YIVO, 1961), 134; Daniel Soyer, *Jewish Immigrant Associations and American Identity* (Cambridge: Harvard University Press, 1997); Hannah Kliger, ed., *Jewish Hometown Associations and Family Circles in New York: The WPA Yiddish Writers' Group Study* (Bloomington: Indiana University Press, 1992), 25–116.

25. Interview with Isidore Wisotsky, YIVO, Irving Howe Papers, RG #570, Box 1, 2.

26. Harry Polis, untitled autobiography, ca. 1966, YIVO, AJA, #292, 14–15.

27. Ibid.

28. Elizabeth Hasanovitz, *One of Them: Chapters from a Passionate Autobiography* (New York: Houghton Mifflin Company, 1918), 15.

29. Jacob Riis, *How the Other Half Lives: Studies among the Tenements of New York* (New York: Telegraph Books, 1985), 85.

30. Liptzin, *Tales of a Tailor*, 22–24; Abraham Rosenberg, *Di Klukmachers un Zayere Iunions* (New York: Kluk Operaytors Iunion Lokal 1, 1920), 3.

31. George Price, untitled autobiographical sketch, undated, YIVO, George M. Price Papers, RG #413, 10.

32. James Oneal, *A History of the Amalgamated Ladies' Garment Cutters' Union, Local 10 Affiliated with the ILGWU* (New York: Local 10, 1927), 295.

33. Polis, untitled autobiography, 15.

34. *Twelfth Annual Report of the Factory Inspectors of the State of New York, 1897* (Albany: Wynkoop Hallenbeck Crawford Co., State Printers, 1898), 45.

35. Lloyd P. Gartner, "The Jews of New York's East Side, 1890–1893: Two Surveys by the Baron de Hirsch Fund," *American Jewish Historical Quarterly* 3 (March 1964): 264–274; George M. Price, *The Russian Jews in America*, trans. Leo Shpall (reprinted from the *Publication of the American Jewish Historical Society* 48 [Sept.-Dec., 1958]: 50).

36. *Twelfth Annual Report of the Factory Inspectors of the State of New York, 1897*, 45; Pope, *Clothing Industry in New York*, 45–53; Melach Epstein, *Jewish Labor in the U.S.A.: An Industrial, Political and Cultural History of the Jewish Labor Movement*, 2 vols. in 1 (New York: Ktav Publishing House, 1969), 98–99.

37. Sorin, *Time for Building*, 74.

38. *A General Survey of the Sanitary Conditions of the Shops in the Cloak Industry* (New York: Joint Board of Sanitary Control, 1911), 7.

39. *Special Report on Sanitary Conditions in the Shops of the Dress and Waist Industry* (New York: Joint Board of Sanitary Control, May 1913), 6–7. Other immigrant groups, principally Italians (the bulk of whom arrived after their Jewish counterparts), also worked in the needle trades. They tended, however, with the exception of waistmaking, to concentrate in needle trades peripheral to ready-made clothing manufacture. Few Jewish workers labored in the trades dominated by Italian workers, like millinery (custom-made dressmaking) and lace-making. These were generally trades that many workers and observers considered distinct from the garment industry. See *Twentieth Annual Report of the Bureau of Labor Statistics for the Year Ended September 30, 1902* (Albany: The Argus Company, Printers, 1903), 54, 68. As Jews moved into certain types of garment manufacture, Italians also quickly formed the majority in certain trades, especially lace and hat making. See Mary Van Kleeck, *Artificial Flower Makers* (New York: Survey Associates, 1913); *Twentieth Annual Report of the Bureau of Labor Statistics*, 91–149. For contrasting experiences of Jewish and Italian workers, see Elizabeth Ewen, *Immigrant Women in the Land of Dollar: Life and Culture on the Lower East Side, 1890–1925* (New York: Monthly Review Press, 1977); Kessner, *Golden Door*, 44–126.

40. E. E. Pratt, *The Industrial Causes of Congestion in New York City* (New York: Longmans, Green, 1911), 19–20.

41. "The Concentration of Garment Shops in Certain Areas and Diminution in the Size of Shops," ILGWU Archives; Union Health Center Papers, Box 5, Folder 11, 59.

42. New York State Department of Labor, *Report of the Growth of Industry in New York* (Albany: The Argus Company, Printers, 1904), 93–94. Long before the arrival of Jewish immigrants, New York was the center of American garment work. From the Early Republic through the twentieth century, New York was at the forefront of change in the garment work. Just before and during the early years of Jewish immigration, New York moved from being a hub of the custom trade to the unmatched center of the ready-made trade. See Pope, *Clothing Industry in New York*, 1–44.

43. *Report of the Growth of the Industry in New York*, 94.

44. Christine Stansell traces the rise of ready-made clothing even further back. The first ready-made trade in New York manufactured cheap garments that were shipped to the South to clothe slaves. Christine Stansell, "The Origins of the Sweatshop: Women and Early Industrialization in New York City," in *Working-Class America: Essays on Labor, Community, and American Society*, ed. Michael H. Frisch and Daniel J. Walkowitz (Urbana: University of Illinois Press, 1983), 78–103. The need for uniforms to clothe the rapidly expanding Union army forced changes in the manufacture of men's clothing. In the decades after the war's end, as the effectiveness of sizing matched changes in clothing styles, men's readymade clothing found a market even among wealthy men. Green, *Ready-to-Wear and Ready-to-Work*, 30–31.

45. Wendy Gamber, *The Female Economy: The Millinery and Dressmaking Trades, 1860–1930* (Urbana: University of Illinois Press, 1997), 10.

46. For the transition to the ready-made trade in women's garment manufacture, see ibid., 216–217.

47. Louis Levine, *The Women's Garment Workers: A History of the International Ladies' Garment Workers' Union* (New York: B. W. Huebsch, 1924), 8–11; Gamber, *Female Economy*, 220–221. The introduction of the cutting knife had important effects on

the composition of the workforce. Soon, as cutting increasingly moved to the factory from the custom shop, cutting became men's work alone. The original short cutting knife was quickly replaced by a long cutting knife, despite the opposition of cutters. The long knife demanded little training but tremendous strength. Oneal, *History of the Amalgamated Ladies' Garment Cutters' Union, Local 10*, 394–396.

48. Cited in Claudia B. Kidwell and Margaret C. Christman, *Suiting Everyone: The Democratization of Clothing in America* (Washington, D.C.: Smithsonian Institute Press for the National Museum of History and Technology, 1974), 79.

49. Oneal, *History of the Amalgamated Ladies' Garment Cutters' Union, Local 10*, 394. On the importance of the sewing machine see Ava Baron and Susan E. Klepp, "'If I Didn't Have My Sewing Machine . . .': Women and Sewing-Machine Technology," in *A Needle, A Bobbin, A Strike: Women Needleworkers in America*, ed. Joan M. Jenson and Sue Davidson (Philadelphia: Temple University Press, 1984), 20–59.

50. "Reports of the Industrial Commission," xxiv; Oneal, *History of the Amalgamated Ladies' Garment Cutters' Union, Local 10*, 132–135; Eileen Boris, *Home to Work: Motherhood and the Politics of Industrial Homework in the United States* (Cambridge: Cambridge University Press, 1994), 49–80.

51. Tcherikower, *Early Jewish Labor Movement*, 165–167.

52. *Fourth Report of the Factory Investigating Commission, 1915, Vol. 2* (Albany: J. B. Lyon Company, Printers, 1915), 181; Katherine Tyng, "The Processes and Organization of the Work in Dress and Waist Manufacture," in *Special Report on Sanitary Conditions in the Shops of the Dress and Waist Industry*, 17–22; Pope, *Clothing Industry in New York*, 70; Susan Glenn, *Daughters of the Shtetl: Life and Labor in the Immigrant Generation* (Ithaca: Cornell University Press, 1990), 100–101.

53. Levine, *Women's Garment Workers*, 168–169.

54. *Report of the Growth of Industry in New York*, 93. The decline in the size and capitalization of shops in the men's industry was similar; see *Report of the Growth of Industry in New York*, 88.

55. *Seventh Annual Report of the Factory Inspectors of the State of New York, 1892* (Albany: James B. Lyon, State Printer, 1893), 113–211.

56. House of Representatives, Committee of Manufactures, 52nd Congress, 2nd Session, "Report on the Sweating System under House Resolution" (Feb. 13, 1892), xii. See also *Fourteenth Annual Report of the Factory Inspectors of the State of New York, 1899* (Albany: James B. Lyons, State Printer, 1900), 112–180.

57. "Reports of the Industrial Commission," xxv; Howe, *World of Our Fathers*, 139.

58. *Third Annual Report of the Factory Inspectors of the State of New York, for the Year Ending December 1st 1888* (Albany: The Argus Company, Printers, 1889), 27; Levine, *Women's Garment Workers*, 14.

59. Green, *Ready-to-Wear and Ready-to-Work*, 37.

60. Yitzchak Yankel Doroshkin, *From Zhitkovitch throughout the World (Episodes of My Life)* (1974), trans. Mindy Gross, YIVO, AJA, #305, 151–154; Oneal, *History of the Amalgamated Ladies' Garment Cutters' Union, Local 10*, 156–157.

61. "Report on the Sweating System," v–vi.

62. *First Annual Report of the Joint Board of Sanitary Control in the Cloak, Suit and Skirt Industry of Greater New York* (New York: Joint Board of Sanitary Control, October 1911), 36–38; *Preliminary Report of the Factory Investigating Commission, 1912, Vol. 1* (Albany: the Argus Company, Printers, 1912), 30–33.

63. *Special Report on Sanitary Conditions in the Shops of the Dress and Waist Industry*, 5–9.

64. Sarah Comstock, "The Uprising of the Girls," *Collier's* 44 (December 25, 1909): 20; Oral History of Leon Stein, Tamiment-Wagner Labor Archives, New York University; Oral History of the American Left (OHAL), Series IV, Section VI, 13; Howe, *World of Our Fathers*, 298.

65. *A General Survey of the Sanitary Conditions of the Shops in the Cloak Industry*, 3–7; Rosenberg, *Di Klukmachers un Zayere Iunions*, 3–6.

66. *First Annual Report of the Joint Board of Sanitary Control*, 37; *Preliminary Report of the Factory Investigating Commission*, 83–86.

67. *Third Annual Report of the Bureau of Statistics of Labor* (Albany: The Argus Company Printers, 1886), 37–39.

68. Pope, *Clothing Industry in New York*, 138–146; *Third Annual Report of the Bureau of Statistics of Labor*, 289.

69. Henry Feingold, *Zion in America: The Jewish Experience from Colonial Times to the Present* (New York: Hippocrene Books, 1974), 142–157; Sorin, *Time for Building*, 109–135. Suzanne Wasserman describes the persistence of ideas about Jewish poverty in "The Good Old Days of Poverty: The Battle over the Fate of New York City's Lower East Side during the Depression" (Ph.D. diss., New York University, 1990).

70. Donald Bigelow, "Introduction," in Riis, *How the Other Half Lives*, xiv.

71. *New York Times*, November 14, 1897; Eva McDonald Valesh, "The Tenement House Problem in New York," *Arena* 7 (April 1893): 580–581; Mark Pittenger, "A World of Difference: Constucting the Underclass in Progressive America," *American Quarterly* 49 (March 1997): 26–65; Matthew Frye Jacobson, *Whiteness of a Different Color: European Immigrants and the Alchemy of Race* (Cambridge: Harvard University Press, 1998), 203–222; Toby Higbie, "Crossing Boundaries: Tramp Ethnographers and Narratives of Class in Progressive Era America," *Social Science History* 21 (Winter 1997): 559–592.

72. *New York Times*, July 30, 1893; *New York Times*, November 14, 1897.

73. *New York Times*, November 14, 1897.

74. "Reports of the Industrial Commission on Immigration," lxvi.

75. United States Immigration Commission, *Dictionary of Races or Peoples* (Washington, D.C.: Government Printing Office, 1911).

76. On languages of civilization, see Gail Bederman, *Manliness and Civilization: A Cultural History of Gender and Race in the United States, 1880–1917* (Chicago: University of Chicago Press, 1995); James R. Barrett and David Roediger, "Inbetween Peoples: Race, Nationality, and the 'New Immigrant' Working Class," *Journal of American Ethnic History* 3 (Spring 1997): 3–44; Matthew Guterl, *The Color of Race in America, 1900–1940* (Cambridge: Harvard University Press, 2001), 14–27; Pittenger, "World of Difference," 39.

77. Jacobson, *Whiteness of a Different Color*, 1–12, 171–200; David Roediger, *Towards the Abolition of Whiteness* (London: Verso, 1994), 181–198; Karen Brodkin, *How Jews Became White Folks and What That Says about Race in America* (New Brunswick, N.J.: Rutgers University Press, 1998).

78. "Reports of the Industrial Commission on Immigration," lxvi.

79. Ibid., lxix.

80. *New York Times*, September 13, 1894; *New York Times*, July 30, 1893.
81. Riis, *How the Other Half Lives*, 79.
82. "Reports of the Industrial Commission on Immigration," lxx; *Herald*, June 23, 1882; *New York Times*, July 30, 1893; *Tribune*, September 4, 1882.
83. *New York Senate Document #36 1885*, 45; "Reports of the Industrial Commission on Immigration," 476.
84. *New York Times*, June 19, 1892; Howe, *World of Our Fathers*, 395–396.
85. "Reports of the Industrial Commission on Immigration," 478.
86. *New York Tribune*, September 4, 1882; *Nation*, February 5, 1891.
87. Valesh, "Tenement House Problem in New York," 580–581; Elizabeth Faue, *Writing the Wrongs: Eva Valesh and the Rise of Labor Journalism* (Ithaca: Cornell University Press, 2002).
88. *New York Times*, January 29, 1905.
89. "Reports of the Industrial Commission on Immigration," 478.
90. *New York Times*, January 29, 1905; *Tribune*, November 25, 1900.
91. Valesh, "Tenement House Problem in New York," 580–581; Markel, *Quarantine!*
92. *New York Times*, January 29, 1905.
93. Riis, *How the Other Half Lives*, 79, 81.
94. Ibid., 81; Theodore Bingham, "Foreign Criminals in New York," *North American Review* (September 1908): 383–384. Daniel J. Walkowitz ties the Bingham report to the rise of Jewish social service. See Daniel J. Walkowitz, *Working with Class: Social Workers and the Politics of Middle-Class Identity* (Chapel Hill: University of North Carolina Press, 1999), 66–72. On Jewish crime, see Jenna W. Joselit, *Our Gang: Jewish Crime and the New York Jewish Community, 1900–1940* (Bloomington: Indiana University Press, 1983).
95. *New York Times*, July 30, 1893.
96. On medical views of Eastern European Jewish immigrants see Alan Kraut, *Silent Travelers: Germs, Genes, and the "Immigrant Menace"* (New York: Basic Books, 1994), 105–135; Markel, *Quarantine!*
97. *New York Times*, January 29, 1905; *New York Times*, July 30, 1893.
98. Markel, *Quarantine!*; Kraut, *Silent Travelers*, 166–196. On the social effects of germ theory, the growth of the public health movement, and the tendency of public health officials to blame immigrants for communicable disease, see Katherine Ott, *Fevered Lives: Tuberculosis in American Culture since 1870* (Cambridge: Harvard University Press, 1996), 100–111; Shiela M. Rothman, *Living in the Shadow of Death: Tuberculosis and the Social Experience of Illness in American History* (Baltimore: Johns Hopkins University Press, 1994), 174–193; Nancy Tomes, *The Gospel of Germs: Men, Women, and the Microbe in American Life* (Cambridge: Harvard University Press, 1999).
99. "Reports of the Industrial Commission on Immigration," lxvi. Eric Goldstein notes that by the time Eastern European Jewish immigrants were arriving in large numbers, German American Jews generally discouraged and disavowed a racialist language. See Eric L. Goldstein, "'Different Blood Flows in Our Veins': Race and Jewish Self-Definition in Late Nineteenth Century America," *American Jewish History* 85 (March 1997): 29–55.
100. Quoted in Sorin, *Time for Building*, 86.
101. Feingold, *Zion in America*, 142–157; Howe, *World of Our Fathers*, 229–234; Kosak, *Cultures of Opposition*, 92–98.

102. Sorin, *Time for Building*, 86–92. On the history of German Jews in New York, see Naomi Cohen, *Encounter with Emancipation: German Jews in the United States, 1830–1914* (Philadelphia: Jewish Publication Society of America, 1984); Hasia Diner, *A Time for Gathering: The Second Migration, 1820–1880* (Baltimore: Johns Hopkins University Press, 1992).
103. "Reports of the Industrial Commission on Immigration," 248–249.
104. Miriam Blaustein, ed., *Memoirs of David Blaustein* (New York: McBride, Nast, 1913), 127–137. On the Educational Alliance, see S. P. Rudens, "A Half Century of Community Service: The Story of the New York Educational Alliance," *The American Jewish Year Book* 46 (1944–1945): 73–88; Sorin, *Time for Building*, 86–88.
105. Howe, *World of Our Fathers*, 119–147.
106. The most insightful analysis of the Kehillah remains Arthur Goren, *New York Jews and the Quest for Community: The Kehillah Experiment, 1908–1922* (New York: Columbia University Press, 1970).
107. "Reports of the Industrial Commission on Immigration," 195–196.
108. Ibid., 476–477.
109. Lawrence Veiller and R. DeForest, eds., *The Tenement House Problem* (New York: Macmillan, 1903); George M. Price, *Tenement House Inspection: A Practical Text Book For Civil Service Candidates* (New York: The Chief Publishing Company, 1904). On the anti-tenement campaign, see Kessner, *Golden Door*, 127–160. For details on depictions of tenements in the popular press, see Rischin, *Promised City*, 82–83.
110. Lilian Wald, *The House on Henry Street* (New York, 1915).
111. Howe, *World of Our Fathers*, 93; Kraut, *Silent Travelers*, 170–171; Markel, *Quarantine!*, 122.

Two "The Great Jewish Métier": Factory Inspectors, Jewish Workers, and Defining the Sweatshop, 1880–1910

1. "Reports of the Industrial Commission on Immigration," Volume 15 (Washington, D.C.: Government Printing Office, 1901), 320; John R. Commons, "The Sweating System in the Clothing Trade," in *Trade Unionism and Labor Problems*, ed. John R. Commons (Boston: Ginn and Company, 1905), 316–335.
2. Leon Fink, *Progressive Intellectuals and the Dilemmas of Democratic Commitment* (Cambridge: Harvard University Press, 1999); Matthew Guterl, *The Color of Race in America, 1900–1940* (Cambridge: Harvard University Press, 2001), 16–27; James R. Barrett and David Roediger, "Inbetween Peoples: Race, Nationality, and the 'New Immigrant' Working Class," *Journal of American Ethnic History* 3 (Spring 1997): 3–44.
3. Daniel T. Rodgers, *Atlantic Crossings: Social Politics in a Progressive Age* (Cambridge: Belknap Press, Harvard University Press, 1998), 235–236.
4. The movement for factory inspection began in the United States only in the 1890s and was aimed especially at the regulation of the labor of women and children. These systems of inspection would be dramatically expanded after the turn of the century and the decision in *Muller vs. Oregon. First Annual Report of the Factory Inspectors of the State of New York for the Year Ending December 1st, 1886* (Albany: The Argus Company, 1887), 41–58; Rodgers, *Atlantic Crossings*; Ulla Wikander, Alice

Kessler-Harris, and Jane Lewis, eds., *Protecting Women: Labor Legislation in Europe, the United States, and Australia, 1880–1920* (Urbana: University of Illinois Press, 1995); Kathryn Kish Sklar, *Florence Kelley and the Nation's Work* (New Haven: Yale University Press, 1995).

5. House of Representatives, Committee of Manufactures, 52nd Congress, 2nd Session, "Report on the Sweating System under House Resolution" (Feb. 13, 1892), iii–xxix; "Reports of the Industrial Commission on Immigration," 316–345. On regulation in Pennsylvania and Massachusetts, see *Thirteenth Annual Report of the Factory Inspectors of the State of New York, 1898* (Albany: Wynkoop Hallenbeck Crawford Co., State Printers, 1899), 779–784.

6. *Seventh Annual Report of the Factory Inspectors of the State of New York* (Albany: J.B. Lyon, 1893), 1–23.

7. *Seventeenth Annual Report on Factory Inspection for Twelve Months Ending September 30, 1902* (Albany: The Argus Company, Printers, 1903), 37; *Thirteenth Annual Report of the Factory Inspectors of the State of New York*, 39–44.

8. *Eighth Annual Report of the Factory Inspector of the State of New York, 1893* (Albany: James B. Lyon, State Printer, 1894), 12.

9. *Seventeenth Annual Report on Factory Inspection*, 37.

10. "Report on the Sweating System," 188.

11. *Fourteenth Annual Report of the Factory Inspectors of the State of New York, 1899* (Albany: James B. Lyons, State Printer, 1900), 42.

12. Jesse Pope, *The Clothing Industry in New York* (Columbia: E. W. Stephens Publishing Company, 1905), 49; Kathie Friedman-Kasaba, *Memories of Migration: Gender, Ethnicity and Work in the Lives of Jewish and Italian Women in New York, 1870–1924* (Albany: State University of New York Press, 1995), 159.

13. Jacob Riis, *How the Other Half Lives: Studies among the Tenements of New York* (New York: Telegraph Books, 1985), 88–100.

14. N. N. Feltes, "Misery or the Production of Misery: Defining Sweated Labour in 1890," *Social History* 17 (October 1992): 441–452; Sheila Blackburn, "'Princesses and Sweated-Wage Slaves Go Well Together': Images of British Sweated Workers, 1843–1914," *International Labor and Working-Class History* 61 (Spring 2002): 24–44.

15. "Report on the Sweating System," v–vi.

16. The first use of the word sweatshop in the United States that I have found is in the *Fifth Annual Report of the Factory Inspectors of the State of New York* (Albany: James B. Lyon, State Printer, 1891), 27–28. The earliest and most complete definition of the "sweat-shop" is in the "Report on the Sweating System," v–vi. For an example of a similar definition of the sweatshop, see "Reports of the Industrial Commission on Immigration," 319–324. For details on the first use of the words "sweatshop" and "sweated," see Pope, *Clothing Industry in New York*, 256–287. As Leon Stein correctly notes: "The Sweatshop is a state of mind as well as a physical fact." Leon Stein, "Introduction," in *Out of the Sweatshop: The Struggle for Industry Democracy* (New York: Quadrangle, 1977), xv–xvi.

17. "Report on the Sweating System," vi.

18. Ibid., 106.

19. John De Witt Warner, "Sweating System in New York City," *Harper's Weekly* 39 (February 9, 1895): 135.

20. "Report on the Sweating System," 95.

21. "Reports of the Industrial Commission on Immigration," 324.
22. *Twelfth Annual Report of the Factory Inspectors of the State of New York, 1897* (Albany: Wynkoop Hallenbeck Crawford Co., State Printers, 1898), 47; George McKay, "The Effect upon the Health, Moral and Mentality of Working People Employed in Overwhelmed Work-Rooms," *Fifth Annual Report of the Factory Inspectors of New York*, 81.
23. Eva McDonald Valesh, "The Tenement House Problem in New York," *The Arena* 7 (April 1893): 580–581.
24. *Twelfth Annual Report of the Factory Inspectors of the State of New York*, 47.
25. "Reports of the Industrial Commission on Immigration," 323–347.
26. Pope, *Clothing Industry in New York*, 47–48; *Eighth Annual Report of the Factory Inspector of the State of New York*, 791. On contemporary racialized images of Jewish immigrants and on rising tides of anti-Semitism, see John Higham, *Send These to Me: Jews and Other Immigrants in Urban America* (New York: Atheneum, 1975), 116–195.
27. *Twentieth Annual Report of the Bureau of Labor Statistics for the Year Ended September 30, 1902* (Albany: The Argus Company, Printers, 1903), 79; "Reports of the Industrial Commission on Immigration," 325.
28. *Oxford English Dictionary, Volume 16* (Oxford: Clarendon Press, 1989), 369–374; William Shakespeare, *A Midsummer Night's Dream* (London: The Arden Shakespeare, 1979), 32 (act II, scene i).
29. Christine Stansell, "The Origins of the Sweatshop: Women and Early Industrialization in New York City," in *Working-Class America: Essays on Labor, Community, and American Society*, ed. Michael H. Frisch and Daniel J. Walkowitz (Urbana: University of Illinois Press, 1983), 78–103.
30. Daniel Pick, *Faces of Degeneration: A European Disorder, c. 1848–c. 1918* (Cambridge: Cambridge University Press, 1989); Mark Pittenger, "A World of Difference: Constucting the Underclass in Progressive America," *American Quarterly* 49 (March 1997): 26–65.
31. McKay, "The Effect upon the Health, Moral and Mentality of Working People Employed in Overcrowded Work-Rooms," 77–80; George McKay, "The Sweating System," in *Eighth Annual Report of the Factory Inspector of the State of New York*, 787–797.
32. "Report on the Sweating System," 108–109.
33. *Ninth Annual Report of the Factory Inspectors of the State of New York, 1894* (Albany: James B. Lyon, State Printer, 1895), 876.
34. Factory inspectors declared filthy habits a particularly "Jewish" characteristic. They insisted that other immigrants, like Swedes and Germans, possessed much healthier habits. State of New York, Department of Factory Inspection, *Testimony of Daniel O'Leary, Factory Inspector of the State of New York, before the United States Industrial Commission, Wednesday, March 8, 1899* (Albany: Brandow Printing Company, 1899), 14–16; *Eleventh Annual Report of the Factory Inspectors of the State of New York, 1896* (Albany: Wynkoop Hallenbeck Crawford Co., State Printers, 1897), 28.
35. "Report on the Sweating System," 199, 187–193.
36. Valesh, "The Tenement House Problem in New York," 582.
37. Riis, *How the Other Half Lives*, 80. Such descriptions of the typical "Hebrew" worker

reflect the United States Immigration Commission's own racial profiles of the "Hebrew, Jewish, or Israelite." United States Immigration Commission, "Dictionary of Races or Peoples," *Reports of the Immigration Commission*, Vol. 5, 61st Congress, 3rd Session, Senate Doc. 748.

38. Such images of Jews as feeble were at the same time separate from and drew on anti-Semitic prejudices. The image of the enfeebled Jewish body recalled older as well as contemporary American and European anti-Semitic depictions of Jews. For some observers, like Jacob Riis, this body type belied anti-Semitic understandings of Jews as thrifty and money-grubbing. At other times, as Jacobson notes, depictions of Jewish "racial" difference was part of a general effort to create racial distinctions among white Americans. See Matthew Frye Jacobson, *Whiteness of a Different Color: European Immigrants and the Alchemy of Race* (Cambridge: Harvard University Press, 1998), 174–182; Robert Singerman, "The Jew as Racial Alien: The Genetic Component of American Anti-Semitism," in *Anti-Semitism in American History*, ed. David A. Gerber (Urbana: University of Illinois Press, 1986), 103–128; Sander Gilman, *Franz Kafka: The Jewish Patient* (New York: Routledge, 1995), 41–100; Karen Brodkin, *How Jews Became White Folks and What That Says about Race in America* (New Brunswick, N.J.: Rutgers University Press, 1998).

39. *Ninth Annual Report of the Factory Inspectors of the State of New York*, 876; "Report on the Sweating System," xxviii–xxix.

40. McKay, "The Effect upon the Health, Moral and Mentality of Working People Employed in Overcrowded Work-rooms," 77–80, 84–85.

41. Ibid., 84–85.

42. *Ninth Annual Report of the Factory Inspectors of the State of New York*, 876.

43. Ibid., 876.

44. "Reports of the Industrial Commission on Immigration," 321.

45. *Twelfth Annual Report of the Factory Inspectors of the State of New York*, 759.

46. "Report on the Sweating System," 199.

47. George McKay, "Evils of the Sweating System," in *Seventh Annual Report of the Factory Inspectors of the State of New York*, 667–669.

48. McKay, "Sweating System," 794.

49. *Third Annual Report of the Factory Inspectors of the State of New York, for the Year Ending December 1st 1888* (Albany: The Troy Press Company, Printers, 1889), 27–28.

50. *Eleventh Annual Report of the Factory Inspector of the State of New York*, 28.

51. "Report on the Sweating System," 199, 224. Katherine Ott describes how by the 1890s the idea of germs had entered common language, dramatically altering the way policymakers and public health advocates talked about contagion. Katherine Ott, *Fevered Lives: Tuberculosis in American Culture since 1870* (Cambridge: Harvard University Press, 1996), 53–68.

52. "Report on the Sweating System," viii. For an excellent study of how the native-born public and government officials expressed their fears of immigrants and their poverty through concerns about epidemic disease, see Howard Markel, *Quarantine! East European Jewish Immigrants and the New York City Epidemics of 1892* (Baltimore: Johns Hopkins University Press, 1997). See also Alan Kraut, *Silent Travelers: Germs, Genes, and the "Immigrant Menace"* (New York: Basic Books, 1994), 50–77.

53. Warner, "The Sweating System in New York City," 135.
54. Consumers' League of New York, "Children Who Work in the Tenements" (March 1908). On the Consumers' League, see Eileen Boris, *Home to Work: Motherhood and the Politics of Industrial Homework in the United States* (Cambridge: Cambridge University Press, 1994), 81–122; Allis Rosenberg Wolfe, "Women, Consumerism, and the National Consumers' League in the Progressive Era, 1900–1923," *Labor History* 16 (Summer 1975): 378–392.
55. John Crowley, "Plague of 1893: The Terrible Scourge of the Tenement House and Reasons for State Control of the Clothing Trade," *Labor Leader* (May 1891); Boris, *Home to Work*, 60–63. Crowley was almost certainly referring to the New York cholera epidemic of 1893, which, as Howard Markel notes, was blamed on Eastern European Jewish immigrants. See Markel, *Quarantine!*
56. "Reports of the Industrial Commission on Immigration," xxx.
57. *Fifth Annual Report of the Factory Inspectors of the State of New York*, 27; George M. Price, *The Russian Jews in America*, trans. Leo Shpall, reprinted from the *Publication of the American Jewish Historical Society* 48 (September-December 1958), 54 (originally published St. Petersburg, Russia, 1893).
58. Quoted in Melach Epstein, *Jewish Labor in the U.S.A.: An Industrial, Political and Cultural History of the Jewish Labor Movement*, 2 vols. in 1 (New York: Ktav Publishing House, 1969), 93.
59. Morris Rosenfeld in his poems described the "*svetshop*" in Morris Rosenfeld, *Songs from the Ghetto*, trans. Leo Wiener (Boston: Small, Maynard and Co., 1900). Uriel Weinreich in his English-Yiddish dictionary translates sweatshop only slightly differently, but still literally, as "*shvitzshop*." See Uriel Weinreich, *Modern English-Yiddish, Yiddish-English Verterbukh* (New York: YIVO Institute for Jewish Research, 1977).
60. Quoted in Epstein, *Jewish Labor in U.S.A.*, 93. See also Bernard Weinstein, *Di Yidishe Iunions in Amerike* (New York: Fareinigte Idishe Gewerkshaftn, 1929), 49–50, and Elias Tcherikower, *The Early Jewish Labor Movement in the United States*, trans. and rev. by Aaron Antonovsky (New York: YIVO, 1961), 168. Epstein suggests that the three characteristics were "Unsanitary conditions, Long or unlimited work hours, Very low wages." Epstein, *Jewish Labor in U.S.A.*, 87.
61. Fannia Cohn, "Unpublished History of the ILGWU," ILGWU Archives; Education Department Papers, Box 2, Folder 8b, Chapter 1, 3; Louis Levine, *The Women's Garment Workers: A History of the International Ladies' Garment Workers' Union* (New York: B. W. Huebsch, 1924), 169; Epstein, *Jewish Labor in the U.S.A.*, 395; Elias Tcherikower, *Geshikte fun der Yidisher Arbeter-Bavegung in di Fareynikte Shtatn, I* (New York: YIVO, 1943), 254–308.
62. "Report on the Sweating System," xiii.
63. Quoted in Irving Howe, *World of Our Fathers: The Journey of the East European Jews to America and the Life They Found and Made* (New York: Harcourt Brace Jovanovich, 1976), 70.
64. Quoted in Epstein, *Jewish Labor in U.S.A.*, 91.
65. "Report on the Sweating System," 93–94.
66. Ibid., 93.
67. Morris C. Feinstone, "A Brief History of the United Hebrew Trades," in

Gewerkshaften: Issued by the United Hebrew Trades on the Occasion of Its 50th Anniversary as a Trade Union Central Body in Greater New York (New York: United Hebrew Trades, 1938), 12.

68. Daniel Bender, "'A hero . . . for the weak': Work, Consumption, and the Enfeebled Jewish Worker, 1881–1924," *International Labor and Working-Class History* 56 (Fall 1999): 1–22. Alan Kraut argues that at the same time that Jewish immigrants recognized their physical weakness, Eastern European Jewish immigrants sought to dispel racialist notions that they were biologically inferior or had a propensity to filth. Kraut, *Silent Travelers*, 136–165.

69. Morris Rosenfeld, "Despair," YIVO; Morris Rosenfeld papers, RG #431, Box 12, Folder 116.

70. Maurice Fishberg, "The Relative Infrequency of Tuberculosis among Jews," reprinted from *American Medicine*, November 2, 1901, Judaica Division, New York Public Library, 4–10; Maurice Fishberg, *Tuberculosis among Jews* (New York: William Wood, 1908), 1–19, reprinted from *Medical Record*, December 26, 1908; Maurice Fishberg, *Health Problems of the Jewish Poor* (New York: Press of Philip Cowen, 1903), 11–13, reprinted from *The American Hebrew*. See Kraut, *Silent Travelers*, 105–135; Deborah Dwork, "Health Conditions of Immigrant Jews on the Lower East Side of New York, 1880–1914," *Medical History* 25 (January 1981), 1–40. Jacobson, *Whiteness of a Different Color*, 175, argues that Fishberg subscribed to racial interpretations of Jewishness. In fact, Fishberg blamed work for the Jewish body.

71. Fishberg, "The Relative Infrequency of Tuberculosis Among Jews," 4–10.

72. Abraham Rosenberg, *Memoirs of a Cloakmaker,* trans. Lynn Davison (New York: n.p., 1920), Martin P. Catherwood Library; Cornell University, 25.

73. Quoted in Epstein, *Jewish Labor in the U.S.A.*, 91.

74. Stella Seligson Papiroff, *With Open Eyes*, undated, YIVO, American Jewish Autobiographies (AJA), RG #102, #368, 32.

75. Rosenberg, *Memoirs of a Cloakmaker*, 25.

76. "Report on the Sweating System," 94.

77. Rosenfeld, *Songs from the Ghetto*, 7–11.

78. Yacob Adler, "The Machine Worker" in Aaron Kramer, ed. and trans., *A Century of Yiddish Poetry* (New York: Cornwall Books, 1989), 91–92.

79. Feinstone, "A Brief History of the United Hebrew Trades," 12.

80. On Epstein, see Howe, *World of Our Fathers*, 574–576.

81. Ott, *Fevered Lives*, 9–29.

82. Hutchins Hapgood, *The Spirit of the Ghetto, Studies of the Jewish Quarter of New York* (1902; reprint, New York: Schocken Books, 1965); Jacob Epstein, *An Autobiography* (London: E. P. Hutton, 1963), 2. The inclusion of Epstein's drawing in a text likely to be read by non-Eastern European Jewish immigrants highlights the sharing of language used to represent the Jewish sweatshop worker. On the idea of seeking a working-class authenticity in popular descriptions of the "ghetto," see Pittenger, "A World of Difference."

83. Price, *Russian Jews in America*, 50–51.

84. Kraut, *Silent Travelers*, 160–162.

85. E. M. Lilien, "An Der Nahmaschine," YIVO, Morris Rosenfeld Papers, RG #431, Box 13, Folder 125.

Three "A Race Ignorant, Miserable, and Immoral": Sweatshop Danger and Labor in the Home, 1890–1910

1. "Reports of the Industrial Commission on Immigration," Volume 15 (Washington, D.C.: Government Printing Office, 1901), 369; Eileen Boris, *Home to Work: Motherhood and the Politics of Industrial Homework in the United States* (Cambridge: Cambridge University Press, 1994), 1–200.

2. The question of married women's work and the parallel question of the male breadwinner and the family wage underpinned not only campaigns against homework, but also campaigns for public health. Part of the goal here is to locate connections between these two campaigns as well as to uncover the gendered discourse that simultaneously tied the sweatshop to tenement homework as well as to public health threats. See Boris, *Home to Work*, 21–124; Eileen Boris, "Regulating Industrial Homework: The Triumph of 'Sacred Motherhood,'" *Journal of American History* 71 (March 1985): 745–763. Rosner and Markowitz note the public health movements' goal of protecting the male breadwinner and restricting married women to the home and to the informal labor market. David Rosner and Gerald Markowitz, "The Early Movement for Occupational Safety and Health, 1900–1917," in *Sickness and Health in America: Readings in the History of Medicine and Public Health*, ed. Judith Walzer Leavitt and Ronald L. Numbers (Madison: University of Wisconsin Press, 1985), 507–552. See also Allison Hepler, *Women in Labor: Mothers, Medicine, and Occupational Health in the United States 1890–1980* (Columbus: Ohio State University Press, 2000). For details on progressive-era debates about women's wage work, see Alice Kessler-Harris, *Out to Work: A History of Wage-Earning Women in the United States* (Oxford: Oxford University Press, 1982), 75–216; Alice Kessler-Harris, *A Women's Wage: Historical Meanings and Social Consequences* (Lexington: University Press of Kentucky, 1990); House of Representatives, Committee of Manufactures, 52nd Congress, 2nd Session, "Report on the Sweating System under House Resolution" (Feb. 13, 1892), xviii, xix. For details on the relationship between Jewish workers and unions dominated by non-Jewish, native-born garment workers, see Louis Levine, *The Women's Garment Workers: A History of the International Ladies' Garment Workers' Union* (New York: B. W. Huebsch, 1924), 68–76.

3. "The Slaves of the 'Sweaters,'" *Harper's Weekly* 34 (April 26, 1890): 335; John De Witt Warner, "Sweating System in New York City," *Harper's Weekly* 39 (February 9, 1895), 135.

4. E. L. Godkin, "Our 'Sweating System,'" *Nation* 50 (June 1890), 483.

5. "Report on the Sweating System," 221.

6. George McKay, "The Effect upon the Health, Moral and Mentality of Working People Employed in Overcrowded Work-Rooms," in *Fifth Annual Report of the Factory Inspectors of the State of New York* (Albany: James B. Lyon, State Printer, 1891), 88–89.

7. Gail Bederman, *Manliness and Civilization: A Cultural History of Gender and Race in the United States, 1880–1917* (Chicago: University of Chicago Press, 1995); Kathryn J. Oberdeck, "Popular Narratives and Working-Class Identity: Alexander Irvine's Early Twentieth-Century Literary Adventures," in *Labor Histories: Class, Politics, and the Working-Class Experience*, ed. Eric Arnesen, Julie Greene, and Bruce Laurie (Urbana: University of Illinois Press, 1998), 201–229.

8. McKay, "The Effect upon the Health, Moral and Mentality of Working People Employed in Overcrowded Work-Rooms," 84–85.

9. "Report on the Sweating System," 198.

10. See Arthur A. Goren, *New York Jews and the Quest for Community: The Kehillah Experiment, 1908–1922* (New York: Columbia University Press, 1970); Paula E. Hyman, *Gender and Assimilation in Modern Jewish History: The Roles and Representation of Women* (Seattle: University of Washington Press, 1995), 93–133; Nancy B. Sinkoff, "Education for 'Proper' Jewish Womanhood: A Case Study in Domesticity and Vocational Training, 1897–1926," *American Jewish History* 77 (June 1988): 572–599; Charlotte Baum, Paula Hyman, Sonya Michel, *The Jewish Woman in America* (New York: The Dial Press, 1976), 163–186; Elizabeth Ewen, *Immigrant Women in the Land of Dollars: Life and Culture on the Lower East Side, 1890–1925* (New York: Monthly Review Press, 1985), 76–91. On the goal of Americanization and its links to marriage among Eastern European Jewish immigrants, see Riv-Ellen Prell, *Fighting to Become Americans: Jews, Gender, and the Anxiety of Assimilation* (Boston: Beacon Press, 1999), 21–87.

11. For a criticism of this "trickle down" model, see Kathy Peiss, *Cheap Amusements: Working Women and Leisure in Turn-of-the-Century New York* (Philadelphia: Temple University Press, 1986), 8–9.

12. Women's economic roles as boarders and shopkeepers has been an important subject for historians of Eastern European Jewish immigrant women; see Susan Glenn, *Daughters of the Shtetl: Life and Labor in the Immigrant Generation* (Ithaca: Cornell University Press, 1990), 74–76; Sydney Stahl Weinberg, *The World of Our Mothers: The Lives of Jewish Immigrant Women* (Chapel Hill: University of North Carolina Press, 1988), 135–136.

13. Glenn, *Daughters of the Shtetl*, 239–240; Kathie Friedman-Kasaba, *Memories of Migration: Gender, Ethnicity, and Work in the Lives of Jewish and Italian Women, 1870–1924* (Albany: State University of New York Press, 1996), 91–134; Weinberg, *World of Our Mothers*, 185–224; Prell, *Fighting to Become Americans*, 105–112.

14. Mabel Hurd Willet, *The Employment of Women in the Clothing Trade* (New York: Columbia University Press, 1902), 86–89.

15. Weinberg, *World of Our Mothers*, 105.

16. Isaac Rubinow, "Economic Condition of the Jews in Russia," *Bulletin of U.S. Bureau of Labor* 15 (1907), 545–547, 523–524; Friedman-Kasaba, *Memories of Migration*, 31–62.

17. Rubinow, "Economic Condition of the Jews in Russia," 523; Hadassa Kosak, *Cultures of Opposition: Jewish Immigrant Workers, New York City, 1881–1905* (Albany: State University of New York Press), 17–18.

18. Glenn, *Daughters of the Shtetl*, 68–70.

19. Rubinow, "Economic Condition of the Jews in Russia," 544–546; Ezra Mendelsohn, *Class Struggle in the Pale: The Formative Years of the Jewish Workers' Movement in Tsarist Russia* (Cambridge: Cambridge University Press, 1970), 1–27; Yoav Peled, *Class and Ethnicity in the Pale: The Political Economy of Jewish Workers' Nationalism in Late Imperial Russia* (New York: St. Martin's Press, 1989), 27.

20. Kosak, *Cultures of Opposition*, 69–74; Weinberg, *Lives of Our Mothers*, 91. On the decline in religious practice in the United States, see Elias Tcherikower, *Geshikhte fun der Yidsher Arbeter-Bevegung in di Fareynikte Shtatn, II* (New York: YIVO, 1945), 418–456.

21. Friedman-Kasaba, *Memories of Migration*, 91–174.

22. Glenn, *Daughters of the Shtetl*, 72–73; Prell, *Fighting to Become Americans*, 104–106; Weinberg, *World of Our Mothers*, 235–236.

23. "Reports of the Industrial Commission on Immigration," 372–373; Miriam Cohen, *Workshop to Office: Two Generations of Italian Women in New York City, 1900–1950* (Ithaca: Cornell University Press, 1993); Rose Laub Coser, Laura S. Anker, and Andrew J. Perrin, *Women of Courage: Jewish and Italian Immigrant Women in New York* (Westport, Conn.: Greenwood Press, 1999), 93–124.

24. *Thirteenth Annual Report of the Factory Inspectors of the State of New York, 1898* (Albany: Wynkoop Hallenbeck Co., State Printers, 1899), 789.

25. "Reports of the Industrial Commission on Immigration," xxvi.

26. Consumers' League of New York, "The Menace to the Home from Sweatshop and Tenement-Made Clothing" (New York, 1901).

27. Allen Forman, "Some Adopted Americans," *American Magazine* 9 (November 1888): 51–52; Thomas Kessner, *The Golden Door: Italian and Jewish Immigrant Mobility in New York City 1880–1915* (New York: Oxford University Press, 1977), 127–160.

28. New York State Legislature, *Report of the Tenement House Committee of 1894* (Albany: J. B. Lyon, 1895); Lawrence Veiller and Robert W. De Forest, eds., *The Tenement House Problem* (New York: Macmillan, 1903); Jacob Riis, *Children of the Tenement* (New York: Macmillan, 1903).

29. *Third Annual Report of the Factory Inspectors of the State of New York, for the Year Ending December 1st 1888* (Albany: The Argus Company, Printers, 1889), 27. While scholars have noted the effects of anti-tenement campaigns on Eastern European Jewish immigrants' living conditions, they have rarely tied the anti-tenement movement to anti-sweatshop campaigns. Doing so places both in the context of middle-class discourses about home and domesticity in the progressive era. Kessner, *The Golden Door*, 132–141; Roy Lubove, *The Progressives and the Slums: Tenement House Reform in New York City, 1890–1917* (Pittsburgh: University of Pittsburgh Press, 1962); Andrew Heinze, *Adapting to Abundance: Jewish Immigrants, Mass Consumption, and the Search for American Identity* (New York: Columbia University Press, 1990), 46, 135–136.

30. *Third Annual Report of the Factory Inspectors of the State of New York*, 27; *Seventh Annual Report of the Factory Inspectors of the State of New York* (Albany: J. B. Lyon, 1893), 2.

31. Melach Epstein, *Jewish Labor in the U.S.A.: An Industrial, Political and Cultural History of the Jewish Labor Movement*, 2 vols. in 1 (New York: Ktav Publishing House, Inc., 1969), 94; Annie S. Daniel, "The Wreck of the Home: How Wearing Apparel Is Fashioned in the Tenements" (New York: New York Consumer's League, n.d.).

32. Jesse Pope, *The Clothing Industry in New York* (Columbia: E. W. Stephens Publishing Company, 1905), 146–147.

33. McKay, "The Effect Upon the Health, Morals and Mentality of Working People Employed in Overcrowded Work-Rooms," 79 (emphasis in the original).

34. "Testimony of Dr. A. S. Daniel," "Report on the Sweating System," 181–186.

35. *Eleventh Annual Report of the Factory Inspectors of the State of New York, 1896* (Albany: Wynkoop Hallenbeck Crawford Co., State Printers, 1897), 28.

36. Eva McDonald Valesh, "The Tenement House Problem in New York," *The Arena* 7 (April 1893), 583.

37. Heinze, *Adapting to Abundance*, 105–146.

38. Corinne L. Gilb, *Oral History of Jennie Matyas*, April-October 1955, Martin P. Catherwood Library, Cornell University, 18.

39. Rose Cohen, *Out of the Shadow: A Russian Jewish Girlhood on the Lower East Side* (1918; reprint, Ithaca: Cornell University Press, 1995), 89.

40. Interview with Isidore Wisotsky, YIVO Institute for Jewish Research, Irving Howe Papers, RG #570, Box 1, 2; Yitzchak Yankel Doroshkin, *From Zhitkovitch throughout the World (Episodes of My Life)* (1974), trans. Mindy Gross, YIVO, American Jewish Autobiographies (AJA), RG #102, #305, 59.

41. *Third Annual Report of the Bureau of Statistics of Labor* (Albany: The Argus Company, Printers, 1886), 289–290.

42. "Report on the Sweating System," 93.

43. Ibid., 93.

44. Ibid.

45. Abraham Rosenberg, *Memoirs of a Cloakmaker*, trans. Lynn Davison (New York: n.p., 1920), Martin P. Catherwood Library, Cornell University, 23.

46. Samuel Shore, "An Epic Achievement," in *Gewerkshaften: Issued by the United Hebrew Trades on the Occasion of its 50th Anniversary as a Trade Union Central Body in Greater New York* (New York: United Hebrew Trades, 1938), 55; Rosenberg, *Memoirs of a Cloakmaker*, 23.

47. Warner, "The Sweating System in New York," 135. On turn-of-the-century anti-homework campaigns, see Boris, *Home to Work*, 21–124; Cynthia Daniels, "Between Home and Factory: Homeworkers and the State," in *Homework: Historical and Contemporary Perspectives on Paid Labor at Home*, ed. Eileen Boris and Cynthia Daniels (Urbana: University of Illinois Press, 1989), 13–32.

48. *Seventh Annual Report of the Factory Inspectors*, 12–13.

49. John R. Commons, "The Sweating System in the Clothing Trade," in *Trade Unionism and Labor Problems*, ed. John R. Commons (Boston: Ginn and Company, 1905), 316–335.

50. "Report on the Sweating System," v–vi. The House Committee defined a hierarchy within the world of sweated garment making with the homework shop at the very bottom.

51. "Report on the Sweating System," viii.

52. Warner, "The Sweating System in New York," 135.

53. "Report on the Sweating System," xxiii.

54. "Reports of the Industrial Commission on Immigration," 373.

55. Boris, *Home to Work*, 49–80. See also Elizabeth Ewen, *Immigrant Women in the Land of Dollar: Life and Culture on the Lower East Side, 1890–1925* (New York: Monthly Review Press, 1977), 121–125; Elias Tcherikower, *The Early Jewish Labor Movement in the United States*, trans. and rev. by Aaron Antonovsky (New York: YIVO, 1961), 170.

56. Warner, "The Sweating System in New York," 135.

57. Ibid., 135.

58. Pope, *Clothing Industry in New York*, 282. It should be noted that Pope, like most contemporary factory inspectors and social reformers, uses the words "homework" and "homeworker" quite specifically to refer to work completed by women in tenement apartments. On the association of homework and women's crafts, see

Nancy L. Green, *Ready-to-Wear and Ready-to-Work: A Century of Industry and Immigrants in Paris and New York* (Durham, N.C.: Duke University Press, 1997), 150–187.

59. *Third Annual Report of the Bureau of Statistics of Labor*, 163–165.
60. "Report on the Sweating System," viii.
61. George M. Price, *Ten Years of Industrial Sanitary Self-Control* (Joint Board of Sanitary Control, 1921), ILGWU Archives; Union Health Center Papers, Box 5, Folder 9, 16.
62. Price (1890), in Tcherikower, *Early Jewish Labor Movement*, 118.
63. Morris Feinstone, "A Brief History of the United Hebrew Trades," in *Gewerkshaften*, 13.
64. Ibid.
65. Glenn, *Daughters of the Shtetl*, 72–73; Weinberg, *World of Our Mothers*, 135–137, 227–228; Cohen, *Out of the Shadow*, 73.
66. On different gendered conceptions of homework in different historical moments, including the idea of homework as flexible forms of production, see Boris and Daniels, *Homework*.
67. It should be noted that male and female Jewish workers efforts to delineate boundaries between home and work began at the height of middle-class reform efforts to pass protective legislation that singled out women and children as unique targets for state safeguarding. On campaigns of protective legislation, see Kessler-Harris, *Out to Work*, 180–214. Elizabeth Faulkner Baker, *Protective Labor Legislation*, Studies in History, Economics and Public Law, vol. 116, no. 2 (New York, 1925); Ulla Wikander, Alice Kessler-Harris, and Jane Lewis, eds., *Protecting Women: Labor Legislation in Europe, the United States, and Australia, 1880–1920* (Urbana: University of Illinois Press, 1995).
68. *Eleventh Annual Report of the Factory Inspector of the State of New York*, 28.
69. Valesh, "The Tenement House Problem in New York," 585–586.
70. "Reports of the Industrial Commission on Immigration," 380.
71. Ibid., 373.
72. The best review of legislation passed in the 1890s can be found in "Reports of the Industrial Commission on Immigration," 373–380.
73. "Report on the Sweating System," xxvi–xxvii; *Twentieth Annual Report of the Bureau of Labor Statistics for the Year Ended September 30, 1902* (Albany: The Argus Company, Printers, 1903), 65.
74. *Seventh Annual Report of the Factory Inspectors of the State of New York*, 54–62; New York State Deputy Factory Inspector Cunningham, "The Sweating System as New York Has Found It," in *Tenth Annual Report of the Factory Inspectors of the State of New York, 1896* (Albany: Wynkoop Hallenbeck Crawford Co., State Printers, 1896), 1328–1331.
75. *Twentieth Annual Report of the Bureau of Labor Statistics*, 65.
76. "Reports of the Industrial Commission on Immigration," 380.
77. Ibid., 380–81.
78. "Report on the Sweating System," 199.
79. "Reports of the Industrial Commission on Immigration," 380–381.
80. Ibid., 374; Boris, *Home to Work*, 21–48.
81. "Report on the Sweating System," 223.
82. Ibid., 92–157.

83. Price, *Ten Years of Industrial Sanitary Self-Control*, 3.
84. "Report on the Sweating System," 94, 126.
85. Tcherikower, *Early Jewish Labor Movement*, 283–284.
86. Levine, *Women's Garment Workers*, 78–81; Kosak, *Cultures of Opposition*, 125–127.
87. Shore, "An Epic Achievement," 55. On the early Jewish labor movement and its difficulties before 1910, see Tcherikower, *Early Jewish Labor Movement*, 272–315; Kosak, *Cultures of Opposition*, 99–130; Levine, *Women's Garment Workers*, 32–99.
88. Price, *Ten Years of Industrial Sanitary Self-Control*, 16–17.
89. ILGWU, *3rd Annual Convention, Report of Proceedings* (1903), 6.
90. "Reports of the Industrial Commission on Immigration," 381.

Four Workers Made Well: Home, Work, Homework, and the Model Shop, 1910–1930

1. Richard Greenwald describes how workers, reformers, and policymakers shaped new forms of industrial relations. He argues that "industrial democracy" was the goal of the alliance. Here it is interpreted as an anti-sweatshop campaign that drew on specific languages of work and gender. Richard Greenwald, "Bargaining for Industrial Democracy? Labor, the State, and the New Industrial Relations in Progressive Era New York" (Ph.D. diss., New York University, 1998).
2. *Third Annual Report of the Joint Board of Sanitary Control in the Cloak, Suit and Skirt and Dress and Waist Industries of Greater New York* (New York: Joint Board of Sanitary Control, December, 1913), 15; Nancy L. Green, *Ready-to-Wear and Ready-to-Work: A Century of Industry and Immigrants in Paris and New York* (Durham, N.C.: Duke University Press, 1997), 49–50; Mary Van Kleeck, *The Artificial Flower Makers* (New York: Survey Associates, Inc., 1913).
3. Italian immigrants enjoyed less mobility than did their Jewish counterparts. As they were less likely to leave the Lower East Side for the more prosperous Bronx or Brooklyn, they were also less likely to work in the larger, safer factories that sprang up outside of the Lower East Side. For important comparative social histories of the Jewish and Italian experience, see Thomas Kessner, *The Golden Door: Italian and Jewish Immigrant Mobility in New York City, 1880–1915* (Oxford: Oxford University Press, 1977); Elizabeth Ewen, *Immigrant Women in the Land of Dollars: Life and Culture on the Lower East Side, 1890–1925* (New York: Monthly Review Press, 1985).
4. *Five Years' Work and Progress of the Joint Board of Sanitary Control in the Cloak, Suit and Skirt and the Dress and Waist Industries: An Experiment in Industrial Self-Control* (New York: Joint Board of Sanitary Control, October 31, 1915), 5.
5. On investigations of industries where Italians worked in large numbers, see New York State Factory Investigating Commission, *Preliminary Report of the Factory Investigating Commission, 1912, Vol. 1.* (Albany: the Argus Company, Printers, 1912).
6. Quoted in George M. Price, *Ten Years of Industrial Sanitary Self-Control* (Joint Board of Sanitary Control, 1921), ILGWU Archives; Union Health Center Papers, Box 5, Folder 9, 18.
7. Louis Levine, *The Women's Garment Workers: A History of the International Ladies' Garment Workers' Union* (New York: B. W. Huebsch, Inc., 1924), 166–167.

8. "Report of the President," *Proceedings of the Tenth Convention of the International Ladies Garment Workers Union* (Boston, 1910), 17.

9. "Report of Local 1," *Proceedings of the Tenth Convention of the International Ladies Garment Workers Union*, 51–52.

10. *Jewish Daily Forward*, July 7, 1910; Greenwald, "Bargaining for Industrial Democracy?" 66–126.

11. Price, *Ten Years Sanitary Self-Control*, 18.

12. Ibid., 19.

13. Levine, *The Women's Garment Workers*, 191–194.

14. The "preferential shop," the Board of Arbitration, and the idea of the industry-wide contract are the most studied elements of the Protocol of Peace. Most examinations have focused on the Protocol of Peace as a foundational experiment in industrial democracy and as an early example of the kind of tripartite collective bargaining involving labor, business, and government that came to characterize the New Deal. For examples of the expansive literature on the cloakmakers' strike and the Protocol of Peace, see Greenwald, "Bargaining for Industrial Democracy?," 181–301; Melvyn Dubofsky, *When Workers Organize: New York City in the Progressive Era* (Amherst: University of Massachusetts Press, 1968), 58–68; Thomas Carpenter, *Competition and Collective Bargaining in the Needle Trades, 1910–1967* (Ithaca: Cornell University / ILR Press, 1972), 1–54; Arthur A. Goren, *New York Jews and the Quest for Community: The Kehillah Experiment, 1908–1922* (New York: Columbia University Press, 1970), 186–213; Steve Fraser, "Dress Rehearsal for the New Deal: Shop-Floor Insurgents, Political Elites, and Industrial Democracy in the Amalgamated Clothing Workers," in *Working-Class America: Essays on Labor, Community, and American Society*, ed. Michael H. Frisch and Daniel J. Walkowitz (Urbana: University of Illinois Press, 1983), 212–255.

15. "Joint Board of Sanitary Control Made Enduring Contribution to Welfare of the Ready-to-Wear Industry," YIVO Institute for Jewish Research, George M. Price Papers, RG # 213.

16. *First Annual Report of the Joint Board of Sanitary Control in the Cloak, Suit and Skirt Industry of Greater New York* (New York: Joint Board of Sanitary Control, October, 1911), 15.

17. *Special Report on Sanitary Conditions in the Shops of the Dress and Waist Industry* (New York: Joint Board of Sanitary Control, May, 1913), 3–8.

18. *Second Annual Report of the Joint Board of Sanitary Control in the Cloak, Suit and Skirt Industry of Greater New York* (New York: Joint Board of Sanitary Control, December, 1912), 7–11.

19. On the rise in public health work during the years of the Protocol of Peace, see Elizabeth A. Toon, "Managing the Conduct of the Individual Life: Public Health Education and American Public Health, 1910 to 1940" (Ph.D. diss., University of Pennsylvania, 1998); Judith Walzer Leavitt, *The Healthiest City: Milwaukee and the Politics of Health Reform* (Princeton: Princeton University Press, 1982); Barbara Gutmann Rosenkrantz, *Public Health and the State: Changing Views in Massachusetts, 1842–1936* (Cambridge: Harvard University Press, 1972); Fitzhugh Mullan, *Plagues and Politics: The Story of the United States Public Health Service* (New York: Basic Books, 1989); John Duffy, *The Sanitarians: A History of American Public Health* (Urbana: University of Illinois Press, 1990); Paul Starr, *The Social Transfor-*

mation of American Medicine: The Rise of a Sovereign Profession and the Making of a Vast Industry (New York: Basic Books, 1982), 180–197; Nell Irvin Painter, *Standing at Armageddon: The United States, 1877–1919* (New York: W. W. Norton & Company, 1987), 253–282.

20. *First Annual Report of the Joint Board of Sanitary Control*, 42.

21. Quoted in Levine, *Women's Garment Workers*, 466.

22. International Ladies' Garment Workers' Union, Educational Department, "Educational Series, No.2" (New York, 1928); YIVO, Bund Archives, ILGWU Collection, RG #1400, Box 13, Folder 54.

23. This rhetorical shift reflected a growing concern in New York about the effects of garment workers on immigrants, especially after the well-publicized 1911 Triangle Shirtwaist Company fire. The deaths of 147 mostly female Jewish and Italian workers raised a fervor of concern about potentially fatal conditions in the garment industry. In the immediate aftermath of the fire, New York state politicians organized the New York State Factory Investigating Commission especially to document conditions in the garment trade. The creation of the commission also helped more Jews and garment workers join the ranks of inspectors and the reform movement. Former garment workers, most notably Clara Lemlich, the outspoken leader of the 1909 Shirtwaistmakers' Strike, became factory inspectors; Lemlich joined the New York State Factory Investigating Commission in 1911. *Preliminary Report of the Factory Investigating Commission, 1912, Vol. 1*, 126–127. On Jewish Progressivism see, for example, Goren, *Kehillah Experiment*; Philippa Strum, *Louis D. Brandeis: Justice for the People* (Cambridge: Harvard University Press, 1984), 159–195; Lloyd P. Gartner, "The Jews of New York's East Side, 1890–1893: Two Surveys by the Baron de Hirsch Fund," *American Jewish Historical Quarterly* 53 (March 1964): 264–274.

24. House of Representatives, Committee of Manufactures, 52nd Congress, 2nd Session, "Report on the Sweating System under House Resolution" (February 13, 1892), 222–223.

25. *First Annual Report of the Joint Board of Sanitary Control*, 10–11. In its first report the JBSC outlined plans to involve workers and their organizing in factory inspections.

26. George Price, untitled autobiographical sketch, YIVO, George M. Price Papers, RG #213; George M. Price, *Russian Jews in America*, trans. Leo Shpall, reprinted from the *Publication of the American Jewish Historical Society* 48 (September-December, 1958).

27. George Price, *Handbook on Sanitation: A Manual of Theoretical and Practical Sanitation: For Students and Physicians* (New York: J. Wiley & Sons, 1901, 1913); Reviews of *Handbook on Sanitation: A Manual of Theoretical and Practical Sanitation* in *The Sanitary Record and Journal*, January 2, 1902, and *American Medicine*, February 22, 1902, both in YIVO Institute for Jewish Research, George M. Price Papers, RG #213; George M. Price, "Factory Hygiene," copy of an address made by Price on "Health Day," December 18, 1914, conference held in connection with the Second Exhibition of Safety and Sanitation at the American Museum of Safety, George M. Price Papers; George M. Price, "Medical Supervision in Dangerous Trades," reprinted from the *Journal of Sociologic Medicine* 16 (April 1915).

28. *Second Annual Report of the Joint Board of Sanitary Control*, 7.

29. For a particularly clear explanation of this hierarchy, see George Price's ten-year review of JBSC's work, *Ten Years of Industrial Sanitary Self-Control*, 3–23. See also George Price, "Industrial Hygiene: Joint Board of Sanitary Control in the New York Ladies Garment Industries," *International Labor Review* (January 1922), in ILGWU Archives, Union Health Center Papers, Box 12, Folder 1.

30. *Fourth Anniversary Bulletin of the Joint Board of Sanitary Control in the Cloak, Suit and Skirt and the Dress and Waist Industries* (New York: Joint Board of Sanitary Control, October 31, 1914), 28–29.

31. *First Annual Report of the Joint Board of Sanitary Control*, 26.

32. Ibid.

33. Ibid., 20–21.

34. Ibid., 87–88. On the interconnection between discourses about dirt, social disorder, and sanitation in other circumstances, see Patricia Cooper and Ruth Oldenziel, "Cherished Classifications: Bathrooms and the Construction of Gender/Race on the Pennsylvania Railroad during World War II," *Feminist Studies* 25 (Spring 1999): 7–41. For a more theoretical account, see Mary Douglas, *Purity and Danger: An Analysis of Concepts of Pollution and Taboo* (New York: Routledge, 1966).

35. *Third Annual Report of the Joint Board of Sanitary Control*, 40.

36. *First Annual Report of the Joint Board of Sanitary Control*, 71.

37. *Fourth Anniversary Bulletin of the Joint Board of Sanitary Control*, 33–35.

38. *Six Years' Work and Progress of the Joint Board of Sanitary Control in the Cloak, Suit and Skirt and the Dress and Waist Industries: An Experiment in Industrial Self-Control* (New York: Joint Board of Sanitary Control, October 31, 1916), 15; "Workers' Health Bulletin" (1915), ILGWU Archives, Union Health Center Papers, Box 10, Folder 10.

39. *Third Annual Report of the Joint Board of Sanitary Control*, 40–41.

40. *First Annual Report of the Joint Board of Sanitary Control*, 71 (emphasis in the original).

41. Ibid., 83–85 (emphasis in the original).

42. *Second Annual Report of the Joint Board of Sanitary Control*, 12; Joint Board of Sanitary Control, *Sanitary Control Monthly Bulletin* 1 (August, 1919), 6.

43. *Six Years' Work and Progress of the Joint Board of Sanitary Control*, 10.

44. *Fourth Anniversary Bulletin of the Joint Board of Sanitary Control*, 15; *Six Years' Work and Progress of the Joint Board of Sanitary Control*, 10.

45. *Fourth Anniversary Bulletin of the Joint Board of Sanitary Control*, 15; George M. Price, "Industrial Hygiene: Joint Board of Sanitary Control in the New York Ladies Garment Industries," reprinted from the *International Labor Review* (January 1922), ILGWU Archives, Union Health Center Papers, Box 12, Folder 1, 125–126. For details on the contemporary public health campaign against homework, see *Second Report of the New York State Factory Investigating Commission*, 90–123.

46. *First Annual Report of the Joint Board of Sanitary Control*, 78–79.

47. *Third Annual Report of the Joint Board of Sanitary Control*, 35.

48. *Fourth Anniversary Bulletin of the Joint Board of Sanitary Control*, 17.

49. *A General Survey of the Sanitary Conditions of the Shops in the Cloak Industry* (New York: Joint Board of Sanitary Control, 1911), 5; *Five Years' Work and Progress of the Joint Board of Sanitary Control*, 5.

50. *Five Years' Work and Progress of the Joint Board of Sanitary Control* , 5.

51. *Third Annual Report of the Joint Board of Sanitary Control*, 15. On this language of reform, particularly in how it related to the eradication of homework, see Eileen Boris, *Home to Work: Motherhood and the Politics of Industrial Homework in the United States* (Cambridge: Cambridge University Press, 1994).

52. "Ten Years of Sanitary Self-Control," *Justice*, May 20, 1921; George Price, *The Modern Factory* (Brooklyn: The Scientific Press, 1914).

53. *A General Survey of Sanitary Conditions of Shops in the Cloak Industry*, 9.

54. Ibid., 25.

55. *A General Survey of Sanitary Conditions of Shops in the Cloak Industry*, 28.

56. Price, *Modern Factory*, 66–69.

57. Yitzchak Yankel Doroshkin, *From Zhitkovitch throughout the World (Episodes of My Life)* (1974), trans. Mindy Gross, YIVO, American Jewish Autobiographies (AJA), RG #102, #305, 155–156.

58. Ibid., 151.

59. An early effort to find an experimental workshop may have originated with Lilian Wald, the nurse and settlement house founder who would later work for the JBSC. Wald organized one small example of an experimental shop. But, as it stood outside of the gendered discourse about homework and sweatshop, her effort garnered little support, attention, or funding. Her shop, a shirtwaist shop, provided shelter and jobs for sick girls, not for male breadwinners. Wald designed the shop as a contrast to the sweatshop. Rose Cohen remembered fondly her time in Wald's shop. She recalled the "boss," Miss Ann O'There, as "so splendid." For Cohen, Wald's shop was a model shop that recalled the utopian visions of the contemporary Russian socialist Nikolai Chernyshevsky: "I was reading at the time a book . . . called, 'What Is To Be Done, or the Vital Question,' by [Chernyshevsky]. In this book there was an ideal sewing shop and I felt as if our little shop too was out of a story." Unfortunately, for Cohen, the shop was short-lived. Soon after she began work there, the employees were scattered among other shops when Wald realized her model shop could not pay for itself. Rose Cohen, *Out of the Shadow: A Russian Jewish Girlhood on the Lower East Side* (1918; reprint, Ithaca: Cornell University Press, 1995), 283. Jo Ann Argersinger notes that in the similar case of the Amalgamated Clothing Workers Union (ACWU), Jewish organizing served to reform the industry and, in the process, rendered women "forgotten." Jo Ann Argersinger, *Making the Amalgamated: Gender, Ethnicity, and Class in the Baltimore Clothing Industry, 1899–1939* (Baltimore: Johns Hopkins University Press, 1999), 60–120.

60. *Sanitary Control Monthly Bulletin* (August 1919), 7.

61. *Workers' Health Bulletin* 3 (1915), ILGWU Archives; Union Health Center Papers, Box 10, Folder 10, 3.

62. *Fourth Anniversary Bulletin of the Joint Board of Sanitary Control*, 15 (emphasis in the original).

63. W. I. Hamilton, "Occupation Research for the Tuberculous," *Industrial Number Bulletin of the National Tuberculosis Association* (January 1922): 1–1–2, 12. On the idea of work as curative, see Daniel J. Walkowitz and Peter Eisenstadt, "The Psychology of Work: Work and Mental Health in Historical Perspective," *Radical History Review* 34 (January 1986): 7–31. On the contemporary sanitarium movement see René and Jean Dubos, *The White Plague: Tuberculosis, Man, and Society* (New

Brunswick, N.J.: Rutgers University Press, 1992), 173–184; Sheila Rothman, *Living in the Shadow of Death: Tuberculosis and the Social Experience of Illness in American History* (Baltimore: Johns Hopkins University Press, 1994), 179–246.

64. *Hatikvah*, April 1927; Alan Kraut, *Silent Travelers: Germs, Genes, and the "Immigrant Menace"* (New York: Basic Books, 1994), 159–163. Capital letters are in the original. For a description of the ILGWU's support for returning consumptive workers to the shop floor, see *Justice*, February 17, 1922.

65. *Jewish Advocate*, September 22, 1927, YIVO; U.S. Territorial Collection, RG #117, Box 52. The working sanitarium suggests the need to revisit the ideas of curing and sanitarium care, in particular, as class- and gender-based notions. For middle-class men and women, sanitarium care was supposed to consist of enforced rest and leisure, with death almost a certainty. For working-class men, like these Jewish garment workers, curing and rehabilitation meant the protection of family life and, thus, of working-class collective morality. The working-class breadwinner had to labor for his cure because of his family responsibilities. On cultural depictions of sanitarium care, see Katherine Ott, *Fevered Lives: Tuberculosis in American Culture since 1870* (Cambridge: Harvard University Press, 1996), 69–86, Rothman, *Living in the Shadow of Death*, 179–225.

66. *The Rocky Mountain News*, August 14, 1927, YIVO, U.S. Territorial Collection, RG #117, Box 52.

67. Edward Hochhauser, director of the Altro Works, "Salvaging the Labor Power of the Tuberculous" *Industrial Number Bulletin of the National Tuberculosis Association*, 9, 12; *Justice*, January 21, 1921. The Navy contract is especially significant because the federal government had avoided giving military contracts to sweatshops, because of worries that disease would be passed on to soldiers.

68. *Report of the Committee for the Care of the Jewish Tuberculous, 1913–1936* (New York, 1937), 19.

69. Ibid., 32–33.

70. Ibid., 46.

71. Ibid.; *Justice*, September 12, 1924.

72. *Report of the Committee for the Care of the Jewish Tuberculous*, 38; Ott, *Fevered Lives*, 146.

73. In recognition of an ethnic ideal, Jewish contractors would hire Italian women rather than Jewish women. Kessner, *Golden Door*, 77; United States Bureau of Labor, *Report on the Condition of Woman and Child Wage Earners in the United States*, Vol. 2 (Washington, D.C., 1911), 221; United States Immigration Commission, *Reports of the Immigration Commission*, Vol. 1, *Abstract of Reports of the Immigration Commission* (Washington, D.C., 1911), 752.

74. *First Annual Report of the Joint Board of Sanitary Control*, 20.

75. "Bulletin of the Joint Board of Sanitary Control in the Cloak, Suite and Skirt Industry" (January, 1912).

76. Pauline Newman, "Twenty-One Years of Health Education among Wage-Earners," ILGWU Archives, Union Health Center Papers, Box 2, Folder 10, 3. The idea of the Jewish labor movement as a struggle to lift immigrant garment workers out of the sweatshops is reflected also in histories of the Jewish labor movement, including those written by former workers and unionists. See, for example, Leon Stein, ed., *Out of the Sweatshop: The Struggle for Industry Democracy* (New York: Quadrangle, 1977); Joseph Brandes, "From Sweatshop to Stability: Jewish Labor between Two World Wars," *YIVO Annual* 16 (1976): 1–149.

77. Address of Meyer London to the ILGWU Cleveland Convention, *Ladies' Garment Worker* (July 1914), 8–9.

78. *Justice*, July 28, 1922, 6. It is interesting that the cloakmakers insisted on putting the word "factories" in scare quotes. Sweatshops, they seem to argue, were not real factories.

79. Abraham Rosenberg, *Memoirs of a Cloakmaker*, trans. Lynn Davison (New York: n.p., 1920), 250.

80. Ibid., 310–311.

81. *Justice*, July 28, 1922, 6.

82. Rosenberg, *Memoirs of a Cloakmaker*, 311. Concern about the "return of the sweatshop" continues to dominate activism and unionism in the garment industry. See Boris, *Home to Work*, 337–366; Edna Bonacich, "Alienation among Asian and Latino Immigrants in the Los Angeles Garment Industry: The Need for New Forms of Class Struggle in the Late Twentieth Century," in *Alienation, Society, and the Individual: Continuity and Change in Theory and Research*, ed. Felix Geyer and Water Heinz (New Brunswick, N.J.: Transaction Publishers, 1992), 165–180.

83. The ILGWU was adamant in their association of piecework with the sweatshop; the union "declared the system of piece-work to be a relic of the abominable sweatshop system." Alexander Trachtenberg, "The 'Glory' of Piece Work," *Justice*, December 9, 1921, 3; Alexander Trachtenberg, "The 'Glory' of Peace [*sic*] Work," *Justice*, December 16, 1921, 3.

84. *Justice*, July 28, 1922.

85. Morris Sigman to William Green, September 20, 1926, ILGWU Archives, Morris Sigman Papers, Box 1, Folder 20; Isidore Nagler to Morris Sigman, October 4, 1926, ILGWU Archives, Morris Sigman Papers, Box 1, Folder 21.

86. "Report of the General Executive Board to the 20th Convention of the International Ladies' Garment Workers' Union" (1929), 7; "Report of the General Executive Board to the 19th Convention of the International Ladies' Garment Workers' Union" (1928), 278.

Five Gaunt Men, Gaunt Wives: Femininity, Masculinity, and the Worker Question, 1880–1909

1. Morris Rosenfeld, "The Sweatshop," in *The Penguin Book of Modern Yiddish Verse*, ed. Irving Howe, Ruth R. Wisse, and Khone Shemruk (New York: Viking, 1987), 84–85 (my retranslation).

2. Susan Glenn, *Daughters of the Shtetl: Life and Labor in the Immigrant Generation* (Ithaca: Cornell University Press, 1990), 239–240; Sydney Stahl Weinberg, *World of Our Mothers: The Lives of Jewish Immigrant Women* (Chapel Hill: University of North Carolina Press, 1988), 134–137; Riv-Ellen Prell, *Fighting to Become Americans: Jews, Gender, and the Anxiety of Assimilation* (Boston: Beacon Press, 1999), 104–107.

3. See Kathie Friedman-Kasaba, *Memories of Migration; Gender, Ethnicity, and Work in the Lives of Jewish and Italian Women in New York, 1870–1924* (Albany: State University of New York Press, 1996), 91–174.

4. On the sexualized atmosphere of the garment workplace, see Charlotte Baum, Paula Hyman, and Sonya Michel, *The Jewish Woman in America* (New York: Dial Press,

1976), 132–136; Weinberg, *World of Our Mothers*, 198–199; Glenn, *Daughters of the Shtetl*, 145–148. Baum, Hyman, and Michel argue that the women often were blamed and blamed themselves for sexual harassment and tension in the workplace. This chapter, in contrast, argues that women understood and challenged the way the sexuality of the workplace ordered and maintained shop floor hierarchy.

5. Franke argues persuasively that most legal definitions of sexual harassment and applications of law do not consider questions of gender. See Katherine Franke, "What's Wrong with Sexual Harassment," *Stanford Law Review* 49 (1997): 691–772, esp. 771–772.

6. Judith Butler argues that through sexual harassment "a person is 'made' into a certain gender." Judith Butler, *Gender Trouble: Feminism and the Subversion of Identity* (New York: Routledge, 1999), xii–xiii.

7. For a theoretical interpretation of such a contradiction, see Joan Wallach Scott, *Only Paradoxes to Offer: French Feminists and the Rights of Man* (Cambridge: Harvard University Press, 1996).

8. On sexual difference as a discursive subject at work, see Joan Wallach Scott, *Gender and the Politics of History* (New York: Columbia University Press, 1988). Judith Butler, *Bodies That Matter: On the Discursive Limits of "Sex"* (New York: Routledge, 1993), 93–119, points out how the performance of (hetero)sexuality serves to give "every body a sex." In this case, it introduces into the shop floor relationships between workers a language of sex and a hierarchy of gender.

9. Nancy Schrom Dye, *As Equals and as Sisters: Feminism, the Labor Movement, and the Women's Trade Union League of New York* (Columbia: University of Missouri Press, 1980), 61–109.

10. Nan Enstad, *Ladies of Labor, Girls of Adventure: Working Women, Popular Culture, and Labor Politics at the Turn of the Twentieth Century* (New York: Columbia University Press, 1999), 84–160. In focusing on contested representations of Eastern European Jewish women during these strikes, Nan Enstad has also described how female Jewish garment workers demanded respect as workers and as ladies. Yet she does so by claiming that they invoked their status as consumers, thereby leading them away from the union and the WTUL. This chapter presents a sharply different interpretation. Enstad argues that working women relied on popular culture in defining the politics of the strike and, thus, ended up with definitions of the political that differed wildly from those of WTUL leaders. In fact, Jewish women also drew on prevailing languages about the dangers of the sweatshop that allowed them to forge unequal but still enduring relationships with the WTUL. It also allowed working women to claim to be victims, serious workers, and ladies. Finally, an examination of how women drew on discourses about the sweatshop to contest the sexuality of the sweatshop and to claim legitimacy as "women workers" reveals that women did seek to win a place in the labor movement. They moved toward the union and forced their way into its anti-sweatshop coalition. They did not retreat, as Enstad seems to argue.

11. Wendy Gamber, *The Female Economy: The Millinery and Dressmaking Trades, 1860–1930* (Urbana: University of Illinois Press, 1997). The gendered confusion was especially prevalent in the women's garment trades. In contrast, men's custom clothing claimed a long heritage of journeyman male tailors. Glenn, *Daughters of the Shtetl*, 106–122.

12. Glenn, *Daughters of the Shtetl*, 115.

13. Mabel Hurd Willet, *The Employment of Women in the Clothing Trade* (New York: Columbia University Press, 1902), 72.

14. *A General Survey of Sanitary Conditions of Shops in the Cloak Industry* (New York: Joint Board of Sanitary Control, 1911), 6–7.

15. Feminist scholars have come to recognize skill as a largely constructed concept tied to hierarchies of gender. See Anne Phillips and Barbara Taylor, "Sex and Skill: Notes Towards a Feminist Economics," in *Feminism and History*, ed. Joan Wallach Scott (New York: Oxford University Press, 1996), 317–330. They cite the case of Eastern European Jewish garment workers in London whose work was so mechanized and differentiated into simple, standardized tasks that there was little actual difference between the training needed to complete different jobs. Yet they still created and maintained strict definitions of skill that fostered a sexual division of labor and a hierarchy of pay. This chapter traces and develops a similar phenomenon among Eastern European Jewish garment workers in New York.

16. Jesse Pope, *The Clothing Industry in New York* (Columbia: E. W. Stephens Publishing Company, 1905), 28.

17. *A General Survey of the Sanitary Conditions of the Shops in the Cloak Industry*, 7.

18. *Special Report on Sanitary Conditions in the Shops of the Dress and Waist Industry* (New York: Joint Board of Sanitary Control, May 1913), 8–10.

19. A number of historians of garment work have examined similar questions. Wendy Gamber traces the way, in the specific case of dressmakers, men seized control of the industry by connecting predetermined style patterns, science, and masculinity. Susan Glenn tends to look at biological idioms advanced by reformers and, perhaps, adopted by workers that naturalized the association of men and machines and women and labor requiring nimble fingers. Gamber, *Female Economy*, 125–228; Glenn, *Daughters of the Shtetl*, 112–117. The goal here is to locate a broader pattern, to foreground the clash between constructions of masculinity and femininity, and to highlight the links between gendered shop floor control, ideas about skill, and roadblocks to women's labor organizing.

20. As Gail Bederman notes, by the turn of the century, manhood was publicly confirmed by a muscular body. This was not always the case for workers. As David Montgomery suggests, participation in male-dominated craft rituals and shop floor socializing confirmed many late nineteenth-century workplaces as manly enclaves. Turn-of-the-century craftsmen, like printers, Ava Baron argues, assured the masculinity of the workplace and the manliness of workers by developing codes of behavior that linked workplace competence to manliness. Gail Bederman, *Manliness and Civilization: A Cultural History of Gender and Race in the United States, 1880–1917* (Chicago: University of Chicago Press, 1995); David Montgomery, *Workers' Control in America: Studies in the History of Work, Technology, and Labor Struggles* (Cambridge: Cambridge University Press, 1979); Ava Baron, "An 'Other' Side of Gender Antagonism at Work: Men, Boys, and the Remasculinization of Printers' Work, 1830–1920," in *Work Engendered: Toward a New History of American Labor*, ed. Ava Baron (Ithaca: Cornell University Press, 1991), 47–69. See also Patricia Cooper, *Once a Cigar Maker: Men, Women, and Work Culture in American Cigar Factories, 1900–1919* (Urbana: University of Illinois Press, 1987), 124.

21. Willet, *The Employment of Women in the Clothing Trade*, 69.

22. The historical literature on workplace harassment is extremely limited. For the few examples of work in this area see Mary Bularzik, "Sexual Harassment at the Workplace: Historical Notes," in *Worker's Struggles, Past and Present: A Radical America Reader*, ed. James Green (Philadelphia: Temple University Press, 1983), 125–131; Enstad, *Ladies of Labor, Girls of Adventure*, 141–145; Kerry Segrave, *The Sexual Harassment of Women in the Workplace, 1600–1993* (Jefferson, N.C.: McFarland and Company, Inc., 1994).

23. *Reports of the Immigration Commission*, "Immigrants in Cities," 61st Congress, 2nd Session, Vol. 1 (Washington, D.C., 1911), Table 70, 231. On the larger phenomenon of women leaving work upon marriage, see Kathy Peiss, *Cheap Amusements: Working Women and Leisure in Turn-of-the-Century New York* (Philadelphia: Temple University Press, 1986), 45–46.

24. *Fourth Report of the Factory Investigating Commission, Vol. II, 1915* (Albany: J. B. Lyon Company Printers, 1915), 177–182. The pattern of women's departure from garment work after marriage was different among Italian women, many of whom continued in the garment industry especially as homeworkers. While Jewish women continued to earn money after marriage as shopkeepers or landladies (many Jewish families kept boarders), the point remains that marriage generally signaled the end of Jewish women's participation in garment work. See Thomas Kessner, *The Golden Door: Italian and Jewish Immigrant Mobility in New York City, 1880–1915* (Oxford: Oxford University Press, 1977), 44–126.

25. U.S. Public Health Service (PHS), "The Health of Garment Workers," *U.S. Public Health Service Bulletin* 71 (May 1915), 28, 46.

26. Quoted in Weinberg, *World of Our Mothers*, 211.

27. Quoted in Alice Kessler-Harris, "Organizing the Unorganizable: Three Jewish Women and their Union," *Labor History* 17 (Winter 1976): 7.

28. Reproduced in Isaac Metzker, ed., *A Bintl Brief: Sixty Years of Letters from the Lower East Side to the Jewish Daily Forward* (New York: Schocken Books, 1971), 103–104.

29. Interview with Fannie Shapiro, in *Jewish Grandmothers*, ed. Sydelle Kramer and Jenny Masur (Boston: Beacon Press, 1976), 13.

30. Pope, *Clothing Industry in New York*, 51.

31. Ephraim Wagner, *The Village Boy* (unpublished autobiography, 1942), YIVO Institute for Jewish Research, American Jewish Autobiographies (AJA), RG #102, #45, 156.

32. Reproduced in Metzker, *A Bintl Brief*, 130–131. Unfortunately, this woman's fiancé did not survive the Triangle fire.

33. Michael Gold, *Jews without Money* (1930; reprint, New York: Carroll & Graf, 1993), 229–231.

34. Willet, *Employment of Women in the Clothing Trade*, 89.

35. On contemporary sexual mores of Jewish immigrants, see Eli Lederhendler, "Guides for the Perplexed: Sex, Manners, and Mores for the Yiddish Reader in America," *Modern Judaism* 11 (October 1991): 321–341; Neil Cowan and Ruth Schwartz Cowan, *Our Parent's Lives: Jewish Assimilation and Everyday Life* (New Brunswick, N.J.: Rutgers University Press, 1996), 144–176. On separate spheres, see Linda K. Kerber, "Separate Spheres, Female Worlds, Woman's Place: The Rhetoric of Women's History," *Journal of American History* 75 (June 1988): 9–39.

36. Abraham Cahan, "A Sweatshop Romance," in *The Imported Bridegroom and Other Stories of the New York Ghetto* (1898; reprint, New York: Garrett Press, 1968), 175.

37. On the workplace as the site of sexual interaction, conversation, desire, and courtship, see Peiss, *Cheap Amusements*, 34–51.

38. Cahan, "A Sweatshop Romance," 166–191.

39. Reproduced in Metzker, *A Bintel Brief*, 48–49.

40. Stella Seligson Papiroff, *With Open Eyes* (n.d.), YIVO, AJA, #368, 32.

41. Willet, *Employment of Women in the Clothing Trade*, 86–87.

42. Quoted in Dye, *As Equals and as Sisters*, 22–23. For a broader vision of the nexus between workplace position and discourses of sexuality, see Joan Wallach Scott, "'L'Ouvrière! Mot impie, sordide . . . ': Women Workers in the Discourse of French Political Economy, 1840–1860," in Scott, *Gender and the Politics of History*, 139–163.

43. Glenn, *Daughters of the Shtetl*, 108; Elizabeth Ewen, *Immigrant Women in the Land of Dollars: Life and Culture on the Lower East Side, 1890–1925* (New York: Monthly Review Press, 1985), 247–248; Oral History of Jennie Matyas by Corinne Gilb, April 20–October 28, 1955, 31, Martin P. Catherwood Library, Cornell University.

44. Constance Leupp, "Assault on Sub-Contractor Starts Shirtwaist Walkout," *The Survey* (December 18, 1909); Sarah Comstock, "The Uprising of the Girls," *Collier's* (December 25, 1909), 20.

45. Dr. Isaac Pomerance, *Autobiographical Notes*, 1952, YIVO, AJA, #274, 26.

46. Sam Liptzin, *Tales of a Tailor: Humor and Tragedy in the Struggles of the Early Immigrants against the Sweatshop*, trans. Max Rosenfeld (New York: Prompt Press, 1965), 60–63. The translation into English is my own.

47. Benjamin Kapp, *Immigrant Physician* (n.d.), YIVO, AJA, #300, 137.

48. Lazarus Marcovitz, *Episodes from Life* (1966), YIVO, AJA #287, 6.

49. Rose Cohen, *Out of the Shadow: A Russian Jewish Girlhood on the Lower East Side* (1918; reprint, Ithaca: Cornell University Press, 1995), 128–129.

50. "Girls' Stories," *Life and Labor* (August 1914): 243–244.

51. Sadie Frowne, "The Story of a Sweatshop Girl," in *Plain Folk: The Life Stories of Undistinguished Americans*, ed. David M. Katzman and William M. Tuttle, Jr. (Urbana: University of Illinois Press, 1982), 55.

52. Liptzin, *Tales of a Tailor*, 60.

53. Harry Lang, *"62": Biography of a Union* (Astoria Press: New York, 1940), 178–179; Baum, Hyman, Michel, *Jewish Woman in America*, 135–136; Enstad, *Ladies of Labor, Girls of Adventure*, 141–145.

54. "Girls' Stories," *Life and Labor*, 243–244; "A Shopgirl," in Metzker, *A Bintel Brief*, 72.

55. Cohen, *Out of the Shadow*, 85.

56. Ibid., 274–275.

57. Letter from "A Shopgirl," 1907, in Metzker, *A Bintel Brief*, 72.

58. Liptzin, *Tales of a Tailor*, 63.

59. "Girls' Stories," *Life and Labor*, 243–244.

60. Frowne, "Story of a Sweatshop Girl," 55.

61. As Jeanne Boydston has pointed out, gender as much as class shapes women's experience at work. Jeanne Boydston, *Home and Work: Housework, Wages, and the Ideology of Labor in the Early Republic* (Oxford: Oxford University Press, 1990), xviii.

62. Liptzin, *Tales of a Tailor*, 60.

63. Cohen, *Out of the Shadow*, 109–110.

64. Peiss, *Cheap Amusements*, 53–55. Peiss explores a different link between immigrant women's imminent marriage, their workplace reproductive roles, and their vastly inferior wages. She argues that by carefully offering attention in exchange for treats and promises of marriage, women could survive on lower wages.

65. *Twentieth Annual Report of the Bureau of Labor Statistics for the Year Ended September 30, 1902* (Albany: The Argus Company, Printers, 1903), 1–35. See also Pope, *Clothing Industry in New York*, 79–137.

66. See Phillips and Taylor, "Sex and Skill," 317–330. On the social construction of skill among contemporary American unionists, see Ileen DeVault, "'To Sit Among Men': Skill, Gender, and Craft Unionism in the Early American Federation of Labor," in *Labor Histories: Class, Politics, and the Working-Class Experience*, ed. Eric Arneson, Julie Greene, and Bruce Laurie (Urbana: University of Illinois Press, 1998), 259–283. Recent reconsiderations of skill as a constructed label often determined by gender rather than as an inherent category have emerged most prominently among European working-class historians; see, for example, Helen Harden Chenut, "The Gendering of Skill as Historical Process: The Case of French Knitters in Industrial Troyes, 1880–1939," in *Gender and Class in Modern Europe*, ed. Laura L. Frader and Sonya O. Rose (Ithaca: Cornell University Press, 1996), 77–107; Laura Lee Downs, *Manufacturing Inequality: Gender Division in the French and British Metalworking Industries, 1914–1939* (Ithaca: Cornell University Press, 1995), 79–118.

67. Glenn also suggests that the garment workplace had a masculinist culture. Glenn, *Daughters of the Shtetl*, 116–117.

68. *Twentieth Annual Report of the Bureau of Labor Statistics*, Table 1, 14–15.

69. Liptzin, *Tales of a Tailor*, 71.

70. Ibid., 72–74. For other examples of how men controlled access to skilled work, see Patricia Cooper, "The Faces of Gender: Sex Segregation and Work Relations at Philco, 1928–1938," in Baron, *Work Engendered*, 320–350.

71. Interview with Louis Panken, YIVO Institute of Jewish Research, Irving Howe Papers, RG #570, 45. On the way that sexual divisions of labor were often explained through claims of physical difference, for example, that women's smaller hands better suited them to particular tasks, see Ruth Milkman, "Redefining 'Women's Work': The Sexual Division of Labor in the Auto Industry during World War II," *Feminist Studies* 8 (Summer 1982): 337–372.

72. Willet, *Employment of Women in the Clothing Trade*, 153.

73. Cohen, *Out of the Shadow*, 123–126.

74. Marcovitz, *Episodes from Life*, 7.

75. This notion of the strike as aimed at male bosses and male workers differs from other interpretations of the strike. The first chroniclers of the strikes saw it as an example of women's labor radicalism. More recent interpretations take a more nuanced view. Annelise Orleck argues that the strikes were a balancing act that forced men to reconsider the position assigned to women. But she sees female strike leaders as backing away from issues of sexuality. Annelise Orleck, *Common Sense and a Little Fire: Women and Working-Class Politics in the United States, 1900–1965* (Chapel Hill: University of North Carolina Press, 1995), 53–86; Maxine Schwartz Seller, "The Uprising of the Twenty Thousand: Sex, Class, and Ethnicity

in the Shirtwaist Makers' Strike of 1909," in *"Struggle a Hard Battle": Essays on Working Class Immigrants*, ed. Dirk Hoerder (DeKalb: Northern Illinois University Press, 1986).

76. For examples of contemporary women's confrontations with constructions of masculinity, see Nancy Hewitt, "'The Voice of Virile Labor': Labor Militancy, Community Solidarity, and Gender Identity among Tampa's Latin Workers, 1880–1921," in Baron, *Work Engendered*, 142–167; DeVault, "'To Sit Among Men,'" 259–283. Susan Porter Benson and Stephen Norwood point out examples of how in largely female trades, women relied on contested notions of femininity to organize collectively and to alter the conditions of labor. See Susan Porter Benson, *Counter Cultures: Saleswomen, Managers, and Customers in American Department Stores, 1890–1940* (Urbana: University of Illinois Press, 1986); Stephen Norwood, *Labor's Flaming Youth: Telephone Operators and Worker Militancy, 1878–1923* (Urbana: University of Illinois Press, 1990). The case of Jewish women in the garment industry in New York is especially interesting because they worked in a gender mixed industry with few inherited constructions of skill.

77. Glenn, *Daughters of the Shtetl*, 167–206. For broader analysis of the structural, political, and cultural barriers to women's participation in the labor movement, see Alice Kessler-Harris, "Where Are the Organized Women Workers?" *Feminist Studies* 3 (Fall 1975): 92–110.

78. Seller, "Uprising of the Twenty Thousand"; Ann Schofield, "The Uprising of the 20,000: The Making of a Labor Legend," in *A Needle, a Bobbin, a Strike: Women Needleworkers in America*, ed. Joan M. Jensen and Sue Davidson (Philadelphia: Temple University Press, 1984), 167–182.

79. Dye, *As Equals and as Sisters*, 92–94.

80. Rose Schneiderman, "The White Goods Workers of New York, Their Struggle for Human Conditions," *Life and Labor* (May 1913): 132.

81. Lang, *"62": Biography of a Union*, 94–139; Louis Levine, *The Women's Garment Workers: A History of the International Ladies' Garment Workers' Union* (New York: B. W. Huebsch, 1924), 218–232.

82. Levine, *Women's Garment Workers*, 151; Orleck, *Common Sense and a Little Fire*, 59–60.

83. "Waistmakers Vote General Strike," *New York Call*, November 23, 1909.

84. Clara Lemlich Shavelson, "Remembering the Waistmakers General Strike, 1909," *Jewish Currents* (November 1982); *New York Call*, November 22, 1909.

85. On the leadership of the 1909 and 1913 strikes, see Dye, *As Equals and as Sisters*, 88–95, 99–100; Lang, *"62": Biography of a Union*, 94–139; Schneiderman, "White Goods Workers of New York," *Life and Labor*, 132–136. Enstad argues that during the 1909 strike there was a divergence between working- and middle-class women. Workers, she suggests, created a distinct idea of ladyhood from their reading of popular culture and as a response to criticism from wealthy critics. Orleck, meanwhile, suggests that working women were not "acted upon" by Progressive activists but exercised real agency in their relationships with the WTUL. In fact, the relationship between workers and the WTUL was a complex cultural negotiation that produced a strategy of ladyhood. This strategy came as much from workers as from WTUL leaders, as one possible response to the sexualization of the workplace. Women did not fully embrace workplace sexuality to the extent that Enstad

suggests, whether that sexuality was real or in the pages of dime novels. Rather, workplace sexuality was also about workplace power. Enstad, *Ladies of Labor, Girls of Adventure*, esp. 84–160; Orleck, *Common Sense and a Little Fire*, 53–80.

86. See, for example, Helen Marot, "A Woman's Strike—An Appreciation of the Shirt-waist Makers of New York," *Proceedings of the American Academy of Political Science, City of New York* 1 (1910): 119–128; "The Shirtwaist Makers' Strike," *Survey* 23 (January 15, 1910): 505–506; Mary Brown Sumner, "The Spirit of the Strikers," *Survey* 23 (January 22, 1910): 550–555; Sue Ainslie Clark and Edith Wyatt, "Working Girls' Budgets: The Shirtwaist Makers and Their Strike," *McClure's* 36 (November 1910): 70–86; Ladies' Waist Makers' Union, *Souvenir History of the Strike* (New York, 1910); "Why the Waistmakers Strike?," *Evening Journal* (November 26, 1909); Comstock, "Uprising of the Girls," *Collier's*, 14–16, 20–21; Schneiderman, "White Goods Workers of New York," *Life and Labor*, 132–136.

87. *Souvenir History of the Strike*, 14–18.

88. Ibid., 10–11; "On the Picket Line," *Life and Labor* (March 1913): 71–73; "Mistresses of Millions are Strike-Leaders," Leonora O'Reilly Papers, Schlesinger Library, Radcliffe College (Microfilm Edition of the Papers of the WTUL, O'Reilly Papers, Reel 11, Frame 972–973); Levine, *Women's Garment Workers*, 226–228; Enstad, *Ladies of Labor, Girls of Adventure*, 128–130.

89. "Why the Waistmakers Strike?," *Evening Journal*.

90. Clark and Wyatt, "Working Girls' Budgets: The Shirtwaist Makers and Their Strike," *McClure's*; Comstock, "Uprising of the Girls," *Collier's*.

91. Martha Bensley Bruere, "The White Goods Strikers," *Life and Labor* (March 1913): 73–75; "Girls' Stories," *Life and Labor*, 243–244.

92. Microfilm edition of the Papers of the WTUL, O'Reilly Papers, Reel 11, Frames 1174–1177, Schlesinger Library, Radcliffe College.

93. Clark and Wyatt, "Working Girls' Budgets: The Shirtwaist Makers and Their Strike," *McClure's*; Comstock, "Uprising of the Girls," *Collier's*, 14–16. Enstad uses this particular source to describe how middle-class women of the WTUL imported into strike publicity their criticism of immigrant women's manners and spending habits. Enstad, *Ladies of Labor, Girls of Adventure*, 84–85, 97.

94. Microfilm edition of the Papers of the WTUL, O'Reilly Papers, Reel 11, Frame 1174.

95. Ibid., Reel 11, Frames 1145–1177. The authors were obviously taken with this particular quote, as it seems to speak to their own ideas about ladyhood. They underlined the quote and highlighted the word "ladies" in their notes.

96. Ibid., Reel 11, Frames 1174–1177.

97. Enstad, *Ladies of Labor, Girls of Adventure*, 48–83.

98. Comstock, "Uprising of the Girls," *Collier's*, 20–21. Annelise Orleck suggests that some female labor organizers actually opposed using sexual harassment as a justification for organizing. Orleck, *Common Sense and a Little Fire*, 72–74. In the end, though, sexual harassment was an increasingly important issue for women in the ILGWU. See "Holding the Fort: The Chicago Garment Workers' Strike," *Life and Labor* (February 1911): 48–52; "Chicago at the Front: A Condensed History of the Garment Workers' Strike," *Life and Labor* (January 1911): 4–15; Leonora O'Reilly, "The Story of Kalamazoo," *Life and Labor* (August 1912): 228–230; Levine, *Women's Garment Workers*, 144–232; Glenn, *Daughters of the Shtetl*, 167–206; Karen Mason, "Feeling the Pinch: The Kalamazoo Corsetmakers' Strike of 1913," in *To*

Toil a Livelong Day: America's Women at Work, 1787–1980, ed. Carol Groneman and Mary Beth Norton (Ithaca: Cornell University Press, 1987), 141–160, esp. 157–159.

99. *New York Call*, December 5, 7, 8, 1909; Orleck, *Common Sense and a Little Fire*, 61–62.

100. Dye, *As Equal and as Sisters*, 91; *New York Call*, October 4, December 4, 1909; Tax, *Rising of the Women*, 220–221.

101. Microfilm edition of the Papers of the WTUL, O'Reilly Papers, Reel 11, Frame 1176.

102. Clark and Wyatt, "Working Girls' Budgets," *McClure's*, 82.

103. Bruere, "The White Goods Strikers," *Life and Labor*, 73–75; "Two Phases of Yuletide, 1909," *New York Call* (December 24, 1909). Enstad analyzes this cartoon and points out that the representation of working-class women in poor dress denied workers "language of entitlement related to dress." This points out the rhetorical disjuncture between workers' and their middle-class allies and leaders; still, though, the cartoon was contained in an issue of the *New York Call* sold by strikers apparently with little resistance on their part. Enstad does not fully address how such strike publicity that included striking women as both the subject and distributor was contested by working-class women, nor does she locate how this image fits into a proletarian (and cross-class) discourse around health, work, and the working-class body. Enstad, *Ladies of Labor, Girls of Adventure*, 103–104.

104. Microfilm edition of the Papers of the WTUL, O'Reilly Papers, Reel 11, Frame 1177. See also Dorothy Dix, "Shirtwaist Strike Shows Woman's Need of the Ballot," in microfilm edition of the Papers of the WTUL, O'Reilly Papers, Reel 11, Frame 996.

105. *Evening Journal*, November 26, 1909.

106. Françoise Basch, "Introduction: The Shirtwaist Strike in History and Myth," in Theresa Serber Malkiel, *The Diary of A Shirtwaist Striker* (1910; reprint, Ithaca: ILR Press, 1990).

107. Theresa Serber Malkiel, "To a Working Woman" (undated pamphlet), Tamiment Library, New York University, Radical Pamphlet Collection, microfilm #5417; Theresa Serber Malkiel, "Woman and Freedom" (undated pamphlet), Radical Pamphlet Collection, microfilm #5420.

108. *New York Call*, April 15–May 14, 1910.

109. Basch, "Introduction," 65–66.

110. Malkiel, *Diary of a Shirtwaist Striker*, 81.

111. Ibid., 82.

112. Ibid., 83.

113. Ibid., 84.

114. Ibid., 96.

115. Ibid.

116. Ibid., 88; *New York Call*, Dec. 4, 1909.

117. Malkiel, *Diary of a Shirtwaist Striker*, 111–112.

118. Ibid., 95.

119. Ibid., 113.

120. Ibid., 122.

121. Ibid., 134.

122. Ibid.

123. Quoted in Paula Scheier, "Clara Lemlich Shavelson," *Jewish Life* (November 1954), 8.

124. Fannia Cohn, untitled draft history of the ILGWU, ca. 1935, ILGWU Archives; Education Department, Box 2, Folder 8b, 12–16.
125. Ibid., 15.
126. Fania M. Cohen [*sic*], "With the Strikers," *Justice* (February 22, 1919). For other examples, see Juliet Stuart Poyntz, "The New Temper of Working Women in the Needle Trades," *Justice* (January 18, 1919); "On Lightheaded Woman," *Justice* (March 8, 1919); Elizabeth Hasanovitz, "1919 Versus 1911," *Justice* (March 29, 1919).
127. "Occasional Notes," *The Ladies' Garment Worker* (June 1911).
128. Orleck, *Common Sense and a Little Fire*, 65.
129. On the way male members of the ILGWU distrusted and marginalized female organizers, see Alice Kessler-Harris, "Problems of Coalition-Building: Women and Trade Unions in the 1920s," in *Women, Work, and Protest: A Century of U.S. Women's Labor History*, ed. Ruth Milkman (Boston: Routledge & Kegan Paul, 1985), 110–138. On relationships between female organizers, see Nancy MacLean, "The Culture of Resistance: Female Institution Building in the International Ladies' Garment Workers' Union, 1905–1925," *Michigan Occasional Papers in Women's Studies* 21 (Winter 1982).
130. Rose Schneiderman, *All for One* (New York: Paul Eriksson, 1967), 50.
131. Orleck, *Common Sense and a Little Fire*, 3.
132. This is an example of what Judith Butler calls the laws of heterosexuality. See Butler, *Gender Trouble*.
133. Orleck, *Common Sense and a Little Fire*, 220–222.
134. Elizabeth Hasanovitz, *One of Them: Chapters from a Passionate Autobiography* (New York: Houghton Mifflin, 1918), 35–36, 305–306. For a study of the difficulties faced by individual female organizers, see Alice Kessler-Harris, "Organizing the Unorganizable: Three Jewish Women and Their Union," *Labor History* 17 (Winter 1976): 5–23.
135. Hasanovitz, *One of Them*, 46.
136. Abraham Reisin, "Equal Rights," *The Ladies' Garment Worker* (November 1917).

Six Inspecting Bodies: Sexual Difference
and Strategies of Organizing, 1910–1930

1. *The Ladies' Garment Worker* (April 1, 1910). It should be noted that they did not assure them a place at the helm of that organization.
2. Ibid.
3. The AR was the ILGWU's most vigorous institutional supporter, collecting more funds for the union during the strikes of 1909 to 1913 than any other group. Melach Epstein, *Jewish Labor in the U.S.A.: An Industrial, Political and Cultural History of the Jewish Labor Movement, 1882–1914* (New York: Ktav Publishing House, 1969), 309.
4. On the relationship between the labor and public health movements see David Rosner and Gerald Markowitz, "The Early Movement for Occupational Safety and Health, 1900–1917," in *Sickness and Health in America: Readings in the History of Medicine and Public Health*, ed. Judith Walzer Leavitt and Ronald L. Numbers (Madison: University of Wisconsin Press, 1985), 507–524.
5. There is a growing literature on the role of gender in perceptions of causes of occupational disease. Historians have also begun to recognize how science and medicine has served to legitimize conceptions of sexual difference. See Allison Hepler,

Women in Labor: Mothers, Medicine, and Occupational Health in the United States, 1890–1980 (Columbus: Ohio State University Press, 2000); Anthony Bale, "Women's Toxic Experience" in *Women, Health, and Medicine in America: A Historical Handbook*, ed. Rima Apple (New York: Garland, 1990); Leslie Doyal, *What Makes Women Sick: Gender and the Political Economy of Health* (New Brunswick, N.J.: Rutgers University Press, 1995).

6. For an overview of the Jewish labor movement in this period, see Joseph Brandes, "From Sweatshop to Stability: Jewish Labor between Two World Wars," *YIVO Annual* 16 (1976): 1–149.

7. Interview with Paul Novick, YIVO, Irving Howe Papers, RG #570, Box 1, 8; Elias Tcherikower, *The Early Jewish Labor Movement in the United States*, trans. and rev. by Aaron Antonovsky (New York: YIVO, 1961), 272–315; Hadassa Kosak, *Cultures of Opposition: Jewish Immigrant Workers, New York City, 1881–1905* (Albany: State University of New York Press, 2000), 99–130.

8. Abraham Rosenberg, *Memoirs of a Cloakmaker*, trans. Lynn Davison (New York: n.p., 1920), 15–21 (Martin P. Catherwood Library, Cornell University).

9. Jesse Pope, *The Clothing Industry in New York* (Columbia: E. W. Stephens Publishing Company, 1905), 211–255; Oral history with Leon Stein, undated, Wagner Labor Archives, Oral History of the American Left (OHAL), Series IV, Section VI, 9.

10. "Address of Meyer London," in "Report and Proceedings of the 12th Convention of the ILGWU" (1914), 136–137.

11. On organizing strategies of the ILGWU after 1913, see Louis Levine, *The Women's Garment Workers: A History of the International Ladies' Garment Workers' Union* (New York: B. W. Huebsch, 1924), 466–505.

12. Maxmilian Hurwitz, *The Workmen's Circle: Its History, Ideals, Organization, and Institutions* (New York: The Workmen's Circle, 1936), 26–27. As in the ILGWU, the push for new services that concentrated on countering the physical effects of garment work came from a new generation of leaders. After 1911, "young" and "old" factions struggled for control of the society. By the conclusion of the struggle in 1917, it became clear that although many of the actual leaders of the "old" faction, the group initially resistant to widening the scope of the AR, remained, the program of the "young" had triumphed.

13. Epstein, *Jewish Labor in the U.S.A.*, 303.

14. A. S. Saks, *Geshikte fun Arbeiter Ring, 1892–1925, Tsveyter Teyl* (New York: Workmen's Circle, 1925), 576–583; Epstein, *Jewish Labor in U.S.A.*, 313–315.

15. Yitzchak Yankel Doroshkin, *From Zhitkovitch throughout the World (Episodes of My Life)* (1974), trans. Mindy Gross, YIVO Institute for Jewish Research, American Jewish Autobiographies (AJA), RG #102, #305, 108–109.

16. "Der Arbeiter Ring un Zeyne Kultur-Oifgabn" (The Workmen's Circle and Its Cultural Programs), "Der Arbeiter Ring Sovenir Den Tsenten Ierlicher Konvenshion Gevidmet" (1910), YIVO, Bund Archives, Workman's Circle Collection, RG #1400, Box 3, Folder 15, 167–187; Saks, *Geshikte fun Arbeiter Ring, Tsveyter Teyl*, 383.

17. Israel Knox, "On the Occasion of Your 25th Anniversary," YIVO, Bund Archives, Workman's Circle Collection, Box 10, Folder 57, 10.

18. A. Rosebury, "A New Departure in Our Union—Sick and Relief Funds," *Ladies' Garment Worker* (May 1915).

19. *Justice* (June 20, 1924).
20. "Declaration of Principles, 1922," in Hurwitz, *Workmen's Circle*, 117–118.
21. "Der Arbeiter Ring Sovenir Den Tsenten Ierlicher Konvenshion Gevidmet," 33; Saks, *Geshikte fun Arbeiter Ring, Ershter Teyl* (New York: Workmen's Circle, 1925), 439–446.
22. Levine, *Women's Garment Workers*, x.
23. "Der Arbeiter Ring Sovenir Den Tsenten Ierlicher Konvenshion Gevidmet," 1.
24. Quoted in notes to Hutchins Hapgood, *The Spirit of the Ghetto: Studies of the Jewish Quarter of New York*, preface and notes by Harry Golden (New York: Schocken Books, 1965), 95.
25. "Krankn benefit funds un klasn kampf" (Sickness Benefit Funds and Class Conflict), "Der Arbeiter Ring Sovenir Den Tsenten Ierlicher Konvenshion Gevidmet," 39–51; "Declaration of Principles," 1st Convention, 1901, in Hurwitz, *Workmen's Circle*, 115–116.
26. *Ladies' Garment Worker* (December 1915).
27. Ibid. (April 1, 1910).
28. See, for example, ibid. (July 1910).
29. "Declaration of Principles," 1st Convention, 1901, 115–116.
30. B. Charney Vladek to William Lescaze, March 31, 1936, Tamiment Institute, Vladek Papers-Addendum.
31. On contemporary campaigns among women for occupational health protections, see Claudia Clark, *Radium Girls: Women and Industrial Health Reform, 1910–1935* (Chapel Hill: University of North Carolina Press, 1997).
32. On the importance of ideas about reproductive dangers and the implementation of occupational health policy, see Patricia Vawter Klein, "'For the Good of the Race': Reproductive Hazards from Lead and the Persistence of Exclusionary Policies toward Women," in *Women, Work, and Technology: Transformations*, ed. Barbara Dygulski et al. (Ann Arbor: University of Michigan Press, 1987); Rosalind Petchevsky, "Workers, Reproductive Hazards and the Politics of Protection: An Introduction," *Feminist Studies* 5 (Summer 1979): 233–246; Allison Hepler, "Shaping the Life of the Pre-Natal: Labor Laws, Liability, and Lead Politics in Twentieth-Century United States," *Social Politics* 6 (Spring 1999): 54–75. For examinations of the way diagnoses of occupational illness depended on social conversations about work and its assumed physical effects, see David Rosner and Gerald Markowitz, *Deadly Dust: Silicosis and the Politics of Occupational Disease in Twentieth-Century America* (Princeton: Princeton University Press, 1991). See also Charles Rosenberg's argument that public understandings of disease depended as much on social conversations about disease as on the words of doctors. Charles Rosenberg, *Explaining Epidemics and Other Studies in the History of Medicine* (Cambridge: Cambridge University Press, 1992), 278–317. For an overview of the general health conditions of New York's Jewish immigrants, see Deborah Dwork, "Health Conditions of Immigrant Jews on the Lower East Side of New York, 1880–1914," *Medical History* 25 (January 1981): 1–40.
33. For an anthropological study that views science as a gendered language that shapes women's imagining of their own bodies, especially during the hours of work, see Emily Martin, *The Woman and the Body: A Cultural Analysis of Reproduction* (Boston: Beacon Press, 1992), 71–138. Roy Porter, "History of the Body," in *New Per-*

spectives on Historical Writing, ed. Peter Burke (University Park: Pennsylvania State University Press, 1992), 206–232.

34. Sidney Schwab, "Neurasthenia among Garment Workers," *American Labor Legislation Review* (January 1911). On the contemporary middle-class discourse around neurasthenia, see T. Jackson Lears, *No Place of Grace: Antimodernism and the Transformation of American Culture, 1880–1920* (Chicago: University of Chicago Press, 1981), 49–57.

35. Elizabeth Grosz and Judith Butler both argue that the body is a subjective "thing" shaped by the language of sexual difference. For Grosz, the "body is the ally of sexual difference." For Butler, it is the body, as a gendered subject, understandable only through its representation in sex/gender discourse. Both see the body as a contested subject whose meaning derives from larger conversations about sex, sexuality, and gender. Elzabeth Grosz, *Volatile Bodies: Toward a Corporeal Feminism* (Bloomington: Indiana University Press, 1994); Judith Butler, *Gender Trouble: Feminism and the Subversion of Identity* (New York: Routledge, 1999).

36. Howard Markel, *Quarantine!: East European Jewish Immigrants and the New York City Epidemics of 1892* (Baltimore: Johns Hopkins University Press, 1997), points out how government and public health policy during cholera and typhus epidemics in New York was shaped by a fear of ethnic Jewish immigrants and the squalor of their surroundings. John Higham, *Strangers in the Land: Patterns of American Nativism, 1860–1925* (New Brunswick, N.J.: Rutgers University Press, 1988), 3–105; Alan Kraut, "Silent Strangers: Germs, Genes, and Nativism in John Higham's *Strangers in the Land,*" *American Jewish History* 71 (December 1981): 269–284; John Higham, *Send These to Me: Jews and Other Immigrants in Urban America* (New York: Atheneum, 1975), 102–137. On medical inspections at Ellis Island and the medicalized fear of Jewish immigrants, see Alan Kraut, *Silent Travelers: Germs, Genes, and the "Immigrant Menace"* (New York: Basic Books, 1994), 49–77; Elizabeth Yew, "Medical Inspection of Immigrants at Ellis Island, 1891–1924," *Bulletin of the New York Academy of Medicine* 56 (June 1980): 488–510.

37. "Members Deceased During 1909," "Der Arbeiter Ring Sovenir Den Tsenten Ierlicher Konvenshion Gevidmet."

38. U.S. Public Health Service (PHS), "The Health of Garment Workers," *U.S. Public Health Service Bulletin* 71 (May 1915): 13–103.

39. PHS, "The Health of Garment Workers," 19, 41.

40. For examples of the ILGWU's use of the PHS survey, see Joint Board of Sanitary Control, *Bulletin* (May 1914), 3; "Work, Health and Disease," in Joint Board of Sanitary Control, *Workers' Health Bulletin* (1915), 11; George Price, "The Physical Examination of Fifty Thousand Garment Workers," *Union Health Center Journal* (March 29, 1924), 33–45.

41. *Third Annual Report of the Joint Board of Sanitary Control in the Cloak, Suit and Skirt and Dress and Waist Industries of Greater New York* (New York: Joint Board of Sanitary Control, December 1913), 69–75; *Justice*, February 8 and February 22, 1924; Price, "Physical Examination of Fifty Thousand Garment Workers."

42. *Third Annual Report of the Joint Board of Sanitary Control*, 69–75; James Oneal, *A History of the Amalgamated Ladies' Garment Cutters' Union, Local 10 Affiliated with the ILGWU* (New York: Local 10, 1927), 264.

43. PHS, "Health of Garment Workers," 87.

44. Ibid., 87–90.
45. Rosner and Markowitz point out that, in general, Progressive Era public health campaigns undertaken jointly by unions and public health officials tended to stress protecting the male breadwinner and returning women to the home. See Rosner and Markowitz, "The Early Movement for Occupational Safety and Health, 1900–1917." On the history of Progressive Era public health practice and the reliance on medical inspection as a form of collective care, see Judith Walzer Leavitt, *The Healthiest City: Milwaukee and the Politics of Health Reform* (Princeton: Princeton University Press, 1982); Fitzhugh Mullan, *Plagues and Politics: The Story of the United States Public Health Service* (New York: Basic Books, 1989); John Duffy, *The Sanitarians: A History of American Public Health* (Urbana: University of Illinois Press, 1990); John Duffy, *A History of Public Health in New York City*, 2 vols. (New York: Russell Sage Foundation, 1974).
46. PHS, "The Health of Garment Workers," 53.
47. *A General Survey of the Sanitary Conditions of the Shops in the Cloak Industry* (New York: Joint Board of Sanitary Control, 1911), 8–12.
48. Ibid., 10.
49. PHS, "Health of Garment Workers," 90. This is not to suggest that women workers did not suffer from painful menstruation, which is, indeed, a problem for highly sedentary workers, only that as a complaint menstrual disorders predominated. For a study of the effect of menstruation on work identity, see Martin, *Woman in the Body*, 92–138.
50. PHS, "Health of Garment Workers," 94.
51. Ibid., 88.
52. *Justice* (October 28, 1921).
53. "Arbeiter Ring Sanitarium, Liberti, Niu Iork, Onveizungen tsu Patsientn," YIVO, Bund Archives, Workman's Circle Collection, Box 10, Folder 57, 3.
54. Alexander Trachtenberg, "The 'Glory of Peace [*sic*] Work,'" *Justice*, December 16, 1921. The ILGWU cited here the Public Health Services study.
55. PHS, "Health of Garment Workers," 94–95.
56. Ibid., 84–85.
57. "A New Departure in Our Union—Sick and Relief Funds," *Ladies' Garment Worker* (May 1915).
58. For an overview of health initiatives in the ILGWU, see Levine, *Women's Garment Workers*, 466–481. For an overview of programs in the AR, see Saks, *Geshikte fun Arbeiter Ring, Tsveyter Teyl*, 831–857. Neither note the way these programs were gendered.
59. "In the Waist and Dress Trade," *Ladies' Garment Worker* (September 1915).
60. "New Activities in Waistmakers' Union, Local 25," *Ladies' Garment Worker* (October 1918).
61. Women workers advanced unique ideas about curing only where they could combine substantial financial resources with a critical mass of female supporters. The AR, organized as it was into branches based on immigrants' Eastern European place of origin, did not offer as comfortable a space as the ILGWU's Local 25. Especially in Local 25 (the waist and dressmakers local), women, bolstered by their majority and their strength in numbers, established forms of curing that offered help to female workers still laboring in factories and those who had left after marriage. See

Juliet Stuart Poyntz, "The Unity Movement—The Soul of a Union," *Life and Labor* (June 1917): 96–98; Hurwitz, *Workman's Circle*. Although the AR did organize women's auxiliary branches, there is little evidence that such branches acted as effective sites of women's power.

62. Juliet Stuart Poyntz, "The Problem of Life for the Working Girl," *Justice* (February 1, 1919).

63. "In the Waist and Dress Trade," *Ladies' Garment Worker* (September 1915).

64. Poyntz, "Problems of Life for the Working Girl." This is an example of what Annelise Orleck describes as women organizers' strategy of "bread and roses." It also represents a shift from a language of class conflict to a language of health. Annelise Orleck, *Common Sense and a Little Fire: Women and Working-Class Politics in the United States, 1900–1965* (Chapel Hill: University of North Carolina Press, 1995).

65. Fannia Cohn, "Concluding Words of the Story of the Educational Department of the International Ladies' Garment Workers Union," 1942, ILGWU Archives, Education Department Papers, Box 6a, Folder 8, 3.

66. Juliet Stuart Poyntz, "The Conquest of Leisure," *Justice* (February 22, 1919); Poyntz, "Unity Movement."

67. Oral history of Sophie Saroff, OHAL, Series I, 1–3; *The Ladies' Garment Worker* (October 1917); *Justice* (March 29, 1919).

68. *Justice* (June 22, 1923).

69. "Waist makers' Splendid Summer Resort," *Justice* (May 10, 1919).

70. *Justice* (July 9, June 25, 1920).

71. "Report of the General Executive Board to the Sixteenth Biennial Convention of the ILGWU" (1922), 88.

72. "Report of the General Executive Board to the Fifteenth Biennial Convention of the ILGWU" (1920), 55–56.

73. *Justice* (March 26, 1920).

74. "Arbeiter Ring Ochter Ierlicher Konvenshion" (May 1908), YIVO, Bund Archives, Workmen's Circle Collection, Box 3, Folder 13, 9–11; "Arbeiter Ring Ierlicher Report" (1911), YIVO, Bund Archives, Workmen's Circle Collection, Box 3, Folder 15, 157.

75. "Ten Years of Fraternal Aid" (New York: Cloakpressers' Union, Local 35), 20.

76. "Twenty Five Years of Relief for the Cloak Pressers"; *Ladies' Garment Worker* (August 1914); "A New Departure in Our Union—Sick and Relief Funds," *Ladies' Garment Worker* (May 1915); Levine, *Ladies' Garment Workers*, 476–478.

77. "Officers Report," "Fourteenth Convention of the ILGWU," 1918, 40–41.

78. Hurwitz, *Workmen's Circle*, 152.

79. For an example of this practice, see Doroshkin, *From Zhitkovitch throughout the World*, 156.

80. "Officers Report" (1918), 41–42.

81. *"Bletlach fun der Geshikte fun Sanatorium far Shvindzichtine,"* in *Der Arbeter Ring Sovenir den Tsenten Ierlicher Konvenshion Gevidmet*, YIVO, Bund Archives, Workman's Circle Collection, Box 3, Folder 15, 136–148.

82. *Arbeter Ring Ierlicher Report*, YIVO, Bund Archives, Workman's Circle Collection, Box 3, Folder 16, 55–56.

83. PHS, "The Health of Garment Workers," 84.

84. *"Report fun Santarium Komite,"* YIVO, Bund Archives, Workman's Circle Collection,

RG #1400, Box 3, Folder 16, Table 3, 116. The AR estimated that consumption infection rates among Jewish garment workers rose from 3.3 per thousand in 1904 to 6.2 per thousand in 1910 when the Liberty Sanitarium opened. Women's numbers at the sanitarium clearly do not reflect this rate of infection. *Arbeter Ring Ierlicher Report*, 71.

85. "Report fun Sanitarium Komite," "Arbeiter Ring Ierlicher Report," 115–133; Saks, *Geshikte fun Arbeiter Ring, Ershter Teyl* (New York: Workmen's Circle, 1925), 357–379.

86. "Klok, skoirt un dres pressers iunion lokal 35, iorlicher report far 1916," YIVO, Bund Archives, ILGWU Collection, Box 15, Folder 61, 36–39; "New Activities in Waistmakers' Union, Local 25," *Ladies' Garment Worker*, October 1918.

87. "Finf un Tsvantsig-iorger Iubelei fun Medikal Department, Arbeiter Ring," YIVO, Bund Archives, Workmen's Circle Collection, Box 10, Folder 57; S. Koner, "Barikht tsum Fuftsen Iorkn Iubeils fun Medikal Department, Arbeiter Ring, 1919–1934," YIVO, Bund Archives, Workmen's Circle Collection, Box 10, Folder 57.

88. *Justice*, December 17, 1920.

89. *Justice*, March 16, 1923.

90. Price, "The Physical Examination of Fifty Thousand Garment Workers," 33–45. On strategies and narratives of curing, see Sheila Rothman, *Living in the Shadow of Death: Tuberculosis and the Social Experience of Illness in American Society* (Baltimore: Johns Hopkins University Press, 1994), 179–246.

91. *Justice* (February 10, 1922).

92. "It Sometimes Happens at the Health Center," *Justice* (December 15, 1922).

93. Union Health Center (UHC), "Report for 1924," ILGWU Archives, UHC Papers, Box 4, Folder 12, 7.

94. UHC, "Report for 1924," 19.

95. *Justice* (June 16, 1922).

96. Ibid.

97. Hurwitz, *Workmen's Circle*, 184–185; *Justice* (October 28, 1921); UHC, "Report for 1924," 11. The UHC reported significant attendance at such lectures.

98. Pauline Newman, "With the Union Health Center," *Justice* (July 4, 1923).

99. Fannia Cohn, "Concluding Words," ILGWU Archives, Education Department Papers, Box 6A, Folder 8, 78.

100. "Ten Years Industrial Self Control: Tenth Annual Report of the Joint Board of Sanitary Control" (New York: Joint Board of Sanitary Control, 1921), 53.

101. *Justice*, December 10, 1920; *The Friend*, August 1928.

102. Interview held with Pauline Newman, January 26, 1965, ILGWU Archives, Recorded Information, Box 1, Folder 2, 6–12.

Seven "Swallowed Up in a Sea of Masculinity":
Factionalism and Gender Struggles in the ILGWU, 1909–1934

1. *Freiheit*, July 11, 1925

2. Anonymous Male #2, December 16, 1974, Wagner Labor Archives, Oral Histories of the American Left (OHAL), #123B.

3. Anonymous Male #1, October 22, 1974, OHAL, #123A. In this chapter, "Communist" and "Communism" are capitalized because of the clear links to the official

American Communist movement and one of its splinter parties, namely the Workers' (Communist) Party. "Socialist" and "socialism" are not capitalized. While many Jewish trade unionists and workers would claim some allegiance to the vague notion of socialism, their connection to the American socialist movement or to the American Socialist Party was distant, if not altogether nonexistent, by the 1920s.

4. Susan Glenn also examines women's increased activism in the ILGWU just before and after the Russian Revolution. She suggests that women's assertion of trade union rights represented an expression of "new womanhood," a phrase few garment workers, male or female, would have understood or used. The analysis here treats the rise of the women's opposition within the context of the ILGWU's factional history. See Susan Glenn, *Daughters of the Shtetl: Life and Labor in the Immigrant Generation* (Ithaca: Cornell University Press, 1990), 207–242. David Gurowsky, "Factional Disputes within the ILGWU, 1919–1928" (Ph.D. diss., State University of New York at Binghamton, 1978), and Stanley Nadel, "Reds versus Pinks: A Civil War in the International Ladies' Garment Workers' Union," *New York History* 66 (January 1985): 48–72, have written the most comprehensive histories of factional struggles in the ILGWU, but, by beginning their narratives in 1919, like most historians, they do not connect left-right struggles with gendered disputes.

5. For two later histories written by partisans of the factionalism that take very different approaches to the question of Communism, see Jack Hardy, *The Clothing Workers: A Study of the Conditions and Struggles in the Needle Trades* (New York: International Publishers, 1935); Joel Seidman, *The Needle Trades* (New York: Farrar and Rinehart, 1942). Unlike observers at the time, both works tend to ignore the role of women.

6. See Alice Kessler-Harris, *Out to Work: A History of Wage-Earning Women in the United States* (New York: Oxford University Press, 1982), 159–160; Roger Waldinger, "Another Look at the International Ladies' Garment Workers' Union: Women, Industry Structure and Collective Action," in *Women, Work and Protest: A Century of U.S. Women's Labor History*, ed. Ruth Milkman (Boston: Routledge and Kegan Paul, 1985), 87–109. In 1920, 40 percent of all unionized women were garment workers and many of these had joined unions after 1910. Within the ILGWU, Local 25 with its 30,000 members was by far the largest of the union's locals and accounted for about one-quarter of all the union's membership. See Leo Wolman, *Growth of American Trade Unions, 1880–1923* (New York: National Bureau of Economic Research, 1924), 97–98.

7. Alice Kessler-Harris examines the informal support networks outside of the union proper that allowed some female organizers to remain active. See Alice Kessler-Harris, "Organizing the Unorganizable: Three Jewish Women and Their Union," *Labor History* 17 (Winter 1976): 5–23.

8. On the relationship of Jewish immigrants to Bolshevism, see Paul Buhle, "Jews and American Communism: the Cultural Question," *Radical History Review* 23 (Spring 1980): 9–37; Gerald Sorin, *The Prophetic Minority: American Jewish Immigrant Radicals, 1880–1920* (Bloomington: Indiana University Press, 1985), 43–46.

9. The rise of a women's opposition within the ILGWU and the left-right split emerged not only because of larger political and social changes beyond the immigrant community in New York, but also because of substantial transformations in the nature of Jewish garment labor. After 1910, Jewish unions and proletarian associations

assumed a permanent place in Jewish workers' daily lives. The financial stability and longevity of the ILGWU were no longer in question. See J. M. Budish and George Soule, *The New Unionism in the Clothing Industry* (New York: Harcourt, Brace and Howe, 1920); Joseph Brandes, "From Sweatshop to Stability: Jewish Labor between Two World Wars," *YIVO Annual* 16 (1976): 1–149.

10. See Alice Kessler-Harris, "Problems of Coalition-Building: Women and Trade Unions in the 1920s," in Milkman, *Women, Work and Protest*, 110–138.

11. Louis Levine, *The Women's Garment Workers: A History of the International Ladies' Garment Workers' Union* (New York: B. W. Huebsch, 1924), 218–226; *Ladies' Garment Worker* (February 1913).

12. *Ladies' Garment Worker* (March 1913).

13. Quoted in Levine, *Women's Garment Workers*, 149.

14. Gertrude Barnum, "The Children's Crusade: The New York Strikers are Winning Fights," *Ladies' Garment Worker* (February 1913).

15. *Ladies' Garment Worker* (September 1913).

16. See, for example, "A bleter ois der geshikte fun der veist makers iunion" [A letter about the history of the waistmakers' union], *Ladies' Garment Worker* (April 1910).

17. *Ladies' Garment Worker* (June 1911).

18. For examples, see *Ladies' Garment Worker* (March 21, August 22, 1914).

19. *Ladies' Garment Worker* (June 1913).

20. M. H. Danish, "1913—January—1914," *Ladies' Garment Worker* (January 1914).

21. Gertrude Barnum, "At the Shirt Waist Factory," *Ladies' Garment Worker* (May 1910). The maternalism of the story is also of particular interest as it relates to the strategies of the Women's Trade Union League (WTUL). The WTUL understood female workers as dreamy, class ignorant girls and relied on maternalist pedagogy to exhort women to join unions. Gertrude Barnum served in the WTUL during the Uprising of the Twenty Thousand.

22. Nan Enstad examines the way male workers regularly used images of the "dressy" girl worker to criticize female unionists. In fact, their discourse of seriousness and criticism of popular culture was a refrain taken up by a few female activists, perhaps seeking to counteract representations of women as novices and uncommitted unionists. Nan Enstad, *Ladies of Labor, Girls of Adventure: Working Women, Popular Culture, and Labor Politics at the Turn of the Twentieth Century* (New York: Columbia University Press, 1999).

23. "Mr. Skinner Climbs Down: A Story of A Girl's Strike and Its Success," *Ladies' Garment Worker* (February 1913).

24. Pauline Newman, "The White Goods Workers' Strike," *Ladies' Garment Worker* (March 1913); Annelise Orleck, *Common Sense and a Little Fire: Women and Working-Class Politics in the United States, 1900–1965* (Chapel Hill: University of North Carolina Press, 1995), 169–193. Annelise Orleck describes these women as the core of activists who introduced new forms of activism in the 1920s. She argues that they created a unique form of "bread and roses" unionism. She does not, however, link women's activism with the rise of a Communist opposition. Nor does her analysis fully explore the discursive limits of women's unionism.

25. Levine, *Women's Garment Workers*, 226–227; Orleck, *Common Sense and a Little Fire*, 79.

26. Oral history of Sarah Borenstein, June 9, 1982, ILGWU Archives, Oral History Collection, Box 20, Folder 25, 8–13.

27. Oral history of Jennie Matyas, April 20–October 28, 1955, conducted by Corinne L. Gilb, Martin P. Catherwood Library, Cornell University, 36.

28. *Ladies' Garment Worker* (March 1913).

29. Oral history of Mary Goff Schuster, September 15, 1982, ILGWU Archives, Oral History Collection, Box 21, Folder 26, 17; Harry Lang, *"62": Biography of a Union* (New York: Astoria Press, 1940), 94–139.

30. Nancy Schrom Dye, *As Equals and as Sisters: Feminism, the Labor Movement, and the Women's Trade Union League of New York* (Columbia: University of Missouri Press, 1980), 1–121.

31. *New York Times*, January 22, 1913.

32. "The Children's Crusade: The New York Strikers are Winning Fights," *Ladies' Garment Worker* (February 1913).

33. Oral history of Jennie Matyas, 35–36.

34. Newman, "White Goods Workers' Strike." Note Newman's use again of the word "school," highlighting the image of the 1913 strikers as novice trade unionists.

35. *Ladies' Garment Worker* (April 1914).

36. For the movement of the WTUL away from organizing, see Dye, *As Equals and as Sisters*, 122–161, and Nancy MacLean, "The Culture of Resistance: Female Institution Building in the International Ladies' Garment Workers' Union, 1905–1925," *Michigan Occasional Papers in Women's Studies* 21 (Winter 1982): 52–53; Orleck, *Common Sense and a Little Fire*, 66–68. Individual women activists, like Rose Schneiderman and Newman, remained tied to the WTUL.

37. Pauline Newman, "Our Women Workers," *Ladies' Garment Worker* (April 1914).

38. Ibid.

39. Pauline Newman to Rose Schneiderman, January 16, 1912, Tamiment Library, Rose Schneiderman Collection, 1909–1914, File 18A.

40. Fannia Cohn, "Education Aids Workingwomen," *Labor Age* (January 1928), 12–13.

41. Constance Denmark, "Our Women Workers," *Ladies' Garment Worker* (August 1914).

42. Cohn, "Education Aids Workingwomen," 12–13.

43. Pauline Newman, "Out of the Past—Into the Future," *Life and Labor* (June 1921), 171–172.

44. Oral history of Jennie Matyas, 78.

45. Oral history of Pauline Newman, conducted by Henoch Mendelsund, 1973, ILGWU Archives, Oral History Collection, Box 2, Folder 4, 17.

46. Cohn, "Education Aids Workingwomen," 12–13. On harassment in the union, see Orleck, *Common Sense and a Little Fire*, 72–74.

47. See, for example, Fannia Cohn, "International Ladies' Garment Workers' Report to the 1917 Conventi on of the WTUL," in *Women in the American Economy*, ed. Eliot and Mary Brownlee (New Haven: Yale University Press, 1976), 221–224; *Ladies' Garment Worker* (July 1913).

48. Denmark, "Our Women Workers," *Ladies' Garment Worker* (August 1914).

49. *Ladies' Garment Worker* (December 1914); Orleck, *Common Sense and a Little Fire*, 169–203.

50. "The Report of Local 25," *Ladies' Garment Worker* (July 1918); Fannia Cohn, "Concluding Words on the Story of the Educational Department of the International Ladies' Garment Workers' Union," ca. 1942, ILGWU Archives, Education Department Papers, Box 6a, Folder 8.

51. Cohn, "Education Aids Workingwomen," 12–13. On the Educational Club and education programs as women's homosocial space, see MacLean, "Culture of Resistance," 73.
52. Oral history of Jennie Matyas, 73.
53. Quoted in MacLean, "Culture of Resistance," 70.
54. Orleck, *Common Sense and a Little Fire*, 74–79.
55. Levine, *Women's Garment Workers*, 352–353.
56. "The Hour of Victory Is Coming!," *Workers' Council Bulletin* (June 1919), YIVO Institute for Jewish Research, U.S. Territorial Collection, RG #117, Box 83.
57. Interview with Charles S. Zimmerman, November 13, 20, 1964, ILGWU Archives, Recorded Information, Box 1, Folder 10, 14–15; Gurowsky, "Factional Disputes," 53–59. On the British roots of the Shop Delegate League, see James Hinton, *The First Shop Stewards' Movement* (London: George Allen & Unwin, 1973). For the general movement in favor of shop steward/delegate systems in the United States and its ties to the Communist left, see David Montgomery, *The Fall of the House of Labor: The Workplace, the State, and American Labor Activism, 1865–1925* (Cambridge: Cambridge University Press, 1987), 425–438.
58. Fannia Cohn, "Short History of the International," ca. 1935, ILGWU Archives, Education Department Papers, Box 2, Folder 8b, 59–60.
59. Oral history of Jennie Matyas, 78; interview with Charles S. Zimmerman, July 1, 1976, ILGWU Archives, Recorded Information, Boxes 8–12, 228.
60. The Shop Delegate Propaganda Committee, "Fellow Workers of the Waist and Dress Unions!" (n.d.), YIVO, U.S. Territorial Collection, RG #117, Box 83."
61. Members of the Ladies' Dress and Waistmakers' Union, Committee "Current Events," "Shall Members of the Union Be Expelled for Criticizing an Official or Any Other Member?" (1918), YIVO, U.S. Territorial Collection, RG #117, Box 83.
62. Ibid.
63. Quoted in Orleck, *Common Sense and a Little Fire*, 183.
64. Workers' Council in the Waist and Dress Industry, "To the Workers of the Waist and Dress Industry" (May 1919), YIVO, U.S. Territorial Collection, RG #117, Box 83.
65. *Justice* (June 1919); Workers' Council in the Waist and Dress Industry, "To the Workers of the Waist and Dress Industry"; Workers' Council of the Waist and Dress Industry, "For Immediate Release" (May 1919), ILGWU Archives, Zimmerman Papers, Box 45, Folder 10 (emphasis in the original).
66. Workers' Council in the Waist and Dress Industry, "To the Workers of the Waist and Dress Industry."
67. "Tentative Plan for Re-Organization of Union on Shop Delegate System" (n.d.), ILGWU Archives, Zimmerman Papers, Box 45, Folder 4.
68. Interview with Charles Zimmerman, 1964, 11.
69. Oral history of Jennie Matyas, 84.
70. "The Present Struggle in the Needle Trade Unions," ca. 1925, ILGWU Archives, Zimmerman Papers, Box 42, Folder 10, 2; "Statement on the Needle Trades Situation by the General Executive Committee, Workers (Communist) Party," April 1925, ILGWU Archives, Research Department Papers, Box 1, Folder 1a.
71. Interview with Charles Zimmerman, YIVO, Irving Howe Papers, RG #570, Box 1, 11–12; Melach Epstein, *Jewish Labor in the U.S.A.: An Industrial, Political and Cul-*

tural History of the Jewish Labor Movement, vol. 2 (New York: Ktav Publishing House, 1969), 130.

72. Workers' Council in the Waist and Dress Industry, "A Reply to Official Lies About the Workers' Council of the Waist and Dress Industry" (1919), YIVO, U.S. Territorial Collection, RG #117, Box 83.

73. Shop Delegate Propaganda Committee, "Fellow Workers of the Dress Industry!" (ca. 1920), YIVO, U.S. Territorial Collection, RG #117, Box 83.

74. Anonymous Female #2, n.d., OHAL, #123C. It is not clear what percentage of Local 25 members were allied with dissident groups. However, it is clear from election results that favored dissident candidates that dissident groups enjoyed large-scale support.

75. Ibid.

76. Interview with Charles Zimmerman, 1964, 52.

77. Anonymous Male #2, OHAL.

78. Anonymous Male #1, October 22, 1974, OHAL, #123A.

79. Levine, *Women's Garment Workers*, 352–353.

80. *Justice* (August 14, 1925).

81. *Justice* (October 2, 1923).

82. *Justice* (February 29, 1924).

83. *Ladies' Garment Worker* (August 1914).

84. Members of the Ladies' Dress and Waistmakers' Union, Committee "Current Events," "Shall members of the Union be expelled for criticizing an official or any other member?"

85. Shop Delegate Propaganda Committee, "Fellow Workers of the Dress Industry!" (ca. 1920) (emphasis in the original). Workers' Council in the Waist and Dress Industry, "A Reply to Official Lies About the Workers' Council of the Waist and Dress Industry."

86. *Justice* (January 7, 1921).

87. "Fellow Workers of the Waist and Dress Unions!" (ca. 1920), YIVO, U.S. Territorial Collection, RG #117, Box 83; Workers' Council, "What Is Your Answer?" (January 1920), YIVO, U.S. Territorial Collection, RG #117, Box 83.

88. Even the International General Executive Board felt a need to answer the criticism of "a group of so-called 'active members' within the local" after the break-up of Local 25. See "Report of the General Executive Board, 1922 International Ladies' Garment Workers' Union Convention" (1922), 50–54; *Justice* (October 1, 8, 1920).

89. Julius Hochman, "Manager Hochman's Final Report on the Dress and Waist Industry," *Justice* (August 24, 1923).

90. Interview with Jennie Matyas in Brownlee, *Women in the American Economy*, 238–240.

91. On the Communists' strategy of seeking elected positions, see Gurowsky, "Factional Disputes."

92. MacLean, "Culture of Resistance," 105.

93. "Report of the General Executive Board to the 19th Convention of the International Ladies' Garment Workers' Union" (1928), 261.

94. "An Open Challenge to the Union Officials of Local 10, Local 25, and the Forward" (n.d.), YIVO, U.S. Territorial Collection, RG #117, Box 83.

95. Recent historians of American Communism have noted how Communism became a language that effectively expressed local working-class discontent. The case here

suggests how, sadly, Communists muted a gendered revolt in their zeal for class-based protest. For interpretations of the way that local Communists interpreted the internationalist, revolutionary rhetoric of Communism in ways that matched the particular circumstances of an area or a group, see Robin D. G. Kelley, *Hammer and Hoe: Alabama Communists during the Great Depression* (Chapel Hill: University of North Carolina Press, 1990); Mark Naison, *Communism in Harlem during the Depression* (Urbana: University of Illinois Press, 1983). The role of women and gender in the American Communist movement has not yet been examined.

96. It was this close connection between the left opposition and the structures and language of American Communism that at once encapsulated the ILGWU opposition as a cohesive unit and provided a visible target for the entrenched, embattled right leadership. As Communist leaders derided, the right leadership raised "the banner of Americanism versus Communism . . . to obscure the real purposes." Joint Board of the Cloak, Skirt, Dress and Reefer Makers' Unions, *The Left Wing in the Garment Unions* (May 1927), YIVO, Bund Archives, ILGWU Collection, RG #1400, Box 3, Folder 10, 14–15. See also "The undersigned, members of the Executive Committee and Manager and Secretary of Local 2" (June 25, 1925), ILGWU Archives, Zimmerman Papers, Box 42, Folder 12.

97. Interview with Charles Zimmerman, 1964, 58.

98. Interview with Charles Zimmerman, 1975, 328–329.

99. "Speech Delivered by Rose Wortis at Yankee Stadium on July 9, 1925," ILGWU Archives, Zimmerman Papers, Box 42, Folder 12, 2. Even in its official reports and minutes, the left acknowledged its roots in the struggle of women between 1914 and 1919; see "Minutes of Joint Action Committee" (June 1925), ILGWU Archives, Research Department Papers, Box 4, Folder 3.

100. Trade Union Educational League, "Di Program fun do Progresive Arbeter fun di Nadl Traydes" (September 1925), YIVO, Bund Archives, American Communism Collection, RG #1400, Box 8, Folder 19. On the TUEL, see Edward P. Johanningsmeier, *Forging American Communism: The Life of William Z. Foster* (Princeton: Princeton University Press, 1994), 150–248.

101. On the relationship between the TUEL and the ILGWU, see "Statement on Situation in Needle Trades, Submitted by Weinstone, Gitlow, and Lifshitz" (March-April 1925), ILGWU Archives, Zimmerman Papers, Box 40, Folder 8; "Report of the National Committee Needle Trades Section, Trade Union Educational League" (ca. 1924), ILGWU Archives, Zimmerman Papers, Box 45, Folder 7; Gurowsky, "Factional Disputes," 95–150.

102. "Letter from Joseph Boruchowitz, Louis Hyman, and Julius Portnoy" (1925), ILGWU Archives, Research Department Papers, Box 4, Folder 4.

103. See "Gigantic Mass Meeting from the Joint Committee of Action, to All Cloak and Dressmakers!" (July 1925), ILGWU Archives, Zimmerman Papers, Box 42, Folder 12. Similarly, when the right criticized the left, they accused the Communists of inflating attendance figures. For examples, see "Statement of Morris Sigman" (August 1925), ILGWU Archives, Morris Sigman Papers, Box 5, Folder 13.

104. *Justice* (August 24, 1923).

105. Anonymous Male #2, OHAL; Louis Levy (Manager-Secretary of Local 1) to S. Cohen, December 11, 1923, YIVO; Saul Shally Papers, RG #1333, Box 1, Folder 1; James Oneal, *A History of the Amalgamated Ladies' Garment Cutters' Union, Local*

10 Affiliated with the ILGWU (New York: Local 10, ILGWU, 1927), 311–316. The Communists in Local 10 successfully fought off the expulsion with only 32 of 1,000 members voting for expulsion.

106. *Justice* (September 10, 21; October 5, 1923); Joint Board of the Cloak, Skirt, Dress, and Reefer Makers' Unions, *Left Wing in the Garment Unions*, 13–15.

107. One female supporter remembered sleeping for weeks in the Local 22 hall to prevent its capture by the right. Female #2, OHAL. For details on the JAC, see interview with Charles Zimmerman, 1964, 53–72; Gurowsky, "Factional Disputes," 150–219.

108. *Justice* (July 5, 10, 31, 1925).

109. Anonymous Female #8, January 2, 1975, OHAL #123J.

110. On the peace agreement, see "The Agreement of Peace in the Cloak and Dressmakers' Union of New York" (September 24, 1925), ILGWU Archives, Morris Sigman Papers, Box 4, Folder 11.

111. Anonymous Male #2, OHAL; "Forward to the Work of Building Our Union!" (July 1925), YIVO, Shally Papers, RG #1333, Box 1, Folder 2. The Workers (Communist) Party noted and criticized the shift from a movement for rank-and-file democracy to a defense of a few leaders; see "Statement on the Needle Trades Situation by the General Executive Committee, Workers (Communist) Party" (1925).

112. Morris Sigman to William Green, September 20, 1926, ILGWU Archives, Morris Sigman Papers, Box 1, Folder 20.

113. *Justice* (July 2, 1926); *Freiheit*, July 2, 1926.

114. *Justice* proudly announced a week later that "Not A Wheel is Turning in New York Cloak Shops," and Sigman proclaimed that "this strike was inevitable." *Justice* (July 9, 1926).

115. *Justice* (November 19, 1926). Zimmerman, Hyman, and Joseph Boruchowitz, an ILGWU vice president and dedicated Communist, proposed and defended a weak agreement that included significant concessions. Large meetings at local halls demonstrated widespread rank-and-file discontent.

116. *Justice* (November 26, 1926).

117. *Justice* (December 17, 1926).

118. *Justice* (December 17, 1926); "Declaration Issued by the Cloak and Dressmakers Assembled at Madison Sq. Garden" (1927), ILGWU Archives, Zimmerman Papers, Box 42, Folder 10.

119. *Justice* (December 24, 1926; January 14, 1927).

120. Hardy, *Clothing Workers*, chap. 3.

121. Anonymous Male #1, OHAL.

122. "The Last Shameful Act of Sigman-'Forward'" (1926), ILGWU Archives, Research Department, Box 7, Folder 12; "To All Locals and Members of the International Ladies' Garment Workers' Union," December 14, 1927, ILGWU Archives, Morris Sigman Papers, Box 4, Folder 12.

123. Anonymous Male #1, OHAL.

124. Isidore Wisotsky, *Such a Life*, unpublished autobiography (n.d.), Tamiment Library, 235; Henry L. Feingold, *A Time for Searching: Entering the Mainstream, 1920–1945* (Baltimore: Johns Hopkins University Press, 1992), 134. For an examination of the challenging and reproduction of gender in 1920s and 1930s gangsterism, see Claire Bond Potter, "'I'll go the limit and then some': Gun Molls, Desire, and Danger in the 1930s," *Feminist Studies* 21(Spring 1995): 41–66.

125. Wisotsky, *Such a Life*, 220–259. The word *mench* in Yiddish carries the meaning of both man and a "responsible/ mature person." Uriel Weinreich, *Modern English-Yiddish, Yiddish-English Verterbukh* (New York: YIVO Institute for Jewish Research, 1977), 541.

126. Fannia Cohn, "Winning Workingwomen to Unionism," *Justice* (July 8, 1927); Fannia Cohn, "Lillian on Sex Lines: 'Inferiority of Women' in the Unions," *Justice* (August 12, 1927); Fannia Cohn, "Women Workers Coming into Their Own," *Justice* (October 7, 1927).

127. Harry Haskel, *A Leader of the Garment Workers: The Biography of Isidore Nagler* (New York: ILGWU, Local 10, 1950), 112–114.

128. *Justice* (October 19, 1928); NTWIU, "The Zimmerman Betrayals Will Not Be Covered Up by Attacks upon the Industrial Union" (n.d.), YIVO, Bund Archives, American Communism Collection, RG #1400, Box 13, Folder 52.

129. "Report of the General Executive Board to the 19th Convention of the International Ladies' Garment Workers' Union," 278; *Justice* (September 1927).

130. NTWIU, "To All Workers in the Open Shops of the Dress Industry" (n.d.), YIVO, Bund Archives, American Communism Collection, RG #1400, Box 13, Folder 52.

Conclusion "Our Marching Orders . . . Advance toward the Goal of Industrial Decency": Measuring the Burden of Language

1. "Proceedings of the 19th Convention of the International Ladies' Garment Workers' Union" (1928), 102–103.

2. "Report of the General Executive Board to the 20th Convention of the International Ladies' Garment Workers' Union" (1929), 9.

3. On New York's Jews in the Great Depression, see Beth Wenger, *New York Jews and the Great Depression: Uncertain Promise* (New Haven: Yale University Press, 1996).

4. "Bulletin of the Joint Board of Sanitary Control in the Cloak, Suit and Skirt Industry" (January 1912). The methodology of reading this document for its own history and for the meaning of its language choice and linguistic silences is influenced by Dipesh Chakrabarty, "Conditions for Knowledge of Working-Class Conditions: Employers, Government and the Jute Workers of Calcutta, 1890–1940," in *Selected Subaltern Studies*, ed. Ranajit Guha and Gayatri Chakravorty Spivak (Oxford: Oxford University Press, 1988), 179–230.

5. "Bulletin of the Joint Board of Sanitary Control in the Cloak, Suit and Skirt Industry" (January 1912).

6. Richard Greenwald, "Bargaining for Industrial Democracy? Labor, the State, and the New Industrial Relations in Progressive Era New York" (Ph.D. diss., New York University, 1998); Joseph McCartin, *Labor's Great War: The Struggle for Industrial Democracy and the Transformation of the American Workplace, 1912–1921* (Chapel Hill: University of North Carolina Press, 1998).

7. "Bulletin of the Joint Board of Sanitary Control in the Cloak, Suit and Skirt Industry" (January 1912).

8. "Bulletin of the Joint Board of Sanitary Control in the Cloak, Suit and Skirt and the Dress and Waist Industries" (May 1914), 2. By mandating fire escapes, the "Fire Safety Division" also encouraged the move away from tenement homework apartments where women worked.

9. "Bulletin of the Joint Board of Sanitary Control in the Cloak, Suit and Skirt and the Dress and Waist Industries" (May 1914), 2.

10. Ibid., 2–3.

11. Ibid., 2.

12. George Price, "Industrial Hygiene: Joint Board of Sanitary Control in the New York Ladies' Garment Industries," *International Labor Review* (January 1922), in ILGWU Archives, Union Health Center Papers, Box 12, Folder 1.

13. "Racketeers Must Be Driven From the Needle Industry!" (January 30, 1933), YIVO Institute for Jewish Research, Bund Archives, ILGWU Collection RG #1400, Box 13, Folder 52; "To All Workers in the Open Shops of the Dress Industry," ca. 1933, YIVO, Bund Archives, ILGWU Collection, RG #1400, Box 13, Folder 52.

14. "Report of the General Executive Board to the 20th Convention of the International Ladies' Garment Workers' Union," 9.

15. "Report of the General Executive Board to the 19th Convention of the International Ladies' Garment Workers' Union," 278.

Epilogue   Anti-Sweatshop Campaigns in a New Century

1. General Accounting Office (GAO), Report to the Chairman, Subcommittee on Commerce, Consumer, and Monetary Affairs, Committee on Government Affairs, Committee on Government Operations, House of Representatives, "Garment Industry Efforts to Address the Prevalence and Conditions of Sweatshops," GAO/HEHS–95–29 (November 2, 1994); Andrew Ross, ed., *No Sweat: Fashion, Free Trade and the Rights of Garment Workers* (New York: Verso, 1997), 12–13.

2. Nicholas Kristof and Sheryl WuDunn, "Two Cheers for Sweatshops," *New York Times Magazine*, September 24, 2000.

3. GAO, "Garment Industry Efforts to Address the Prevalence and Conditions of Sweatshops."

4. Julie Su, "El Monte Thai Garment Workers: Slave Sweatshops" in Ross, *No Sweat*, 143–150; Peter Liebhold and Harry R. Rubenstein, *Between a Rock and a Hard Place: A History of American Sweatshops, 1820–Present* (Los Angeles: UCLA Asian American Studies Center and Simon Wiesenthal Center Museum of Tolerance, 1999), 61–80.

5. Liza Featherstone and United Students Against Sweatshops, *Students against Sweatshops* (London: Verso, 2002).

6. Ross, *No Sweat*; "Sweat & Tears Still in Fashion in City," *Daily News*, July 8, 2001; Liebhold and Rubenstein, *Between a Rock and a Hard Place*, 15–60.

7. Edna Bonacich, Lucie Cheng, Norma Chinchilla, Nora Hamilton, and Paul Ong, eds., *Global Productions: The Apparel Industry in the Specific Rim* (Philadelphia: Temple University Press, 1994).

8. For a comparative study of turn-of-the-century and contemporary sweatshops, see Daniel Soyer, "Garment Sweatshops, Then and Now," *New Labor Forum* 4 (Spring-Summer 1999), 35–46.

9. Featherstone, *Students against Sweatshops*, 9–18; Linda Shaw, "The Labor behind the Label: Clean Clothes Campaigns in Europe," in Ross, *No Sweat*, 215–220.

10. Kitty Krupat, "From War Zone to Free Trade Zone: A History of the National Labor Committee," in Ross, *No Sweat*, 53–60.

11. http://www.nikebiz.com.
12. Ethel Brooks, "The Ideal Sweatshop? Gender and Transnational Protest," *International Labor and Working-Class History* 61 (Spring 2002): 93.
13. Krupat, "From War Zone to Free Trade Zone," 60–61.
14. UNITE!, "Make This a Holiday Season of Conscience: Shop 'Sweat Free'" (November-December 1997), 15–22; Eyal Press, "Sweatshopping," in Ross, *No Sweat*, 221–226.
15. Charles Kernaghan, "Paying to Lose Our Jobs," and NLC, "An Appeal to Walt Disney," in Ross, *No Sweat*, 78–112. See also Charles Kernaghan to NLC Contacts, "Urgent Action Alert/Request for Immediate Solidarity; Women maquiladora workers under attack in El Salvador," May 18, 1995 (in author's possession).
16. *New York Daily News*, July 8–11, 2001.
17. *New York Daily News*, July 8, 2001.
18. NLC, "An Appeal to Walt Disney," 100.
19. Jill Andresky Fraser, *White Collar Sweatshop: The Deterioration of Work and Its Rewards in Corporate America* (New York: W. W. Norton, 2001); Barbara Garson, *The Electronic Sweatshop: How Computers Are Transforming the Office of the Future into the Factory of the Past* (New York: Penguin, 1989); Michael Belzer, *Sweatshops on Wheels: Winners and Losers in Trucking Deregulation* (Oxford: Oxford University Press, 2000).
20. Bruce Raynor, "Serfs of the Service Economy," *New York Times*, November 16, 1999.
21. National Mobilization Against Sweatshops, "What's Behind the Chinatown Dining Experience?" (in author's possession).
22. Chandra Mohanty, "Women Workers and Capitalist Scripts: Ideologies of Domination, Common Interests and the Politics of Solidarity," in *Feminist Genealogies, Colonial Legacies, Democratic Futures*, ed. J. Jacqui Alexander and Chandra Mohanty (New York: Routledge, 1997), 3–29.
23. Kristof and WuDunn, "Two Cheers for Sweatshops."
24. Brooks, "The Ideal Sweatshop?," 105.
25. Testimony of Charles Kernaghan, National Labor Committee, to the Democratic Policy Committee Congressional Hearings, April 29, 1996 (New York: NLC, 1996). See also Miriam Ching Yoon Louie, *Sweatshop Warriors: Immigrant Women Workers Take On the Global Factory* (Cambridge: South End Press, 2001).
26. Brooks, "The Ideal Sweatshop?," 94.
27. Aihwa Ong, *Spirits of Resistance and Capitalist Discipline: Factory Women in Malaysia* (Albany: State University of New York Press, 1987); James C. Scott, *Domination and the Arts of Resistance: Hidden Transcripts* (New Haven: Yale University Press, 1990).
28. Featherstone, *Students against Sweatshops*, 80–91; Xiaolan Bao, "Sweatshops in Sunset Park: A Variation of the Late Twentieth Century Chinese Garment Shops in New York City," *International Labor and Working-Class History* 61 (Spring 2002): 69–90.

Index

Note: Italicized page numbers indicate illustrations.

About the Author

Daniel E. Bender is an assistant professor of history at the University of Waterloo and has taught at Princeton and Michigan State Universities. His work has appeared in *International Labor and Working-Class History*, the *Radical History Review*, and the *Journal of Women's History*. He is the co-editor, with Richard Greenwald, of *Sweatshop U.S.A.: The American Sweatshop in Historical and Global Perspective*. He is married to Mimi Halpern and lives in Waterloo, Ontario.